TECHNIQUES OF AUTORADIOGRAPHY

TECHNIQUES OF AUTORADIOGRAPHY

by

ANDREW W. ROGERS

Medical Research Council, Neuroendocrinology Research Unit, Department of Human Anatomy, University of Oxford (Great Britain)

Second revised and enlarged edition

ELSEVIER SCIENTIFIC PUBLISHING COMPANY
AMSTERDAM/LONDON/NEW YORK/1973

ELSEVIER SCIENTIFIC PUBLISHING COMPANY
335 Jan van Galenstraat
P.O. Box 1270, Amsterdam, The Netherlands

AMERICAN ELSEVIER PUBLISHING COMPANY, INC.
53 Vanderbilt Avenue
New York, New York 10017

SECOND EDITION 1973

Library of Congress Card Number: 72–87964

ISBN 0-444–41057–0

With 92 illustrations

Printed in The Netherlands

Preface to the Second Edition

Autoradiography has progressed considerably since the first manuscript of this book was written. In fact I have been embarrassed to find the first edition deficient or misleading in many places and downright wrong in several. I have therefore largely rewritten the book, encouraged by those who felt the first edition was useful, and trying to benefit from the criticisms of those who did not.

The book is now in three sections. The first deals with the principles underlying the method; the second with the collection and interpretation of data from autoradiographic experiments; the third with the techniques of preparing autoradiographs. The major changes will be found in the second section, since the questions now being asked of autoradiography have become considerably more sophisticated in recent years.

Each chapter is intended to stand on its own. This has inevitably meant a certain amount of repetition, but I feel this is perhaps better than assuming that every reader will read the whole book from beginning to end.

It is a great pleasure to acknowledge the collaboration of Dr. **J.M. England** in producing a new section on the statistical analysis of autoradiographic data. In the section on electron microscope autoradiography, I have relied heavily on the advice of Dr. Miriam Salpeter, in whose laboratory at Cornell University this manuscript was started, while I was a guest on sabbatical leave there, and of Dr. M.A. Williams, of Sheffield. The section on diffusible materials has benefited greatly from discussions with Dr. W.E. Stumpf and Dr. W.B. Kinter. To them and to many others who have made available to me their data for building up this account of the present state of the art of autoradiography, I wish to record my thanks.

I am grateful to the following authors for permission to reproduce material which was used in the first edition: to Dr. H. Levi for Figs. 10, 11, 12, 13 and 85 from work carried out together; to Dr. M.M. Salpeter for kindly providing Figs. 2, 86, and 91, and for permission to reproduce Figs. 23, 25, 87, 88 and 90; to Dr. L.G. Caro for Figs. 3 and 22; to Dr. Z. Darzynkiewicz for Fig. 37; to Dr. R. Ross for Fig. 39; to Dr. L. Lajtha for Fig. 81; to Dr. S. Ullberg for Fig.

77; to Dr. L. Schwartz for Fig. 78. The range-energy data in the Appendix is based on material published by Dr. P. Demers. The table of data on radio-isotopes is taken from data published by the United Kingdom Atomic Energy Authority.

My thanks are due to the Editors of the following journals for permission to reproduce material already published by them, which had been used in the first edition: *Proceedings of the Royal Danish Academy of Sciences,*, Figs. 10, 11, 12, 13 and 85; the *Journal of Cell Biology*, Figs. 3, 22 and 88; *Laboratory Investigation*, Figs. 23, 25, 87 and 90; the *Journal of Anatomy*, Fig. 52; *Experimental Cell Research*, Fig. 56; *Radiation Research*, Fig. 29; the *Journal of Histochemistry and Cytochemistry*, Fig. 39: and *Leitz Mitteilungen*, Figs. 47, 49 and 51.

Of the new material in this second edition, I wish to express my thanks to Dr. M.M. Salpeter for permission to use Figs. 17, 18, 19, 20, 24, 63, 64, 67, 74, 74 and 75; to Dr. S. Bleecken for Fig. 21; to Dr. W.B. Kinter for Figs. 40 and 41; to Dr. J.M. England for Fig. 70 and new tables in the Appendix; and to the Research Laboratory of Ilford, Ltd., for kindly providing Fig. 1.

My thanks are due to the editors of the following journals for permission to use material already published by them: *Philosophical Transactions of the Royal Society*, Figs. 17, 18, 19 and 68; *Journal of Microscopy*, Figs. 54, 55, 57, 58 and 59; *Journal of Cell Biology*, Figs. 24, 73 and 74; *Journal of Clinicial Investigation*, Figs. 40 and 41; *Zeitschrift für Allgemeine Mikrobiologie*, Fig. 21; *Journal of Anatomy*, Fig. 43; *Journal of Endocrinology*, Fig. 44; and *Academic Press*, Fig. 30.

I am most grateful to Mrs. Betty Hammond for the care with which she has typed the mauscript. Miss Christine Court has once again provided several excellent diagrams, while Miss Tania Williams and Miss Barbara Liddiard have helped in many ways with the preparation of material for this edition. My wife has not only shown great tolerance during the gestation of the book, but has carried out an extensive literature search.

Finally, my thanks are due to the Medical Research Council, to the late Prof. G.W. Harris, F.R.S., and to Dr. A.G.M. Weddell for their interest and support while working here in Oxford.

Oxford, April 1972   ANDREW W. ROGERS

BIBLIOGRAPHY OF AUTORADIOGRAPHY

1 F. Passalacqua, *Biol. Latina*, 8, *Suppl.* 4 (1955) 7. Covering publications from 1924–54.
2 G.A. Boyd, *Autoradiography in Biology and Medicine*, Academic Press New York 1955. Covering period up to 1954.
3 M.E. Johnston, *Univ. Calif. Radiat. Lab.*, *8400*, July 1958. Covering period 1954–57.
4 M.E. Johnston, *Univ. Calif. Radiat. Lab.*, *8901*, August 1959. Covering period 1958–59.

CONTENTS

PART 1: THE THEORETICAL BASES OF AUTORADIOGRAPHY

CHAPTER 1

The Uses of Autoradiography

HISTORICAL INTRODUCTION

The first undoubted autoradiograph was obtained almost exactly 100 years ago. In 1867, Niepce de St. Victor[1] published an account of the blackening produced on emulsions of silver chloride and iodide by uranium nitrate and tartrate. It is curious that the blackening of photographic emulsions by radioactive material should have been observed in this way so long before the realisation that radioactive phenomena even existed. Niepce found this blackening to occur, even when the uranium salt was separated from the emulsion by sheets of glass of different colours. He interpreted his results in terms of luminescence.

In 1896, Henri Becquerel[2] repeated and extended Niepce's observations, again in the belief that he was investigating mechanisms of fluorescence. He used crystals of uranyl sulphate, and showed that, after exposing them to sunlight, they were able to blacken a photographic plate through two layers of black paper. On one occasion, it seems that the sun did not shine for several days, and the uranyl sulphate remained in a closed drawer together with the photographic plate. This plate was also found to be blackened. Through this experiment, and the work of the Curies in 1898, radioactivity was first demonstrated. So autoradiography is in fact older than the knowledge of radioactivity itself, and contributed directly to its discovery.

After these first, almost accidental, autoradiographs of crystals of uranium salts, autoradiography remained a curious observation rather than a scientific technique for a quarter of a century. Not until 1924 did Lacassagne and his collaborators begin to use this response of photographic emulsions to ionising radiations in order to study the distribution of polonium in biological specimens[3,4]. Their work, which followed sporadic experiments by other investigators, was the first systematic and successful attempt to exploit the phenomenon observed by Becquerel as a means of observing the sites of localisation of radioactivity within biological specimens.

References p. 8

[1]

The development of autoradiography as a biological technique progressed very little from Lacassagne's work until after the 1939-45 war. Physicists were using photographic methods of recording and studying radioactive phenomena, but the application of similar techniques to biological material was limited by two factors. The first, and most important, was that the few naturally occurring radioactive substances were of very little biological interest. In the second place, autoradiography was dependent on emulsions prepared for photographic purposes: the few autoradiographs that were made involved pressing the specimen against a photographic plate. The first fifty years of autoradiography saw very little accomplished, apart from the study, on a macroscopic scale, of the distribution of various salts of radium, thorium, or uranium in a few plants and animals[5].

The revolutionary advances in physics during and after the Second World War brought a new impetus to autoradiography. The study of cosmic rays and of the particles which could increasingly be generated in the laboratory created the demand which led to the production of nuclear emulsions – photographic emulsions with specialised characteristics, which recorded the tracks of charged particles with greater precision and sensitivity. From the work of such men as C.F. Powell[6,7], a wealth of new information became available, both on the techniques of handling this new recording medium, and on the interpretation and analysis of the observed particle tracks. Several fundamental particles were first described on the basis of their tracks in nuclear emulsions.

Controlled nuclear fission brought a further impetus to autoradiography. The advent of the atomic bomb made it vitally important to know the distribution in plants and animals of the fission products of radioactive fallout. At the same time, new radioactive isotopes became available, opening up new possibilities in the investigation of biological systems. It is not surprising that the physicists and biologists working in these new fields should have adopted the techniques and emulsions of the particle physicists.

In 1940, Hamilton, Soley and Eichorn[8] demonstrated the uptake of radioactive iodine by the thyroid gland, and Leblond[9] soon afterwards prepared autoradiographs showing its distribution in the gland. These were still made with the old technique of placing the sectioned specimen in direct contact with a lantern plate. By 1946, Bélanger and Leblond[10] had evolved a technique with liquid emulsion that gave considerably better resolution. The molten emulsion was removed from the lantern slides, and painted on the specimens with a fine paintbrush. It was not long before Arnold[11], who was studying the retention of long-lived isotopes in the body, adapted this technique for use with nuclear emulsions. The following year (1955), Joftes and Warren[12] described dipping slides in molten nuclear emulsion, a technique which has been widely used, and is the basis for present-day liquid emulsion methods.

During the same decade, a parallel group of techniques was emerging. The lantern slide provided the starting point once again, and several authors [13, 14] attempted to improve the contact between emulsion and specimen by stripping the emulsion off its glass support and applying it directly to the specimen. As was the case with liquid emulsions, a new technique employing a nuclear emulsion soon made its appearance. At the suggestion of S.R. Pelc, Kodak Ltd. began the manufacture of a special autoradiographic stripping film[15, 16]. Since the publication of these two papers, the stripping film technique, which brought great advances in resolution and in reproducibility over any of the techniques that had been tried up to that time, has probably yielded more autoradiographic information than any other single method.

Both the liquid emulsion and the stripping film techniques produce emulsion layers a few microns thick over the surface of the specimen. Charged particles coming from the specimen only leave one or two silver grains to show their passage in this type of preparation. A few autoradiographers, however, saw possibilities in the more direct application to biology of the physicists' techniques of recording particle tracks. This approach is direct and simple in the case of α particles, which leave a very characteristic track that is easy to record and recognise. β Particles are not so amenable to track methods, but, thanks to the pioneering work of physicists such as Hilde Levi[17-19] and C. Levinthal[20], β-track autoradiography has developed into a technique of great quantitative precision.

The last decade has seen a rapid transformation of cellular biology due to the development of the electron microscope. It was inevitable that attempts should be made to link the techniques of autoradiography to this new method of observing biological material. The first, and rather unpromising, autoradiographs viewed in the electron microscope were published in 1956 by Liquier-Milward[21]. Since then, new techniques have been proposed, and new nuclear emulsions produced, to meet the requirements of this approach for extremely high resolution. It is now possible to resolve the site of incorporation of radioactive material to within 500–700 Å in favourable circumstances, and further improvements are certain to come.

Radioactivity is no longer the property of a few rare elements of only minor biological interest. An increasingly wide range of compounds is now available labelled with a radioactive isotope, opening up new possibilities in the study of living systems. In consequence, the blackening of an emulsion of silver halides by uranium salts observed by Niepce a century ago has evolved into a wide spectrum of techniques for recording and measuring radioactivity in biological material.

RADIOACTIVE ISOTOPES

What place do radioactive isotopes have in the study of living systems?

The majority of techniques available to the biologist are basically analytical. In other words, by their application a mixture of individuals (which may be molecules or cells or animals) can be separated into groups on the basis of some common similarity between the members of each group. The techniques of biochemical analysis, such as chromatography, for instance, can give detailed and quantitative information on the molecules out of which cells and cell products are made. The techniques of histology and histochemistry provide an analysis of the cells and tissues of the body on the basis of their appearance and chemical constitution.

In living systems molecules and cells, and even whole organisms, undergo rapid and often surprising transformations. An aminoacid may be synthesised into a protein, which is subsequently degraded, yielding the original aminoacid again. The large, multinucleate megakaryocyte forms the small blood platelets. By their very nature, analytical procedures are cumbersome and unreliable for the study of these transformations. The relative sizes of the aminoacid and protein compartments of a cell are a poor measure of the rate of transformation of the one into the other.

If, however, aminoacid molecules labelled with a radioactive isotope can be introduced into such a system, and their recognition combined with subsequent analysis, the synthetic pathways by which they are incorporated into specific proteins may be studied, and the rates of these transformations measured with considerable precision.

This is the basic pattern of the tracer experiment. Whatever the material under examination, the pattern is the same. A population that is heterogeneous is separated into homogeneous groups by an analytical technique after the addition to it of labelled members of one group. The possible transformations that may occur between that group and the others are then determined by looking for the distribution of radioactivity in the analysed population.

The chief value of radioactive isotopes in biological research has been to provide precisely this dynamic information to supplement the analytical techniques as they have been applied at every level from the molecular upwards. In every field of biology, the combination of radioisotope techniques with the analytical methods available has added another dimension to the observations that can be made. It is difficult to see how the work of the past 20 years on oxidative respiration, photosynthesis, or the control of protein synthesis by the nucleic acids, to quote only these examples, could have been carried out without the advances in nuclear physics that made radioactive isotopes so freely available.

In addition to this use of isotopes in the tracer experiment, there have evolved a number of techniques in which radioactivity has been exploited in a purely analytical way. The precision with which relatively small numbers of labelled atoms may be detected and measured has led to methods of analysis more sensitive than those otherwise available. In radioactivation analysis, for example, a method has developed for measuring the yield of certain elements in biological specimens at a sensitivity which is often far higher than that available with any other existing technique. The principle involved is neutron irradiation of the specimen in order to induce radioactivity in the element under study. The characteristic radiation from this activity is then detected and measured[22].

Another example of the use of radioactive isotopes as the basis for an analytical technique comes from histochemistry. In 1961, Ostrowski and Barnard[23] suggested the use of isotopically labelled enzyme inhibitors as histochemical reagents. Following their application to the tissue under study, the distribution of radioactivity could be observed by autoradiography. From this pattern, the distribution of the enzyme to which the inhibitor was bound could be inferred, and measurements of the radioactivity present in a particular cell or structure could be used to estimate the number of molecules of enzyme present there. Reference will be made to this interesting approach later, in the chapters dealing with quantitative measurements by means of nuclear emulsions, and to some of the results that have been obtained through its application.

Apart from tracer experiments and the analytical techniques based on radioactive isotopes, the third main group of experiments that involve the use of isotopes comes under the heading of radiobiology. Studies on the distribution and retention within the body of ingested radioisotopes and on the effects of radiation on the surrounding cells and tissues combine elements of the tracer experiment with the analytical approach.

These are the three principal ways in which radioactive isotopes are used in studying living systems. The techniques available for recording and measuring radioisotopes will next be considered, to try and pinpoint the characteristics of nuclear emulsions which make them suitable for particular experiments, and to relate these features to the other methods of detecting radiation.

AUTORADIOGRAPHY IN RELATION TO OTHER TECHNIQUES
OF DETECTING RADIOISOTOPES

The methods available for the detection and measurement of radioactivity can be classified under three headings.

The first of these is the group of electrical methods that depends on the production of ion pairs by the emitted radiation. The geiger tube, the ionisation chamber, and the gas-flow counter are all examples of this approach, in which the ionisation caused by the passage of a particle or γ ray through the sensitive volume of the counter is recorded as an electrical pulse, which can be then amplified and registered.

The second group relies on the property, possessed by a number of materials, of absorbing energy from the incident radiation, and re-emitting this in the form of visible light. In a scintillation counter, these minute flashes of light are detected and converted into electrical pulses by a photomultiplier tube, and may then be amplified and registered in the same way as in the ionisation detectors.

These two groups of techniques have much in common. A β particle entering the sensitive volume of the counter produces a transient effect which is converted into an electrical pulse. These pulses can be handled by data processing systems rapidly and reliably. The pulse counting techniques, whether based on ionisation or scintillation, can provide accurate measurements of the radioactivity in a source, but each measurement is a sum of the radiation entering the sensitive volume of the counter. Variations in radioactivity from one part of the sample to another are not detected.

Autoradiography differs from the pulse counting techniques in several important respects. Each crystal of silver halide in the photographic emulsion is an independent detector, insulated from the rest of the emulsion by its capsule of gelatin. Each crystal can respond to the passage through it of a charged particle, with the formation of a latent image that persists throughout the counting or exposure period, and is made permanent by the process of development. The record provided by the nuclear emulsion is cumulative, and spatially accurate.

By responding in this strictly localised fashion to incident charged particles, a nuclear emulsion is ideally suited to studies of the distribution of radioactivity within a sample, a function that the pulse counters cannot perform. But while the emulsion can and does respond in a quantitative fashion to radiation, it is often a slow and difficult process measuring the overall activity of a sample in this way, by comparison to the speed and simplicity of the pulse counters.

There is thus little point in autoradiographing a specimen that is homogeneous. But where the specimen is made up of different components the measurement of the radioactivity present in bulk samples by pulse counting techniques only gives a mean value for the whole specimen. An extreme case of heterogeneity within the specimen is provided by animal or plant tissues. Pulse counting from a gram of homogenised liver gives a rapid and accurate assessment of the total radioactivity present, but no evidence on whether it is intra- or extracellular, in parenchymal cells or other cell types, nuclear or cytoplasmic, and so on. The earliest experiments in autoradiography were concerned solely with the localisation of radioactivity within a specimen, and this probably remains the most frequent goal of biologists using nuclear emulsions.

The strict localisation of the response of a nuclear emulsion to those grains through which an incident particle passes, means that it is possible to study sources of very small size within a larger specimen. It is possible to observe the nucleus of a single cell, and determine whether or not it is labelled, or an individual chromosome in a squash preparation of a dividing cell.

It may be impossible to isolate sources as small as these from the tissue to present them to a pulse counting system. Even if microdissection is possible, the levels of radioactivity in such minute specimens are usually too low for detection against the background of the pulse counter. In such cases, there is no alternative to using the nuclear emulsion itself as a measuring instrument.

Nuclear emulsions have a very high efficiency for β particles, particularly those with low energies. Fortunately, many of the elements of interest to the biologist have suitable isotopes – tritium, carbon-14, sulphur-35 and iodine-125 for example. If the volume of emulsion to be examined is restricted to the immediate vicinity of the source, the effective volume of detector may be as little as 100 cubic microns. Reducing the detector volume also reduces the probability of observing a background event, due to cosmic rays, for instance. It may be weeks or months before background in such small volumes of emulsion builds up to restrictive levels. It is possible, therefore, to combine a high efficiency for low energy β particles with very long counting times. With suitable techniques, sources the size of a single cell or smaller can be accurately measured at decay rates as low as 1 disintegration per day. By contrast, most commercially available pulse counters have backgrounds of 10–20 counts per minute.

In summary, then, autoradiography supplements the data provided by pulse counting techniques when the specimen is relatively large, indicating the distribution of radioactivity between the various parts of the specimen. With sources of cellular dimensions, pulse counting is often impossible, and measurements of radioactivity may have to be made by autoradiography.

References p. 8

Quantitative methods of autoradiography have made great strides in recent years, and it is now often possible not only to compare the levels of radioactivity in microscopic sources, but even to measure them in absolute terms[24]. Absolute measurements of radioactivity have even been made on subcellular structures by electron microscope autoradiography[25].

In these and other applications, the use of nuclear emulsions to detect ionising radiations provides the biologist with information that often no other technique can give. The techniques of autoradiography still appear to be developing and diversifying, as new problems emerge to which the characteristics of the method can be matched.

REFERENCES

1   N. Niepce de St. Victor, *Compt. Rend.*, 65 (1867) 505.
2   H. Becquerel, *Compt. Rend.*, 122 (1896) 420, 501, 689, 1086.
3   A. Lacassagne and J.S. Lattes, *Bull. Histol. Appl. et Tech. Microscop.*, 1 (1924) 279.
4   A Lacassagne, J.S. Lattes and J. Lavedan, *J. Radiol. Électrol.*, 9 (1925) 1.
5   F. Passalacqua, *Biol. Latina*, 8 (1955) 7, Suppl. IV.
6   C.F. Powell and A.P.S. Occhialini, *Nuclear Physics in Photographs*, Clarendon, Oxford, 1947.
7   C.F. Powell, P.H. Fowler and D.H. Perkins, *The Study of Elementary Particles by the Photographic Method*, Pergamon, London, 1959.
8   J.G. Hamilton, M.H. Soley and K.B. Eichorn, *Univ. Calif. (Berkeley) Publ. Pharmacol.*, 1, No. 28 (1940) 339.
9   C.P. Leblond, *J. Anat.*, 77 (1943) 149.
10 L.F. Bélanger and C.P. Leblond, *Endocrinology*, 39 (1946) 8.
11 J.S. Arnold, *Proc. Soc. Exptl. Biol. Med.*, 85 (1954) 113.
12 D.L. Joftes and S. Warren, *J. Biol. Phot. Assoc.*, 23 (1955) 145.
13 A.M. McDonald, J. Cobb and A.K. Solomon, *Science*, 107(1948) 550.
14 G.A. Boyd and A.I. Williams, *Proc. Soc. Exptl. Biol. Med.*, 69 (1948) 225.
15 I. Doniach and S.R. Pelc, *Brit. J. Radiol.*, 23 (1950) 184.
16 R.W. Berriman, R.H. Herz and G.W.W. Stevens, *Brit. J. Radiol.*, 23 (1950) 472.
17 H. Levi, *Exptl. Cell Res.*, 7 (1954) 44.
18 H. Levi, *Exptl. Cell Res.*, Suppl. 4 (1957) 207.
19 H. Levi, A.W. Rogers, M.W. Bentzon and A. Nielson, *Kgl. Danske Videnskab. Selskab, Mat.-Fys. Medd.*, 33, No. 11 (1963).
20 C. Levinthal and C.A. Thomas, *Biochim. Biophys. Acta*, 23 (1957) 453.
21 J. Liquier-Milward, *Nature*, 177 (1956) 619.
22 J.M.A. Lenihan and S.J. Thomson (eds.), *Advances in Activation Analysis*, Academic Press, London and New York, 1969.
23 K. Ostrowski and E.A. Barnard, *Exptl. Cell Res.*, 25 (1961) 465.
24 A.W. Rogers, Z. Darżynkiewicz, K. Ostrowski, E.A. Barnard and M.M. Salpeter, *J. Cell Biol.*, 41 (1969) 665.
25 M.M. Salpeter, *J. Cell Biol.*, 32 (1967) 379.

CHAPTER 2

Nuclear Emulsions and the Photographic Process

The response of photographic emulsions to light is still not fully understood. Research is still in progress into the fundamental mechanisms by which light activates the crystals of silver halide, and into the complexities of development. Fortunately, the research worker who uses nuclear emulsions does not need a complete understanding of the photographic process. It is sufficient to have a working hypothesis which fits the principal phenomena which he will meet. Such a hypothesis is available, and there exists enough accepted theory upon which autoradiography may be reasonably and successfully based.

In his book on autoradiography, G.A. Boyd[1] states that "the biologist is better trained to understand the working of a photographic emulsion than that of an electronic circuit." I am not sure that I fully understand either, though I must admit to finding the literature on photographic emulsions far more interesting. Ever since the development of photographic emulsions based on silver bromide and gelatin in 1850, the production of photographic material has contained an element of empiricism, which has been reinforced by the secrecy with which the commercial process has been surrounded. This process includes stages like "the second ripening" which are reminiscent of attempts to make liqueurs in the kitchen, and odd scraps of information such as that pork gelatin is unsatisfactory for the production of silver bromide emulsions. But in spite of its empirical nature, the production of photographic emulsion is now a carefully controlled process, and, if the results of autoradiography are not precise and reproducible, the fault is usually to be found in the experiment and not in the emulsion.

THE PHOTOGRAPHIC PROCESS

Many salts can be activated by light. The type of photographic emulsion with which autoradiography is concerned is a suspension of crystals of silver bromide in gelatin. When light falls on such an emulsion, a change is produced in the bromide crystals. This change is not directly visible, but on treatment of the emulsion with a developing agent, those crystals affected by light become converted into grains of metallic silver, whereas crystals which have not been illuminated remain unchanged. In photographic terms, the film that has been exposed possesses a "latent image", which can be converted into a true image by development. In autoradiography, the term latent image has come to refer to the change produced by light or radiation of other sorts within the individual halide crystal, and this is the context in which it will be used throughout this book.

Silver bromide crystallises in a cubic pattern, with the ions of silver and bromide regularly spaced, each silver ion in the centre of 6 bromide ions, and *vice versa.* But light does not produce a latent image in a perfect crystal. Defects in the regular lattice of the crystal are essential for photosensitivity, and the controlled production of these defects is vital to emulsion manufacture. These defects form sensitivity specks, which are often at the surface of the crystal, but also occur more deeply.

Our understanding of the process of formation of a latent image is based on the theory produced in 1938 by Gurney and Mott[2]. They proposed that the initial effect of light on a crystal of silver bromide is to raise the energy of the outermost electron of a bromide ion so that it leaves its orbit. The bromide ion thus becomes an atom of bromine. The electron thus liberated is able to travel through the crystal from one ion to the next, in a conductivity band, until it becomes trapped at one or other of the sensitivity specks or defects in the crystal lattice. At this site, a silver ion becomes converted into an atom of silver. The latent image within a crystal is thus the presence within a sensitivity speck of a number of atoms of metallic silver.

In the presence of a developing agent, this nucleus of metallic silver catalyses the conversion of the entire crystal into metallic silver. The bromide crystals which have not been reduced to silver are finally dissolved out of the emulsion by the photographic fixative, leaving a pattern of silver grains reproducing the pattern of light falling on the emulsion.

The tracks of charged particles are recorded in a nuclear emulsion by fundamentally the same process, except that the electrons initially liberated in the crystal derive their energy from the passage of the particle through the crystal, and not from photons of visible light.

Each stage in this process will now be considered in rather more detail. Those readers who wish to explore the fundamental mechanisms of photography are referred to the short list of books at the end of this chapter[3,4].

SILVER BROMIDE CRYSTALS

Probably the chief difference between the emulsions produced for light photography and those for nuclear work is the much higher ratio of silver bromide to gelatin in the latter. The higher this ratio becomes, the higher the density of the emulsion, and hence the greater its stopping power for charged particles – in other words, particle tracks will become relatively shorter.

For a given bromide to gelatin ratio, the silver bromide may form relatively few, large crystals, or be divided into a large number of smaller crystals. It is clear that the latter alternative will give more information per unit volume of emulsion: there are more possibilities for crystals to be activated or not, and the events occurring within the emulsion will be reproduced with greater accuracy, or resolution. Nuclear emulsions, designed to record the tracks of sub-atomic particles, tend to have smaller crystals than the emulsions designed for photography for this reason. With fewer, larger crystals, however, more blackening of the processed emulsion will result from small numbers of particles, since one such large crystal may yield as much silver on development as many smaller ones, without requiring any more ionisation to produce a latent image within it.

It is possible to obtain nuclear emulsions in a wide range of crystal sizes from $0.02-0.5$ μ diameter, and with equally wide variations in the sensitivity of the individual crystals. In general, the more precise the resolution of events in the emulsion that the experiment demands, the smaller the crystal diameter that will be appropriate. In X-ray films, the crystal diameters are in general far larger, ranging from $0.2-3.0$ μ. The significance of these differences between the two types of emulsion will be discussed further in relation to the definition of efficiency (see p. 73 and p. 270).

In general terms, the smaller the mean diameter of the silver halide crystals in an emulsion, the more difficult it becomes to achieve a high sensitivity. It is clear that a very small crystal can only contain a correspondingly small part of the trajectory of a charged particle, so that the total energy liberated within the crystal by the particle is relatively small. There must be a limiting crystal diameter below which the passage of a β particle is unlikely to be recorded. This stage may not yet have been reached, but, as will be seen in the chapter on electron microscope autoradiography (p.332), the emulsions with the smallest crystal diameters at present available are less sensitive than those with larger crystals.

Fig. 1 shows crystals of three Ilford emulsions, as seen under the electron microscope. The variation in crystal diameter from one to another is clearly

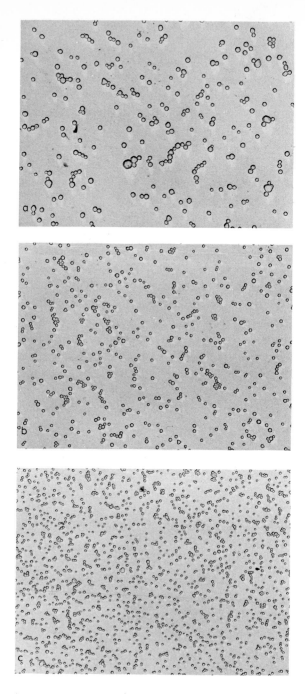

Fig. 1. Electron micrographs of silver halide crystals from Ilford nuclear research emulsions. The crystals have been shadowed so that the length of the shadow is twice the height of the crystal. 1a, G5 emulsion; 1b, K5 emulsion; and 1c, L4 emulsion. (X 7500) (Micrographs kindly made available by the Research Laboratory, Ilford Ltd.)

seen. One other major difference between nuclear emulsions and those used for photography is the uniformity of their crystals. In conventional photography, a certain amount of variation in size and in sensitivity from one crystal to another can be tolerated, and may even be a positive advantage, giving greater contrast rather than an all-or-none, soot-and-whitewash type of picture. In nuclear emulsions, however, uniformity in size and sensitivity are important characteristics of the silver bromide crystals.

GELATIN

The functions of gelatin are more important and more varied than might at first be thought. This complex protein is derived from the skins of cattle, and the emulsion manufacturers go to great lengths to ensure that their supplies are uniform in many different respects.

In the first place, gelatin forms a supporting medium for the silver bromide crystals, isolating them from each other so that one crystal may not catalyse the development of its neighbours. If an emulsion is centrifuged while molten, each crystal will apparently move within its own shell of gelatin, so that the concentrated silver bromide crystals will still remain isolated from each other. As a supporting matrix, gelatin must permit the access of reagents to the crystals, and, in the completed autoradiograph, allow for clear visibility of the developed grains. At the stage of formation of the latent image, and even more so later when development is in progress, the deposition of metallic silver within the crystal is accompanied by the migration of bromine atoms out of the crystal. Gelatin acts as an acceptor of bromine, permitting these processes to take place without too high a probability of recombination between the bromine and the photolytic electron in the one case, and bromine and the silver atoms in the other.

In short, gelatin matters, and attempts to replace it with other materials have so far failed.

Two properties of gelatin deserve special mention. It undergoes sol–gel transformations reversibly at little above room temperature. It can thus be melted and poured conveniently. It is also capable of considerable changes in volume on hydration or drying. If it is spread on a plane support, these changes will usually appear as variations in thickness of the emulsion layer. Rapid drying may cause severe deformation of gelatin, and can even crack a glass support. The gelatin may also apply pressure to the silver bromide crystals, causing the appearance of latent images through mechanical stresses alone. All drying procedures should be gentle and slow, to achieve the best results.

References p. 29

Ilford add a plasticising agent to their emulsions to reduce the shrinkage that would otherwise occur on drying, which may be washed out of the emulsion in any procedure that involves soaking or diluting the emulsion before exposure. If this happens, the stress background will be considerably higher. Waller[5] has suggested adding 1% of glycerol to any aqueous bath in which the emulsion is soaked. This certainly reduces the stress background in nuclear emulsions, and this step is frequently included in the detailed techniques described later.

THE LATENT IMAGE

A latent image is formed within a silver halide crystal when sufficient atoms of silver are present there to ensure development of the crystal. There is no fixed number of atoms of silver needed for this to occur: with most nuclear emulsions under reasonable conditions of development, the number probably lies between 10 and 1000. Most crystals have several sensitivity specks, and more than one of these may contain an adequate number of silver atoms. In other words, the initial amount of silver catalysing the deposition of silver within the crystal during development may vary widely from one activated crystal to another, giving developed grains of different sizes, from crystals of identical size, under identical conditions of development.

In a highly sensitised emulsion, very little energy is required to produce a free electron which can travel through the crystal lattice to a sensitivity speck. This reaction is not specific to light and to ionising radiations, but may occur in response to a whole range of agents. Mechanical pressure has already been mentioned in discussing the properties of gelatin, and beautiful fingerprints may be made with nuclear emulsions. Heat, too, may provide sufficient energy to cause latent image formation. Probably some of the random silver grains which form the inevitable background in any autoradiograph are due to thermal excitation. Many chemicals, particularly reducing agents, are capable of acting on silver bromide crystals with the appearance of a latent image, even in very low concentrations.

Once a latent image has formed at a sensitivity speck, it is not necessarily there forever. It is possible for the silver atoms to recombine with the bromine atoms to give silver bromide once more. This occurs as a random process, so that it is more likely where a long period of time elapses between formation of the latent image and development. There are certain conditions which strongly favour this recombination, or latent image fading, as it is called. Heat will increase its probability, as will the presence of excess water. Many oxidising agents will also greatly accelerate the rate of fading of the latent image. Latent image fading tends to be more severe in emulsions with a small crystal diameter.

It is possible to expose nuclear emulsions at temperatures down to −196°. Under constant conditions of development, the number of developed grains produced by a uniform dose of radiation decreases linearly, until at −76° it falls to 35% of the number that is seen with exposures at 4° (ref. 6). At low temperatures, the size of the latent images is smaller, or the distribution of latent image silver more disperse. Over quite a range of temperatures, however, this effect can be balanced by a slight increase in the time of development, without a significant increase in background.

Finally, it must be emphasised again that latent images form at sites within a crystal that were determined by faults in the regular lattice of silver bromide introduced during manufacture. The position of a latent image within a crystal need have no relation to the path of a charged particle through the crystal. This assumes considerable importance in discussions of autoradiographic resolution at the electron microscope level (p. 62).

From these rather bewildering observations, it is possible to draw some general rules which indicate the conditions of handling of nuclear emulsions which are likely to be the most successful. For many of the recommendations made for the handling of nuclear emulsions are designed to prevent fading of the latent image, and the creation of latent images by means other than radiation. Light and mechanical pressure must obviously be avoided. Emulsions should be heated as little as possible, for the shortest possible time. Drying must be slow, uniform, and gentle: stress from shrinkage of the gelatin is reduced if the emulsion is dried slowly, after it has gelled. During exposure, the emulsion should be cooled to reduce thermal background. Exposure should be as short as possible, the emulsion should be kept dry and, if latent image fading is likely to affect results adversely, in an atmosphere from which oxygen is excluded. Throughout preparation and exposure, every effort must be made to prevent contaminating chemicals from coming into contact with the emulsion. Vessels used to hold emulsion should be of glass, plastic, or high grade stainless steel, and must be kept scrupulously clean. Only distilled water should be used.

Finally, since so many agents can cause formation and fading of the latent image, the presence or absence of developed silver grains in an autoradiograph of itself means absolutely nothing. Only a well-designed experiment, with adequate controls, will give a meaningful result.

DEVELOPMENT OF THE LATENT IMAGE

Two principal methods of developing the latent image exist. The first, which is by far the more commonly used, is known as chemical development: the second, physical development, will be briefly discussed on page 24.

All chemical developers act in the same general way. They are reducing agents, usually possessing the appropriate reducing potential when in slightly alkaline media. Since the process of development results in the generation of hydrobromic acid, developing solutions usually contain some sort of buffering system for maintaining the optimum pH.

Almost any agent with the appropriate reducing properties will act as a developer. Sugars, haemoglobin, and even old Burgundy wines have been used[7]. The commonly used developers generally contain hydroquinone, metol, or amidol. Slight differences between the effects of these agents exist. Hydroquinone tends to produce thick filaments of silver: amidol and metol produce finer filaments. p-Phenylenediamine is a developer that also attacks the silver bromide crystals directly, a sort of combined developer and fixer. In this way, its use results in very small developed grains. Presumably, as development slowly proceeds at the latent image, etching of the surface of the crystal also goes on, finally separating the latent image and its attached grain from the remaining silver bromide, and preventing the further growth of the grain.

Some developers only affect latent images at the surfaces of the crystals, others will also develop internal latent images. This may be of importance when latent images are being lost during exposure by oxidation. This process appears to affect surface latent images more rapidly than internal ones, and reliance on a developer than cannot reach internal latent images may lose many grains that should have been developed[8]. In most cases, however, the choice of developer makes only marginal differences to the final autoradiograph. The important thing is to understand the principles underlying development, so the most appropriate conditions can be selected for each experiment.

Development proceeds rapidly at the site of a latent image. The silver bromide is converted to silver atoms, which are deposited on the site of latent image formation, and bromide ions, which diffuse out from the crystal. Silver deposition results in an elongated, thin ribbon, probably by the addition of more silver at the latent image spot, and displacement of the rest of the ribbon away from it. This ribbon, rather like tooth-paste squeezed out of a tube, coils to form a tangled mass which looks like a solid "silver grain" in the light microscope. Under the electron microscope, however, its structure may be clearly seen (Fig.2).

Recent studies by Bachmann and Salpeter[9] show that the developed grain may not necessarily coincide in position with the parent crystal, although the silver grain always makes contact with the crystal at the site of the latent image.

Fig. 2. Electron micrograph of silver grains of Ilford L4 emulsion developed with Microdol X. The characteristic appearance of silver grains after chemical development is seen – irregular coiled ribbons of metallic silver. (× 36 000) (Material provided by Dr. M.M. Salpeter)

The size to which such a grain may grow is limited by the total amount of silver present in the parent crystal, provided that the neighbouring crystals remain isolated from the catalytic effect of this coil of silver. But development may be stopped at any stage short of this maximum grain size. The fully developed grain is slightly bigger than its parent crystal.

Development also takes place in the absence of a latent image, but far more slowly. Ultimately, however, every crystal in the emulsion will be converted to silver if development is allowed to go on long enough.

If development is stopped short at a given point, differences in the number and size of the original silver deposits in crystals containing latent images may be reflected in differences in the size of the developed grains. Clearly, those crystals with several, large, nuclei of silver will develop faster than those with one, relatively small, latent image. Development is not an "all-or-none" effect, but a variable phenomenon. Crystals containing a latent image are "developed" when the mass of silver in the grain is brought to a sufficient size to be seen. Under constant conditions of development, a latent image of N atoms of silver may be needed to do this. By altering one parameter of development, latent images of $N/2$ atoms may be sufficient to produce visible grains. Under identical conditions of processing, a change in the methods of observing the emulsion may bring into view grains that were previously too small to be seen.

If one takes an emulsion in which ionising particles have produced latent images in a given number of the crystals, a plot of the number of grains against development time would follow the general course illustrated in Fig. 3. Some of

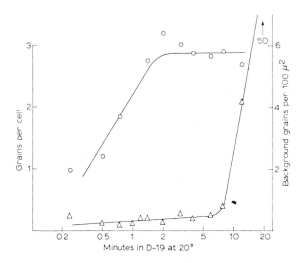

Fig. 3. The kinetics of development of Ilford L4 emulsion in D-19 developer. The grain count per labelled bacterium (○) remains constant after about 2 min development. The background grain density (△) slowly increases up to 6 min, and very rapidly at longer development times. (From Caro and Van Tubergen, 1962)

the grains due to radioactivity in the source appear after minimal development, their number increases with time, and then reaches a plateau. The randomly distributed background grains build up slowly at first, but increase logarithmically at longer development times. The latent images in crystals hit by beta particles are fairly large, it seems, and lie within a reasonably narrow size range. The distribution of latent image sizes in background crystals is quite different, with a few crystals only possessing latent images that can be developed in a short time, but more and more grains appearing as prolonged development lifts to visibility crystals with fewer and fewer atoms of latent image silver. The art of development is the selection of conditions which will give the best ratio of grains from radioactive particles to background grains.

During the period in which the number of silver grains in the tracks is not increasing, the size of these grains may still be increasing. Ahmad and Demers[10] have investigated the effect of this increase in size on the opacity of the grains, measured photometrically, and it is clear that, while the number of grains in a track often has this long plateau, any characteristic of the grains that can be measured photometrically varies continuously with developing time. This point will be discussed again later in considering the value of photometric estimations of grain density (p. 182).

A number of factors can affect the precise shape of the development curve. Perhaps the most important variable is temperature. At about 5° or below, the course of development is so slow that for practical purposes it can be considered arrested. As the temperature rises, under otherwise constant conditions, the speed of development increases. This effect is made use of in the temperature cycle development of thick emulsion layers. At room temperature, the rate of diffusion of developer into the thick emulsion is slow by comparison with the rate of development, so that the surface may be heavily over-developed before the developer has even penetrated to the deeper layers. Such thick emulsions are soaked first in developer at 5°, to ensure access of developer to all layers, and then warmed up to permit development to proceed.

The concentration of developing agent will also affect the rate of development, which will be reduced by dilution and increased by a raised concentration. One other variable is not often appreciated. This is the effect of agitating the slides while they are in developer. This speeds up the rate of development to a surprising degree.

It is clear, then, that several variables determine the precise shape of the development curve — the choice of developer, its dilution, the temperature of development, and the amount of agitation. How does one select the correct combination?

The first thing to be realised is that the degree of development that is optimal will vary from one experiment to another. There is no "correct time". Fig. 4 shows a series of autoradiographs prepared under identical conditions and developed for increasing periods of time, viewed by two alternative methods of illumination. It is clear that the use of transmitted illumination to view the autoradiographs makes necessary the presence of larger silver grains, in order that they may be recognised clearly. At the same time, very small background grains will not be seen. A longer development time can be chosen than would be advisable with dark-field illumination. In the same way, the magnification at which the autoradiograph is to be viewed influences the choice of an ideal development time. At very low magnifications, large grains only will be seen, and a longer time will be chosen. Under oil immersion, this degree of development might produce grains so big that they obscure important detail in the specimen, while the second population of smaller background grains might be just visible.

The development schedule must be appropriate to the experiment. The best way to determine the optimum conditions is to take a series of slides with the sort of specimen that will form the main experiment, expose them under identical conditions, and then, having arbitrarily chosen a likely developer, dilution, and temperature at which to work, develop the autoradiographs for

Fig. 4(A2).

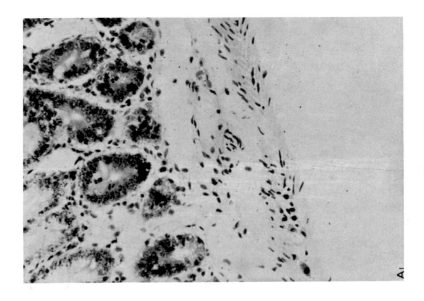

Fig. 4(A1).

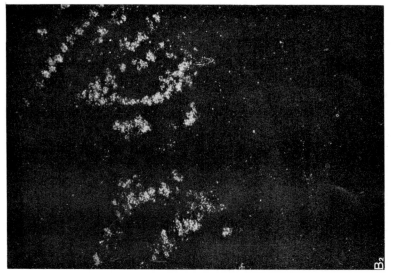

Fig. 4(B2).

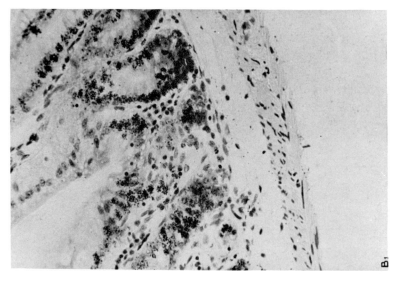

Fig. 4(B1).

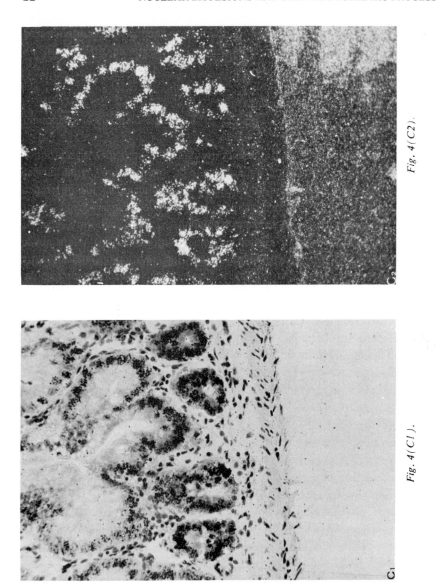

Fig. 4(C2).

Fig. 4(C1).

Fig. 4. Photomicrographs of the intestine of the galago after the administration of [^{3}H]-thymidine. Identical sections covered with Ilford G5 emulsion have been developed in Amidol for increasing times. The same field from each slide is presented with transmitted (*1*), and incident dark-field illumination (*2*). (*A*) after 3 min development, the grains are small and hard to see by transmitted light *(1)*, clear and distinct by incident light *(2)*. (*B*) Centre, after 7 min development, the grains are better seen by transmitted light (*1*), large by incident light (*2*). (*C*) After 11 min development, the grains are clear and distinct by transmitted light (*1*), still with a low background. By incident light (*2*), however, many tiny background grains can be seen. Sections stained with Harris' haematoxylin. (× 170)

increasing times. View the slides under the conditions that will be used to view the experimental autoradiographs, and select the time that gives the clearest trace with an acceptably low background.

It may be that the whole process of development is too rapid — that the first slide has no trace, while background fog is already appearing on the second. In this case, the arbitrarily chosen parameters must be altered to slow down development, to lengthen out the plateau between the development of activated crystals and the production of background fog. Diluting the developer or reducing the temperature of development are the two alternatives. Similarly, if the development time that is optimal seems unnecessarily long, development can be speeded up by increasing the temperature or the amount of agitation.

Development times and conditions are given in all the techniques that are described fully in the second part of this book. It cannot be emphasised too strongly that these are only suggestions, based on the darkroom conditions and methods of microscopy in one laboratory. They are undoubtedly not applicable to every autoradiographic experiment. The same is true of development schedules published in the literature, and of manufacturers' recommendations. The optimal time and conditions of development depend so critically on the requirements of the experiment itself, and on the methods of viewing the finished autoradiograph, that there is no alternative to determining them directly in the laboratory.

Welton[11] has presented an interesting analysis of some of the variables affecting the development of Kodak AR-10 stripping film with D19b developer. Her results suggest that temperatures up to $23°$ may be used without shortening the plateau of development unduly by the rapid increase of background grains. To try to give some idea of the relative importance of the other factors involved, diluting the developer with its own volume of distilled water may increase the development time by about 50%. Continuous, gentle agitation may halve the time in developer that gives best results, by comparison with no agitation at all.

To get reproducible results, it is obviously necessary to control these various factors. It is possible to get moderately reproducible results by checking the temperature of the developer, and adopting some routine of agitation, such as 10 shakes per minute. These variables can be simply controlled to much greater accuracy. By using a thermostatically controlled developing tank with nitrogen burst agitation, we have considerably reduced the variation between batches of autoradiographs caused by slight differences in the conditions of development[12].

The only satisfactory way to get good results in the conditions of your own autoradiographic experiment is to carry out the simple investigation into developing conditions outlined above. Few publications state the conditions of development at all fully, and none specify the frequency of agitation of the developer. It is, incidentally, not enough to find the best conditions for one emulsion, and to expect them to apply to another. Even the nuclear emulsions produced by one manufacturer may vary in this respect. The optimal development for Ilford K2 in my laboratory produces unacceptable background fog with similar layers of Ilford G5.

Development is arrested, when working with thin emulsion layers, by rinsing the slide in distilled water. This dilutes out the developer to such a low concentration that development stops. With thicker emulsion layers this process becomes less and less effective, and it is usual to reinforce the dilution by also changing the pH to the acid side of neutrality. A 1% solution of acetic acid will do this very satisfactorily.

PHYSICAL DEVELOPMENT

In chemical development, as outlined above, the silver bromide crystal provides the silver which becomes deposited on the latent image. In physical development, the process is somewhat different.

Silver is deposited from solution on the the minute speck of metallic silver already present at the latent image. This may be done before fixation with developers such as amidol at an acid pH, with the addition of silver nitrate or silver sodium sulphite to provide a source of silver. Probably the more usual method is to dissolve out the silver bromide by fixation in sodium thiosulphate first, and then to develop in a solution of p-phenylenediamine, sodium sulphate, and silver nitrate.

Physical development results in the formation of very small silver grains, which are spherical or comma-shaped when seen under the electron microscope, instead of the long coiled filaments produced by conventional chemical developers. This type of development has been suggested for use with electron microscope autoradiography for this reason, by Caro and Van Tubergen[13]. The small grains, which make contact with the presumed site of the latent image, give better overall resolution than large grains, since the position of the latent image responsible for the latter cannot be determined with certainty (see p. 62).

Physical development only has this one, rather specialised, application to autoradiographic techniques in use at the present time.

FIXATION OF THE EMULSION

After chemical development, fixation dissolves away the silver bromide crystals that remain in the emulsion. This is usually carried out in a solution of sodium thiosulphate (hypo). The thiosulphate ion forms a series of soluble complexes with ionic silver, without affecting the developed grains. It is possible to increase the rate of fixation by agitating the solution, as with development, and by increasing its temperature. The end-point of fixation is generally taken as twice the period required for the emulsion to become transparent.

The concentration of sodium thiosulphate is not critical, in the range of 25–35%. It is usual to work with a 30% solution, but it is quite unnecessary to weigh out the hypo to the third decimal place.

It is important to remember that nuclear emulsions contain a higher percentage of silver bromide than do photographic emulsions, and that the speed of fixation drops off rapidly as the products of fixation accumulate in the solution. As a rough guide, no more than 24 autoradiographs with thin emulsion layers on $3'' \times 1''$ slides should be fixed in 250 ml of hypo. With thicker emulsion layers, larger volumes and frequent changes of hypo are necessary. The rate-limiting factor appears to be the diffusion of the silver–thiosulphate complexes out of the emulsion.

Rapid fixers of various sorts are often used in photography instead of plain hypo. They are based on the use of ammonium thiosulphate, and they can reduce the fixation time by as much as 75%. Unfortunately, ammonium thiosulphate dissolves the silver grains slowly, in addition to its more rapid attack on the silver bromide crystals. In very thin emulsion layers, its use is acceptable, as it is in contact with the emulsion for so short a time that the developed grains are probably not significantly eroded. But, in the thicker emulsion layers, where the fixation times may be very long indeed and a more rapid action would be very welcome, the silver grains themselves may be so reduced in size that they are no longer visible if a rapid fixer is used. If plain hypo is used for fixation, it is important that it should be freshly made up, and discarded after use.

Hardeners may be added to acid fixing-baths. These reduce the swelling of the gelatin in the subsequent washing, and hence its liability to mechanical injury. In most microscope work, it is possible to avoid physical damage to the emulsion during washing, and to protect it subsequently under a cover-glass, so that hardeners are only an added complication. With thick emulsions, hardeners in the fixing-bath can considerably increase the time needed for fixation. They may have a place in the processing of autoradiographs of large objects, such as chromatograms.

References p. 29

In a nuclear emulsion, which is usually 50% by volume silver bromide crystals, very few of which become converted into silver grains, it is obvious that removal of the undeveloped crystals by fixation will reduce the volume of the emulsion considerably. After fixation, dehydration in alcohols, and mounting in a conventional histological medium under a coverslip, an emulsion layer may be as little as one third its original thickness during exposure. This may make the recognition and following of particle tracks in thick emulsion layers very difficult, and it is often useful to impregnate the emulsion with glycerin or some similar agent in order to reswell it to a thickness nearer that during exposure, if track recognition is necessary.

By the process of fixation, then, the silver bromide remaining in the emulsion after development is brought into solution. Afterwards, the products of fixation must be washed out of the emulsion layer. This is usually done in running tapwater. A flat, shallow dish and rapidly running water will give the shortest washing time. At this stage, the gelatin usually swells considerably, and great care must be taken not to damage or displace the emulsion. If the emulsion layer is very thin, as in electron microscope work, or not very firmly attached, as when an impermeable layer of polyvinyl chloride covers the specimen, washing must be extremely gentle. It may help to keep the specimen horizontal while washing, or to use several changes of stationary water. It is a good idea to keep the temperature of all the solutions used to process autoradiographs within a few degrees of each other, preferably at or below 20°.

Even with prolonged washing, it is difficult to remove the last traces of thiosulphate from emulsion layers. Thiosulphate ions appear to become adsorbed to the surface of silver grains[14]. In most instances, this does not matter to the autoradiographer. If the emulsion is transferred after fixation to an acid medium, however, the developed grains may be eroded with the formation of silver sulphide. I have known the grains to vanish completely from an autoradiograph, causing considerable consternation, following the use of certain staining procedures, or even histological mounting media. It is possible to reduce thiosulphate adsorption by the silver grains by treating the emulsion with a solution of potassium iodide before fixation[14].

SPECIAL TECHNIQUES

Several procedures from commercial photography have been adapted for autoradiography, or their use suggested. Some of them are briefly mentioned here, and their possible relevance to autoradiographic techniques discussed.

(a) Hypersensitisation

Herz[15] has suggested the use of emulsions in which the sensitivity has been increased by treatment with triethanolamine before exposure, and this technique has also been dealt with by Waller[5]. This treatment is capable of giving an increase of approximately 30% in the number of grains per 100 μ of particle track for high energy electrons in Ilford nuclear emulsions.

This increase in sensitivity has been seldom used in autoradiography. One would expect this treatment to increase the background, and make the emulsion less predictable in performance, but this may not be serious in practice. Unfortunately, Barkas[16] reports that hypersensitised emulsions develop background fog very fast at room temperature, and are best stored at $-20°$.

There might be situations in which this increase in sensitivity would be valuable, such as in electron microscope autoradiography, where long exposure times are necessary.

(b) Intensification of the latent image

It is possible to increase the size and the catalytic activity of the latent image present in an undeveloped crystal by depositing another metal, such as gold, on it. Under constant conditions of development, this has the effect of increasing the rate of conversion of that crystal to a grain of metallic silver.

In most autoradiographic applications, gold latensification, as this process is sometimes called, does not offer any real advantage. In electron microscope autoradiography, however, particularly when the two emulsions with the smallest available diameter of crystal are being used (see p. 332), latent image intensification is an extremely valuable technique[17, 9]. Here, exposure times of 10-12 weeks may still be insufficient to produce enough developable latent images to give a satisfactory autoradiograph. It can make all the difference between success and failure of an experiment to be able to amplify latent images below the limits of normal development techniques so that they also produce developed grains.

This technique is described in Chapter 18, where the methods of Bachmann and Salpeter are discussed more fully.

(c) Modifications of the developed grains

It is possible to produce autoradiographs with coloured silver grains by various techniques of development[3]. One can also modify the developed and fixed image in many ways, to produce larger grains, for instance, or to make them radioactive[18]. Few attempts have been made to apply these techniques to autoradiography, but they exist, and may find applications to special situations.

(d) Xerography, and the use of Polaroid film

Dobbs[19] has discussed the use of xerography in autoradiography. While interesting, the experiments he quotes do not offer any improvement over existing methods that I can see at present. Jackson and Kahn[20] have found Polaroid film convenient in the autoradiography of chromatograms.

(e) Silver bromide precipitation on the specimen

Silk, Hawtrey, Spence and Gear[21] have described a method which involves depositing silver on the specimen, and converting this to the bromide *in situ* with bromine vapour. From what has been said earlier about the functions of gelatin in nuclear emulsions, it seems unlikely that a layer of silver bromide of this nature would act as a reliable and reproducible recording medium. The autoradiographs they published are not very striking, their experiments, which seem poorly controlled, do not agree with the results of other electron microscope techniques, and their method has not been repeated by anyone else. From first principles, this would seem an unlikely approach to take.

Recently, a rather more sophisticated method has been described for making a silver bromide emulsion in the laboratory[22]. This involves the formation of silver particles in gelatin on the specimen, and their subsequent bromination after treatment with collodion to restrict redistribution of the silver into fewer larger particles. A mean crystal diameter of 100 Å is claimed, giving very good resolution in electron microscope autoradiography. The important factors of sensitivity and reproducibility are not mentioned.

(f) Eradication of unwanted latent images

It is possible to remove existing latent images in a nuclear emulsion, by exposing it to conditions which favour latent image fading[16]. This may be valuable if emulsion has been accidentally exposed to radiation or to any other factor which could cause unwanted background. The techniques available for doing this are discussed in more detail on p. 105.

(g) Image reversal

In a study on particulate fallout debris from thermonuclear explosions, Sisefsky[23] has used a method of reversal development which essentially produced clear areas in an otherwise blackened emulsion at the site of radioactivity. This permitted direct examination of the radioactive particles without interference from overlying silver grains.

(h) The removal of unwanted emulsion layers

This may be necessary if the emulsion has been ruined, perhaps by exposure to light, and the specimen is difficult to replace. It has also been used, after photography of the autoradiographic trace, to permit more accurate examination of the underlying specimen. The gelatin of the emulsion can simply be removed by digestion for 2–5 min in 1% potassium hydroxide at room temperature. This will often leave developed grains still in contact with the specimen. These can be removed by treatment with 7.5% potassium ferricyanide for 15 min, 3 changes of 30% sodium thiosulphate for 5 min each, and thorough washing in running water.

REFERENCES

1 G.A. Boyd, *Autoradiography in Biology and Medicine*, Academic Press, New York, 1955.
2 R.W. Gurney and N.F. Mott, *Proc. Roy. Soc. (London) Ser. A.*, 164 (1938) 151.
3 C.E.K. Mees and T.H. James (Eds.), *The Theory of the Photographic Process*, 3rd ed., Macmillan, New York, 1966.
4 J.W. Mitchell (Ed.), *Fundamental Mechanisms of Photographic Sensitivity*, Butterworth, London, 1951.
5 C. Waller, *1st European Symposium on Autoradiography, Rome, 1961.*
6 T.C. Appleton, *J. Histochem. Cytochem.*, 14 (1966) 414.
7 M. Abribat, *Sci. Ind. Phot.*, 15 (1944) 204.
8 A.W. Rogers and P.N. John, in L.J. Roth and W.E. Stumpf (Eds.), *The Autoradiography of Diffusible Substances*, Academic Press, New York, 1969
9 L. Bachmann and M.M. Salpeter, *Lab. Invest.*, 14 (1965) 303.
10 I. Ahmad and J. Demers, *Can. J. Phys.*, 37 (1959) 1548.
11 M.G.E. Welton, *J. Phot. Sci.*, 17 (1969) 157.
12 B. Liddiard and A.W. Rogers, In preparation.
13 L.G. Caro and R.P. Van Tubergen, *J. Cell Biol.*, 15 (1962) 173.
14 G.I.P. Levenson and C.J. Sharpe, *J. Phot. Sci.*, 4 (1956) 89.
15 R.H. Herz, *Lab. Invest.*, 8 (1959) 71.
16 W.H. Barkas, *Nuclear Research Emulsions*, Part 1, Academic Press, New York, 1963.
17 M.M. Salpeter and L. Bachmann, *J. Cell Biol.*, 22 (1964) 469.
18 G.W.W. Stevens, *Brit. J. Radiol.*, 23 (1950) 723.
19 H.E. Dobbs, *Intern. J. Appl. Radiation Isotopes*, 14 (1963) 285.
20 D.D. Jackson and M. Kahn, *Intern. J. Appl. Radiation Isotopes*, 20 (1969) 742.
21 M.H. Silk, A.O. Hawtrey, I.M. Spence and J.H.S. Gear, *J. Biophys. Biochem. Cytol.*, 10 (1961) 577.
22 B.H.A. Van Kleeff, W.E. de Boer, R. Kokke and T.O. Wikén, *Exptl. Cell Res.*, 54 (1968) 249.
23 J. Sisefsky, FOA 4 C 4417-18 (1970), Swedish Research Institute of National Defence.

CHAPTER 3

The Response of Nuclear Emulsions to Ionising Radiations

It might be thought unnecessary in a book of this sort to describe the particles and electro-magnetic radiations emitted by radioactive isotopes. It is certainly beyond the scope of this book to deal with their physical characteristics comprehensively. But biologists using radioisotopes frequently have gaps in their knowledge. I have been shown an electron microscope autoradiograph by a research worker who assured me that the coiled thread of metallic silver forming each developed grain was in fact the complete track of a β particle. The particles of major interest to the biologist will be reviewed briefly, concentrating on their characteristics as they can be seen in nuclear emulsions.

RADIOACTIVE ISOTOPES

Each atom consists of a dense, positively charged nucleus and a number of negatively charged electrons in orbit around it, like planets around the sun. The chemical properties of each atom are determined by the number of electrons around it, which depends in turn on the number of positive charges in the nucleus. The nucleus contains two types of particle, the proton, which carries a single positive charge, and the neutron, which is of similar mass, but is uncharged. The naturally occurring atoms of each element must clearly have the same number of protons in the nucleus. They also have a constant number of neutrons, and if for any reason the ratio of protons to neutrons is altered, the atomic nucleus becomes unstable. For each element, then, a number of different isotopes may exist, as the ratio of protons to neutrons is varied, but only one of these isotopes is normally stable – that which is naturally occurring. The unstable or radioactive nuclei disintegrate, ejecting charged particles until they reach a new balance of neutrons to protons which is stable.

Each radioactive isotope has well-defined characteristics. The manner in which disintegration takes place, in other words the types of radiation or particle emitted, their energies, and the daughter nucleus which is produced, is constant for each atom of that isotope. The probability or time-scale of disintegration is also characteristic for the isotope: this is usually expressed as the half-life, or time over which half the nuclei of that isotope will disintegrate. This time is independent of the total number of radioactive nuclei present, so that for a given mass of radioactive material, half the unstable nuclei will disintegrate in one half-life, half of the remainder in the next, and so on. Half-lives may range from fractions of a second to thousands of years.

The radioactivity of a given mass of material is measured in units called Curies: 1 Curie equals 3.7×10^{10} disintegrations per second. This is a statement of the rate at which unstable nuclei are distintegrating. Obviously, to achieve the same disintegration rate, an isotope with a long half-life will require far more unstable nuclei than one with a short half-life.

The events which take place when an unstable nucleus disintegrates affect the atom itself, and the surrounding atoms. If a nucleus attempts to change its ratio of protons to neutrons by ejecting a charged particle, it is clear that its own residual charge must alter. Since this charge determines the number of orbital electrons, and hence the chemical nature of the atom, disintegration produces an atom of another element. The charged particle is ejected with a certain amount of energy, and both the particle and the energy must in the last analysis be absorbed by surrounding atoms. The patterns of energy loss by α and β particles will be considered in the next section.

Any mass of a radioactive isotope is a diminishing asset, decaying at the rate indicated by its half-life. But a specific chemical compound labelled with a radioactive isotope is even more vulnerable. At each disintegration, a molecule is disrupted by an abrupt switch of one atom to a different chemical state, while surrounding molecules are bombarded by ejected particles. In some cases, compounds may be produced which will catalyse the breakdown of molecules in which radioactive disintegration has not yet taken place. Radiation decomposition is a complex phenomenon, and is discussed at length by Bayly and Weigel[1].

In the following section, the interactions of charged particles with nuclear emulsions will be considered. This is basically the same as the behaviour of these particles in any other medium, except that the density of the medium affects the probability of interaction for a given length of particle track. Nuclear emulsions have a high density, about 3.8 during exposure: in tissues and in most histological embedding media, which have a density about 1.1, track lengths will be correspondingly greater and the density of events along the track more widely spaced.

PARTICLES AND RADIATIONS

The previous chapter has presented the mechanism by which a silver bromide crystal responds to photons of light falling on it. The absorbed energy of the photon raises one electron to a higher energy level, and this enables the electron to move through the crystal structure until it is trapped at a sensitivity speck, resulting in the conversion of a silver ion to elemental silver. This minute deposit of silver within the crystal forms the latent image, which catalyses the conversion of the crystal to metallic silver in a chemical developing solution. Ionising radiations can also impart energy to the silver bromide crystals through which they pass, producing a series of latent images.

In considering the effects of ionising radiations on nuclear emulsions, the radiations themselves must be separated into two categories. The first of these is the group of charged particles, including the α and β particles which form the main radiations of interest to autoradiographers. These particles, by virtue of the charge they carry, can exert an effect at a distance on the electrons in orbit about the atomic nuclei of silver and bromine which make up the crystal. If positively charged, they can attract electrons out of orbit: if negatively charged, their passage near to an electron may be enough to repel it out of orbit. In passing through matter, the charged particles lose energy in a closely spaced series of charge effects on the electrons that come within their field. In addition, they will also lose energy in less frequent interactions with positively charged atomic nuclei. This loss of energy in many little packets results in the production of many latent images distributed along the course of the particle through the emulsion. On development, these silver grains mark out the track of the particle.

The second category includes the uncharged particles, such as the neutron, and the electro-magnetic radiations, such as the X and γ rays. Uncharged particles only lose energy by direct collision with electrons or nuclei. Since such collisions are relatively unlikely, these particles may travel for considerable distances through nuclear emulsion without leaving a latent image to indicate their passage. The path taken by such particles through emulsion cannot be traced, though the infrequent collisions in which they are involved may produce recognisable patterns. In much the same way, the electro-magnetic radiations lose energy only in direct "collisions", imparting energy to orbital electrons in relatively few, widely spaced events, such as the processes of photoelectric absorption or of Compton scattering, or the production of a positron and an electron within the field of an atomic nucleus. The details of these interactions may be found in textbooks of atomic physics. Their result, from the viewpoint of the user of nuclear emulsions, is that electro-magnetic radiations leave no recognisable track, but produce sporadic electron tracks throughout the emulsion.

Clearly, it is the charged particles which produce recognisable tracks that are most usefully studied by means of nuclear emulsions, and a few of these will now be considered in more detail.

THE α PARTICLE

α Particles are relatively massive. Each one is identical to the nucleus of a helium atom, consisting of two protons and two neutrons. It therefore carries two positive charges. As one might expect, such large particles are not common in the radioactive disintegration of the lighter atomic nuclei. They are emitted by a few isotopes of elements with a high atomic number, and, in particular, from the naturally occurring series of actinium, uranium, and thorium. Each isotope which emits α particles does so at one or more specific energy levels: in other words, all the α's emitted by one isotope have the same initial energy (or, sometimes, two distinct initial energies), and this energy of emission is characteristic of that isotope. All α particles have initial energies greater than 4 MeV, and very few have energies greater than 8 MeV, so that they form a relatively homogeneous group when one comes to consider their tracks in nuclear emulsion.

Each α particle has a rest mass nearly 8 000 times that of an electron. It is not surprising, therefore, that a collision between these two particles will knock the electron off its course, without noticeably influencing the path of the α particle, like a collision between a cannonball and a table-tennis ball. Even in a collision with the nucleus of a hydrogen atom, an α particle will only be slightly deviated from its path.

By virtue of its two positive charges, an α particle will attract orbital electrons over a considerable distance, in atomic terms, while there will be mutual repulsion between it and other atomic nuclei which it may approach. An α particle dissipates energy very rapidly indeed in these effects on electrons, so that its range in matter is short, despite its high initial energy. Another way of describing the same thing would be to say that α particles cause tremendous havoc to the electron shells of the atoms through which they pass. In terms of the photographic process, this implies that they create a great number of latent images, affecting every silver halide crystal through which they pass.

So the track of an α particle in nuclear emulsion will be very dense, with every crystal along its path activated, and will be quite straight, apart from a slight chance of deviation toward its termination, if it collides with an atomic nucleus after it has already been slowed down. The track will also be relatively short: in Ilford G5 emulsion, all α's of initial energies between 4 and 8 MeV will

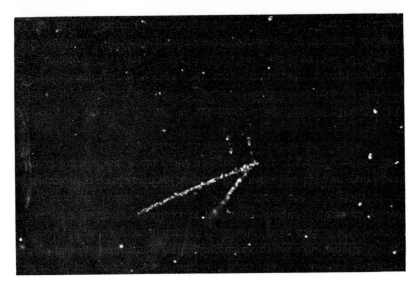

Fig. 5. 2 α tracks and 1 β track originating from the same point, recorded in Ilford G5 emulsion. Note the width and density of the straight α tracks, the wide grain spacing of the tortuous β track. (× 720)

have ranges between 15 and 40 μ. The track will be fairly wide, as the energised electrons resulting from the many collisions along the path of the α particle will themselves often travel short distances through the emulsion, causing latent images in adjacent crystals. These secondary electrons are often called δ rays, and they give the α track an irregular, fringed edge at very high magnifications.

This high rate of energy loss results in many latent images being formed in every crystal hit, and each latent image has a high probability of containing a large number of atoms of elemental silver. An emulsion of low sensitivity will be sufficient to record the tracks of α particles, and, similarly, mild development will make these grains visible.

Fig. 5 shows two α tracks, radiating outwards from a single source. These tracks are quite characteristic. They are easy to record. They may be extrapolated back towards the specimen to indicate the exact source with great precision. They are easy to count, and quantitative procedures are simple and reliable. It is a great pity that so few of the isotopes of interest to the biologist emit α particles. Fig. 6 shows an autoradiograph of the spleen of a patient who had been given an intravenous dose of a thorium-containing compound several years previously. The tracks are so unmistakeable that their distribution can be

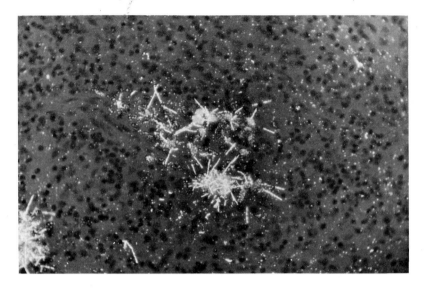

Fig. 6. Photomicrograph of a human spleen. The patient had been injected intravenously with a thorium-containing compound 14 years previously. Crystalline deposits of thorium salts can be seen, with many α tracks radiating out from them. Stained with Harris' haematoxylin, autoradiograph prepared by dipping in Ilford G5 emulsion. (× 170) Photograph taken with combined transmitted and incident lighting. (The tissue was obtained by courtesy of Dr. H. Levi)

plotted with great precision. In the course of autoradiography, α tracks will often be seen forming part of the background. α-Emitting isotopes occur as impurities in glass, and also in the emulsion itself.

β PARTICLES

β Particles are really electrons of nuclear origin. They have the same mass as electrons, and the same single negative charge. The ejection of a β particle from the nucleus is the commonest way in which artificially induced radioactive nuclei achieve stability, and most of the radioisotopes of interest to biologists fall into this group.

Unlike α particles, the β particles emitted by one particular isotope do not all have the same initial energy. They show a spectrum of energies, ranging from a maximum value down to zero. The maximum energy (E_{max}) is characteristic of the particular isotope. The shape of the energy spectrum varies, too, from one isotope to another. Some, like phosphorus-32, are bell-shaped, with relatively few β's at the high and low ends of the energy spectrum, and a peak in between: others, like calcium-45 or carbon-14, have the peak probability of emission nearer the low energy part of the spectrum. Several spectra are illustrated in Fig. 7. Marshall[2] presents useful data on the calculation of energy spectra for isotopes emitting β particles.

The range of maximum energies is far greater for β particles than for α's. Tritium has an E_{max} of 18 keV, while for some isotopes the figure is over 3 MeV. It is clear at once that β tracks will be far more variable in length than those from the much more homogeneous group of α particles.

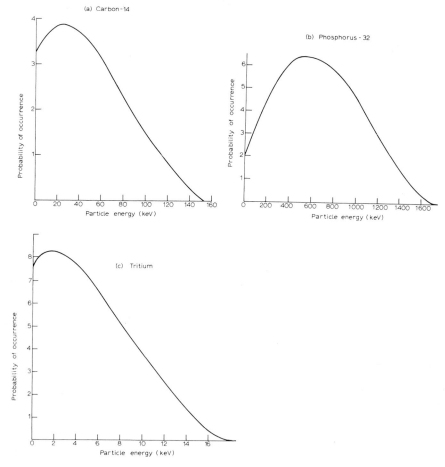

Fig. 7. Energy spectra of 3 β-emitting isotopes. *(a)* carbon-14, E_{max} 155 keV; *(b)* phosphorus-32, E_{max} 1.7 MeV; *(c)* tritium, E_{max} 18.5 keV.

This variability becomes even more pronounced when one considers the passage of a β particle through matter. Having the same mass and charge as an orbital electron, a β particle may impart sufficient energy to it to eject it from its orbit, but, since we are now dealing with a collision between two table-tennis balls, the β particle itself will be deflected from its course. This mutual repulsion between the β particle and the electrons near which it passes is the principal means by which the β particle loses energy. It produces a random, buffeting effect on the path of the β particle, with large numbers of small deviations of course, at times summating to give a curved path, at times cancelling out to approximate the path to a straight line (Figs. 8, 14). Very occasionally, the collision between the β particle and an electron imparts sufficient energy to the latter to send it careering off as a δ ray with a track that can be recognised (Fig. 9). Since the β particle and the δ ray are both electrons, they cannot be distinguished from each other by their behaviour. By convention, the one with the shorter track is called the δ ray, and the other is considered to be the original β

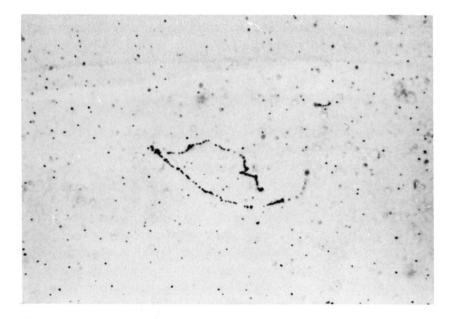

Fig. 8. A photomicrograph of a β track, recorded in Ilford G5 emulsion. The grain spacing in the track is wider, and the grains on average are smaller in diameter, at its origin: the larger, densely packed grains at the termination of the track can be readily distinguished. The very acute angle in the track represents a nuclear collision: several other nuclear collisions can be seen in the terminal quarter of the track. The initial energy of this particle was about 190 keV. (× 700)

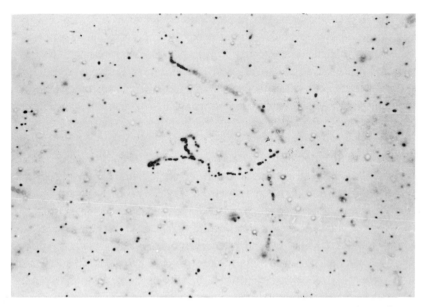

Fig. 9.   Part of the track of a β particle, recorded in Ilford G5 emulsion. The track appears
to branch, giving rise to two track terminations, with large, closely packed silver grains. This
is a collision with an orbital electron, which has had sufficient energy imparted to it to
produce a recognisable track. By convention, the longer branch is considered the track of
the β particle, the shorter one that of the orbital electron − the δ ray. (× 700)

particle. Where a recognisable δ ray occurs, the β particle undergoes an abrupt
change of course and loses a considerable amount of energy to the δ electron:
the two tracks separate at practically 90°.

A β particle may also lose energy in large packets by passing close to an
atomic nucleus. The positive charge of the nucleus accelerates the β particle as it
approaches, may cause it to change direction, and exerts a braking effect on it as
it departs. The energy lost by the β particle in this process appears in X-rays
(Bremsstrahlung) which are not recorded by the emulsion as a recognisable
track. The net effect of a nuclear collision, as far as it can be seen in the
emulsion, is that there is a sudden and often considerable change of course, a
sharp angle in the track, which is usually quite distinct from the gradual curves
that result from random buffeting by orbital electrons (see Fig. 8).

The rate at which β particles lose energy is much lower than that of α
particles, so their ranges in emulsion are much greater. The term "range" has
been used in two rather different contexts in the literature. In some cases, the
point-to-point distance travelled by the β particle is meant, in others, the net

distance which it travels from the source. Since the path of a β particle is so tortuous, and may even twist back towards its origin, these two measurements may be very different. In order to prevent confusion, the point-to-point distance travelled by the β particle is best referred to as its track length, and its penetration into matter as its radius, since this is the radius of the sphere around the origin of the particle that contains the entire track. It is clear that the radius cannot be greater than the track length.

The track length of a β particle of initial energy 20 keV is about 3 μ in Ilford G5 emulsion: for an initial energy of 6 MeV, the length becomes about 10 mm. For an α particle of 6 MeV, the comparable figure is 26 μ. It is obvious that the rate of energy loss is so much lower for β particles that one cannot expect anything like the same density of latent images along their path. In fact, the β particle may pass through many crystals without imparting sufficient energy to them to create a latent image. Other crystals will have the minimum energy given them to render them developable: still others will receive considerable amounts of energy, resulting in the deposition of much more metallic silver within them than the bare minimum needed for development. So the track of a β particle through nuclear emulsion consists of silver grains, some small, some larger, with many gaps. It is never quite straight, but always shows small deviations, and there will be occasional abrupt changes of direction (nuclear collisions), and, more rarely, places where the track branches into two (δ ray formation). The distribution of small and large grains and of gaps along the track is more or less random, and there will sometimes be several grains closely spaced, sometimes regions where the grains are widely separated (Figs. 8 and 14).

But the distribution of grains along the track is not completely random. As can be seen from Figs. 8 and 9, the grains tend to be larger, and more closely spaced, towards the end of a track. This part of the track also tends to be more tortuous than the rest of it. Both these phenomena have the same cause. Over a wide range of energies above 500 keV, the rate at which a β particle loses energy is practically constant. As the β particle is slowed down to below 500 keV, the rate at which it loses energy increases, gradually at first, then more rapidly until, right at the very end of the track, the rate of energy loss is about 8 times as high as it was at 500 keV. Inevitably, the number and size of latent images per micron of track also increase towards the end of the track.

The higher the sensitivity of the emulsion, the more grains will be recorded per micron of track. A relatively insensitive emulsion can record the last few microns of a β track, where the rate of energy loss is high; but it would fail to yield more than a few widely spaced grains earlier in the track where the β particle is still highly energetic, and losing its energy more slowly. These grains represent crystals of silver halide in which by chance sufficient energy has been dissipated for the formation of a latent image, and they might well be so widely spaced that they could not be identified as a continuous track. Similarly, the development of an emulsion becomes critically important with energetic β particles. Powerful development will lift more latent images to the level of visible grains in the track. This will at the same time increase the frequency of background grains, making a high grain density in the track necessary for its recognition.

By comparison with α particles, then, β particles are much more difficult to record. Technically, the emulsions required must be much more sensitive, and development must be more strictly controlled. The long and irregular β tracks are more difficult to recognise, and cannot be extrapolated back with certainty to indicate their point of origin. It is impossible to know, when a β particle enters the emulsion, whether one has the complete track of a β of X KeV, or the final portion of the track of a very much more energetic particle. Most of these difficulties are inherent in the properties of the β particles themselves, and so cannot be side-stepped.

Many of the factors governing the recording of β particles in nuclear emulsions have now been investigated. Zajac and Ross[3] and Levi, Rogers, Bentzon and Nielsen[4] present most of the experimental data available for β particles of initial energies less than 400 keV, and the agreement between these two sets of results is good.

From a combination of these results, Levi *et al.* have calculated equations describing many of the basic properties of β particles in this energy range. The track length in Ilford G5 emulsion is related to the initial energy of the particle by the equation,

$$\log \bar{L} = 1.59 \log E - 1.51$$

where $\bar{L}$ is the mean track length in microns, and E is the initial particle energy in keV. The number of grains produced under plateau conditions of development by β particles is related to initial energy by the equation

$$\log \bar{G} = 1.19 \log E - 0.74$$

where $\bar{G}$ is the mean number of developed grains per track (Fig. 10). The relationship between the number of grains in the track and the track length is given by (Fig. 11),

$$\log \bar{G} = 0.747 \log \bar{L} + 0.385$$

There is considerable scatter about the mean value for both the track length and the number of grains per track, the coefficient of variation in both cases being about 20%.

From this data, it is possible to calculate the probable initial energy of a β

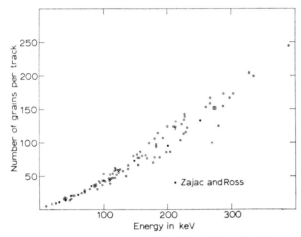

Fig.10. The relationship between the number of grains per track and the initial energy of the β particle. Open circles represent individual tracks recorded in Ilford G5 emulsion: solid circles represent mean values for groups of particles in Kodak NT-4 emulsion, determined by Zajac and Ross (1949). (From Levi *et al.*, 1963). (NT-4 emulsion was formerly available from Eastman Kodak Company.)

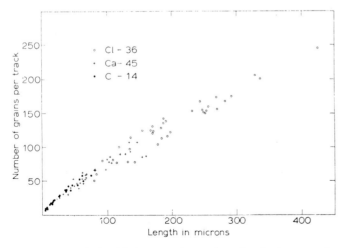

Fig.11. The relationship between the number of grains in a β track and the grain-to-grain track length, measured in Ilford G5 emulsion. (From Levi *et al.*, 1963)

References p. 46

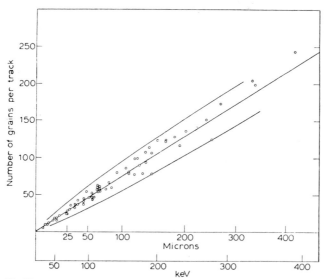

Fig.12. The numbers of grains in β tracks are related to the grain-to-grain track length, and to the initial energies of the β particles. Open circles represent individual tracks recorded in Ilford G5 emulsion: the lines represent the mean and 95% confidence limits of measurements made by Zajac and Ross (1949) on groups of monoenergetic electrons recorded in Kodak NT-4 emulsion. (From Levi *et al.,* 1963) (NT-4 emulsion was formerly available from Eastman Kodak Company.)

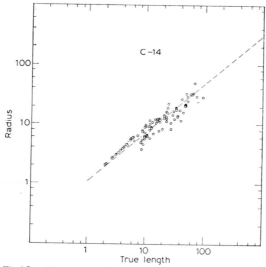

Fig.13. The relationship between the track radius and the grain-to-grain track length for β-particles from carbon-14. The radius is that of the smallest sphere, with the first grain of the track as its centre, that contains every grain in the track. This relationship is energy dependent, and should not be used for other isotopes. (From Levi *et al.,* 1963)

particle from either its track length or the number of grains in its track in Ilford G5 emulsion. These relationships are summarised graphically in Fig. 12.

The track radius, defined as the radius of the smallest sphere centred at the origin of the β particle which contains every silver grain in the track, is a much more variable parameter, as might be expected from the very irregular track patterns which β particles characteristically produce. In the rather narrow range of initial energies between 20 and 150 keV, the relationship between track length and radius can be expressed as (Fig. 13)

$$\log \overline{R} = 0.816 \log \overline{L} - 0.042.$$

It is thus possible to calculate the radius of the sphere about a point source which will contain a given percentage of the tracks originating from the source. For instance, a sphere of radius 20 μ will contain every silver grain in 90% of the tracks originating from a point source of carbon-14 at its centre. The remaining 10% of the tracks will leave this sphere of G5 emulsion at some point. The corresponding radius around a point source of calcium-45 is 45 μ.

If one considers the individual silver grains produced by β particles originating from a point source of carbon-14 surrounded by emulsion on all sides, 29% of them will lie within a radius of 5 μ from the source, 50% within 9 μ, 75% within 17 μ, and 90% within 25 μ.

The measurement of radioactivity in terms of the number of disintegrations taking place within a source in a given exposure time is technically very difficult, and will be discussed in detail in Chapter 12. But it is clearly possible, on the basis of this mass of data on the behaviour of β particles in Ilford G5 emulsion, to count the number of tracks or even the number of individual silver grains within a given volume of emulsion, and to estimate from this the disintegration rate within a labelled source at a known distance from the volume examined.

It cannot be emphasised too strongly that nuclear emulsions provide a recording medium for charged particles which is versatile, sensitive, and reliable. Biologists have hardly begun to exploit the full potentialities of this detector, as can easily be realised by looking at the highly sophisticated measurements made by physicists with similar basic techniques[5-7]

Apart from the β-emitting isotopes used experimentally, the autoradiographer will meet background β particles from a number of sources. Potassium-40 is a naturally occurring β emitter encountered in glassware, and carbon-14 will be found in the gelatin of the emulsion. In addition, all the stray background ionising radiations that man is heir to can produce δ rays, or secondary electron tracks.

These, then, are the particles which will concern the autoradiographer in practically every experiment. β Particles are often likened to drunks, starting out with a long stride and a spurious confidence, weaving through matter with increasingly frequent changes of direction, and hesitant, shorter steps until the original impetus is lost and the track ends. Whatever recording system is used, from a monolayer of minute crystals to a layer of emulsion 100 μ or more in thickness, the characteristics of β particles must be understood if the patterns of silver grains produced by them are to be interpreted sensibly.

γ RAYS

There is little more to be said about these. As stated on p. 32 they betray their presence only by infrequent secondary electrons, which may produce background grains or even tracks, indistinguishable from those of β particles. γ Rays are only a source of additional background to the autoradiographer, unless he is working with macroscopic specimens at very low resolution.

For this latter type of work, it is clear that the emulsion should be highly sensitised, and its crystals should be large, to give the maximum blackening for the incident radiation. It is often possible to increase the efficiency of recording for γ rays significantly by placing a layer of material of high atomic number, such as lead, directly against the emulsion, sandwiching the latter against the specimen. This dense material acts as an intensifier, increasing the probability of secondary electrons, which are the actual particles registered by the emulsion.

OTHER IONISING RADIATIONS

(a) Internal conversion electrons

Some isotopes, such as iodine-125, emit γ rays of very low energy. These have a certain probability of ejecting from orbit one of the inner electrons around the actual nucleus that is disintegrating. The ejected electron behaves just like a β particle, the principal difference being its mode of origin. The only practical difference is that internal conversion electrons are all of the same energy from a given isotope, instead of showing the spectrum of energies of a β emitter.

Many internal conversion electrons have a very low energy, which is ideal for autoradiographic purposes.

An excellent discussion of isotopes emitting internal conversion electrons, together with a list of those isotopes likely to be of interest in autoradiography, has been presented by Forberg, Odeblad, Söremark, and Ullberg[8].

(b) Positrons

A few isotopes produce positrons, which have the same mass as electrons, but carry a single positive charge: sodium-22 is an example. These lose energy in repeated buffetings by orbital electrons, in rather the same way that β particles do. The typical tail of the β track is not produced, however, since the positron ends its brief existence by annihilating with an orbital electron, giving off two quanta of γ rays of 511 keV each.

(c) Cosmic rays

These consist of highly energetic charged particles which bombard the upper atmosphere continually. At ground level, cosmic radiation is a mixture of secondary and subsequent products of this bombardment. Some components of this radiation are easily recognised in thick layers of nuclear emulsion, by their

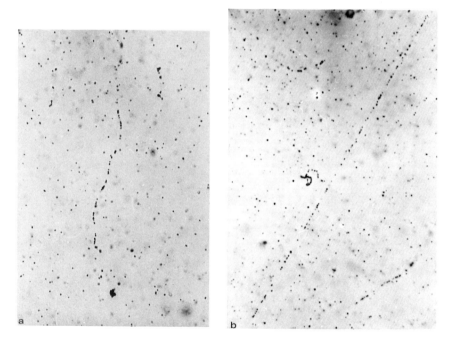

Fig.14. Photomicrographs of portions of the track of *(a)* a β particle, *(b)* a high energy cosmic ray. The latter is quite straight, and can often be followed for very long distances through a thick emulsion layer. A δ ray can be seen originating from it. By contrast, the β particle has a characteristic track, with many changes of direction as a result of buffeting by orbital electrons. Even in the absence of dramatic changes of direction due to nuclear collisions (Fig. 8), these small deviations produce an irregular track which can usually be recognised without difficulty. Tracks recorded in Ilford G5 emulsion. ($\times$ 540)

References p. 46

straight tracks of great length, marching through the emulsion with occasional δ tracks originating from them (Fig. 14b).

REFERENCES

1   R.J. Bayly and H. Weigel, *Nature,* 188 (1960) 384.
2   J.H. Marshall, *Nucleonics,* 13 (1955) No.8, 34.
3   B. Zajac and M.A.S. Ross, *Nature,* 164 (1949) 311.
4   H. Levi, A.W. Rogers, M.W. Bentzon and A. Nielsen, *Kgl. Danske Videnskab. Selskab, Mat.-Fys. Medd.,* 33 (1963) No. 11.
5   P. Demers, *Ionographie,* University Press of Montreal, 1958.
6   C.F. Powell, P.H. Fowler and D.H. Perkins, *The Study of Elementary Particles by the Photographic Method,* Pergamon, London, 1959.
7   W.H. Barkas, *Nuclear Research Emulsions,* Part 1, Academic Press, New York, 1963.
8   S. Forberg, E. Odeblad, R. Söremark and S. Ullberg, *Acta Radiol. (Ther.),* 2 (1964) 241.

CHAPTER 4

The Resolution of Autoradiographs

In the previous chapter, we have seen that any isotope that emits β particles does so over a wide spectrum of energies, and that the path taken by each β particle is unpredictable, and may have many abrupt changes of direction. The initial course taken by a β particle ejected from the source appears to be randomly determined, so that there is an equal probability of the track starting off in any direction.

If one considers a point source emitting β particles, which is surrounded on all sides by a layer of nuclear emulsion thicker than the maximum track length of the particles, clearly the source will lie at the centre of a sphere of developed grains, and the density of grains will decrease as one proceeds outwards from the source towards the perimeter of the sphere (Fig. 15a). The diameter of the sphere will be determined by the greatest track radius, as defined in the last chapter, which is related to the maximum energy of β particles emitted. The distribution of silver grains within the sphere will be a complex function, influenced by the shape of the energy spectrum of the isotope, amongst other factors.

For the purposes of calculation, it is usually assumed that the density of silver grains falls off as one proceeds away from the source as the inverse of the square of the distance. In fact, the density decreases more rapidly than the inverse square law would suggest, as shown by Levi, Rogers, Bentzon and Nielsen[1].

If one slices such a sphere of emulsion in half (Fig. 15b), the source now has silver grains on one side only. This is the situation when the source is supported on, for instance, a glass slide, and covered with an emulsion layer thicker than the maximum range of the emitted particles. This model, where the emulsion is on one side of the source only, and is thick relative to the ranges of emitted particles, is used in track autoradiographs, and also very frequently in the autoradiography of tritium at the light microscope level: it will be discussed in more detail later (pp.68, 304 and 313). Replacing the emulsion over half the space angle around the source by glass distorts the shape of the hemisphere of grains slightly.

References p. 70

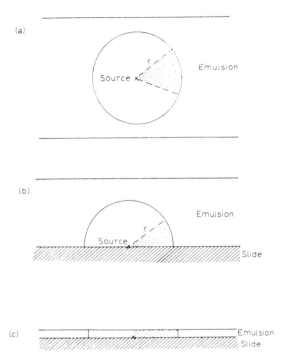

Fig.15. Diagrams illustrating the three source–emulsion relationships most commonly encountered. In (*a*) the source is completely surrounded by emulsion to a thickness greater than the maximum track radius (*r*). In (*b*) the source is mounted on a support, usually a glass slide, and covered with emulsion on one side only by a thick layer of emulsion. In (*c*) the typical grain density autoradiograph, the layer of emulsion over the source is thin relative to the track length.

Particles that enter the glass will have a longer path than they would have done in emulsion. If they are scattered back across the glass–emulsion interface, they will produce grains in the emulsion which have a wider distribution about the source than is seen when the source is completely surrounded by emulsion.

If one now considers a thin section through the centre of the sphere of emulsion (Fig. 15c), this approximates more nearly to the usual histological autoradiograph. The source, supported on a glass slide, is covered on the other side by a thin layer of emulsion, and many of the particles emitted will travel through the emulsion into the air beyond. If the emulsion is viewed perpendicularly to the plane of the slide, the source appears as the centre of a circular area of silver grains. Once again, altering the density of the medium that originally occupied the rest of the sphere from that of emulsion to that of air has the effect of increasing the diameter of this circle, and lowering the grain densities within it.

The three models illustrated in Fig. 15 cover practically every type of auto-radiograph. In track autoradiography, sources may be suspended in emulsion or covered on one side only with a relatively thick emulsion layer, to give the sphere or hemisphere type of geometry. A tritium source covered by an emulsion layer 3 or more microns thick is another example of the hemisphere model. Most autoradiographs produced for the light or electron microscope are examples of the grain density model, where the emulsion layer is thinner than the maximum track length. Since the grain density model is the most widely used, it is not surprising that most of the studies of resolution have been made for evaluating this type of autoradiograph.

DEFINITIONS OF RESOLUTION

If one considers the type of preparation shown in Fig. 15c, a plot of the grain density along a line passing through the source would look rather like the curve shown in Fig. 16.

The grain density is highest over the source, falling off symmetrically as the distance from the source increases on either side. It is clear that it is very

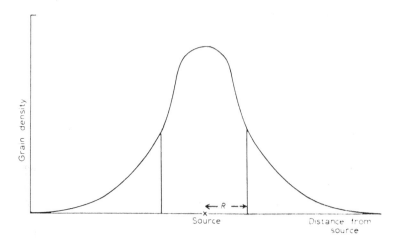

Fig.16. A diagram illustrating the distribution of silver grains around a source in a grain density autoradiograph. On a line across the emulsion, running through the source, the grain density is highest immediately over the source, falling off symmetrically on either side of it. *R* indicates the resolution, defined here as the distance from the source at which the grain density falls to half that directly over the source itself.

References p. 70

difficult to define the precise diameter of the circular area of silver grains around the source. The grain density falls away gradually to background levels and the end point is impossible to determine with certainty. Resolution is therefore usually defined in terms of some other function of the grain density which is more convenient to measure in practice.

Unfortunately, different authors have chosen different functions of the grain density curve as the basis for definitions of resolution. The choice of definition has a considerable influence on the numerical value given to the resolution in any particlar set of experimental conditions. Before comparing the resolution claimed by one author with that stated elsewhere, it is a good idea to make sure that they are both talking about the same thing. In particular, it is important to distinguish between definitions based on point sources, and those based on linear or extended plane sources: and between definitions based on grain density (the number of grains per unit area of emulsion) and on the percentage of the total grains produced by the source.

Let us view Fig. 15c from above. The point source has a high density of grains over it: concentric rings of emulsion taken further and further from the source have fewer and fewer grains in them. If one takes concentric rings of uniform width, one can count the number of grains in each ring, and plot this figure against distance from the source to produce a curve of grain distribution around the source, from which some definition of resolution can be derived. Alternatively, one can calculate the grain density in each ring. But since the area of each ring is much larger than the area of the ring immediately inside it, it is obvious that the curve of *grain density* will fall off much more steeply than the curve of *grain distribution.* A definition of resolution based on some function of the grain density about a point source will necessarily give smaller values for the resolution than a definition based on grain distribution about a point source.

A linear source of radioactivity can be considered as an infinite number of point sources arranged along a line, and each point source will produce grains in just the same pattern as a single point source (Fig. 16). But instead of the grain distribution falling off in a radially symmetrical fashion, the grains in the direction of the line fall near the line, while only those produced in a direction perpendicular to the line will lie as far from the line as they do from their actual point of origin. If we divide the emulsion into bands of equal width, similar to the concentric rings around the point source, and count the number of grains in each band, this measure of resolution will fall off more rapidly than the grain distribution around a point source in identical conditions of autoradiography. But since the area of each band is the same, there is now no difference between curves of grain distribution and curves of grain density.

Clearly, the definition of resolution determines the actual, numerical value to be attached to it in any given set of conditions.

In photography, resolution is usually defined in terms of the distance that must separate two objects before they can be distinguished from each other. If two sources were to lie very close to each other, the silver grains produced by the one would overlie the other, and *vice versa,* giving a density curve with a single peak like that shown in Fig. 16. As the sources are moved further apart, this peak would broaden and become lower, and finally the grain density midway between the two sources would be lower than the two peaks over the sources. Gomberg[2] examined this situation, defining resolution as the distance which must separate two sources of equal strength if the grain density between them falls to half that seen over each source. The same model has formed the basis for an extensive theoretical treatment of resolution by Bleecken[3-5].

A widely accepted definition of resolution was proposed by Doniach and Pelc[6]. With a grain density curve similar to that in Fig. 16, they defined the resolution as the distance from the source at which the grain density is one half that seen directly over the source. They presented a series of calculations of resolutions based on a point source, and on a linear source at right angles to the plane of the emulsion.

Nadler[7] used a rather similar definition. He worked with extended planar sources, and calculated the distance from the edge of the source at which the grain density fell to one half of that above the edge itself.

Bachmann and Salpeter[8] defined resolution as the radius of the circle about a point source which contains half the silver grains produced by that source, the half-radius (*HR*). This definition is a useful one when one comes to the analysis of autoradiographs at the electron microscope level. Here, one is faced with a number of scattered grains, and the problem is to identify their source. If a circle of the same size as the resolution circle is placed around each grain, there is by definition a 50% probability that the point of origin of the β particle lies within it.

In addition to the references given above, theoretical treatments of resolution in the grain density type of autoradiograph have been presented by Gross, Bogoroch, Nadler and Leblond[9], Lamerton and Harriss[10], Caro[11], and Pelc[12].

Recent work by Salpeter, Bachmann and Salpeter[13] on resolution at the electron microscope level has been based on a linear source, with measurements of grain distribution in bands of equal width parallel to the source. They have carried out these measurements under many different conditions, and determined the pattern of distribution of developed grains around the line, and the distance from the line that contains half the grains produced by it — the half-

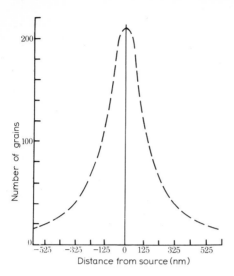

Fig.17. The distribution of silver grains around a linear source of tritium, autoradiographed with Ilford L4 emulsion and developed with Microdol X. The *HD* value is the distance from the line which delimits the area containing half the grains produced by the source – in this case the *HD* is 145 nm. (Data taken from Salpeter *et al.*, 1969)

distance (*HD*) (Fig. 17). Although changing the thickness of the specimen, or the crystal diameter of the emulsion, produced considerable changes in the *HD*, they found that the *shape* of the curve of distribution of grains around the line was identical in all cases. This observation allowed them to produce a generalised curve of grain distribution in units of *HD* which has since been shown to fit autoradiographs at the light microscope level also[14]. A mathematical treatment of resolution[13] has also been presented.

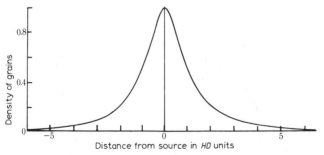

Fig.18. The distribution of silver grains around a linear source of tritium, measured in units of *HD*. This generalized curve describes the distribution found in all the experimental conditions examined by Salpeter *et al.*, 1969.

This generalised curve of grain distribution (Fig. 18) is a valuable step forward. It is a relatively simple matter to calculate the predicted grain distributions around sources of various sizes and shapes, once the distribution around a linear source is known. In Fig. 19, grain densities are shown for hollow circular sources and for solid discs of various radii, and many other shapes are calculable. One only needs to determine the relevant value of HD for one's own autoradiographs to be able to predict grain distributions around any labelled biological structure that can be approximated to a fairly simple geometical shape. The concepts of

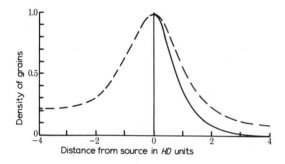

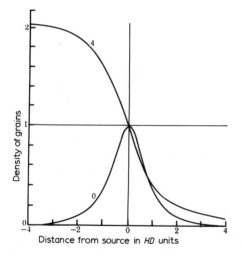

Fig.19. Generalized curves showing the distributions of silver grains around sources of different shapes. Positive values on the abscissa represent areas outside the edge of the source, negative values areas inside the edge of the source. (*a*), the solid line relates to a point source, the broken line to a hollow circular source of radius 4 *HD* units. (*b*) line 0 relates to a point source, line 4 to a solid disc of radius 4 *HD* units. (From data of Salpeter *et al.*, 1969)

HD and *HR* will be discussed several times in the rest of this book, particularly in connection with the interpretation of autoradiographs.

FACTORS THAT GOVERN THE RESOLUTION OF GRAIN DENSITY
AUTORADIOGRAPHS

The mathematical treatment of resolution appeals to some people. It is a complex affair, and every treatment has to start from simplifying assumptions. Since these are likely to be different in each paper, there is an endless field for argument and for the exercise of mathematical expertise. Fortunately for the poor biologist, all the theoretical models proposed to date agree in indicating that certain geometrical factors in the preparation of the autoradiograph have an important bearing on how good or bad the resolution will be. What is more, experimental test systems, such as the test charts developed and used by Stevens[15], have confirmed the effects of altering these factors on the resolution.

Whatever definition of resolution you adopt, and whatever system of autoradiography, the following factors will help to determine the resolution you obtain. They can be divided into factors operating in the source itself, and factors concerned with the nuclear emulsion.

(a) Factors in the source

(i) The choice of isotope.   Clearly, if the maximum energy of the β particles coming from the source is increased, there will be particles producing silver grains at greater distances from the source. The whole curve of distance *versus* grain density shown in Fig. 16 will be broader, and the resolution will be poorer. In grain density autoradiographs, there is a very definite improvement in resolution to be gained from using an isotope with lower energies. If, as with iodine, several isotopes are commercially available, it is common sense to use the one with the lowest energy of emission if high resolution is needed. The great value of tritium in autoradiography lies in its very low maximum energy (18 keV).

(ii) The distance between source and emulsion.   If the source is separated from the emulsion, instead of being in direct contact with it, this is similar in principle to examining a thin section which does not pass through the centre of the sphere of emulsion described in Fig. 15. The grains lying over the source when this section is viewed from above are now at a distance from it, instead of being immediately adjacent, and they have a correspondingly lower probability of being hit. So the peak of the grain density curve will be lower. At the same time, the grains which lie a little to one side will be nearly the same distance

from the source as those which are directly over it: they will therefore have nearly the same chance of being hit. By contrast, when the emulsion is in contact with the source, the probability of being hit falls off considerably at even short distances from the source. So the curve of grain density will be flatter as well as lower, when emulsion and source are separated.

It is sometimes necessary to interpose a thin layer of inert material, such as polyvinyl chloride, between the source and emulsion, in order to prevent chemical interaction between them affecting the autoradiograph. Any such layer, however thin, will result in poorer resolution. In situations where it must be used, an interposed layer must be kept as thin as possible.

(iii) The thickness of the source.   If the source, instead of being the dimensionless point source that we have been considering so far, has an appreciable thickness, the situation that results is really a special case of separation of source from emulsion. The rod-shaped source, lying perpendicular to the plane of the emulsion, can be regarded as a series of point sources. The uppermost of these will have the characteristic curve of resolution seen in Fig. 16. The next below will, in effect, be separated from the emulsion by the first layer of source, and its resolution will be correspondingly worse, and so on down the rod. The resultant resolution of the complete rod will be a composite of the resolutions at each level, and will inevitably be poorer than that of a point source in direct contact with the emulsion.

(b) Factors in the emulsion

(i) The thickness of the emulsion.   The effect of increasing the thickness of the emulsion layer is rather similar to increasing the thickness of the source. Reference to Fig. 15 will show that a thin section of emulsion through the centre of the sphere of emulsion of Fig. 15a will give grain densities which decrease rapidly with increasing distance from the source. A section of emulsion parallel to this, at some distance from the source, will have grain densities that are still maximal over the source itself, but which decrease relatively slowly as one moves away from the point over the source. Superimposing several of these sections of emulsion at different levels, the resultant grain density does not fall off nearly so abruptly with distance from the source as is the case with a thin emulsion layer in contact with the source.

(ii) The size of the silver halide crystals.   We have seen in Chapter 2 that the latent image produced in a silver halide crystal as a consequence of the passage of a β particle will lie at a preformed sensitivity speck, and not necessarily on the

path of the crystal. The developed grain that results will have a point of contact with the parent crystal at this latent image site, but may not coincide with the position of the crystal.

If the size of crystal is smaller, the position of the developed grain must correspond more closely to the trajectory of the particle. This will result in improved resolution.

(iii) The length of exposure. In a situation such as that shown in Fig. 16, it is clear that the probability of a crystal being hit by a β particle is far higher directly over the source than it is several microns away from it. It is equally true that the probability of a crystal over the source receiving two hits from different β particles is much higher. Such a crystal, unfortunately, cannot produce two developed grains in consequence.

If exposure is held to a relatively short time, so that no crystal has a significant chance of a double hit, the grain distribution will show the sharp peak characteristic of Fig. 16. If exposure continues until the probability of double hits over the source becomes considerable, the grain density over the source will not increase proportionally to the increase occurring away from the source, resulting in a broader, flatter curve, and poorer resolution. Ultimately, all the crystals over the source will be hit, and further increases in exposure will only give more grains in the areas of low grain density away from the source.

Complete saturation of the emulsion in this way is fairly obvious. But deviations from a linear response in the volume of emulsion immediately over the source occur at much lower grain densities than is commonly realised. The resolution is often better in autoradiographs with low grain densities, quite apart from the advantages to be gained, from the point of view of statistics, in working with many lightly labelled sources rather than a few heavily labelled ones (see p.223).

(iv) The sensitivity of the emulsion. On p.39, it was explained that β particles have a lower rate of energy loss per micron of track at higher energies, up to about 500 keV. In other words, at higher energies they have a smaller probability of losing enough energy in a silver halide crystal to make it develop. If the emulsion has a low sensitivity, or if development is incomplete, an even higher threshold of energy loss per crystal must be reached before a developed grain will result.

Immediately over the source, β particles will enter the emulsion at the complete spectrum of energies of the isotope being used. At a distance from the source, only relatively low energy portions of the ends of the tracks will be encountered. If the emulsion is so insensitive that high energy particles do not have a reasonable probability of causing developed grains along the initial part of the track, relatively few grains will appear over the source. This is equivalent to requiring more than one hit per crystal to give a grain over the source, while, in the areas away from the source, one hit per crystal will be enough. This would clearly distort the shape of the curve of grain density against distance, giving poorer resolution. Although this is likely to be only a minor effect by comparison with the other factors that have been listed, it is worth taking into account in experiments where the very highest resolving power is required.

(v) The size of the developed silver grains.   There is some evidence that a developed silver grain may not correspond in position with the halide crystal from which it grew[8]. Obviously the two must make contact at the latent image, if nowhere else, but the fully developed grain is considerably larger than the parent crystal and may lie to one side or other of the latter. The smaller the size of the developed grain, the nearer will its centre be to the latent image. Where the highest possible resolution is needed, in electron microscope autoradiography, developing methods that produce small grains have a small but significant influence on the overall resolution.

To sum up, the eight factors listed above are the variables available for manipulation. Some are of cardinal importance, others only marginal in their influence on resolution. Separation of source from emulsion is probably the most effective way of producing an autoradiograph with poor resolution. The choice of isotope, the thickness of the specimen, and the thickness of the emulsion layer all have considerable effect on resolution in one or other type of autoradiograph. By contrast, crystal diameter, developed grain size, and sensitivity of emulsion have effects which are much smaller, and are not worth consideration unless the more dramatic ways of producing poor resolution have already been looked after.

RESOLUTION AND THE AUTORADIOGRAPHY OF MACROSCOPIC SPECIMENS

When a grain density autoradiograph is made from a specimen the size of a section through the body of a mouse, the sort of information that is looked for is the distribution of the labelled compound between organs, or between maternal and foetal tissues. In the autoradiography of chromatograms, the spots may be several cm^2 in size. The highest possible resolution is not only not needed, it can be a real nuisance, making the collection of data more difficult. A smooth integration of grain density over the surface of an organ may be a positive advantage.

Such autoradiographs are usually viewed without magnification, so that the β particles leaving the surface must produce a considerable mass of developed silver if they are to be recognised at reasonably low rates of labelling.

The techniques for producing grain density autoradiographs from macroscopic specimens are discussed in Chapter 14, and it will be seen that many of the recommendations given there seem to be designed to give rather poor resolution. X-ray film is the recording medium of choice: its large crystal diameter (of the order of 3 microns) means that a single β particle can produce quite a mass of developed silver. X-ray film has an anti-abrasion coating to prevent the emulsion layers being scratched during handling. This is sufficiently thick to reduce the efficiency for the very low energy β particles of tritium to almost zero. So higher energy isotopes are often the ones of choice. The thinness of the source is determined by the difficulties of preparing and handling a large specimen. In a situation where so many factors are already set to produce an autoradiograph of fairly low resolution, it makes no sense to bother about the size of the developed grain.

The thickness of the emulsion layer is controllable in one sense, however. X-ray films are normally two emulsion layers, on either side of a central support of cellulose acetate or some similar material. The emulsion layer nearer the source will have an image with higher resolution than the one further away. The final autoradiograph can often be sharpened up a bit by soaking off the far emulsion layer after processing is complete.

RESOLUTION IN LIGHT MICROSCOPE AUTORADIOGRAPHY

There are really two separate geometrical situations here, the hemisphere model which can be achieved with tritium and one or two other isotopes with very low energies of emission, and the grain density model that can also be obtained with low energy isotopes, but is almost obligatory with isotopes of the maximum energy of carbon-14 or higher.

(a) Tritium

With a maximum energy of 18.5 keV the β particles from tritium have a range that seldom exceeds 2 microns in biological specimens, or 1 micron in nuclear emulsion. Tritium can give autoradiographs with very high resolution.

Clearly, any separation of source from emulsion is likely to prevent any β particles at all from reaching the emulsion, unless it is very thin. So, for reasons

Isotope	Section thickness (μ)	Emulsion	Developer	HD (μ)
^{3}H	0.5	AR-10	D-19	0.35
	0.4	L4	D-19	0.3
	1.0	L4	D-19	0.35
	0.5	NTB-2	Dektol	0.38
^{14}C	0.5	L4	D-19	0.8
	0.5	AR-10	D-19	2.0

Fig.20. HD values for various combinations of section thickness, emulsion and isotope, at the level of light microscope autoradiography. Liquid emulsions were applied as dense or overlapping monolayers, as judged by the interference colour of the dried emulsion layer. (Data kindly provided by Dr. M.M. Salpeter)

other than resolving power alone, separation is to be avoided if at all possible. From above a thickness of about 2 microns, only an insignificant number of β particles will reach the emulsion in most biological specimens, so that variations in specimen thickness above 2 microns will not affect the resolution at all. Below this value, there is a clear improvement in resolution with thinner sources (Fig. 20) and the highest resolution to date has probably been obtained with single bacterial chromosomes[16] (Fig. 21).

The effect of increasing the emulsion thickness is interesting. If the source is covered with a monolayer of silver halide crystals of an emulsion such as L4, probably about 60% of the β particles will be stopped in the emulsion: the next layer of crystals might stop a further 20%, and so on. Above a thickness of 2 microns, so few β particles will ever penetrate that they can effectively be ignored. The lateral scatter of the β particles in the monolayer of crystals nearest the source will be greater than in any subsequent layer, as illustrated in Fig. 15b. So adding layers of emulsion above the first will give a very slight *improvement* in resolution up to about 2 microns, and will have no effect whatever on the autoradiograph above that thickness. This latter effect can be seen in the data in Fig. 20.

Reducing the crystal diameter in the emulsion improves resolution, though the improvement is not very obvious in Fig. 20. It also minimises the chance of

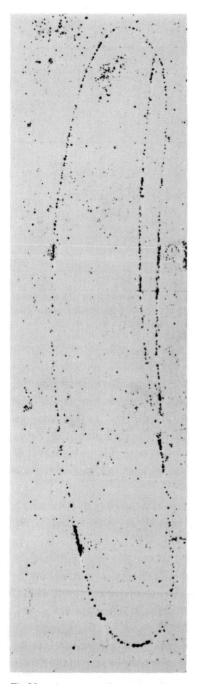

Fig.21. An autoradiograph of a chromosome of *E. coli,* labelled *in vivo* with [³H] thymidine for two generations and then extracted and autoradiographed with Kodak AR-10. About one-third of the chromosome has replicated. The scale indicates 100 μ. (From Bleecken, Strohbach and Sarfert, *Z. Allgem. Mikrobiol.* 6 (1966) 121)

crystals over the source receiving double hits. If the particles from a point source have only a small probability of reaching more than the nearest 3 or 4 crystals, double hits will become a nuisance far sooner than if the same volume of emulsion is occupied by 12–15 smaller crystals.

Emulsion of low sensitivity will record low energy β particles satisfactorily, so this factor does not influence resolution, nor does one at the light microscope level have to worry too much about the size of the developed grain.

HD values for tritium at the light microscope ievel are in the range of 0.3–0.5 micron (Fig. 20) which agrees well with the data calculated on a rather different basis by Hill[17].

(b) Isotopes of higher maximum energy

At the light microscope level, these are usually autoradiographed by the grain density model (Fig. 15c). The lower the maximum energy of the isotope, the better the resolution.

There is really very little to add in considering this group. The highest possible resolution will be given by a very thin source covered with a monolayer of silver halide crystals. The emulsion should have the smallest crystal diameter compatible with visibility in the light microscope, and with a high enough sensitivity to record the beginnings of tracks from β particles at the upper end of the energy spectrum. The exposure time should be controlled to keep low the probability of double hits over the source. At the light microscope level it probably is not worth keeping the size of the developed grains small by special means.

Careful measurements of resolution are hard to come by. Budd and Salpeter[14] have found an *HD* value of 2.0 μ for carbon-14, using a source 0.5 microns thick and a layer of *AR*-10 emulsion. One might expect an *HD* value of about 8 μ for phosphorus-32 in the same experimental conditions (Fig. 20).

(c) The autoradiography of diffusible materials

When the labelled source is freely diffusible in the biological specimen, movement of radioactivity from its position during life can contribute to the final distribution of silver grains. In a poorly controlled specimen, diffusion during freezing and subsequent freeze-drying can give a horrible spread of radioactivity. If freezing is rapid and subsequent handling avoids thawing at any stage, there is no reason why the resolution obtained with diffusible materials should not be comparable with that of fixed and embedded histological specimens[18, 19]. An interesting observation has been made by Clarkson and Sanderson[20], who studied cryostat sections of plant material. After freeze-drying, a section of

10 microns nominal thickness would remain at its original thickness over cellulose cell wall, but would dry down to a very thin layer of almost molecular dimensions over the lumen of conducting vessels. This effect can obviously introduce considerable variations in resolution into a single section. While animal tissues are usually rather more homogeneous, the same effect must occur to some extent over cytoplasm and extracellular fluid.

RESOLUTION IN ELECTRON MICROSCOPE AUTORADIOGRAPHY

Autoradiographic resolution has received more intensive and anxious attention from electron microscopists than from anyone else. The discrepancy between the resolving power of the electron microscope itself – in the range of 5–10 Å – and that of the photographic emulsion as a detector for β particles is so great that the measurement of autoradiographic resolution, the study of the factors that influence it and the devising of methods to manipulate those factors have occupied a lot of time and effort. Since all studies at this level start with the thinnest possible emulsion layer, a packed monolayer of crystals of small diameter, they all are concerned with the grain density model (Fig. 15c). In fact, our understanding of the factors affecting resolution in this system at the light microscope level owes a great deal to studies in electron microscope autoradiography.

The first major attempt to tackle this problem was made by Caro[11]. Starting with a thin biological specimen in direct contact with a monolayer of silver halide crystals, he identified three factors which contribute to the scatter of silver grains around a radioactive source. The first is the geometric relationship between source and emulsion, which determines the pattern or distribution of the paths of the β particles through the emulsion layer. Next is the fact that a latent image forms in a hit crystal at a performed sensitivity speck, and not necessarily on the path of the particle itself. The third factor is the uncertain relationship between the centre of the developed grain and the latent image. By employing a physical developer, p-phenylenediamine, Caro reduced his last source of uncertainty considerably, producing tiny, comma-shaped grains which indicated the site of the latent image with considerable precision.

Caro[11] did not evaluate the second and third sources of error which he identified, but concentrated on the geometric error, which appeared to contribute the major part of the uncertainty in identifying the source of radioactivity in the specimen. He broke this geometric error down into three components: (1) the possibility that a β particle will have sufficient energy to reach a crystal at a given distance from it; (2) the effective size of the crystal, taking into account its shielding from the source by adjacent crystals; (3) the solid angle subtended to the source by the unshielded portion of the crystal. Assuming a point source of tritium 500 Å away from a packed monolayer of crystals 1000 Å in diameter, Caro found that the grain density at a distance X from the source (D) could be approximated to the grain density over the source itself, (D_o), by the equation

$$D = D_o \, e^{-1.6 X}$$

Using the same approach, Caro[11] was able to calculate predicted grain densities around labelled bacteriophages, and found experimentally a reasonably good agreement with prediction. He also calculated predicted grain densities for two thicknesses of source and two diameters of crystal (Fig. 11). These curves show that reducing the crystal diameter from 1000 Å to 100 Å (far smaller than

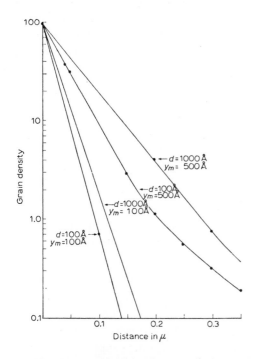

Fig.22. The expected distribution of silver grains around a point source labelled with tritium. d indicates the diameter of the silver halide crystals forming a monolayer over the source: y_m indicates the vertical distance from the source to the crystals. The distributions calculated from Caro's formula indicate the improvement in resolution likely from a thinner source or a smaller crystal diameter. (From L.G. Caro, 1962)

any available emulsion with useful sensitivity) would only improve the resolution by a relatively small amount. By contrast, reducing the specimen thickness
from 500 Å to 100 Å would have a much greater impact on resolution.

This paper focussed attention on many points of significance. Caro[11] drew
attention to the undoubted benefit that would result from smaller crystals in
terms of increased information per unit area of emulsion, for instance, even if
the predicted resolution, strictly defined, did not seem to improve very
dramatically. He defined resolution as twice the distance at which the grain
density falls to half its value directly over a point source, and on this basis
predicted a value of 860 Å for a tritium source 500 Å away from a packed
monolayer of 1000 Å crystals.

Bachmann and Salpeter[8] produced the next significant treatment of
resolution in electron microscope autoradiography. Their method of
autoradiography differed slightly from Caro's: in particular, they introduced a
carbon layer of 50–60 Å between specimen and emulsion. The three factors
identified as contributing to the scatter of grains about a point source by Caro[11]
were again recognised, but this time an attempt was made to evaluate the influence of crystal and grain diameters on resolution. The photographic error (E_p)
due to the combination of these two factors was taken to be

$$E_p = \sqrt{\frac{a^2}{5} + \frac{b^2}{12}}$$

where a is the diameter of the silver halide crystal and b the diameter of the
developed grain. Fig. 23 shows their calculated values of E_p for two emulsions
and several developing routines. It appears from their calculations that the

Emulsion	Developer	Diameter of halide crys- tals	Size of de- veloped grains	Mean pho- tographic error	Efficiency
Ilford	Microdol X	1 000–1 600	2 000–3 000	900	1 : 10
L4	p-Phenylenediamine	1 000–1 600	400– 700	600	1 : 13
Kodak	Dektol	300– 550	800–1 500	400	1 : 37
NTE	Gold latensification and Dektol	300– 550	800–1 500	400	1 : 12
	Gold latensification and Elon–ascorbic acid	300– 550	400– 600	280	1 : 9

Fig.23.   The effects of different development routines on the photographic component of
resolution and on the efficiency, for monolayers of emulsion exposed to tritium. (Data
taken from Bachmann and Salpeter, 1965) All distances are in Angstrom units.

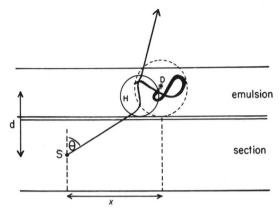

Fig.24. Diagrammatic model of an electron microscope autoradiograph. The source, S, is taken to lie on the mid-plane of the section: the β particle leaves the source at an angle θ, following an almost straight path to the emulsion layer where it hits a crystal, H. The centre of the developed grain is at D. The specimen to emulsion thickness is d, taken from the mid-plane of the section to the mid-plane of the emulsion: x is the projected distance from the source to the middle of the developed grain. (Data provided by Dr. Salpeter)

diameter of the crystal is more important than that of the developed grain in its influence on resolution.

Bachmann and Salpeter[8] next considered the distribution of β particle trajectories in the plane of the emulsion, or the geometric error (E_g). Fig. 24 shows their model. D is the centre of the developed grain, X the lateral distance between the source (S) and D, and ϑ the angle between the vertical and the path of the β particle. The distance between S and the emulsion is d, which is a sum of $t_e/2 + t_s/2 + t_i$ where t_e is the thickness of the emulsion layer (the diameter of the silver halide crystals), t_s the source thickness and t_i the thickness of the intervening layer of carbon. The density of β particles crossing the emulsion plane at any point lies between the limiting values of $\cos^3 \vartheta$ and $\cos^2 \vartheta$, and the fraction of the total emitted β particles that cross the emulsion plane in a circle of radius $\tan \vartheta$ is $1 - \cos \vartheta$. The geometric error was defined as the value of X at which $1 - \cos \vartheta = 0.5$ or the radius of the circle around the source through which half the β particles reaching the emulsion would travel. The resolution, or *HR*, which was discussed on p.51 and was the radius of the circle around a point source which contains half the silver grains produced by it, was calculated to be

$$HR = \sqrt{E_p^{\,2} + E_g^{\,2}}$$

	Specimen I	Specimen II
Section thickness	350	1000
Carbon layer	50	50
Emulsion	NTE	L4
Emulsion thickness	600	1300
Development	Gold–Elon	Microdol X
Photographic error	280	900
Geometrical error	720	1650
Total error	770	1850

Fig.25.   The factors affecting resolution calculated for Specimen I, which was prepared to give the highest possible resolution, and Specimen II, the most usual electron microscope autoradiograph prepared with L4 emulsion. The photographic and geometrical errors are discussed on pp.64 and 65. The total error should be near the *HR* value, determined experimentally. It is clear that geometrical factors contribute more than photographic to the total error in both specimens. (Data derived from Bachmann and Salpeter, 1965) All distances in Angstrom units.

In Fig. 25, the *HR* is calculated for two types of specimen. It will be seen at once that the resolution appears to be much worse than that calculated by Caro[11] and given above. But it must be remembered (see p.50) that the *grain density* about a point source falls off much more rapidly than the *grain distribution.* If Bachmann and Salpeter's calculations are used to estimate the geometrical error in terms of grain density, similar to Caro's, a value much nearer to his will be found.

This theoretical treatment illustrates well the contributions to resolution that are made by such factors as specimen thickness, and diameters of halide crystal and developed grain. The predicted values of *HR* for tritium range from 770 Å with Kodak NTE and the best conditions that can probably be obtained at present with sectioned biological material, to 1850 Å for a thicker section covered with a monolayer of L4.

In a later paper, Salpeter, Bachmann and Salpeter[13] looked for experimental verification of these predicted values of *HR*. This paper is basically empirical. It proved more convenient to study the grain distribution around a radioactive line source than to construct point sources, so a "hot line" was autoradiographed under a number of conditions, and the shortest distance from the centre of each developed grain to the line measured, up to 2 microns on either side. The equivalent concept to the HR for a point source, the HD (or distance from the line within which 50% of all the grains from it lie) has been found, and is listed for the various conditions studied in Fig. 26. Values of HR are not identical with the HD : $HD = HR/1.7$. When this correction is made, it will be seen that the theoretical predictions suggest a slightly better resolution (by 5–30%) than was found in practice. Once again, Fig. 26 shows clearly the improvements in resolution that follow from reducing the section thickness, and the diameters of halide crystal and developed grain. It was on the basis of these distribution curves that Salpeter, Bachmann and Salpeter[13] derived their universal curves for grain density studies (see pp.51–53).

So an HD of about 800 Å can already be obtained with sectioned material, and if only the section thickness and the halide crystal diameter could be considerably reduced, further improvements in resolution would follow. Unfortunately resolution cannot be considered in isolation from all the other factors that make an autoradiograph interpretable: the conflicting demands of

Isotope	Emulsion	Section thickness	Development	HD
^{3}H	L4 monolayer	1200	Microdol X	1650
			Paraphenylenediamine	1450
		500	Microdol X	1450
			Paraphenylenediamine	1300
	NTE double layer	1200	Dektol	1250
		500	Dektol	1000
	NTE monolayer	1200		1000
		500		800
^{14}C	L4 double layer	1000	Microdol X	2850
		500		2350
	L4 monolayer	1000		2300
		500		1800
	NTE double layer	1000	Dektol	2500
	NTE monolayer	1000		2000
^{55}Fe	L4 monolayer	1000	Microdol X	1300

Fig.26. Experimentally determined *HD* values for various combinations of isotope, specimen, emulsion and developer. The distances are all in Ångstrom units. Values for tritium are taken from Salpeter, Bachmann and Salpeter, 1969; those for carbon-14 from Salpeter and Salpeter, 1969; the one for iron-55 from D.M. Parry (personal communication).

efficiency and of adequate contrast and radioactivity in the specimen frequently prevent the highest resolution from being achieved. These problems are discussed more fully on p.252.

THE RESOLVING POWER OF TRACK AUTORADIOGRAPHS

The grain density model of autoradiography that has been discussed above is by far the most commonly employed. In some experimental situations, however, there are advantages in using much thicker emulsion layers, and studying the tracks of the β particles, rather than variations in the density of developed grains. This corresponds to the sphere and hemisphere concepts of Fig. 15 and it has interesting consequences for the resolution obtainable.

Let us consider a source mounted on a glass slide, and covered with nuclear emulsion to a thickness greater than the maximum range of the particles emitted — such a situation with carbon-14, for instance, would require a thickness of about 50 μ. If the track density is kept fairly low, by exposing for a short time, it is possible to recognise the individual tracks and to distinguish their beginning from their termination. Each track can therefore be traced back to the point at which it entered the emulsion. It is possible to plot the distribution of points of entry around a source, just as the distribution of individual grains was plotted in Fig. 16. The resolving power of this system then becomes, by analogy, the radius

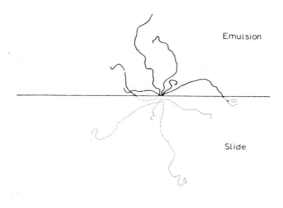

Fig.27. The distribution of β-particle trajectories around a source mounted on a glass slide and covered by a thick layer of emulsion. Half the particles initially enter the emulsion, half the glass. Scattering across the glass—emulsion interface occurs in both directions, but points where particles cross this plane are randomly distributed over a relatively large area.

of the circle around the source which contains one half of the points of entry of β particles originating from the source.

If the source is assumed to be very small, is in direct contact with the emulsion, and is mounted on a plane surface, it is clear that about half the particles emitted will enter the emulsion directly from the source, the other half being directed into the glass slide (Fig. 27). A small proportion of those fired into the emulsion will subsequently be scattered back into the slide, leaving a curved section of track visible. Similarly, some of the tracks entering the glass slide will be scattered into the emulsion at a distance from the source. But if one considers all the tracks that appear in the emulsion, the majority enter directly from the source, and present no particular problem in recognition. The problem of high resolution in track autoradiographs becomes one of defining these points of entry with the greatest possible precision.

In this situation, some of the recommendations for obtaining high resolution in grain density autoradiographs require modification. To begin with, there is little improvement in resolving power with using a lower energy isotope. In fact, with high energy emitters, such as phosphorus-32, the tracks tend to be much straighter near their origin than with lower energies, such as carbon-14. It is easier to extrapolate a straight track back towards its origin than a crooked one. With particles of higher energy there will be a smaller percentage of very tortuous short tracks, with which the uncertainty as to the precise point of entry may be considerable.

The separation of source from emulsion will still reduce the resolving power considerably, and increasing thickness of the source will have a similar effect. The thickness of the emulsion layer now is an advantage, however: it does not need critical control, provided only that it is thick enough to enable one to determine which is the beginning of the track and which the end. Background particles entering the emulsion from the air surface should be recognised and rejected with confidence.

The dimensions of the silver halide crystals cannot, unfortunately, be reduced very far, as it is usually not practicable to view a thick emulsion layer except with conventional transmitted light, but their sensitivity becomes a matter of critical importance. If, at the start of a high energy track, the grains are on average 4 μ apart, there may be tracks which appear to start quite a way from the source. If the sensitivity is so much higher that the average grain spacing becomes 1 μ, the first grain in each track will correspond much more closely to the point of entry of the β particle.

The exposure time will have to be kept short, as, if there are many tracks criss-crossing in one microscope field, the problems of identification become impossibly complex.

References p. 70

Given a highly sensitised emulsion and correct development, the resolving power of track autoradiography is probably comparable to that of conventional thin emulsion layers for carbon-14 and sulphur-35, and considerably better for higher energy isotopes such as phosphorus-32.

Alpha tracks. These are straight and short, and very easy to extrapolate back into the source. (Figs. 5 and 6). The only problem they raise in considering resolution is that, with a nuclear emulsion of high sensitivity, the tracks become so broad, due to the δ rays, that it is a cylinder that is extrapolated back, rather than a line. For the best resolving power, an emulsion of low sensitivity and fairly small grain size offers the best precision – for instance, Ilford KO.

RESOLUTION AND THE INTERPRETATION OF AUTORADIOGRAPHS

It should be quite clear by now that the resolution of an autoradiographic system is a measure of the scatter of developed grains over and around radioactive sources in the specimen. It is *not* a statement of the minimum size of source that can be identified. It may be quite possible to determine the source in a complex specimen when the structures within the specimen are smaller than the *HD*. The use of the *HD* value in interpreting the grain distribution in autoradiographs is considered in greater detail in Chapter 11.

REFERENCES

1   H. Levi, A.W. Rogers, M.W. Bentzon and A. Nielsen, *Kgl. Danske Videnskab. Selskab, Mat.-Fys. Medd.,* 33 (1963) No. 11.
2   H.J. Gomberg, *Univ. of Mich. Project* AT (11-1)-70, No. 3, 1952.
3   S. Bleecken, *Naturforsch.,* 23B (1968) 1339.
4   S. Bleecken, *Naturforsch.,* 23B (1968) 1350.
5   S. Bleecken, *Naturforsch.,* 23B (1968 1478.
6   I. Doniach and S.R. Pelc, *Brit. J. Radiol.,* 23 (1950) 184.
7   N.J. Nadler, *Can. J. Med. Sci.,* 29 (1951) 182.
8   L. Bachmann and M.M. Salpeter, *Lab. Invest.,* 14 (1965) 1041.
9   J. Gross, R. Bogoroch, N.J. Nadler and C.P. Leblond, *Am. J. Roentgenol., Radium Therapy, Nucl. Med.,* 65 (1951) 420.
10 L.F. Lamerton and E.B. Harriss, *J. Phot. Sci.,* 2 (1954) 135.
11 L.G. Caro, *J. Cell Biol.,* 15 (1962) 189.
12 S.R. Pelc, *J. Roy. Microscop. Soc.,* 81 (1963) 131.
13 M.M. Salpeter, L. Bachmann and E.E. Salpeter, *J. Cell Biol.,* 41 (1969) 1.
14 G.C. Budd and M.M. Salpeter, *In preparation.*
15 G.W.W. Stevens, *Brit. J. Radiol.,* 23 (1950) 723.

16   J. Cairns, *J. Mol. Biol.*, 6 (1963) 208.
17   D.K. Hill, *Nature,* 194 (1962) 831.
18   T.C. Appleton, *J. Histochem. Cytochem.*, 14 (1966) 414.
19   R. Creese and J. MacLagan, *J. Physiol.*, 210 (1970) 363.
20   D.T. Clarkson and J. Sanderson, Personal communication.

CHAPTER 5

The Efficiency of Autoradiographs

We have seen in the previous chapters that β particles can cause developable latent images in nuclear emulsions. Since the β particles cause the developed grains, it is reasonable to assume that a simple relationship exists under any given set of conditions between the number of β particles leaving the specimen during exposure and the number of silver grains produced by them. In the ideal case, there should be a direct proportionality between the radioactivity of the specimen and the number of silver grains produced by it.

Unfortunately, many factors can influence the efficiency with which an emulsion records β particles. The great advantage which autoradiography has for the biologist is the retention of structural patterns in the specimen; but this implies immediately that differences in geometry and density will also be preserved from point to point in the specimen. In Geiger or scintillation counting, care is taken to reduce every sample to a uniform specimen so that the efficiency of counting is the same for all samples. With the pulse counting techniques, each sample is presented to the same detector: in autoradiography, each sample is covered with very many halide crystals, each an individual detector. So the concept of efficiency assumes great importance in autoradiography. It is very easy to count silver grains and to compare the numbers counted over various specimens in the cheerful assumption that the efficiency of autoradiography has been the same in every case. It is often depressingly difficult to autoradiograph several specimens with the same efficiency.

In this chapter, the various factors which can influence the efficiency of autoradiography will be considered. The interpretation of autoradiographs is a more complex matter, involving the resolution, or scatter of silver grains about the source, as well as the efficiency: this will be considered in a later chapter.

DEFINITIONS OF EFFICIENCY

Just as resolution has been variously defined by different autoradiographers, so there are several definitions of autoradiographic efficiency. The definition that is most commonly met with relates the number of silver grains produced in a layer of nuclear emulsion to the number of particles entering it. This is quite a convenient definition for experiments into efficiency. It is relatively simple to take an extended, uniformly labelled source and to determine the number of particles per unit area per unit time that leaves its surface, using some type of electronic pulse counter. The same source can then be exposed to an emulsion layer, and the number of developed grains counted. The efficiency can then be calculated directly.

In the majority of radioisotope techniques, however, efficiency means something rather different. It is the number of events recorded, as pulses in the case of a Geiger counter, related to the number of radioactive disintegrations taking place in the source.

This is a more complex concept, as it introduces many variables in the source itself. If the source is relatively thick by comparison to the range of the β particles emitted, many of them will never reach the recording device at all. Though efficiency, defined in this way, is much more useful to the biologist, this definition is not often applied to autoradiography. This is unfortunate, since knowledge of the efficiency, in these terms, of the system being used is basic to the quantitative interpretation of autoradiographs.

In this book, I shall use "efficiency" to mean the emulsion response relative to the number of radioactive disintegrations taking place in the source during exposure. The term "grain yield" will be used for the mean number of grains produced per β particle entering the emulsion. The grain yield should be a constant for any given grain density autoradiograph: the efficiency, however, can vary enormously from point to point within a single specimen.

This definition of efficiency must be interpreted in different ways with different autoradiographic systems. In a grain density autoradiograph prepared for examination under the light or electron microscope, the number of grains is the emulsion response to be related to the disintegration rate. When the emulsion is examined by the unaided eye, however, individual silver grains are not seen. The intensity of blackening of the film becomes the parameter that is related to the number of β particles emitted by the source during exposure. The effects of this substitution of blackening for grain number will be discussed below in relation to macroscopic specimens. When one comes to track autoradiographs, the unit to be observed and counted is not the individual silver grain, but the arrangement of grains to form a track. In this case, efficiency becomes the ratio between the number of tracks produced in the emulsion and the number of radioactive disintegrations taking place in the source.

FACTORS AFFECTING THE EFFICIENCY OF GRAIN DENSITY
AUTORADIOGRAPHS

(a) Factors in the source

(i) The choice of isotope.   The initial energies of the β particles emitted by
the specimen influence the efficiency of grain density autoradiographs in many
ways. Rather than attempt to summarise these effects here, they will be
considered in the following sections, in relation to the particular factor under
discussion. It will be seen that switching to an isotope of lower maximum energy
may improve the efficiency in some respects while making it worse in others: the
overall gain or loss in efficiency will depend on all the factors operating to
produce the autoradiograph.

(ii) The distance between source and emulsion.   Separating the source from
the emulsion will, in general, reduce the efficiency. The degree to which this
effect operates will depend largely on the initial energy of the β particles. With
tritium, for instance, the particle track is so short anyhow that even the thinnest
inert layer will screen off a significant porportion of β particles from the emulsion. Perry *et al.*[1] have shown that 675 mμ of formvar are sufficient to reduce
the grain count over a tritium-labelled cell by 85%. With higher particle energies,
this effect becomes less important, until, with phosphorus-32, separation by
several microns of material of density about 1.1 will not produce a significant
reduction in efficiency. There is no appreciable difference, for instance, between
a film that has been exposed in direct contact with a paper chromatogram
containing phosphorus-32, and one that has been separated from the source by a
single thickness of paper.

Curves for the external absorption of β particles are available in the literature,
relating the density of the intervening layer (measured in mg/cm^2) to the
proportion of β particles which penetrate through to the other side. Maurer and
Primbsch[2] present such a curve for tritium, based on measurement with biological material: Pelc and Welton[3] have published a theoretical curve which is
practically identical.

(iii) The thickness of the source.   A flat, planar source which is only a few
Ångstrom units thick in contact with a nuclear emulsion, will produce a given
number of β particles entering the emulsion per hour. A source twice as thick,
but otherwise identical, will project β particles into the emulsion at twice the
rate. But if one continues this process of increasing the thickness of the source,

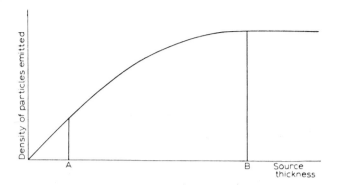

Fig.28. The effect of increasing source thickness on the density of β-particles leaving the surface of the source. In the initial part of the curve, up to A, source thickness is nearly proportional to particle density, and the source is "infinitely thin": above B, increases in source thickness do not affect particle density, and the source is "infinitely thick".

and plots source thickness against counting rate (Fig. 28), the counts will soon fall below the line which indicates a direct proportionality between the two. Above a given thickness, adding a further layer ot radioactive material to the bottom of a source does not produce the expected increase in counting rate, since this layer is separated from the emulsion by the overlying layers, which absorb some of the β particles coming from the lowest layer before they can be counted. With still greater source thicknesses, the departure from linearity becomes more and more marked until the addition of further radioactive material has no effect whatever on the count rate, which remains constant.

This phenomenon is known as self-absorption, and the general curve shown in Fig. 28 is found with any isotope emitting β particles, though the precise thicknesses vary with the energy spectrum of the isotope. In the initial part of the curve, where the increase in count rate is nearly enough linear for all practical purposes, the source is said to be infinitely thin. On the plateau, the source is said to be infinitely thick. At infinite thinness, the observed count rate is proportional to the amount of radioactivity in the source: at infinite thickness, the count rate is proportional to the concentration of radioactivity within the source, but is independent of its absolute amount.

It is obvious that the thickness of the source must affect the efficiency, except at infinite thinness. How important is this factor with various isotopes?

With phosphorus-32 and tissue sections 5 μ thick, one is working at infinite thinness. With carbon-14, a simple and direct method of calculating self-absorption has been presented by Hendler[4]. Using his figures, and assuming the density of fixed biological material to be 1.3, a section 1 μ thick would absorb 5.5% of the emitted β particles – or, stated in the more usual terms, there would be 94.5% transmission of the particles emitted in the direction of the emulsion. At 5 μ, there is 82.5% transmission and at 10 μ, 70.3%. It is clear that in this energy range self-absorption is having a very significant effect. In other words, the efficiency is critically dependent on the source thickness.

Tritium represents the extreme case where self-absorption is the most important single factor in considering autoradiographic efficiency.

Falk and King[5] used uniformly tritiated methacrylate to investigate self-absorption, and their results are shown in Fig. 29. There is no evidence of an initially linear relationship between thickness of methacrylate and observed grain densities, suggesting that infinite thinness had already been left behind at 0.5 μ. After 3 μ, there is little increase in grain density, and infinite thickness is reached at 5 μ. These sections should have approximately the same density as fixed biological material. The dramatic effects of self-absorption on the efficiency of these autoradiographs can be clearly seen, with values ranging from over 15% at 0.5 μ to 2% at 10 μ.

Pelc and Welton[3] have computed self-absorption curves for tritium which match well with Falk and King's[5] data. Careful analyses of self-absorption with tritium are presented by Maurer and Primbsch[2] and by Perry et al.[1] with bio-

AUTORADIOGRAPHIC EFFICIENCY AS A FUNCTION OF SECTION THICKNESS WITH A SOURCE UNIFORMLY LABELLED WITH TRITIUM

Section thickness (μ)	Grain count per 100 μ^2	Efficiency (%)
0.5	1.22 ± 0.11	15.72
1.0	1.72 ± 0.09	11.08
2.0	2.18 ± 0.10	7.04
3.0	2.61 ± 0.10	5.62
4.0	2.99 ± 0.15	4.82
5.0	3.25 ± 0.15	4.19
6.0	3.28 ± 0.15	3.52
7.0	3.20 ± 0.18	2.94
8.0	3.25 ± 0.12	2.62
9.0	3.26 ± 0.14	2.34
10.0	3.16 ± 0.12	2.03

Fig.29. Grain densities over sections of methyl methacrylate, uniformly labelled with tritium, and exposed to Eastman Kodak NTB-2 emulsion under identical conditions. The efficiencies have been calculated on the basis of the known specific activity of the methacrylate. (Material reproduced from Falk and King, 1963)

logical material. Maurer and Primbsch[2] showed that the density of nucleolus, nucleus and cytoplasm differed, even in fixed and sectioned material, from 0.018 mg/cm^2 for nucleus to 0.095 mg/cm^2 for nucleolus. So not only is self-absorption critically important with tritium, but it can and does vary from point to point within a biological specimen. As an example, self-absorption reduces the number of β particles reaching the emulsion to 40% relative to an infinitely thin specimen if the radioactivity is distributed in fixed and sectioned nuclear material 3 μ thick: comparable figures for cytoplasm would be 2 μ, and for nucleolus 0.6 μ. An interesting discussion of these problems of density and thickness of the source was published by Perry[6].

(b) Factors in the emulsion

(i) The thickness of the emulsion. In a situation where the emulsion thickness is less than the maximum length of the β track, it is obvious that increasing the thickness of the emulsion will increase the total number of developed silver grains. For high energy β emitters like phosphorus-32, and emulsion layers in the range of $1-20\,\mu$, it is reasonable to assume that there is a linear relationship between the thickness of the emulsion layer and the efficiency of the system. For carbon-14, the first 2 μ of emulsion will effectively reduce the number of β particles entering the next layer, and so on, and the effect of increasing the emulsion thickness will not be linear.

This factor, then, also varies in importance with the maximum energy of β particle from the isotope under examination. With tritium, this is so low that the maximum track length in nuclear emulsion is about 3 μ, and the maximum radius, or penetration into the emulsion, probably about 1 μ. In this case, it is irrelevant how thick the emulsion layer is, provided it does not drop below 2 μ. As will be seen in chapter 13 (p.250), this means that liquid emulsion techniques, in which the emulsion thickness is not strictly controlled, can be used for quantitative measurements with tritium. With isotopes of higher energies, however, more accurate control of emulsion thickness is essential if grain counts are to be compared between one source and another.

(ii) The dimensions and packing of the silver halide crystals. If one compares a layer 4 μ thick of an emulsion with silver halide crystals 0.5 μ in diameter with a similar layer of crystals of equal sensitivity, but of diameter 0.1 μ, it is obvious that a β particle travelling through the latter layer will hit many more crystals. The layer of emulsion made up of small crystals closely packed can carry more information per unit volume, and produce more developed grains per

β particle. Provided the decrease in crystal size is not achieved at the expense of sensitivity, such an emulsion is more efficient than one with larger crystals.

(iii) The sensitivity of the emulsion.   In chapter 3 (p.37), the track characteristic of a β particle travelling through nuclear emulsion was described. Not every crystal along the trajectory of the particle will have sufficient energy imparted to it to produce a developed grain, though every crystal hit will have some energy dissipated in it. If an emulsion is highly sensitised, less energy is needed to make an activated crystal develop into a grain. In such an emulsion, the grains will be closely spaced along the track of the particle. With lower sensitivities, only those grains that have had a large amount of energy dissipated within them will be developed.

Tritium is once again a special case. The energies of these particles are so low that they have a small probability of affecting more than one grain anyhow. At these low energies, the rate of energy loss is very high, and a relatively insensitive emulsion will record tritium with almost the same efficiency as a highly sensitised one — and often with a lower background. This is the rationale behind the use of Ilford K2 instead of K5 for tritium, or NTB-2 instead of NTB-3, a procedure which will be mentioned again on p.256.

(iv) The conditions of exposure and development.   Fig. 3 illustrates the time course of development of an emulsion layer, with increasing development producing a higher grain density over a labelled source up to a level at which a plateau is reached. Even on this development plateau, the number of developed grains per source increases slightly. It is clear that comparisons between different emulsions must be made under reasonably comparable conditions of development if they are to mean anything. Young and Kopriwa[7], for instance, claim that Gevaert NUC-307 is more sensitive than Ilford L4 by a factor of 1.14: if one looks carefully, the Gevaert emulsion was developed for twice as long as the Ilford, in a concentrated as opposed to a very dilute developer, to a point where the background was 2.7 times higher. Development can affect efficiency, but increased development times are not a good method of getting higher efficiencies since they may disproportionately increase the background.

Some developers produce higher efficiencies than others. Some appear to limit development to relatively large latent images while others preserve and develop minimal latent images. Gold latensification, which will be discussed further in relation to electron microscope autoradiography (pp.27 and 350) is one method of bringing very small latent images to development. In general, however, the differences in efficiency between developers are not great. This factor only assumes significance in electron microscope autoradiography, where the use of very small silver halide crystals means that most of the latent images are minute, and yet, since efficiency is crucially important, every latent image should be developed.

Several papers report variation in efficiency with the temperature of exposure of the autoradiograph[8,9]. Under constant conditions of development, the higher the temperature of exposure the higher the efficiency. It seems that the latent images formed at lower temperatures are smaller or more disperse. The same is also true of the background, however, and it would appear that efficiencies and background levels very similar to those obtained at 4° exposure can be achieved in autoradiographs exposed at −79° by slightly increasing development.

(v) The duration of exposure. Each halide crystal can only produce one developed grain. If many crystals are hit by more than one β particle, the efficiency will clearly be lower than if an identical autoradiograph is exposed for a shorter time.

Perry[6] has an excellent discussion on the probability of double hits. Biologists like myself are often surprised to find that this probability is finite, though very small, for each β particle after the first that travels through an emulsion layer. It does not become large enough to require correction factors until about 10% of the available crystals have already been hit. With grain density autoradiographs and isotopes of the maximum energy of carbon-14 or higher, it is reasonable to consider crystals at all depths in the emulsion as available. With tritium this clearly is not so, and double hits are a far more serious problem, as a point source in contact with the emulsion can only affect the few crystals that lie within 1 μ radius. If n_{max} is the total number of crystals that can be affected by a source, the observed grain count n_{obs} is related to the number that should have been seen in the absence of double hits, n_{true}, by

$$n_{obs} = n_{max}\left[1 - \left(\frac{n_{max}-1}{n_{max}}\right)^{n_{true}}\right]$$

(vi) Instability of the latent image. It frequently happens that similar autoradiographs are exposed for different times, and that the efficiency in the longer exposure is found to be lower than in the shorter. As we saw in Chapter 2, latent images can regress during exposure, an effect that is favoured by the presence of excessive moisture and of oxidising agents. Generalised latent image fading can be due to incomplete drying of the emulsion, and the presence of atmospheric oxygen: in this case, it tends to affect large areas of emulsion, often being more

Fig.30. An emulsion layer fogged by light and "exposed" under conditions used for autoradiography in contact with a cryostat section of rat submandibular gland for several days before development. Note the anatomical distribution of fading of the latent images, over the

severe over the section, where presumably drying was less thorough. It may vary from slide to slide, and will tend to be worse with longer exposures. This effect should be excluded from any quantitative experiment by the use of suitable control slides (see p.263).

Latent image fading over the specimen, due to a chemical interaction between parts of the specimen and the emulsion, can also occur. This negative chemography will produce wildly varying efficiencies over a single section in extreme cases (Fig. 30), and should also be excluded by control slides in which a high and uniform density of latent images has been created *before* exposure begins.

These comprise the majority of factors which can influence the efficiency of an autoradiograph. Others exist, though their effect is not sufficiently documented to enable one to estimate their relevance. Salpeter and Szabo[10] , for example, have found a curious drop in efficiency with increasing density of β particles in electron microscope autoradiographs. This cannot be explained by latent image fading, double hits or self-absorption. At present, it seems to be a function of certain emulsion–developer combinations.

Enough should have been said in the preceding pages to emphasise the wide variations in efficiency that can exist, not only from one experiment to another but from one point to another in the same biological specimen. The relative importance of these factors will now be discussed for each major group of autoradiographic techniques.

THE EFFICIENCY OF AUTORADIOGRAPHS OF MACROSCOPIC SPECIMENS

Specimens such as chromatograms or sections through large objects like whole mice or rat brains are usually viewed with the naked eye, or at very low magnifications. At this level, individual silver grains cannot be seen, and blackening in the film is the response that indicates radioactivity. Nuclear emulsions tend to have very small crystal diameters relative to other photographic materials, so that a high density of developed grains is needed to give a visible blackening. In X-ray emulsions the crystal diameter may be ten times greater than in a nuclear emulsion, so that the mass of silver formed by one developed grain is obviously very much more.

With isotopes of the energy of carbon-14 or higher, X-ray film is the obvious choice. Fig. 78 gives a rough idea of the radioactivity needed in a given spot of carbon-14 to give reasonable blackening in a stated exposure time. The large crystal size and the emulsion thickness of about 20 μ provide a recording medium which is very efficient, and which has sufficient resolution for most macroscopic work.

References p. 88

But X-ray films have a coating over the emulsion layer to reduce damage by handling. This anti-abrasion coating is sufficiently thick to screen off most of the β particles from tritium. The combination of this separation of source from emulsion with the self-absorption that is likely in a relatively thick specimen makes the efficiency of this method far lower for tritium, probably by a factor of about 100 compared to carbon-14. In consequence, several techniques have been described as alternatives to simple apposition to X-ray film: these are discussed in more detail in Chapter 14. They include apposition to a nuclear emulsion with a large crystal diameter; the impregnation of chromatograms with a liquid X-ray emulsion[11]; and conversion of the low energy β particles, which have such a short range, to light photons by immersing chromatogram and X-ray film in scintillation fluid[12].

If the choice is available, it is better to avoid the use of tritium in favour of isotopes of higher energy, for the autoradiography of macroscopic specimens.

THE EFFICIENCY OF GRAIN DENSITY AUTORADIOGRAPHS FOR THE LIGHT MICROSCOPE

In light microscope autoradiographs with tritium, the most significant variables affecting efficiency are self-absorption and the separation of source from emulsion. The latter should be avoided wherever possible. A few figures from the literature will illustrate the dramatic influence of self-absorption on efficiency. Small bacterial cells such as *E.coli* may be autoradiographed at an efficiency as high as 27% (ref. 13). Mammalian spermatozoa labelled in the DNA of the head, which is about 0.5 μ diameter, can give an efficiency of 17% (ref. 14). Sections of rat liver labelled more or less uniformly with a tritiated amino acid give efficiencies around 5% at 5 μ thickness, and 2–3% at 10 μ (ref. 15).

Few if any of the β particles will penetrate further than 1 μ into the emulsion, and some data from Salpeter and Szabo[10] suggest that a packed monolayer will stop as much as 60% of the β particles from tritium. Provided only that the emulsion is thicker than 2 μ, variations in emulsion thickness have no effect on efficiency. Since the particles are all of low energy, there is little gain from the use of highly sensitised emulsions. The probability of double hits may be high with small sources, since only those crystals within a radius of 1 μ from the source will contribute to n_{max} in the equation on p.79. From this point of view, there is an obvious advantage in using an emulsion with small crystal size.

Though it is usual to equate self-absorption with the thickness of the specimen, the results of Maurer and Primbsch[2] demonstrate how important variations in density can be in the specimen. Any extractive procedure that reduces specimen density without removing the radioactivity of interest will improve efficiency.

With isotopes of higher maximum energy, source—emulsion separation and self-absorption have progressively less effect on efficiency. As an example, if a bacterium labelled with carbon-14 has an efficiency of 60% in a given autoradiographic system, a section of density 1.3 and thickness 5 μ would register at 50% efficiency, and increasing the thickness to 10 μ would reduce the efficiency to 42%. With phosphorus-32, self-absorption can be effectively ignored in this range of source thickness.

On the other hand, variations in emulsion thickness now assume much greater importance. With phosphorus-32 one can assume a direct proportionality between efficiency and the thickness of the emulsion layer in grain density autoradiographs. With carbon-14, absorption in each micron of emulsion will reduce the number of β particles entering the next micron by about 10%. Sensitivity of the emulsion affects efficiency: with particle energies above about 500 keV the highest possible sensitivity will be needed, and even so many of the latent images will be relatively small, requiring considerable care in exposure and development. Since each source now can affect a far larger volume of emulsion than in the case of tritium, the probability of double hits significantly reducing the efficiency becomes less.

There have been few accurate measurements of efficiency with isotopes other than tritium at the light microscope level. Andresen et al.[16] present careful data on carbon-14, using Kodak AR-10. As a rough guide, grain density autoradiographs with carbon-14 should achieve an efficiency of 40—50% with sections 5 μ thick and emulsion layers in the range of 3—5 μ. The efficiency for phosphorus-32 in similar conditions might be between 30 and 40%.

THE EFFICIENCY OF AUTORADIOGRAPHS FOR THE ELECTRON MICROSCOPE

Efficiency matters a great deal in these autoradiographs. The demands of high resolution produce a specimen which is extremely thin, and thus contains relatively small amounts of radioactive material, and place it next to a monolayer of silver halide crystals. The smaller the crystals the better the resolution. But such a thin recording medium cannot be as efficient as the layers several microns thick used for light microscope work. Electron microscope autoradiography is always a compromise between the highest possible resolution (which is seldom good enough) and an efficiency sufficiently high to produce enough silver grains to analyse. It is in this context that the various methods of development have been most intensively studied in relation to efficiency.

Specimen and emulsion are so thin that it is possible to treat tritium in the same fashion as isotopes of higher energy. For specimens up to 1000 Å thick and of density up to 1.3, it is possible to ignore self-absorption even with tritium[17]. Vrensen[18] has published data which suggest that self-absorption may have a significant effect with tritiated sections between 400 and 1000 Å thick. A careful re-examination of this work by Salpeter and Szabo[10] has shown that self-absorption can be ignored in this range, and has indicated a curious effect which probably explains Vrensen's data. At very low densities of β particles, the efficiency of L4 when developed with either Microdol X or D-19 developers is significantly higher than at higher particle densities. This appears to be a function of the distances between adjacent latent images at development. With Elon-ascorbic acid development after gold latensification, the efficiency stays equally high at very low and at higher particle densities. It is entirely possible that the effect attributed to section thickness by Vrensen was in fact due to the wide spacing of latent images in the case of the thinner sections, and was not due to self-absorption. Certainly, Salpeter and Szabo have shown that if exposure is controlled to give grain densities in the same range for both groups of sections, the efficiency is the same whether sections of 500 or 1000 Å are used.

Efficiency is related to emulsion thickness. Vrensen[18] has claimed an increase in efficiency from using a double layer of silver halide crystals without a serious loss of resolution, and there may be situations where his compromise is justified. The results of Salpeter and Szabo suggest that the increase in efficiency of a double layer of L4 is of the order of 20% over that achieved by a monolayer, with a tritium-labelled source.

The crystal size has a complex effect on efficiency. It is very difficult to manufacture emulsions with a crystal diameter below 1000 Å with a sensitivity for β particles equal to that of Ilford L4. As the sensitivity of the crystals falls, the efficiency of the monolayer as a recording medium also falls. On the other hand, the probability of double hits rises far more rapidly with large crystal diameters. Ilford L4 has a mean crystal diameter of 1400 Å, and a packed monolayer has 45–50 crystals per square micron. By comparison, Kodak NTE has a mean crystal diameter of about 400 Å, and a monolayer contains over 400 crystals per square micron.

Latent image stability improves with larger crystal diameters in general. Even with L4, Salpeter and Bachmann[19] find it necessary to place a layer of evaporated carbon between section and emulsion to prevent latent image loss, probably caused by osmium compounds in the section. This layer should be about 50–60 Å thick, and should not affect the efficiency significantly by β absorption, even with tritium, while the gain in efficiency by promoting latent image stability is considerable with long exposures.

Many developers have been examined in the attempt to bring to development the smallest possible latent images. Since small developed grains can give better resolution than large ones, this search has often been combined with attempts to arrest development before the crystal is fully converted to silver. This can lead to a spuriously high value for efficiency. It is possible with L4 to start to develop several latent images independently in the same crystal: if development is manipulated to prevent these uniting in one large grain, and yet each speck of silver is counted as a separate grain, efficiencies several times higher than is justified may be quoted. The crystal represents the unit of information in the emulsion, not the latent image.

Intensification of latent images by treatment with gold salts prior to development is probably the most successful single procedure in achieving high efficiencies by modifications of development. Fig. 23 presents the efficiencies obtained in Salpeter's laboratory for different combinations of emulsion and developer. Other values are published by a number of authors[18, 20, 21].

There is less information available for isotopes of higher energy. Calcium-45 in the form of small crystalline deposits of calcium fluoride has been investigated by Huxham, Lipton and Howard[22], who claim an efficiency of about 3% with L4. Caro and Schnös[21], using L4 and p-phenylenediamine developer, claim 2.5% efficiency for phosphorus-32.

THE EFFICIENCY OF TRACK AUTORADIOGRAPHS

If one now considers track autoradiographs, where the emulsion is thick relative to the maximum track length of the β particles being emitted, there are several factors that differ from those discussed above. The problems of self-absorption and emulsion sensitivity, however, are the same.

The key to the differences that do exist lies in the definition of a β track. This is usually accepted as four or more silver grains arranged in a linear fashion. This pattern is sufficiently improbable in random background grains to exclude the chance of counting fortuitous groups of individual grains as tracks. But all isotopes which emit β particles have a spectrum of energies extending right down to zero, and some of these particles will have insufficient energy to produce 4 silver grains in a row. With phosphorus-32, this fraction is so low that it is negligible. With carbon-14, 14% of the β particles will not produce a track[23]. With tritium, the fraction that does produce a track is very small[24].

So, if one considers the effect of particle energy on efficiency in track auto-

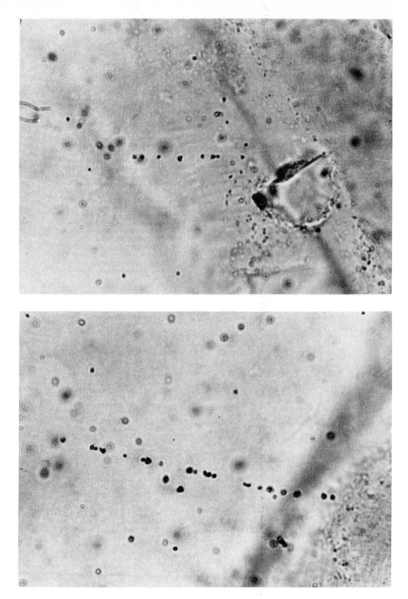

Fig.31.   A photomicrograph of a β-track autoradiograph prepared with Ilford G5 emulsion in conditions permitting the fading of latent images. Portions of two tracks from phosphorus-32 can be seen. In one, the silver grains have a normal size distribution and normal spacing. In the other, the grains are smaller and more widely spaced than usual. The latter track was presumably formed early in exposure, the former one late in exposure. The coexistence of normal and "faded" tracks in the same autoradiograph is clear evidence of latent image fading. (× 850)

radiographs, the higher the maximum energy, the higher the efficiency. With particulate sources suspended in a nuclear emulsion, Levinthal and Thomas[25] have shown that 100% efficiency can be obtained with phosphorus-32. With phosphorus-32 in a 5 μ section, covered on one side by emulsion, the efficiency will be approximately 50%. With carbon-14 in a similar situation, the efficiency will be nearer 30%, after allowing for self-absorption and the necessity to produce a track 4 grains long. The efficiency of track autoradiographs does not vary with emulsion thickness, provided always that the emulsion is thick enough to record the tracks adequately. Track autoradiographs are less critically affected by latent image fading. The exposure time is usually very short, as the interpretation of track patterns becomes very difficult if the track density is high. Further, latent image fading affects those crystals with minimal latent images first, and its initial effect on a β track is to reduce the grain density along the track, still leaving those grains which had more energy dissipated in them to indicate the passage of the particle. Thus the track may still be recognised and counted in the presence of mild latent image fading (Fig. 31).

THE CONFLICTING DEMANDS OF RESOLUTION AND EFFICIENCY

Some of the factors that contribute to a high efficiency have already been identified as desirable from the viewpoint of high resolution. Separation of source from emulsion makes for a poor autoradiograph in both respects; while the highest efficiency and resolution come with a source that is extremely thin. A high probability of double hits reduces both efficiency and resolution.

In other respects, a compromise may have to be reached if the system giving the highest resolution fails to give sufficiently high grain densities for reasonable analysis. Obviously a very thin section will contain less radioactivity than a thicker one cut from the same specimen, and a monolayer of crystals is a less efficient recording medium than a layer of the same emulsion 5 μ thick. In order to get a sensible autoradiograph within a tolerable exposure period, it may be necessary to accept a thicker specimen or a thicker emulsion layer, or both. Strict control of latent image fading and careful development, with gold latensification if necessary, may improve the situation.

One further technique has recently been advocated to give higher efficiencies the conversion of the energy lost by the β particles into light by means of scintillation compounds[26]. This has been in use for many years in the autoradiography of chromatograms[12], but has not been applied to autoradiographs at the light or electron microscope level, on the assumption that photon emission at points along the β track could only increase efficiency at the expense of a considerably poorer resolution. The increases in efficiency claimed are very considerable – 1.9 times with tritium and 40 times with sulphur-35 in tissue sections coated with NTB-2 emulsion. At present it is too early to assess the full potential of this technique, which needs further investigation.

REFERENCES

1   R.P. Perry, M. Errera, A. Hell and H. Durwald. *J. Biophys. Biochem. Cytol.*, 11 (1961) 1.
2   W. Maurer and E. Primbsch, *Exptl. Cell Res.*, 33 (1964) 8.
3   S.R. Pelc and M.G.E. Welton, *Nature*, 216 (1967) 925.
4   R.W. Hendler, *Science*, 130 (1959) 772.
5   G.J. Falk and R.C. King, *Radiation Res.*, 20 (1963) 466.
6   R.P. Perry, in D.M. Prescott (Ed.), *Methods in Cell Psysiology*, Vol. 1, Academic Press, New York and London, 1964.
7   B.A. Young and B.M. Kopriwa, *J. Histochem. Cytochem.*, 12 (1964) 438.
8   T.C. Appleton, *J. Histochem. Cytochem.*, 14 (1966) 414.
9   W. Sawicki, K. Ostrowski and J. Rowiński, *Stain Technol.*, 43 (1968) 35.
10 M.M. Salpeter and M. Szabó, *J. Histochem. Cytochem.*, 20 (1972) 425.
11 J. Chamberlain, A. Hughes, A.W. Rogers and G.H. Thomas, *Nature*, 201 (1964) 774.
12 A.T. Wilson, *Biochim. Biophys. Acta*, 40 (1960) 522.
13 S. Bleecken, *Atompraxis*, 10 (1964) 1.
14 W.L. Hunt and R.H. Foote, *Radiation Res.*, 31 (1967) 63.
15 H.K. Oja, S.S. Oja and J. Hasan, *Exptl. Cell Res.*, 45 (1967) 1.
16 N. Andresen, C. Chapman-Andresen, H. Holter and C.V. Robinson, *C.R. Lab. Carlsberg Chim.*, 28 (1953) 499.
17 L. Bachmann and M.M. Salpeter, *J. Cell Biol.*, 33 (1967) 299.
18 G.F.J.M. Vrensen, *J. Histochem. Cytochem.*, 18 (1970) 278.
19 M.M. Salpeter and L. Bachmann, *J. Cell Biol.*, 22 (1964) 469.
20 B.M. Kopriwa, *J. Histochem. Cytochem.*, 15 (1967) 501.
21 L.G. Caro and M. Schnös, *Science*, 149 (1965) 60.
22 G.J. Huxham, A. Lipton and B.M. Howard, *Austr. J. Exptl. Biol., Med. Sci.*, 47 (1969) 299.
23 H. Levi, A.W. Rogers, M.W. Bentzon and A. Nielsen, *Kgl. Danske Videnskab. Selskab, Mat.-Fys. Medd.*, 33 (1963) No. 11.
24 H. Levi, *Scand. J. Haematol.*, 1 (1964) 138.
25 C. Levinthal and C.A. Thomas, *Biochim. Biophys. Acta*, 23 (1957) 453.
26 R.J. Przyblyski, *J. Cell Biol.*, 43 (1969) 108a.

CHAPTER 6

Autoradiographic Background

In every autoradiograph, silver grains appear in the developed emulsion which are not due to radiation from the experimental source, but to other causes. These grains constitute the background. The recognition and measurement of radioactivity depend on the comparison of the grain or track density over an experimental source with the density found over a source that is known to be unlabelled. Clearly, the amount and the variability of background determine the minimum level of radioactivity that can be recognised.

To most people starting work with radioactive isotopes and autoradiography, background seems to be synonymous with cosmic radiation. When I first began this type of work, I went to great trouble to obtain permission from the National Coal Board to expose my slides at the bottom of a coal mine. This added a touch of the bizarre to the whole procedure, but I was rather crestfallen to find that the background was considerably higher in these slides which had been so carefully shielded from cosmic radiation than in control slides exposed in the refrigerator in the laboratory. In fact, cosmic rays form a comparatively insignificant component of background in most instances.

The major factors that contribute to autoradiographic background will vary from one laboratory to the next, from one technique to another, even between experiments carried out in the same laboratory with the same technique. The more important causes of background are discussed below, together with suggested ways of investigating their relative importance in any given experiment.

(a) Development and background

In Chapter 2 (p.19) we have already seen that if the strength, the temperature, or the duration of development are progressively increased, more and more silver grains will be developed, regardless of the degree of exposure of the emulsion to radiation. Taking development time as an example (Fig. 3), beyond a threshold time, the number of silver grains lying along the tracks of particles

References p. 106

[89]

which have passed through the emulsion does not increase significantly. At some development time longer than this, many tiny background grains appear, growing larger and more numerous as development is extended further. These effects have been studied, for instance, by Ahmad and Demers[1], and by Caro and Van Tubergen[2].

The optimal development time varies with the emulsion used, with the developer, and with many other factors, and there may be no alternative to finding it for the conditions that will be used in a particular series of experiments, using the methods outlined in Chapter 2.

A high background caused by overdevelopment can often be recognised by simple examination of the developed emulsion. The background grains will usually be randomly scattered throughout the emulsion, and noticeably smaller than the grains due to radiation. In cases where the background is very high, the processed emulsion may have a pinkish-grey colour when looked at with the unaided eye.

(b) Background due to exposure to light

The emulsions available for autoradiography vary considerably in their sensitivity to visible light, but all of them will show increasing background with increasing exposure to light. Appropriate safelighting conditions are recommended by the manufacturer for each emulsion, and these should be carefully followed. For the Ilford G, K, and L emulsions, the light brown Ilford "S" safelight is satisfactory. This seems very bright to anyone used to working with Kodak AR-10, or the Eastman Kodak NTB emulsions, which require the dark red Wratten No. 2 filter. The safelight filter only ensures that the wavelength of the light falling on the emulsion is that to which it is least sensitive. The light intensity is determined by the power of the bulb, which is usually taken to be 15 W, and by the distance between light source and emulsion. There is absolutely nothing to be gained by using very murky working conditions, and then carrying out each procedure 6 inches from the safelight in order to see what to do.

In effect, emulsions are at their most sensitive when adequately dried. (Strictly speaking, the fading of the latent image is very rapid in a wet emulsion, giving a similar end result to a loss of sensitivity.) In the liquid emulsion techniques, for instance, a level of light intensity can be tolerated while the emulsion is molten and diluted with water that would be likely to cause an increase in background once the emulsion layers are fully dried. It is reasonable to use lower levels of lighting, or to work further from the safelight, when putting the dried autoradiographs away for exposure, or while developing them, than in the initial stages of preparing the emulsion.

Undue exposure to light can be simply recognised when it is at the stage of gross fogging. The silver grains occur throughout the emulsion, and there may be curious geometrical patterns visible, due to the partial shielding of one slide by the next one, or by some neighbouring object. The section itself may give a certain amount of protection to the overlaying emulsion. The less obvious degrees of fogging can be difficult to recognise on examination of the emulsion alone. If light is suspected as a cause of high background, there may be no alternative to preparing and developing a series of emulsion layers on plain slides, without any biological specimen, varying the intensity of lighting to see if there is any significant effect on the background.

Methods have been described for preparing and processing autoradiographs in total darkness[3]. If correct safelighting and handling procedures are employed, I have found no appreciable improvement in background levels from working in absolute darkness.

(c) Background due to pressure

Nuclear emulsions are sensitive to pressure, and beautiful fingerprints can be produced in them as patterns of developed grains. In some laboratories, this response to pressure is used routinely for "writing" numbers and letters on the dried emulsion layer with a pointed instrument. On development, they will appear clearly in black.

Obviously, scratches, fingerprints, and other gross insults to the emulsion must be avoided. But there are other examples of stress or pressure causing a high background which are not so immediately evident. Gelatin contracts on drying, and, if this process is carried out too fast, or taken too far, developed grains will be produced. This type of artefact can show itself in two ways. Where the emulsion is in contact with the glass slide, it may be subjected to sliding, lateral stresses as it shrinks, producing background grains which are often arranged in curious patterns when viewed under low magnification. These grains tend to lie in the emulsion layer nearest to the glass support. Very thin emulsion layers will tend to dry much more rapidly than thicker ones, and they will often have a higher background for this reason. In slides dipped in very dilute liquid emulsion, and dried in a vertical position, the background often increases sharply towards the top of the slide, where the emulsion layer is thinnest.

The other type of stress or pressure artefact is usually limited to the area over a specimen, such as a tissue section. The upper profile of a tissue section is usually very irregular: if the section was cut at a thickness of 5 μ, it will be 5 μ thick only in places. Over the blood vessels, for instance, and other tissue spaces, the thickness drops abruptly to zero, and the same is true of the edges of the section. With liquid emulsion techniques in particular, these irregularities fill with emulsion, producing many changes in thickness and occasional wedges, where the emulsion dips right down to the glass support. These places seem particularly vulnerable to stress artefacts on drying, and a line of silver grains, closely following such a change in contour in a section, should always be regarded with suspicion. If the line of silver grains is regular and confined to one plane in the emulsion, if it follows the change in contour very accurately, it is almost certainly an artefact. There are several papers in the literature which claim to demonstrate the localisation of radioactivity along the course of fibres of various sorts, in which the published microphotographs are beautiful examples of this type of artefact. Even the β particles from tritium have a measurable range in emulsion, and the silver grains from a uniformly labelled linear source would occur at many levels through the emulsion. They would be distributed at distances up to at least $2\ \mu$ on either side of the source, and would show some statistical variability in density from place to place along the source. Fig. 32 illustrates the very different appearance of the stress artefact.

Several precautions can be taken to avoid these pressure artefacts. The glass support should, wherever possible, be coated with a thin layer of gelatin (the subbing solution, described on p.108) before the emulsion is applied. This not only improves the adhesion of emulsion to glass, but reduces the stress artefacts due to lateral displacements on drying. For routine work, emulsion layers should not be less than $3\ \mu$ thick.

The crucial step in controlling these pressure artefacts, however, comes in drying the emulsion after applying it to the specimen. Many workers have their own drying routines, and these can vary greatly in detail. Most of them have certain features in common, which emphasise the factors that must be most carefully controlled. The first of these is the speed of drying. Sawicki and Pawinska[4] have made some interesting observations with Kodak AR-10. If the film is dried very slowly over 24 h, by placing it in a closed but permeable box over calcium chloride in a desiccator, the observed background lies between 0.09 and 0.24 grains per $100\ \mu^2$. If, under otherwise identical conditions, the film is dried rapidly in front of a fan, the background values are from 4 to 7 times higher.

With liquid emulsion techniques, the emulsion is kept warm in order to keep it molten for application to the specimen. Particularly if it is applied as a very thin layer, it will dry almost immediately. Caro and Van Tubergen[2] have drawn attention to the changes in distribution of silver halide crystals that can occur as a result of this rapid drying of a thin, warm emulsion, and have recommended cooling the emulsion to its gelling point prior to application. This procedure

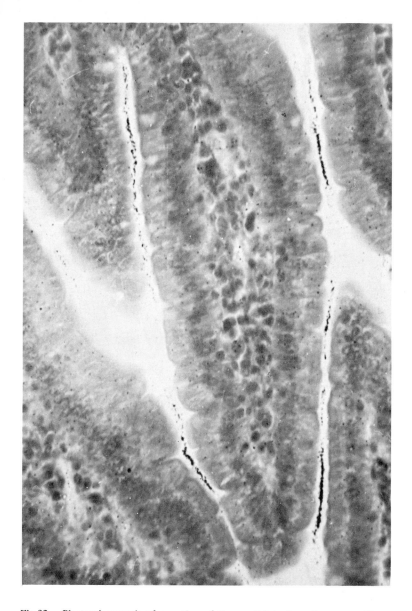

Fig.32. Photomicrograph of a section of the small intestine of a mouse. The section was coated with a thin layer of Ilford K2 emulsion, which was rapidly dried at 30°, in front of a fan. Exposure for 1 week was followed by development in the usual way. Note the high background of randomly distributed silver grains, and the dense lines of silver following the edges of the tissue. Both the random background and the edge artefact reflect the physical stressing of the halide crystals caused by rapid drying of the emulsion. (X 440)

References p. 106

should be equally effective in reducing the stressing of the crystals during drying. Certainly, the emulsion should be cooled immediately it is on the specimen, and should be dried very gently in the gel state.

In quantitative work, it may be necessary to take special precautions against latent image fading. Messier and Leblond[5], using Eastman-Kodak emulsions and the dipping technique, found it necessary to expose their autoradiographs at extremely low relative humidities in order to prevent latent image fading. With Ilford emulsions, I have found that this sort of drying produces unacceptably high background levels. Ilford recommend a relative humidity of 40–45% during exposure, and the background is considerably less under these conditions, while fading of the latent image is not a problem for exposures up to about 3 weeks. There may well be genuine differences between the behaviour of the Ilford and Eastman-Kodak emulsions in this respect, and the high background from vigorous drying seen in the former may not occur with the latter. The whole problem of latent image fading and its control will be discussed in more detail later (p.228).

One further step to reduce the probability of stress artefacts on drying has been suggested by Waller[6]. Emulsions, as supplied from the factory, normally contain various plasticising agents which tend to reduce the shrinkage of the gelatin on drying, and these agents may be leached out if the emulsion passes through aqueous media before exposure. Waller recommended that all aqueous solutions that come into contact with emulsions prior to exposure should contain added glycerol to a final concentration of 1%. The detailed descriptions of technique given in later chapters often include this addition of glycerol.

If it is necessary to expose an emulsion under extremely dry conditions or in vacuo, Ilford will provide their emulsions with added plasticiser.

(d) Chemography

In most of the autoradiographs that biologists prepare, emulsion comes into contact with biological material of some sort during exposure. Many reactive groups, in particular those that are reducing agents, are capable of producing a latent image in silver halide crystals by direct, chemical action.

Tissue that has been through the processes of fixation, dehydration, embedding in paraffin wax, sectioning, and subsequent dewaxing is less likely to give rise to this type of artefact than fresh tissue sectioned on a cryostat, for instance. But in most situations the possibility of chemography exists, and one of the most striking things about this particular source of background grains is its unpredictability. One series of sections out of a score processed in apparently the same way will show it, where the others do not.

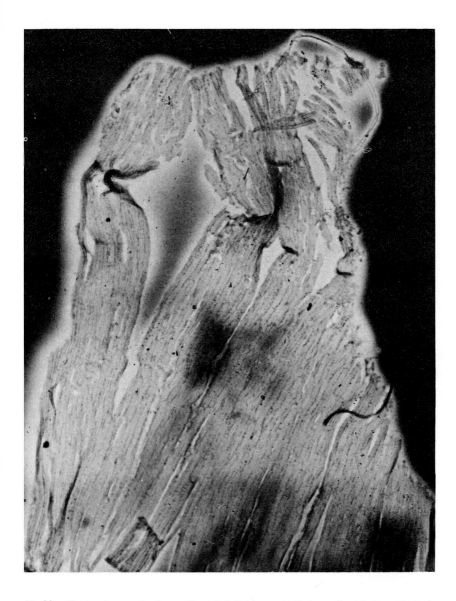

Fig.33. Photomicrograph of a section of skeletal muscle that was fixed in formalin before embedding in paraffin wax. The section was coated with Ilford K2 emulsion, which was fogged by light before being exposed in the dark for 18 days. Development followed in the usual way. It can be seen that blackened emulsion surrounds the section, but, over the section itself, gross fading of the latent images caused by light has occurred. This is an example of negative chemography. (X 27)

The opposite effect to this, negative chemography, may also occur. Certain reactive groups in the specimen may result in very rapid fading of the latent image in the adjacent crystals, resulting in an area of emulsion that is virtually incapable of registering the passage of a charged particle. Fig. 33 (p.95) shows a dramatic example of this type of chemography. The material is muscle, fixed in formalin, embedded in paraffin, and autoradiographed by the dipping technique, using Ilford K2 emulsion. The photomicrograph shows a control slide which had been fogged by light before being exposed, together with the rest of the slides, for two weeks. The emulsion has been very effectively bleached, with complete loss of the latent image, in the regions over the section only. It is often almost impossible to trace down the variable that produces this effect in one block, but not another.

A further example of chemography is provided by Fig. 34. This shows an autoradiograph of a section of a human femur, obtained at post-mortem. In the course of a long illness, this patient received many injections of the short-lived isotope calcium-47. It had been suggested that this material might have been contaminated with traces of the longer-lived calcium-45, and that enough might have accumulated in her bones to give an autoradiograph. So a portion of femur was placed in contact with an X-ray film, and the autoradiograph obtained. The result looks quite impressive. There is obviously heavy blackening present, and it seems to follow an anatomical distribution. It is clear, however, that there are also some areas of this "autoradiograph" that are lighter than the background away from the bone. This indicates that these areas are being bleached by some compounds unknown, presumably originating in the tissue. If negative chemography is occurring, the blackening also may be an artefact. The bone was therefore dipped in a solution of nitrocellulose, coating it with an inert and relatively impermeable layer which was still thin enough for the majority of the β particles to penetrate. The autoradiograph that was then obtained, under otherwise identical conditions of exposure, was completely negative. It was obvious that all the blackening seen in the first picture was artefactual, due to chemography. Since it was blackening unrelated to radiation from the source, it was, by definition, background.

It is one of the most significant characteristics of chemography, that it frequently has an anatomical distribution, giving rise to a very plausible "autoradiograph". It is quite common also to have this combination of blackening with bleaching in the same specimen. Neither observation should be very surprising, since presumably the chemical groups responsible vary in concentration from one part of a biological specimen to another in some sort of anatomical fashion. The spread and severity of this artefact may increase with increasing

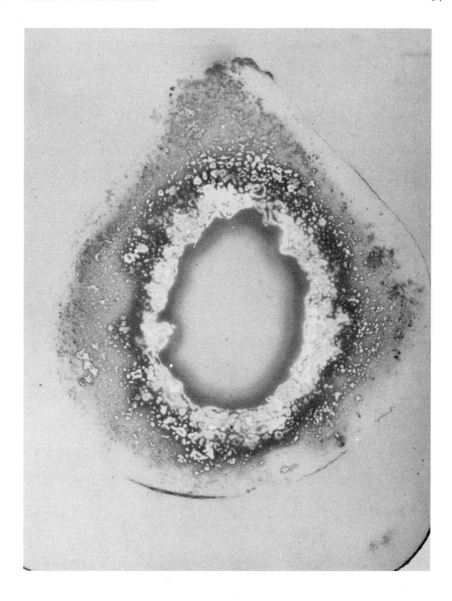

Fig.34. Autoradiograph of a cut surface of human femur, placed in contact with an X-ray film. All the blackening, as well as the areas which are less black than background, are caused by chemography. A second autoradiograph of the same material with source separated from emulsion by a thin, impermeable membrane failed to produce any blackening whatever. (× 4)

exposure time. It is obvious that this artefact is so serious a pitfall in the interpretation of an autoradiograph that adequate control measures must be taken in every single experiment. This point is discussed further in considering the design of autoradiographic experiments (p.263).

Chemography depends on the diffusion of reactive molecules into the emulsion from the specimen, and their reaction there with the silver halide crystals. The rates of both these processes are temperature dependent, so it is possible to reduce the severity of this artefact by exposure at low temperature[7]. If development is kept constant, a lower exposure temperature produces a poorer efficiency in the emulsion[8]. The latent images formed at temperatures below about −20° appear to be smaller or more diffuse. They are still there, however, and I have found that the very severe drop in efficiency reported by Welton[8] can be effectively restored by slight increases in either the temperature or duration of development.

The choice of developer may have a surprising influence on the severity of chemography[7]. Chemical effects on the silver halide crystals are presumably maximal at the crystal surface, and a developer that relies on surface latent images only will be much more sensitive to latent image loss from chemography than one that attacks internal latent images also.

It is sometimes possible, with experience, to suspect the presence of chemography by simple examination of the emulsion under high magnification. If the grain density is significantly lower over the specimen than away from it, negative chemography should be suspected. The silver grains due to positive chemography are often large, irregular, and sometimes clumped together. Their distribution over the specimen is often thicker and more even that one would expect from radioactivity, and there is no suggestion of their arrangement in segments of tracks. But these are not fully reliable criteria, and the only real protection against chemography lies in the adequate design of the experiment, with the correct use of control procedures.

(c) Contamination of the emulsion

Just as certain reactive groups in the specimen may affect the performance of the emulsion, so may traces of contaminating chemicals in the emulsion itself. Nuclear emulsions are finely controlled in manufacture, and carefully designed, and great care should be taken to keep them free from contamination.

Glass, certain plastics, and high grade stainless steel are the only materials that should be allowed to come into contact with nuclear emulsion, and they should all be scrupulously clean. Metallic ions are a frequent cause of trouble, particularly copper, and copper water baths and other metal objects, such as spoons or forceps, should be avoided at all costs. Distilled or deionised water should be used for all solutions.

It is often difficult to clean glassware that has held emulsion. The most satisfactory procedure I have found is to soak it first in normal sodium hydroxide, which digests away the gelatin. After washing, chromic acid will remove any remaining traces of silver salts. Thorough washing for several hours in running tap water, followed by distilled water, will be needed to remove the acid.

A different type of contamination may occur if the darkroom is not kept clean. This is particularly likely to happen if it is shared with amateur photographers. Developer and fixer get spilt on the floors and benches, and allowed to dry. Subsequent movement, or switching on a fan, stirs up dust containing all manner of strange compounds which may settle on emulsion layers which are in process of drying. This type of background can be more easily appreciated if two slides without specimens on them are coated with emulsion, and the one fogged by exposure to light. After leaving them in the darkroom with the fan on for an hour, they should be put away for several days, then developed and examined critically. It is often a salutory experience to note just how many strange specks are visible on the surface of the emulsion, and how likely they are to produce areas of blackening or bleaching.

Serious research with autoradiographic techniques requires a separate darkroom. Any spilt solutions should be mopped up at once and the area washed. Periodic cleaning of the darkroom and washing of the working surfaces is a good idea.

(f) Environmental radiation

It is obvious that extraneous sources of radiation will produce background in nuclear emulsions. Cosmic rays form only one component of this.

At ground level, cosmic rays form a wide spectrum of particles, from very high energy ones that penetrate long distances through matter to low energy secondary electrons. Any shielding material interposed between the emulsion and the sky will screen off some of this radiation. The cosmic ray background will be lower in the basement of a 6-storey building than in an adjacent single-storey hut. A small box of lead bricks two inches thick will reduce the cosmic ray intensity still further.

Some rocks contain appreciable amounts of radioactive isotopes, as do the building materials made from them. But these naturally occurring sources of radiation are likely to be of academic interest only in most instances. X-ray machines, and laboratories using γ-emitting isotopes, are much more dramatic sources of background. On a smaller scale, the glass of the microscope slide contains potassium-40 and traces of α-emitting isotopes, while the gelatin of the emulsion itself has minute amounts of carbon-14 in it. If the isotope under study emits γ rays or β particles of very high energy, it is possible for adjacent slides to irradiate one another during exposure, producing very significant levels of background.

With track autoradiographs, many of these sources of radiation can be distinguished from that of the specimen by the pattern of track they produce. With thin emulsion layers, however, it is likely that only the densely ionising α particles can be satisfactorily recognised.

Background caused by environmental radiation may occasionally be recognisable from examination of the emulsion. The silver grains will be arranged along the tracks of individual particles, and these will be randomly distributed throughout the emulsion, without reference to the specimen.

Environmental radiation, then, provides the irreducible minimum of background to most experiments. But the other factors listed in this chapter usually are responsible for the majority of the background grains seen in an autoradiograph. Their effect is superimposed on the slow increase of background due to cosmic radiation. In all cases of unduly high background, these other factors, singly or in combination, are likely to be responsible. If the low levels of grains due to cosmic radiation are demonstrably the major component of the background in a series of autoradiographs, and this background is still unacceptably high, then it may become necessary to investigate methods of shielding the emulsion during exposure.

(g) Spontaneous background

The nuclear emulsions used in autoradiography are very highly sensitised products. In all of them, an occasional silver halide crystal will develop a latent image speck spontaneously. The more highly sensitised the emulsion, the more likely this event becomes. It is a good rule never to use an emulsion that is more highly sensitised than is strictly necessary. Low energy β particles from tritium, for instance, will be recorded in a less sensitive emulsion than that needed for β particles of much higher energies. α Particles will leave their characteristic tracks in even less sensitive media. The very highly sensitised emulsions, such as Ilford K5 or Eastman Kodak NTB-3, will have a higher rate of formation of spontaneous background, will be sensitive to a wider range of environmental radiations, and will be less tolerant to the raised temperatures necessary in melting and to the stresses of drying, than will K2 or NTB-2. The overall background of the former under similar conditions will always be higher, so that it seems only reasonable to reserve their use for experiments with β particles of fairly high energy, which really require their higher sensitivity.

High temperatures increase the rate of formation of spontaneous background, so that emulsions are ideally stored before use and during exposure just above freezing point. The hydrated emulsions in gel form that are used in liquid emulsion techniques should not be frozen before application and drying.

The rate of formation of spontaneous background tends to increase with the age of the emulsion. Nuclear emulsions should always be used as soon after manufacture as possible, though, with good conditions of storage, they usually remain in reasonable condition for up to 2 months.

(h) Causes of background specific for stripping film

In the stripping film technique, the emulsion layer has to be stripped off its support before its application to the specimen. If this is done in conditions of low humidity, static electricity may be generated, with a crackling noise and even visible flashes of light accompanying the stripping process. This cause of background can often be recognised by the presence of dense lines of developed grains running parallel to each other across the developed emulsion. The control of this artefact lies in the control of temperature and humidity in the darkroom, which is discussed further in Chapter 15. It is an interesting idea to chain one's technician to the water pipes in the darkroom to try to earth the plate during stripping, but I am afraid it is not really effective.

A recent paper from the Kodak Research Laboratories (Kodak Ltd.) has drawn attention to another source of high background in AR-10 stripping film[9]. The concentration of soluble bromide ions in the emulsion is carefully controlled during manufacture to achieve a good balance between sensitivity and the rapid growth of background. When the film is floated out on distilled water before picking it up on the specimen, diffusion into the water reduces the effective concentration of soluble bromide to the point that background may build up to unacceptable levels in exposures of 10 weeks or even less. By stripping the film on to distilled water containing 10 mg/l potassium bromide and 50 g/l glucose, background growth can be restrained without loss in sensitivity.

INFORMATION TO BE OBTAINED FROM THE EXAMINATION OF BACKGROUND

It is a good idea to take time for the systematic study of background levels in every batch of autoradiographs made. A great deal can be learnt about the techniques in use, even without making detailed grain counts. In particular, if slides from one batch of autoradiographs are exposed for varying times, a lot of useful information can be gained from their examination.

References p. 106

Figs. 35 and 36 illustrate the results that may be found in generalised form, with grain count per unit area plotted against exposure time. In the ideal autoradiograph (line A), there are no background grains present at the start of exposure, and their number should increase slowly but linearly with time. This situation is almost never achieved, however, and nearly every series will show a certain level of background right at the beginning of exposure (line B).

If the background is unduly high at the start of exposure (line C), several possibilities exist. The emulsion could be old, or have a high level of background due to its previous history. Undue exposure to safelighting, or drying that is too rapid may also be responsible.

If the increase in background with time is linear but rapid (line D) this suggests that the level of environmental radiation is too high. With higher energy isotopes, it may be that one slide is irradiating its neighbours during exposure.

In many instances, the initial rate of increase of background will level off after a short time (line E). In other words, an equilibrium will be reached between the rate of formation of latent images on the one hand, and the process of latent image fading on the other. The extreme case of latent image fading

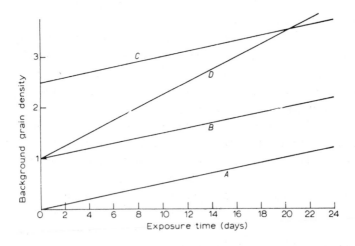

Fig.35. Graphs illustrating the rate of growth in background levels with increasing exposure times, in the absence of latent image fading. *A*, the ideal situation, with no background at the start of exposure, and slow build-up during exposure, due to environmental radiation. *B*, the more usual finding, with appreciable background levels at the start of exposure. *C*, high levels of background at the start of exposure, suggesting old emulsion, or faulty technique in preparing the autoradiograph. *D*, reasonable background levels at the start of exposure, but rapid increase during exposure, suggesting high levels of environmental radiation.

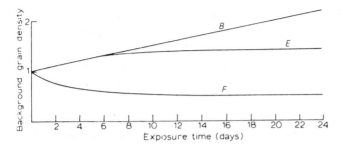

Fig.36. Graphs illustrating the effect of latent image fading on background levels. *B* is the normal result one might expect in the absence of fading. In *E*, very slow fading produces a deviation from linearity after several days' exposure, and a plateau in background levels after about 2 weeks. In *F*, more rapid fading results in an initially rapid fall in background levels, as the latent images created in preparing the autoradiograph fade, followed by a plateau at a very low level.

(line F) produces an initial decrease in background, as the latent images formed in preparing the autoradiograph disappear. The curve then levels off as the equilibrium between formation and the fading process is reached.

THE MEASUREMENT OF BACKGROUND

In quantitative studies, the grain counts observed over the specimen will include background grains, and should be corrected by subtracting the mean number of background grains found in similar volumes of emulsion away from the radioactive areas in the specimen. This is often done by counting grains in areas of emulsion well away from the specimen. This is not a strictly correct procedure, though the error it introduces is often small.

From what has already been said about the various causes of background, it is clear that it may vary significantly from areas over the section to areas away from it. The uneven upper profile of the specimen may result in deviations from the normal emulsion thickness. Failure to dry the emulsion adequately before exposure may affect the area where there is a specimen beneath the emulsion more severely than the emulsion alone, resulting in more latent image fading over the section. But the biggest variable is chemography, which may result in considerable differences in density of background grains between the two sites.

The ideal way to estimate background is to expose an inactive, but otherwise identical, specimen to the same emulsion. Background counts can then be taken from emulsion over areas of non-radioactive specimen matched to the areas from which the experimental counts are obtained.

Up to the present, few autoradiographers have chosen the number of areas to be counted in order to get a realistic estimate of the mean background upon any rational basis. A recent paper by England and Miller[10] discusses how the effort of data collection can best be distributed between labelled sources and background, to achieve a desired level of statistical accuracy. The graphs from their paper can be referred to in the Appendix (p.356).

In any comparison of the radioactivity present in two or more sets of sources, the mean background level is the statistic that should be looked for. In one very important group of experiments, however, this information is not sufficient. In many situations, the number of labelled cells is the parameter measured, rather than the level of radioactivity of the cells themselves. The percentage of labelled cells in various parts of the cell cycle after incorporation of tritiated thymidine is often found as a basis to estimate cell kinetics. The injection into an animal of cells labelled *in vitro* may also be followed by counts of labelled cells in various tissue compartments at later times. In both types of experiment, the definition of "a labelled cell" is obviously important. If one assumes that any cell with more than the mean background grain density is "labelled", random fluctuations in background will result in many unlabelled cells being wrongly accepted. The usual procedure seems to be to take a figure, such as 4 grains per cell, and to accept as "labelled" any cell which reaches or exceeds this level. This rough-and-ready rule of thumb is liable to generate misleading data in both directions – false positives and false negatives. The random, statistical fluctuations in background will produce occasional volumes of emulsion with high grain densities, up to 10–15 grains over areas the size of a single cell[11], in the absence of radioactivity. If large areas of tissue are being scanned to find the occasional "labelled" cell, this upper end of the distribution spectrum of background counts may make a very significant contribution to the data collected. On the other hand, if genuinely "labelled" cells have a mean grain count of 10–15 grains per cell, there may be a finite probability of finding radioactive cells with fewer than 4 grains over them. Ideally, one wishes to know the distribution of background counts over areas the size and shape of a cell, and to compare this with the distribution of observed counts over the cell population being examined. Stillström[12] first presented statistical methods for this type of analysis, and Bresciani and Thompson[13] have a computer programme which does much the same sort of thing. This problem is also discussed in detail by England and Miller[10], and by Moffatt et al.[11] who demonstrate the very considerable difference that a critical analysis can make to the percentage of labelled cells in experimental situations.

In photometric estimation of grain densities, the background reading contains an element independent of the presence or absence of silver grains, due to light scattered by the optical system of lenses, emulsion, specimen and slide. This will be discussed further in Chapter 10. With television scanning systems of grain counting, Mertz[14] has drawn attention to an interesting method of reducing the effective background in tritium autoradiographs. As was pointed out in Chapter 3 (p.39), β particles of very low energy have a high rate of energy loss. The latent images created in crystals hit by tritium β's tend to be large, and, in most conditions of development, the silver grains will also be large relative to the average background grain. In using the Quantimet image analyser, Mertz has found that he can count the great majority of tritium grains while rejecting most of the background ones by particle size analysis.

BACKGROUND ELIMINATION

Many of the causes of an unacceptably high background operate during exposure and development. These can and should be controlled by the auto-radiographer. Occasionally, due to causes outside his control, the emulsion has a high background before the start of exposure. It may be, for instance, that the emulsion has been obtained from abroad. The combination of several days in transit at fairly high ambient temperatures with heavy exposure to cosmic radiation at high altitude in an aircraft may result in an unacceptable level of background. In this situation, several methods exist for wiping the slate clean again, so to speak, before exposure begins, based on the deliberate fading of the latent images. The formation of a latent image is a reversible process, and fading of the latent image is favoured, as we have seen, by the presence of oxidising agents, or of a high relative humidity.

The simplest method of background eradication is to expose the auto-radiographs in air at a fairly high relative humidity. Latent image fading proceeds together with the formation of new latent images by the radiation from the specimen. At the end of a reasonably long exposure time, such as two weeks, the probability of any latent images surviving from the start of exposure is remote. Only those produced in the last few days will stand much chance of develop-ment. The result will be an autoradiograph with relatively low background. For studies of the localisation of radioactivity, this method is quite acceptable. It is a poorly controlled way of achieving background eradication, however, and is out of the question in quantitative work, since it is quite impossible to estimate the effective duration of exposure.

Waller[6] recommends keeping the emulsion for a period of 1 h at 100% relative humidity and a temperature of 37°. This is sufficient to accelerate fading in any pre-existent latent images, and has the advantage that it does not alter the emulsion in any way, whereas the several methods that have been proposed involving chemical treatment of the emulsion may affect the sensitivity adversely. This technique is discussed in some detail, together with others that have been suggested, by Barkas[15].

Another technique has been described by Caro and Van Tubergen[2]. After preparation, the slides are placed in a closed glass container, at the bottom of which are several layers of filter paper, moistened with a few drops of 6% hydrogen peroxide. After 2.5–3 h, the slides are removed and dried carefully, and exposed in the usual way. This treatment can give a very impressive reduction in background. The sensitivity of the emulsion does not seem to be affected by this procedure. Hydrogen peroxide is known to cause fogging of emulsions in certain circumstances, however, and I have had some complete failures with this technique, without being able to pinpoint any differences in procedure.

With track autoradiographs, the process of pouring the molten emulsion effitively eradicates the background. Any particle tracks in the emulsion become "scrambled" by the pouring, and are converted into scattered individual grains. The number of background tracks should always be practically nil at the start of exposure.

REFERENCES

1   I. Ahmad and J. Demers, *Can. J. Phys.*, 37 (1959) 1548.
2   L.G. Caro and R.P. Van Tubergen, *J. Cell Biol.*, 15 (1962) 173.
3   E.B. Barnawell, M.R. Banerjee and F.M. Rogers, *Stain Technol.*, 45 (1970) 40.
4   W. Sawicki and M. Pawinska, *Stain Technol.*, 40 (1965) 67.
5   B. Messier and C.P. Leblond, *Proc. Soc. Exptl. Biol. Med.*, 96 (1957) 7.
6   C. Waller, *The Properties of Nuclear Emulsions in Relation to Autoradiography*, 1st European Symposium on Autoradiography, Rome, 1961.
7   A.W. Rogers, P.N. John, in L.J. Roth and W.E. Stumpf (Eds.), *Autoradiography of Diffusible Substances*, Academic Press, New York and London, 1969.
8   M.G.E. Welton, *J. Phot. Sci.*, 17 (1969) 157.
9   C. O'Callaghan, G.W.W. Stevens and J.F. Wood, *Brit. J. Radiol.*, 42 (1969) 862.
10 J.M. England and R.G. Miller, *J. Microscopy*, 92 (1970) 167.
11 D.J. Moffatt, S.P. Youngberg and W.K. Metcalf, *Cell and Tissue Kinetics*, 4 (1971) 293.
12 J. Stillström, *Intern. J. Appl. Radiation Isotopes*, 14 (1963) 113.
13 F. Bresciani and K. Thompson, *Brookhaven National Laboratory Reports*, BNL-8360 (1963).
14 M. Mertz, *Histochemie*, 17 (1969) 128.
15 W.H. Barkas, *Nuclear Research Emulsions*, Part 1, Academic Press, New York, 1963.

PART 2: THE PLANNING AND INTERPRETATION OF AUTORADIOGRAPHIC EXPERIMENTS

CHAPTER 7

Histological Techniques and Autoradiography

Autoradiography is a bridge linking biochemical observations on the synthetic ability and specific reactivity of biological tissues with their microanatomy. To give the fullest possible information, the steps by which the tissue is prepared for histology should be clearly defined in biochemical terms, and the recognition of histological detail should be unimpaired by the techniques of autoradiography. These ideals may not always be realised. This chapter will discuss some of the problems raised by making biochemical inferences from histological material, and by the attempt to make histological techniques compatible with the use of nuclear emulsions as detectors for radioactivity.

CLEAN WORKING CONDITIONS

Before considering the stages of histological preparation of a specimen in detail, it should be noted that autoradiography requires a degree of cleanliness and care, at every stage in the handling of the specimen, that is seldom needed in the production of histological preparations alone. It is a useful, and often sobering, exercise to take some stained sections produced in the normal way by the methods in use in the laboratory, and to examine them critically, by transmitted and by incident light, for "silver grains". Frequently, many black specks of the approximate dimensions of a developed grain will be seen by transmitted light, and their number will almost certainly be more by incident dark-field lighting. This "background", in the absence of an emulsion layer, can be completely ignored in normal microscopy, but it becomes highly embarrassing in an autoradiograph.

It is a good idea to train the technician who will prepare material for autoradiography to keep one complete set of glassware and solutions for this purpose alone. In this way, reproducible cleanliness can usually be obtained. These solutions should be covered, to prevent dust accumulating on their surface, and to prevent changes in concentration due to evaporation or imbibition of water, and should be renewed frequently. Wet slides should never be allowed to dry in a position where dust, or chemicals in use in the general laboratory, can settle on them, but should be dried in a protected, dust-free position.

Glassware used for emulsion work should be very carefully cleaned. Vessels that have contained liquid emulsion are often difficult to deal with. After washing in hot water to remove as much emulsion as possible, they should be soaked in normal sodium hydroxide solution for several hours. After washing in hot water, they should be immersed in cleaning acid, washed in cold running water overnight, and finally rinsed in distilled water. Even so, glassware that is frequently used for emulsion work tends to acquire a characteristic, hazy appearance, due to the surface deposition of silver.

Microscope slides require special cleaning. Even the commercially obtained "pre-cleaned" slides are usually too dirty. Slides should be soaked overnight in cleaning acid, made by dissolving 100 g potassium bichromate in about 850 ml water, and adding 100 ml concentrated sulphuric acid: the acid should be added very slowly, with constant stirring. After the acid bath, the slides are washed for several hours in cold running tapwater, followed by 2 changes of distilled water for 30 min each. They are then dipped once in the following solution at room temperature:

Gelatin	5.0 g
Chrome alum	0.5 g
Water to make	1000 ml

The slides should then be allowed to drain and dry while in a dust-free atmosphere.

This gelatine solution (or "subbing" solution) should be filtered immediately before use. It is unwise to try and keep it for more than about 48 h, even in a refrigerator. It is usually convenient to produce a large number of subbed slides at one time, and to keep them in clean, covered containers of plastic or glass until they are required. These subbed slides are usually clean enough for autoradiography, and the layer of gelatin provides good adhesion both for the section and the emulsion. It may be difficult to make good smears of cell suspensions on subbed slides, in which case gelatinisation should be omitted, and special care will be required in processing and mounting the autoradiographs to prevent movement or loss of the emulsion.

Solutions used in preparing material for autoradiography should be made up from reasonably fresh stocks of chemicals of known purity.

Emulsions are sensitive to many forms of chemical contamination, and I have known cases of chemography which have been traced back ultimately to old or low-grade reagents. Tapwater may have to be replaced with distilled or ion-free water in preparing the solutions used in histology up to the stage of auto-radiography.

Common sense must guide the degree to which cleanliness is pushed: it can become an obsession, slowing down work unreasonably. But one should be aware that the steps of preparing a tissue for autoradiography can introduce contamination, and include these steps in the investigation if the controls for chemography indicate that this artefact is present.

THE PRESERVATION AND EXTRACTION OF RADIOACTIVITY IN HISTOLOGICAL PREPARATION

In order to prepare a thin enough section of a solid tissue for observation in the light or electron microscope, it must first be embedded in some supporting matrix of sufficient hardness to allow sectioning. The materials in general use at the light microscope level, paraffin wax and the newer polymers such as araldite and Epon, are not miscible with water, and the embedding of tissues in them is preceded by the precipitation of much of the macromolecular moiety by histo-logical fixation, followed by the withdrawal of the water present by soaking the tissue in increasing concentrations of alcohol. It is often assumed that this type of processing leaves in the embedded tissue the proteins and nucleic acids, while removing the ions and many other small molecules, together with much of the fat. With increasing sophistication, it has become necessary to re-examine this assumption critically.

In general terms, three categories of experiment can be listed, which make rather different demands on the steps of histological preparation.

(a) Precursor incorporation studies

In this group of experiments, a radioactive precursor is presented to the tissue to determine the sites at which it is synthesised into the molecule under study. The autoradiograph is expected to show only the sites of synthesis into a larger molecule, and the histological processing to perform a selective extraction, removing all the unincorporated precursor.

The retention of radioactivity in the tissue after administration of labelled amino acids was examined by Vanha-Perttula and Grimley[1], amongst others. They compared fixation with either formaldehyde or glutaraldehyde, followed by buffer washing, post-fixation in osmium tetroxide and dehydration, with the standard biochemical step of precipitation in trichloracetic acid, at a time after the administration of the labelled amino acid when very little of the radio-activity would be expected as free amino acid. When [^{3}H] leucine was used as a precursor, the TCA precipitate contained all but 13.9% of the total radioactivity. Formalin fixation and subsequent processing retained all but 14.5%, while glutaraldehyde permitted the loss of only 3.5%. Quantitatively, it looks as if formaldehyde and the subsequent processing leave the equivalent of a TCA precipitate in the tissue section, though several questions remain unsolved. The chemical form of the radioactivity that was lost was not established: it may have been free amino acid, or represent incorporation into other molecules such as polypeptides or proteins of low molecular weight. Whatever its form, it is clear that the fixative glutaraldehyde retained much of this material in the tissue. Peters and Ashley[2] have demonstrated that glutaraldehyde can link free amino acids to the fixed and precipitated protein, giving spurious results for incorporation into proteins: this effect will be particularly serious at very short times after the administration of the amino acid. A similar effect has been found, though to a lesser extent, for formaldehyde[1].

Mitchell[3], studying the retention of a labelled protein in tissues, found very variable losses in fixation and embedding from one tissue to another. Losses in processing were particularly severe in neonatal animals, with formalin fixation. The failure of formalin to retain protein quantitatively in tissues has also been described by Merriam[4].

With the nucleic acids, it is reasonable to assume that DNA will be retained by fixation in formaldehyde or glutaraldehyde: the latter fixative can link free thymidine to precipitated material, though this effect is small by comparison to that seen with amino acids[1]. With precursors of RNA, the position is far less clear. Sirlin and Leoning[5] have shown that 4S RNA is effectively retained after fixation with formaldehyde or Carnoy's, and work reported by Edström[6] on isolated neurones shows that Carnoy's fixative can quantitatively retain RNA. Schneider and Maurer[7] and Schneider and Schneider[8] have reported loss of RNA after formalin fixation, and the figures obtained by Vanha-Perttula and Grimley[1] and [^{3}H]uridine show 22% of the total radioactivity in their system extracted by glutaraldehyde and the subsequent buffer washes, and 24% loss with formaldehyde. It would seem that Carnoy's fixative is the one of choice for RNA retention, but further work is needed to define the precise patterns of retention of this group of macromolecules after different fixation procedures. Monneron and Moulé[9] have studied the retention of soluble precursors of RNA by fixation, which was quite considerable after osmium tetroxide as a primary fixative. Routines of fixation with glutaraldehyde or formaldehyde, extensive buffer washes over 2 days at 0°, and post-fixation in osmium tetroxide were free from this artefact.

There is little work available on the quantitative retention of polysaccharides after fixation. With mannose as a precursor, losses of about 20% have been found with glutaraldehyde and formaldehyde[1]: binding of the precursor does not seem to be a problem in this one example.

Perhaps because the steps of dehydration and embedding require the use of fat solvents, the retention of lipids through histological processing has been more extensively studied than any other tissue component. It is summarised in a recent review by Williams[10] High retention rates for phospholipids with osmium tetroxide, either as a primary or a secondary fixative, have been demonstrated right through to the embedded tissue. The figures for other fats are less encouraging.

(b) Distribution studies of drugs and hormones

The second group of autoradiographic experiments in this context involves the injection of labelled drugs or hormones into the biological system, and the use of autoradiography to identify the sites at which the labelled material is "bound". Here the assumption is sometimes made that histological processing will remove all the "free" reagent. This situation has seldom been examined with the care that is required, and little evidence is available on the retention of active agents at their sites of binding, or on possible spurious incorporation of unbound radioactivity by fixation. Nor is the assumption always justified that sites of binding represent sites of action of drugs and hormones.

Amongst the steroid hormones, oestradiol binds tightly to a protein present in the cytosol of target cells, but, as Stumpf and Roth[11] have shown, the hormone-protein complex cannot be quantitatively demonstrated except by autoradiographic techniques designed for freely diffusible compounds. Similarly, the drug methotrexate, which binds very tightly to folate reductase, requires techniques for diffusible compounds for its demonstration[12]. On the other hand, the quantitative demonstration of the covalently bound enzyme inhibitor DFP has been carried out on fixed and embedded material[13]. Three factors seem to be involved. The first is the nature of the binding to the tissue component. Covalent binding usually survives processing: non-colavent bonds seldom survive. However high the affinity of the labelled compound for its binding site, the transfer of the tissue through relatively large volumes of aqueous solutions in the early stages of fixation will remove label. Secondly, fixation may produce stereochemical changes on the binding site, with loss of the labelled molecule. Finally, the binding site itself may not be completely precipitated by fixation.

(c) Ions and other diffusible molecules

Studies of the distribution of labelled ions and small, freely diffusible molecules are clearly impossible with conventional histological techniques. Methods have been described for the preliminary precipitation of particular ions in tissue prior to fixation (*e.g.* Halbhuber and Geyer[14]), but these have their own source of error which must be considered.

It may be possible to modify the conventional histological procedure in some way to minimise the loss of radioactivity. The use of fat solvents may be avoided by cutting frozen sections, or by embedding in a water-soluble wax[15], for example. Alternatively, techniques for the autoradiography of freely diffusible materials can be used, as described in Chapter 8. These may quite simply be combined with extractions with specific solvents, if removal of unbound radio-activity is required.

In selecting a method of fixation for tissue for autoradiography, the possibility of interaction between tissue and emulsion must not be overlooked. Fixatives, such as Zenker's, which contain salts of mercury or lead should be avoided, as they tend to cause positive chemography[16]. Those containing picric acid, such as Bouin's may be used provided the section is treated with ammoniacal alcohol or a solution of lithium carbonate to remove all traces of yellow colouration before autoradiography. Even with formaldehyde and glutaraldehyde, extensive washing should follow fixation: otherwise desensitisation of the emulsion may result from traces of free fixative in the tissue (see Fig. 33).

HISTOLOGICAL SECTIONS

The majority of autoradiographs are based on histological sections of embedded tissue. It is surprising how little attention has been paid to the difficulties of producing sections of known thickness. In a recent series of experiments, I was shaken to find a variance in grain counts over sections labelled with carbon-14 so great that I was unable to detect differences between experimental groups that had been obvious on parallel experiments with liquid scintillation counting. A block of paraffin wax was therefore prepared, uniformly impregnated with radioactive testosterone, and serial sections cut on our microtome under the normal conditions were dissolved and counted individually in the liquid scintillation counter. The variability in section thickness was such that the standard deviation of the counts from single sections was nearly 30% of the mean figure. Tests of several combinations of microtome and technician in surrounding laboratories showed a range of values about this figure. By investing in an expensive and large microtome, and paying considerable attention to the details of knife sharpening and sectioning, we can now obtain sections at a nominal $4\,\mu$ in which the standard deviation of a series of thickness measurements is not more than 7.5% of the mean value.

Sections cut at a nominal 1 or $2\,\mu$ from material embedded in plastic is even more difficult to obtain at a uniform thickness. With blocks of uniformly labelled methacrylate, we have had series in which the standard deviation has been as high as 70% of the mean thickness. We have also found wide differences in mean thickness between one series and another, particularly when different microtomes and operators are involved.

Probably the most detailed examination of sectioning is presented by Hallén[17], who developed an ingenious method of measuring section thickness. He concluded that "even if the sectioning is performed under ideal conditions the variation of thickness between and within the sections is remarkably large". In many experiments this variation will impose a corresponding uncertainty on the grain counts obtained from the sections. Some care and attention to the technique of sectioning may reduce this source of variability, but cannot eliminate it. Either the experimental design must ensure that grain counts from each group are based on a relatively large number of sections, or some method must be employed to select for autoradiography sections from a narrow range of thicknesses. Reference to the section in Chapter 5 on self-absorption will show that with carbon-14, sulphur-35 or isotopes of higher energy variations in source thickness around a mean of $5\,\mu$ will introduce corresponding changes in grain count; while at $1\,\mu$ sources labelled with tritium will show variation in grain count related to thickness.

Unfortunately section thickness is not often measured. With a uniformly labelled block, as described above, the mean volume of each section can be estimated, provided that the section is complete. This method gives no information, as variations in thickness due to compression of the section, and variations within each section cannot be measured. For plastic sections up to $2\,\mu$ thick, mounted on a glass slide, interference measurements in reflected light provide a quick and simple way of finding the thickness in absolute terms. Sections in paraffin wax can also be measured in the same way prior to dewaxing, provided they do not exceed about $6\,\mu$, but their upper profile after dewaxing is so irregular that this type of measurement, or indeed any estimate at all, becomes very difficult indeed. Hallén's apparatus[17], while not commercially available, is not too complicated, and provides accurate estimates up to $20\,\mu$, or even up to $200\,\mu$ with reduced accuracy.

Estimates of section thickness at the electron microscope level are usually made on the basis of the interference colour of the section, so that the variability of thickness is considerably less for those sections selected for autoradiography. Even in this case, Williams[10] has drawn attention to the variations that can occur between different observers and in different conditions of observation. In a laboratory where the apparatus for measuring section thickness by interference in reflected light is available and frequently used, it is possible to improve on the figures presented by Williams[10] (Dr. Salpeter, personal communication). Williams has also drawn attention to variations in thickness within sections[10], which could introduce errors into the analysis of grain distributions at the electron microscope level.

Strict self-absorption corrections require a detailed knowledge of the density of tissue components after fixation, embedding, and sectioning. This is a problem that has been skated around in the literature, and little information is available apart from estimates in very general terms.

The step of mounting the section on the slide requires a little care, as the gelatin layer on the subbed slide differs somewhat in its characteristics from the usual adhesives such as glycerine and albumin. When mounting the section on the slide, it is a good idea to allow the gelatin subbing to hydrate fully before drying down again in contact with the section. It is possible to pick sections up from a water surface and to dry the slide again so quickly that there is virtually no adhesion between gelatin and section, and dipping in liquid emulsion can either introduce emulsion into spaces between section and slide, or float the section off altogether. I find it best to place the subbed slide, with a few drops of distilled water on it, on a level hotplate, and to float the wax section on the surface of the water until it has flattened out. This gives the gelatin an opportunity to hydrate, and it will stick firmly to the section on removing the water.

Paraffin wax sections require dewaxing before applying the emulsion. Scrupulous care should be taken over this process: traces of wax left on the slide will produce very uneven coating with liquid emulsion, and prevent adhesion if stripping film is used. Clean solutions, changed frequently if many slides are being processed at once, will ensure that the surface of the slide wets evenly with distilled water when dewaxing is complete.

STAINING THE AUTORADIOGRAPH

The correlation of labelling with the underlying tissue is only possible if structural detail can be easily recognised. This usually requires some form of staining of the section at the light microscope level. Phase contrast can be used very successfully to view autoradiographs, particularly if the tissue is familiar to the microscopist, but most workers still prefer staining, which improves the range of detail that can be recognised and provides a closer correlation to normal histology.

There are two possibilities in staining: the first is to introduce the stain before applying the emulsion layer; the second to stain after photographic processing is complete.

(a) Prestaining

This choice has some advantages, and many limitations. Staining before autoradiography is identical to the normal routine of histology – the same reactive groups are present in the section, which should look just like a standard histological specimen after staining. The gelatin of the emulsion layer will not be stained, and in general it is easier to get precise and vivid staining than if the emulsion layer is already present. Some reactive groups are lost in photographic processing, particularly enzymes, which often cannot be demonstrated histochemically after autoradiography.

Unfortunately, prestaining has to be approached with caution. It introduces another step between the collection of the tissue from the animal and the application of the emulsion. It must be demonstrated that this step does not remove significant radioactivity from the specimen, or introduce a source of chemography, which will affect the performance of the emulsion layer later. The loss of radioactivity on prestaining is well documented with the Feulgen reaction for DNA[18, 19]: it seems to be maximal at the washing stage after acid hydrolysis[19]. Bryant[20] has described a curious phenomenon on hydrolysis, in which radioactivity appears to be displaced from onion tip nuclei in the S-phase and simultaneously increased over metaphase cells. The periodic-acid–Schiff reaction also can cause trouble, though this has been attributed to Schiff's reagent rather than to the acid hydrolysis[21] : if the hydrolysis is carried out before autoradiography and the Schiff staining afterwards, grain counts are not reduced.

There are many examples in the literature of stains applied before autoradiography affecting the emulsion layer. To quote only two examples, prestaining with Celestin Blue causes severe positive chemography[22] , as do attempts to stain plastic embedded sections with toluidine blue.

One further problem with prestaining is that the photographic processing often alters or removes the stain. This effect, which is quite significant with the haematoxylins, for instance, can be reduced in severity by the selection of processing conditions which do not involve wide changes in pH. Amidol will act as a suitable developing agent when buffered to a pH only slightly on the alkaline side of neutrality: a distilled water stopbath can be followed by fixation in sodium thiosulphate, using the same buffer system that was employed for the developer. Recipes for suitable solutions will be found on p.327.

In summary, staining the section before autoradiography is acceptable if control experiments show that grain counts over stained and unstained sections are identical, and there is neither positive nor negative chemography. In these circumstances, if removal of stain in processing can be avoided, the clarity and precision of staining will usually be better than with post-stained material.

(b) Post-staining

If the section is stained through the photographic emulsion after processing is complete, there is clearly no problem about the removal of radioactivity, or possible chemography, nor will the stain be affected by processing. This approach has two potential headaches, the first the removal of silver grains or even the emulsion itself from the specimen, the second the difficulty of adequate staining after processing has modified the reactive groups present in the specimen and covered it with a layer of gelatin.

The removal of developed silver grains in staining is often related to the pH of the solutions used. Photographic fixation in sodium thiosulphate leaves each developed grain surrounded with a shell of adsorbed thiosulphate ions (p. 26) which cannot be removed even by long washing times in water. On transfer to an acid solution these ions can erode and remove the silver grains completely. I have known this happen after staining with several of the haematoxylins, on differentiation with acid alcohol. It has been described on acid hydrolysis prior to Schiff staining[21] . This effect can be minimised by iodide treatment of the emulsion prior to fixation[23] , but it is probably best avoided by controlling the pH of all staining solutions, so that the acid conditions likely to produce this attack on the developed grains do not occur.

Removal of the emulsion itself can occur with staining methods that require heat or very alkaline solutions. The staining of plastic sections with toluidine blue, which usually involves heating for a short time to 60°, is one example.

The processed emulsion layer may provide quite a barrier to precise staining. Reagents have to diffuse through the gelatin to reach the specimen, and the gelatin may retain traces of thiosulphate, affecting the reagents or providing an environment of an inappropriate pH. It may make staining less variable if autoradiographs are soaked in a buffer at the optimum pH for the staining reaction before the reagents are applied. The gelatin frequently takes up the stain, which is not surprising since it is protein, like much of the histological specimen. Stains for specific reactive groups in the tissue are often used in an attempt to colour the section without affecting the gelatin: methyl green—pyronin for nucleic

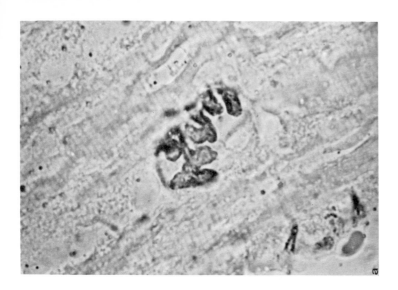

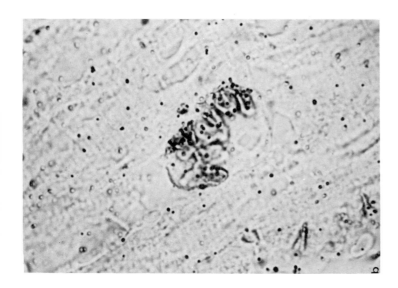

Fig.37. An endplate of mouse diaphragm, which was labelled *in vitro* with tritiated DFP, sectioned on a cryostat and autoradiographed with Ilford K2 emulsion. After processing, the DFP was removed with pyridine-2-aldoxime and the reactivated acetylcholinesterase demonstrated histochemically. (× 800) (Material prepared by Dr. Z. Darżynkiewicz)

References p. 121

acids, for instance, has been used by Ficq[24] tnrough layers of emulsion 50 μ or more thick. The very non-specific counterstains of conventional histology, such as eosin or chromotrope, are the worst for colouring the gelatin. Grossly over-staining the specimen, followed by a rapid removal of excess stain, will tend to bring down the levels of staining in the emulsion before the section is affected.

Some reactive groups are lost from the specimen in autoradiography and photographic processing, and histochemical reactions will at times be much weaker than in normal material. It is all too easy to assume that a particular reaction will be impossible through the emulsion, and this assumption should always be examined in a critical and optimistic spirit. Peroxidase activity can be demonstrated by post-staining[25], and even fairly complex sequences such as the reactivation of organophosphate – inhibited acetylcholinesterase by pyridine-2-aldoxime, followed by Karnovsky's technique for the demonstration of sites of cholinesterase activity, can be successfully carried out, as has been shown by Dr. Darżynkiewicz[26] (Fig. 37).

In general, post-staining will be found preferable to prestaining. Before a method is used on experimental material, it should be demonstrated that grain densities over stained and unstained specimens are identical.

A few general points remain to be made about the selection of stains. If the autoradiograph is to be viewed by transmitted light, a light colour, such as pink or yellow or light green, may be preferable to dark blues or purples which can produce darkly stained granules in the tissue rather similar to silver grains. If reflected light is to be used, giving a dark-field effect for viewing, methods that produce a light-scattering precipitate in the tissue should be avoided, and also stains, such as eosin, which give a considerable fluorescent glare by this method of illumination.

Several lists of stains which have proved compatible with autoradiography are available[16, 27–29]. In many cases, several slightly differing recipes are available in the histological literature for a single staining method, and local differences in the sources of dyes and reagents may also occur. It is sensible to check that a chosen technique does not interact with the autoradiograph in the conditions within one's own laboratory before adopting it.

The staining of autoradiographs prepared for the electron microscope is discussed on p.337.

IMPERMEABLE MEMBRANES

It may be essential to stain the specimen before autoradiography by a method that causes chemography, or with a stain that is altered by photographic proces-sing. It may be impossible to remove a source of chemography from a section. In

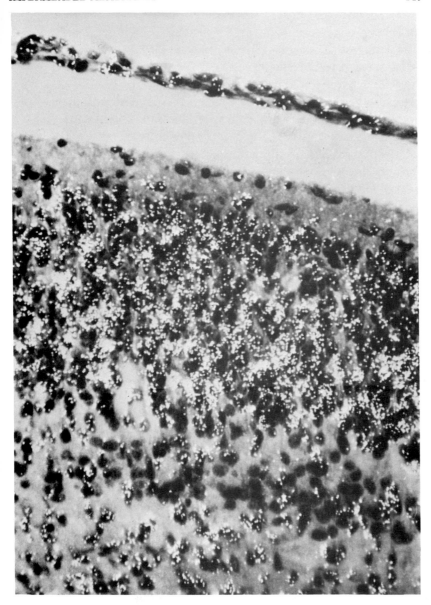

Fig. 38. Photomicrograph of the cerebral cortex of a rat at the 18th day of foetal life, following the injection of tritiated thymidine 2 days previously. The section was stained with Harris' haematoxylin and covered with a PVC membrane before autoradiography, with a thin layer of Ilford G5 emulsion. The presence of the membrane must have reduced the autoradiographic efficiency, but a clear trace was nevertheless obtained in 13 days' exposure. Photograph taken with Leitz Ultropak × 22 objective, with simultaneous transmitted bright-field and reflected dark-field illumination. (× 300) (Material produced in collaboration with Dr. M. Berry)

References p. 121

such cases, a thin, impermeable membrane can be applied over the specimen before putting on the emulsion. Such a membrane should be very thin, to reduce to a minimum the separation of source from emulsion: it should also be reasonably strong, impermeable, and chemically inert.

Chapman-Andresen[30] investigated a number of possible materials, and described a nylon membrane which had suitable characteristics. More recently, Sawicki and Darżynkiewicz[31] described a very satisfactory membrane of polyvinyl chloride (Fig. 38). Unfortunately, the starting materials for both these techniques have been discontinued by their manufacturers. A suitable alternative has been found by Keyser and Wijffels[32], a copolymer that includes vinylchloride and vinylidenechloride, called Ixan SGA, manufactured by Solvay S.A., of Brussels.

To prepare the Ixan solution, use the following method:

Dissolve 9.7 g Ixan SGA in 30 g butyl acetate. This may take up to 48 h. When fully dissolved, add 57.9 g trichlorethylene with constant stirring, 0.8 g cyclo-hexanone, and 1.6 g dibutyl phthalate. The latter acts as a plasticiser for the membrane, which can be made firmer and more brittle by reducing its concentration, or more pliable by increasing it. This stock solution keeps indefinitely, provided evaporation is prevented.

To prepare membranes, let one drop of the solution fall on to a clean water surface in a dish about 9″ by 6″. The drop will spread on the water, and the solvents evaporate, leaving a membrane which contracts a little in the next half-minute or so. This membrane can then be picked up on the specimen in much the same way as stripping film (Fig.80). A membrane showing a red–green interference colour of the first order will be about 105 mμ thick, and should not reduce the grain count over a tritiated source by more than about 20%. The efficacy of such a membrane in preventing chemography and retaining stain in the section was examined by Keyser and Wijffels for a number of different stains[32].

A membrane such as this is hydrophobic, and emulsion layers will not adhere to it as well as to a subbed slide. Thin layers of liquid emulsion can be kept in place on membrane-covered slides if they are kept horizontal through photographic fixation and washing, and if both these steps are carried out very gently. The use of a hardening stopbath (p.295) might also reduce the chances of losing the emulsion. With stripping film loss of emulsion is even more likely, and it may be necessary to sub the slide with gelatin (p.108) over the membrane, accepting the increased separation of source from emulsion, if this technique is to be used.

Once the membrane has stabilised, it is not easy to dissolve it again in organic solvents, so that sections should be stained before applying the membrane.

HISTOLOGICAL METHODS FOR PARTICULAR APPLICATIONS

Thin sections of tissue embedded in plastic can be very difficult to stain after autoradiography, while many of the stains used for them cause severe chemography. Methods for staining them have been discussed by Stevens[33] ; and staining may be facilitated by treating the sections with sodium hydroxide followed by periodic acid before autoradiography[34] . Many laboratories prefer to view such material by phase contrast. (See also NOTES ADDED IN PROOF, p. 360)

Prescott and Bender[35] have described fully a method for the autoradiography of squash preparations of chromosomes. With this material, several workers have found it necessary to view the chromosomes and the silver grains separately, photographing the one before examining the other[36, 37] . This is an added complication to the technique, and should be avoided if possible. The strategy of photographing the specimen before applying the emulsion, and examining the autoradiographs with the photograph available, may make possible the combination of autoradiography with some other cytochemical technique, such as fluorescence microscopy, which might otherwise be very difficult[38] .

PREPARING AUTORADIOGRAPHS FOR MICROSCOPY

Before viewing, autoradiographs are usually mounted under a coverglass to protect the emulsion layer from scratching. Processed stripping film is almost impermeable to many of the conventional mounting media, and attempts to prepare it under a coverglass may lead to a mass of tiny bubbles forming over the tissue section. Since it already carries a thick layer of gelatin over the emulsion, it is often stored and examined without a coverglass. If a coverglass is preferred, one remedy that usually prevents the formation of bubbles in the specimen is to dip the slides once in a 2% solution of polyvinyl alcohol during dehydration[39] .

Track autoradiographs are easier to interpret if they are viewed with the emulsion in a swollen, hydrated state (p. 317): the same may be true of grain density autoradiographs if there is any danger of confusing silver grains with stained granules in the tissue section.

REFERENCES

1   T. Vanha-Perttula and P.M. Grimley, *J. Histochem. Cytochem.*, 18 (1970) 565.
2   T. Peters and C.A. Ashley, *J. Cell Biol.*, 33 (1967) 53.
3   J. Mitchell, *Austr. J. Exptl. Biol. Med. Sci.*, 44 (1966) 225.

4   R.W. Merriam, *J. Histochem. Cytochem.*, 6 (1958) 43.
5   J.L. Sirlin and U.E. Leoning, *Biochem. J.*, 109 (1968) 375.
6   J.E. Edström, *J. Neurochem.*, 1 (1956) 159.
7   G. Schneider and W. Maurer, *Acta. Histochem.*, 15 (1963) 171.
8   G. Schneider and G. Schneider, *Proc. 2nd. Int. Congr. Histochem. Cytochem. Frankfurt/Main*, 1964, p. 169.
9   A. Monneron and Y. Moulé, *Exptl. Cell Res.*, 56 (1969) 179.
10 M.A. Williams, *Advan. Opt. Electron Microscopy*, 3 (1969) 219.
11 W.E. Stumpf and L.J. Roth, *J. Histochem. Cytochem.*, 14 (1966) 274.
12 Z. Darżynkiewicz, A.W. Rogers, E.A. Barnard, D.-H. Wang and W.C. Werkheiser, *Science*, 151 (1966) 1528.
13 A.W. Rogers, Z. Darżynkiewicz, E.A. Barnard and M.M. Salpeter, *Nature*, 210 (1966) 1003.
14 K.-J. Halbhuber and G. Geyer, *Acta Histochem.*, 31 (1968) 222.
15 H.F. Steadman, *Section Cutting in Microscopy*, Blackwell, Oxford, 1960.
16 G.A. Boyd, *Autoradiography in Biology and Medicine*, Academic Press, New York, 1955.
17 O. Hallén, *Acta Anat., Suppl.* 25 (1956).
18 R. Baserga and K. Nemeroff, *Stain Technol.*, 37 (1962) 21.
19 W. Lang and W. Maurer, *Exptl. Cell Res.*, 39 (1965) 1.
20 T.R. Bryant, *Exptl. Cell Res.*, 56 (1969) 127.
21 W. Sawicki and J. Rowinski, *Histochemie*, 19 (1969) 288.
22 E.M. Deuchar, *Stain Technol.*, 37 (1962) 324.
23 G.W.W. Stevens and P. Block, *J. Phot. Sci.*, 7 (1959) 111.
24 A. Ficq, in J. Brachet and A.E. Mirsky (Eds.), *The Cell*, Vol. I, Academic Press, New York, 1959.
25 R.A. Popp, W.D. Gude and D.M. Popp, *Stain Technol.*, 37 (1962) 243.
26 A.W. Rogers, Z. Darżynkiewicz, K. Ostrowski, E.A. Barnard and M.M. Salpeter, *J. Cell Biol.*, 41 (1969) 665.
27 J.M. Thurston and D.L. Joftes, *Stain Technol.*, 38 (1963) 231.
28 L.F. Bélanger, *Stain Technol.*, 36 (1961) 313.
29 C.P. Leblond, B.M. Kopriwa and B. Messier, in R. Wegmann (Ed.), *Histochemistry and Cytochemistry*, Pergamon, London, 1963.
30 C. Chapman-Andresen, *Compt. Rend. Trav. Lab. Carlsberg, Ser. Chim.*, 28 (1953) 529.
31 W. Sawicki and Z. Darżynkiewicz, *Folia Histochem. Cytochem.*, 1 (1964) 283.
32 A. Keyser and C. Wijffels, *Acta Histochem., Suppl.* 8 (1968) 359.
33 A.R. Stevens, in D.M. Prescott (Ed.), *Methods in Cell Physiology*, Vol. II, Academic Press, New York, 1966.
34 A. Hendrickson, S. Kunz and D.E. Kelly, *Stain Technol.*, 43 (1968) 175.
35 D.M. Prescott and M.A. Bender, in D.M. Prescott (Ed.), *Methods in Cell Physiology*, Vol. 1, Academic Press, New York, 1964.
36 A. Fröland, *Stain Technol.*, 40 (1965) 41.
37 M. Callebaut and P. Demalsy, *Stain Technol.*, 42 (1967) 227.
38 D. Masuoka and G.F. Placid, *J. Histochem., Cytochem.*, 16 (1968) 659.
39 M.J. Schlesinger, H. Levi and R. Weyant, *Rev. Sci. Instr.*, 27 (1956) 969.

CHAPTER 8

The Autoradiography of Radioisotopes in Diffusible State

The methods for preparing sections of tissue for autoradiography derived from the conventional histological process of embedding in paraffin wax or a resin such as araldite were discussed in Chapter 7. For certain types of experiment, particularly for study of the incorporation of a labelled precursor into a macromolecule, these histological techniques have a lot to recommend them. The histological fixation precipitates and retains the marcromolecule, while the range of solvents used in fixation and dehydration prior to embedding effectively wash out of the tissue any precursor that has not been synthesised into macromolecules.

But there are many situations in which the process of section preparation removes radioactivity that is of interest. The degree of loss varies widely: it may be only a few percent of the total with some proteins, it may go as far as complete removal with labelled ions. The mechanism of loss also varies: it may be limited to diffusion in aqueous solutions, or it may be due to the solubility of, for instance, lipids in non-aqueous solvents such as ethanol and xylene. Since the extent and mechanism of loss of radioactivity show this enormous variation from one experiment to another, it is not surprising that the literature contains a bewildering range of techniques that have been applied at one time or another to the localisation of radioactivity that is diffusible, when studied by conventional methods of histology and autoradiography. In some cases, relatively simple modifications of the process of embedding the tissue have proved sufficient: in others, nothing short of a method with the complete absence of solvents of any sort has been satisfactory: in many other cases, unfortunately, no clear evidence is offered on the suitability or otherwise of the technique used.

In consequence, the literature on the autoradiography of diffusible materials forms a dense jungle, bewildering and contradictory. No attempt will be made here to review it. Instead, I shall try to indicate the principles that should guide one in the selection of a technique, and give in some detail descriptions of a few methods that have found fairly general acceptance. In many ways, this is the most difficult area in autoradiography, but it is also one of the most interesting to the biologist, opening up possibilities for measuring the distributions of drugs and hormones in tissues, the concentrations of sugars and amino acids in cells, and even the concentrations and diffusion rates of electrolytes between various cell compartments.

The problems posed by diffusible materials, and the techniques for coping with them, are best considered under two headings – those concerned with the preparation of the specimen for autoradiography, and those to do with the exposure of the specimen to the emulsion.

THE PREPARATION OF SPECIMENS FOR AUTORADIOGRAPHY

The complexity of the process between collecting the specimen and the start of autoradiography varies considerably with the type of experiment. The specimen must be thin enough to view at the appropriate magnification. With a suspension of separate cells, this may present very few problems, but most specimens are solid tissues which require sectioning before microscopy is possible. In order to cut suitably thin sections, the tissue must have a certain hardness and uniformity. This can be achieved either by dehydrating the tissue and impregnating it uniformly with paraffin wax, or with a plastic of some sort, or the necessary consistency can be reached by freezing the tissue, effectively embedding it in ice. Embedding in wax or plastic provides conditions for sectioning which are better than those given by freezing. The uniformity of section thickness is better, the techniques are simpler, and the final product, the section, looks more acceptable to the histologist. So this type of section should be used wherever possible. Unfortunately, the range of solutions needed includes an aqueous fixative, dehydration in increasing concentrations of alcohol, and replacing the alcohol with a solvent such as xylene or benzene before impregnation with the embedding agent. The method which gives the best sections involves the greatest risk of removing the very radioactivity which is to be autoradiographed. The first question facing one is the following.

DO CONVENTIONAL HISTOLOGICAL METHODS REMOVE THE RADIOACTIVITY UNDER STUDY?

This can be tested in several ways. Labelled tissue fragments can be taken through all the solvents used in fixing and embedding, and the solutions analysed afterwards. If all the radioactive material is to be retained in the tissue, the presence of any detectable radioactivity in any of the solvents is enough to show that some modification of the process is necessary. If the extraction of radio-activity in one form is permissible, but retention in another is required, analysis of the solvents may be needed to establish the chemical form of the extracted radioactivity: extraction of inorganic iodide and retention of an iodinated compound, for instance. An alternative procedure is to measure the radioactivity remaining in the tissue fragment at each stage.

In general, these are rather insensitive controls. The volume of tissue is often small relative to that of the processing solutions, so that a total loss of as much as 10% of the radioactivity through the entire process may be difficult to detect. While a uniform reduction of 10% in the radioactivity of all tissue elements might not invalidate the experiment, complete removal from one tissue compartment, such as the extracellular fluid, would produce a totally different auto-radiograph. This type of testing also fails to show whether there has been any redistribution of radioactivity within the tissue during processing.

A more time-consuming but more reliable control is to compare autoradio-graphs prepared by conventional means with those made from identical material treated by one of the techniques which prevents any loss or displacement during processing – the techniques which will be discussed in full later in this chapter (pp.131–135). In many instances, if such a technique has to be set up at all, it may be quicker to use it for the whole experiment in the first place, rather than as a control to validate some other approach. In other cases, such as attempts to study the distribution of inorganic ions like sodium and iodide, it will be obvious that conventional histological methods should be replaced by frozen sectioning, and there is no point bothering with experiments into the rate of loss in different solvents.

If there is an indication that radioactivity of interest to the experiment is being lost in tissue processing, two lines of action can be taken. The steps of tissue processing can be examined carefully to see if modifications to the method can cure the problem. Alternatively, a technique based on frozen sections can be adopted.

MODIFICATIONS TO CONVENTIONAL PROCESSING

There are many reasons why these should be preferred to frozen sections, provided that they meet the requirements of retention of radioactivity. The techniques are simpler, the histology is better, the section thickness is more reproducible and can be more accurately controlled and measured: the geometry of section and emulsion is more predictable with plastic embedding, and there is also the possibility of extending studies to the electron microscope level.

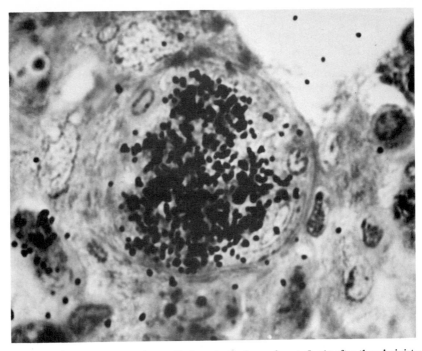

Fig.39.   Photomicrograph of a small artery in the lung of a rat, 5 min after the administration of tritiated aspirin. The tissue was frozen in isopentane at the temperature of liquid nitrogen, freeze-dried, and infiltrated *in vacuo* with Epon. The section, 1 μ thick, was autoradiographed with Kodak NTB-2 emulsion. Note the excellent localisation of this highly soluble drug to the lumen of the vessel. (X 1600) (From Wilske and Ross, 1965)

It may be sufficient to alter the fixation so as to retain radioactivity through processing. Williams[1] has illustrated how variable the retention of lipids can be with different fixation techniques. Loss of fat-soluble components may be prevented by using embedding media that are water-miscible, thus avoiding dehydration in alcohols and clearing in xylene or some similar reagent. Steedman[2] describes some of the water-miscible waxes available for light microscopy.

The most widely used modification of the methods for embedding tissues is to freeze-dry the tissue fragments, and then impregnate them directly with the embedding agent. Branton and Jacobson[3] described such a method with paraffin wax as the embedding medium. Wilske and Ross[4] tried the same thing with Epon as embedding agent (Fig. 39), and their method was further developed by Nadler *et al.*[5]. A detailed study of the application of this approach to the autoradiography of steriods has been presented by Attramadal[6-8]. Perhaps the most dramatic demonstration of its possibilities comes from Kinter and his co-workers[9], who have produced electron microscope autoradiographs of the distribution of [³H] galactose in hamster intestine.

Nadler et al.[5] showed an almost complete loss of inorganic iodide from the thyroid gland during fixation in Bouin's fluid and embedding in paraffin wax in the conventional way: with freeze-drying, fixation in osmium vapour and impregnation with Epon, this loss was reduced to about 5%. Similar figures are presented by Attramadal[6] for labelled steroids. The loss of radioactivity on fixation, dehydration and embedding in Epon was 75–80% for the uterus. Osmium tetroxide fixation produced very little loss of activity by comparison with formaldehyde, while glutaraldehyde perfusion with osmium post-fixation retained practically all the activity: in spite of this promising beginning to the process, losses on dehydration were very high, producing comparable total extractions whatever fixative was used. The losses from liver were lower, in the range 45–50%. With freeze-drying, vapour fixation and impregnation with Epon, the total loss from the tissue was about 4% (ref. 7). It is interesting to note that collecting the sections on water and floating them out produced a significant further loss of radioactivity – 10% in the case of thyroidal iodide[5], and 2.5% with labelled steroids in the uterus[6].

In Kinter's laboratory, the loss of radioactivity from sections while in contact with water was even more serious when either [³H] galactose or [³H] phlorizin was used[9]. Diffusion artefacts could be recognised in the autoradiographs, due not only to translocation of radioactivity while collecting and floating out the sections, but also to movement during dipping in liquid emulsion. These artefacts were ascribed to water-permeable channels in the araldite sections, and to loss from the surface of the section. Considerable improvement was obtained by incorporating a silicone fluid in the araldite: this was thought to close off the water-permeable channels in the sections. Surface loss to the water on floating out remained high at 25% of the total radioactivity, but did not increase above this level on prolonged floating. The autoradiographs showed much better resolution and no obvious diffusion artefacts when silicone was used. Even this surface loss can be reduced if the sections are cut on a dry glass knife[10].

Several interesting features emerge from these experiments. First, very substantial reductions in the extraction of radioactivity can often be achieved by freeze-drying and vapour fixation instead of fixation and dehydration in solution, but there is almost always some loss of radioactivity. Next, the severity of this loss varies, as would be expected, with the chemical nature of the labelled material and with the precise processing method: in addition, it varies considerably from tissue to tissue under identical conditions of treatment. Thirdly, the

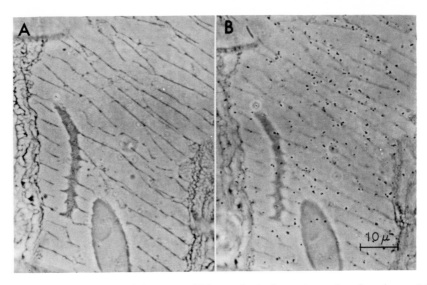

Fig.40 A blood vessel of Necturus, which was slowly frozen to produce large ice crystals separated by eutectic lines, which contained all the solutes, including [³H]glucose. The tissue was then freeze-dried, and embedded in Epon and autoradiographed. A, focused on the section; B, with the silver grains in focus. Of the silver grains over the plasma, 85% lay within 1 μ of the centre of a eutectic line. (× 1400) (From C.E. Stirling, A.J. Schneider, M.-D. Wong and W.B. Kinter, *J. Clin. Invest.*, 51 (1972) 438)

retention of radioactivity through to the embedded block is not the end of one's worries since losses in cutting and mounting the sections may be surprisingly high.

Considering these findings, it is only possible to place reliance on the autoradiographs if one assumes that the radioactivity lost comes randomly and equally from all tissue compartments, and that it is not accompanied by significant translocation of the radioactivity left behind in the section. These assumptions are not easy to prove. However, Fig. 40 shows an autoradiograph prepared by Kinter of [³H]glucose in salamander plasma. On freezing, which was deliberately a slow process, large solute-free ice crystals have been produced bounded by "eutectic lines" of precipitated proteins and other solutes. Grain counting has shown that 85% of the silver grains lie within 1 micron of the centres of these lines, giving very respectable resolution and a clear indication that in this model system no signficant translocation of the surviving radioactivity has taken place.

Freeze-drying and impregnation with an embedding agent are not universally applicable. Dr. Kinter informs me that the techniques which have given such useful information on the distribution of labelled sugars in his laboratory are far

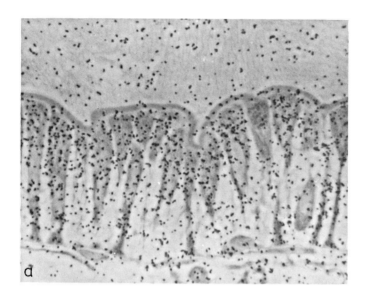

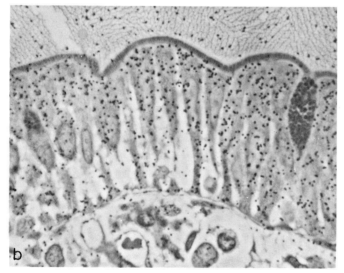

Fig.41 Autoradiographs of biopsies of human intestinal mucosa, incubated in a medium containing [³H]galactose. The fragments were then freeze-dried, embedded in Epon and sectioned at 1 to 2 μ. (*a*) Grain densities considerably higher than are found over the incubating medium occur over the cytoplasm of columnar absorptive cells, but not over their nuclei or over a goblet cell. (*b*) After similar incubation in the presence of phlorizin, grain densities over columnar cells were only 50% of those seen in the absence of this glucoside. (× 800) (From C.E. Stirling, A.J. Schneider, M.-D. Wong and W.B. Kinter, *J. Clin. Invest.*, 51 (1972) 438)

from satisfactory for autoradiographs of labelled sodium. In each case, then, the onus of proof is on the experimenter, who must show how far his procedure retains the radioactivity under study in the tissue, and must consider possible translocation of label. Each detailed procedure, each labelled compound and each tissue may give different results. The critical steps seem to be the impregnation with embedding agent, the collection and floating out of sections and the coating with emulsion. In spite of these obstacles, when the technique is carefully established, it can give very valuable results (Fig. 41).

METHOD FOR FREEZE-DRYING AND PLASTIC EMBEDDING

Step by step accounts of the method are published, with slight differences, by several authors[4,5,7,9]. The following short account is based on the process as used in Dr. Kinter's laboratory.

Small fragments of the tissue to be sectioned are placed on pieces of aluminium foil and rapidly frozen in propane cooled in liquid nitrogen to about $-184°$. The size of fragment is critical to adequate preservation of cytological detail — 1 mm cube is about the upper limit. The foil and tissue, after draining off excess propane, are then transferred to a freeze dryer cooled to liquid nitrogen temperature and the apparatus is pumped down to 10^{-5} torr (10^{-5} mm Hg). After a total of 50 h, the temperature is raised to $-70°$, and thence by stages to room temperature over a further 40—48 h.

The tissue fragments, which are very fragile by this time, are transferred to a desiccator containing phosphorus pentoxide and 0.1—0.5 g osmium tetroxide: after evacuating the air, the tissue is left for 12 h to fix in the osmium vapour. Next, the tissue is placed in the side-arm of a Thunberg tube, which has about 0.5 ml of embedding medium in the lower arm. This is pumped down to 0.2 torr for an hour, and then evacuated a second time before allowing the tissue to fall into the embedding medium. After warming the tube to 60° it is evacuated for a third time, sealed, and kept at 60° for 12 h. The tissue is transferred to a capsule containing degassed medium with catalyst added, and cured for 2 h at 0.2 torr at room temperature, followed by 36 h at 48°.

The embedding medium consists of 54 volumes Araldite 502 (Ciba), 45 volumes dodecenyl succinic anhydride and 1 volume of silicone fluid 200 (Dow—Corning): the latter is dispersed in the other constituents by vigorous shaking for 10—12 min. The catalyst is 2 volumes of benzyldimethylamine. The sections can be cut in the normal way on an ultramicrotome: alternatively, a dry glass knife can be used with the back of the knife (the surface extending from the cutting edge away from the block face) coated with Teflon. Using Wantz

T-fix (Du Pont), spray the back of the knife briefly, and heat the the knife on a hotplate at $70°$ for 5 min. Sections collected dry may be flattened with chloroform, either as a drop of fluid or as vapour.

METHODS BASED ON FROZEN SECTIONS

We have seen that methods based on the use of conventional embedding media, while capable of giving interesting results in particular cases, fail to retain all the radioactivity in tissue fragments in many instances. A number of techniques have been described which attempt to preserve all the radioactivity, whatever its chemical form, through the process of sectioning by the simple expedient of avoiding all contact between the tissue and solvents of any sort. These methods in general have the great advantage that loss of radioactivity from the tissue may be confidently excluded. Technically they are more difficult than producing sections from an embedded block, and the reproducibility of section thickness and quality of histological picture will usually compare unfavourably with the latter. The idea common to these methods is that the tissue should be rapidly frozen, and kept in the frozen state through sectioning and autoradiography so that translocation or diffusion of radioactive material is kept to a minimum. Alternatively, the frozen sections may be freeze-dried before exposure, permitting their return to room temperature under controlled conditions of humidity.

The frozen section approach has been widely used. It is the basis of many studies on the distributions of drugs and hormones by whole-body autoradiography, and will be discussed in this context in more detail in Chapter 14. In one form or another, it has provided most of the data from the autoradiography of diffusible materials at the light microscope level to date. So far it has not been possible to extend the technique to the electron microscope, though this may come in the next few years. Cryostat sections are difficult to cut by comparison to embedded tissues, as mentioned above: in addition to this, the retention of the tissue and section in the frozen state for relatively long times may favour the growth of ice crystals, with disruption of cellular structure and the movement of labelled solutes. Sectioning a frozen block of tissue carries the risk of thawing at the line of pressure of the knife edge. The frozen section contains all the reactive groups that were present in that volume of tissue *in vivo,* and is much more likely to interact chemically with the emulsion than a comparable section in Epon or araldite.

In spite of these difficulties, some of which will be discussed in more detail later on, techniques based on frozen sections have given a lot of information, and are the best we have at present for the autoradiography of labelled compounds that are lost in embedding.

OBTAINING FROZEN SECTIONS

The freezing of tissues and cutting of frozen sections are discussed in a number of articles in *The Autoradiography of Diffusible Substances*[11] , which should be consulted as a useful introduction. In principle, freezing should be very rapid if ice crystals are to be avoided. This means cooling in a medium of high thermal conductivity at a very low temperature, and, even more important, restricting the size of the block tissue: 1 mm cube is reasonable, and 2 mm in any one diameter should be a maximum. Once frozen, tissues may be stored indefinitely provided care is taken to keep the temperature below about $-70°$ and to prevent the tissue drying out by sublimation. Tissue blocks may be cut at almost any temperature from $-20°$ downwards: the lower the temperature the thinner the section that can be conveniently cut. A thin frozen section can so easily thaw, with spread of labelled solutes in a totally uncontrolled fashion, that a frozen cabinet with reasonable working space around the microtome (a cryostat) is essential for this type of work.

Many slight variations in method have been described: the following is the procedure used in my laboratory (Fig. 42). A small beaker of isopentane is cooled in liquid nitrogen until it begins to become viscous. The tissue fragment, removed as rapidly as possible from the animal and trimmed down to an appropriate size, is placed on a small square of blue card on which identifying numbers can be written in pencil, and is dropped into the isopentane. It is transferred to liquid nitrogen after a minute or so, the coloured card making it easy to see the tissue. It can remain in liquid nitrogen as long as required. When the tissue is needed for sectioning, a plate of aluminium about 6″ × 4″ × ¾″ is cooled with solid carbon dioxide to well below 0°, and a container of acetone and solid carbon dioxide prepared, with the blockholder from the cryostat microtome standing with its stem in the acetone. A scalpel and two pairs of forceps are precooled on the aluminium plate. With cooled forceps, the card with tissue attached is brought out of the liquid nitrogen and placed on the plate. The isopentane around the tissue will thaw, but the tissue itself will remain firmly frozen. With the scalpel, the tissue is separated from the card and positioned on the plate so that it can be quickly picked up in a predictable orientation. Next, one drop of a slurry of carboxymethylcellulose in distilled water is placed on the face of the blockholder: the concentration is not critical, provided only that it forms a fairly thin paste. This drop will freeze up from its base fairly rapidly,

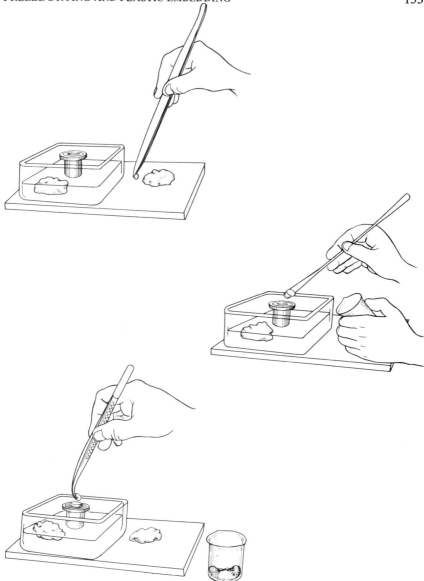

Fig.42. A diagram illustrating a method that can be used to mount frozen tissues on blockholders for sectioning in a cryostat, without permitting them to thaw. (*a*) With pre-cooled forceps, the tissue block is transferred from liquid nitrogen to a metal plate, pre-cooled with solid carbon dioxide. (*b*) A drop of a slurry of carboxymethylcellulose is placed on the cleaned blockholder, which stands with its stem in a mixture of acetone and solid carbon dioxide. (*c*) When the drop of carboxymethylcellulose has frozen completely, except for a thin layer at its apex, the tissue block is placed on the drop with precooled forceps, where it freezes into contact immediately.

References p. 147

and the advancing edge of the frozen zone can be easily recognised. When all but a thin skim of carboxymethylcellulose at the surface of the drop is frozen, the tissue is picked up with precooled forceps and placed on the drop. The frozen tissue will adhere at once to the carboxymethylcellulose, and remain frozen throughout the procedure, except for a surface layer at the base of the tissue block. This step is obviously a critical one, and calls for slickness. If the tissue is allowed to thaw while sitting in a puddle of carboxymethylcellulose, it will be useless for autoradiography and should be thrown away at once.

Once mounted on the blockholder, the tissue should be placed in the cryostat cabinet as soon as possible, and sectioned within a few hours. After 4–5 h, the tissue will become increasingly difficult to section as the small fragment dries out by sublimation.

There are many commercially available cryostats, which are not all suitable to this particular application. It is crucially important that the very thin frozen section should not thaw, even transiently, so that any design of cryostat that permits warm air to reach the region of the knife should be avoided. It is a fairly simple job to modify many commercial designs to convert the cabinet to a closed working area with glove ports[12] : some manufacturers will provide this modification on request.

The better the design of the microtome in the cryostat, the easier it will be to cut reproducible and thin sections: a rotary microtome is clearly preferable. There is often a gain in reproducibility of sectioning from motorising the microtome: a slow cutting stroke is often required, and this is difficult to reproduce by hand without hesitations and changes of speed. The quality and angle of the knife are crucially important. I have found that machine sharpened knives are a great help: the bevel angle remains constant from one knife to the next. Once the optimum knife angle has been determined, knives sharpened by machine can be changed without any alteration in sectioning characteristics. The temperature of sectioning should be $-20°$ or less to keep the section frozen. At $-20°$, thicker sections in the range of $10–20\,\mu$ can be cut reasonably well: at -25 to $-30°$, it becomes easier to cut below $5\,\mu$. It should be possible to cut at 3 or $2\,\mu$ and collect practically all the sections without undue difficulty. Stumpf and Roth[13] have shown that sections down to $1\,\mu$ can be cut at temperatures down to $-90°$, and even occasional ones at $0.5\,\mu$: for routine autoradiography at the light microscope level these very low temperatures are not essential, provided care is taken to prevent temperature fluctuations around the knife.

It has been suggested that the tissue must thaw at the knife edge, like ice under a skate, with consequent redistribution of radioactivity. This seems undeniable. However, the zone of thawing is probably very narrow and re-

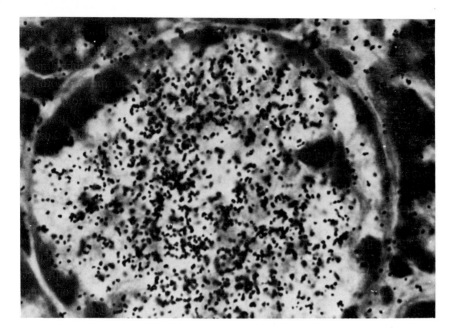

Fig.43. An autoradiograph of the submaxillary salivary gland of the mouse after an injection of [^{125}I] iodide. The tissue was sectioned at 3 μ in a cryostat and autoradiographed by the technique of Stumpf and Roth. Note the excellent resolution, with heavy grain density over the cytoplasm of cells of the convoluted granular tubule, but not over the nuclei, and a clear edge to the high grain density following the basal cell membrane. (X 400) (From Rogers and Brown–Grant, 1971)

freezing must occur almost instantaneously on the surface of the knife. Certainly many series of autoradiographs of radioiodide produced in my laboratory have given good localisation with no evidence of a smearing of radioactivity from regions of high grain density to adjacent areas (Fig. 43). As an added precaution against this effect, it may help to cool the knife to a considerably lower temperature than the rest of the cryostat cabinet: this can be done by packing small chips of solid carbon dioxide against it.

A completely enclosed cryostat may contain air that is so dry that a build-up of static electricity on constant use may make the sections very difficult to handle. I have seen them hopping about between glass and metal surfaces inside the cryostat like a team of performing fleas. It helps to earth the knife.

THE AUTORADIOGRAPHY OF SECTIONS CONTAINING DIFFUSIBLE
RADIOISOTOPES

Let us assume that we have obtained a tissue section without any loss or
displacement of the radioactive material within it. What problems arise in bringing this section in contact with an emulsion layer and subsequently processing
the emulsion?

(a) The autoradiography of embedded sections
It is tempting to treat these as if they were sections of fixed radioactive
material, and to forget that loss or movement of labelled material may still
occur.

If the tissue has been embedded in paraffin wax, perhaps after freeze-drying[3],
the temptation to dewax the section in xylene and to rehydrate them in a graded
series of alcohols must be resisted: if the radioactivity will survive this extraction
process, it can hardly be called "diffusible". Wax sections are best exposed by
laying the ribbon of sections on a preformed emulsion layer, and gently flat-
tening them with pressure. After exposure, the sections will have to be dewaxed
before development, or removed from the emulsion altogether, to permit
reagents to reach the emulsion beneath the sections. This can be done by dewaxing in xylene and careful washing, but sections are often lost at this stage.
All in all, autoradiography is difficult with sections like this, and this method of
embedding is best avoided.

Sections of tissue embedded in araldite or Epon are easier to autoradiograph,
as there is no need to remove the embedding plastic. Several methods are available. The sections may be mounted on slides and dipped in liquid emulsion or
covered with stripping film in the conventional way (see pp.310 and 289)[4]. But,
as mentioned above, loss of radioactivity from the section can occur at this stage
with many diffusible materials[7,5], and the experimenter must satisfy himself and
others that such loss is not occurring before he can use such direct and simple
methods.

Sections can be mounted on one slide and exposed by placing the slide
face-to-face with another that has been coated with emulsion by dipping or by
stripping film. This quick and simple method has the disadvantage that section
and autoradiograph must be separated before photographic processing and viewing, with a consequent loss of resolution. Attempts to leave the section on the
emulsion when separating the slides only make it difficult for the processing
solutions to reach the emulsion under the section.

Perhaps the most satisfactory approach is to form a thin emulsion layer on a wire loop, using the Caro technique (p.348), and to place this when dry over the section[14], mounted on some support such as a microscope slide. Reasonably reproducible geometry can be obtained without the section coming into contact with liquid emulsion or with water.

(b) The autoradiography of frozen sections

The handling of these very delicate sections is complicated by the fact that thawing produces gross redistribution of diffusible substances. The utmost care is needed if physical damage to the section is to be avoided, and thawing from warm instruments or air or even pressure prevented. There are two basic choices. Either the frozen section can be placed in contact with a preformed emulsion layer, cooled to at least $-15°$, or the section can be freeze-dried. After this latter step, it may be brought to room temperature under conditions of controlled humidity and placed in contact with a preformed emulsion layer.

The first and more direct method was described by Appleton[15]. He used slides coated with stripping film, applied so that the emulsion layer faced away from the glass: the technique can just as well be followed after dipping the slides in liquid emulsion. The emulsion-coated slides are cooled, and gently touched against the cryostat section as it lies on the knife immediately after cutting. This method requires the cryostat to be in the darkroom, and really implies sectioning under safelighting. It is quite possible to section under full lighting and switch to safelighting to pick up the sections, but I find this alternation of light and dark more difficult to get used to than working throughout under safelighting. Cryostat cutting is never easy, but if care is taken to adjust the microtome so that satisfactory sections are being cut before switching off the main light, and if the safelight is positioned so that it is reflected by the knife surface to the operator, it is a reasonable technique. One advantage offered by the Ilford emulsions is their tolerance of a rather brighter level of safelighting than can be used with Eastman Kodak NTB or Kodak AR-10 emulsions (p.255).

Appleton recommended keeping the emulsion-coated slides at -5 to $-10°$, and stated that a temperature differential of several degrees between emulsion and knife was essential for good contact between section and emulsion. This has not been my experience, and I feel the margin of safety to prevent thawing of the section is too small if emulsion at $-5°$ is used. If the emulsion-coated slides are kept in the cryostat cabinet at the temperature of the microtome itself, the dangers of thawing are less, and we have had no difficulty in picking up the section from the knife. The emulsion only needs to be touched gently against the section: why the section prefers the emulsion to the knife is not clear, but it is fortunate that it does. Pressing the slide against the section usually makes it stick firmly to the knife, and risks thawing the section by pressure. If the section does thaw, it will leave a frost mark on the knife which can easily be seen, and enables one to reject the section.

The Appleton technique has the advantage of simplicity. The frozen section is directly placed in contact with a frozen emulsion layer. It is reasonably easy to produce ribbons of sections on the emulsion, and serial sections are quite possible. It has been criticised on the ground that the section probably thaws, at least transiently, at the instant of picking up from the knife. While it is possible for this to happen, I do not believe it is necessary or, in reasonable hands, a frequent event.

Contact between section and emulsion may not be uniformly close with the Appleton technique. Some sections seem to curl away from the emulsion during exposure. An alternative, called the "modified sandwich technique", has been suggested by Kinter and Wilson[16]. Here, the cryostat sections are picked off the knife with a mounted needle or bristle and gently flattened on a slide with a very smooth surface such as Saran or Teflon. This slide is brought face-to-face with a slide coated with emulsion, and kept in contact throughout exposure. All these steps, of course, take place at temperatures well below freezing. At the end of exposure the slides are separated, and the section remains in contact with the emulsion.

The second approach with freeze-dried frozen sections was described by Stumpf and Roth[17]. The frozen sections are collected from the knife with a mounted bristle or fine forceps, and placed in a small container for transfer to a freeze-drier. A simple and convenient system for freeze-drying is the cryosorption pump[18]. It appears from data presented by Stumpf and Roth that a vacuum of about 10^{-3} torr at $-70°$ for a period of 12 h is sufficient to dry tissue sections to constant weight. We usually leave sections in the cryosorption apparatus overnight. It is a good idea to fit a vacuum gauge to the apparatus, as the undetected presence of a leak may result in the sections thawing and the material being wasted on allowing them to come to room temperature. Stumpf and Roth have shown that the freeze-dried sections can take up moisture again from the ambient air on bringing them to room temperature and opening the pump. The weight increases by about 1% of the dry weight for every 10% relative humidity in the air. At high humidities, this may well produce movement of labelled material. It is as well to control the relative humidity of the air used to break the vacuum to 20–30% and to store the sections in a desiccator until they are ready for mounting on the emulsion.

To place the freeze-dried section on the emulsion layer, slides are first coated with emulsion, either by dipping or with stripping film, and carefully dried. Then, in safelighting, the sections are placed on a very smooth surface, such as Teflon, slightly smaller in area than the emulsion-coated slides. This Teflon support is brought to the edge of the bench so that it overhangs slightly, and an emulsion-coated slide is placed emulsion down on the support. Slide and support are picked up together, gently pressed between finger and thumb, and the support allowed to fall away. The sections remain on the surface of the emulsion. A detailed account of the full method has recently been given by Stumpf[19].

THE EXPOSURE AND PROCESSING OF AUTORADIOGRAPHS OF FROZEN SECTIONS

With the Appleton technique it is essential to expose at temperatures low enough to prevent thawing: with the Stumpf and Roth technique it is not essential, but still preferable to do so. The presence of a drying agent is a good idea. The temperature of exposure will be discussed later, in connection with the prevention of chemography (p.141).

Frozen sections are no appreciable barrier to the diffusion of reagents into the underlying emulsion. The main problem is to keep them in contact with the emulsion. With the Appleton technique, the slides should be brought out into the darkroom while still cold. Condensation will form on the slides, which should be left to warm up to room temperature and to dry out. This wetting and drying helps to fix the sections to the emulsion. Stumpf[19] achieves the same end by breathing on the sections several times and letting them dry off. Even with this precaution, sections may sometimes float off the emulsion. If this is going to happen it is most likely to occur in photographic fixation or the subsequent wash. Coating emulsion and section with a thin layer of gelatin after development but before fixation prevents this.

The sequence in which we routinely process our autoradiographs is as follows:

(*i*) The slides are brought out of the deep freeze in which they were exposed, placed on the bench, and allowed to warm up and dry in a gentle current of cool air.

(*ii*) The slides are then placed in 4% formaldehyde in phosphate buffer (pH 7.4) for 15 min at room temperature to fix the sections.

(*iii*) After rinsing in 3 changes of distilled water for 1 min each, the slides go into developer and stopbath.

(*iv*) After the stopbath, the slides are dipped once in 0.5% gelatin in distilled water, and allowed to dry in air.

References p. 147

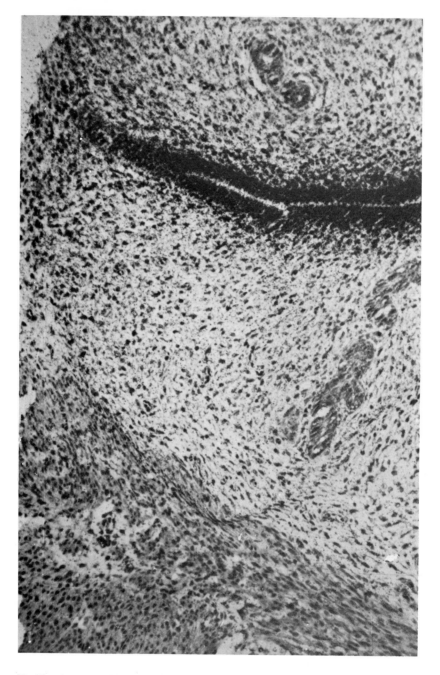

Fig.44. An autoradiograph of the uterus of an ovariectomised rat 24 h after a single injection of progesterone. The rat was given [^{125}I] iodide 2 h before sacrifice. A cryostat section of the uterus was autoradiographed by a modified Appleton technique. Note the high grain density over the luminal epithelium (× 130) (From Brown-Grant and Rogers, 1972)[33]

(*v*) Photographic fixation follows, with gentle washing in tap-water to finish.

The end product is usually quite adequate for histology and photography (Figs. 43 and 44). If reflected light is to be used to view the final autoradiograph or as a basis for photometric grain counting, it is essential to have the emulsion on top of the stained section and immediately under the coverslip. This can be done by picking up the section from the cryostat knife on a coverslip coated with emulsion, rather than a slide.

Unfortunately, a coverglass has a very small heat capacity, and it is difficult to control its temperature accurately during the handling involved in picking up the section, so that the section may sometimes thaw, with a consequent redistribution of radioactivity. It is possible to get the best of both worlds by fixing coverglasses to slides with a drop of histological mounting medium, and then coating them with emulsion. The slide provides the required heat capacity, and makes handling simpler, and, after staining, the coverglass can be loosened from the slide in xylene, and can be mounted emulsion side downwards, on a clean slide for microscopy.

CHEMOGRAPHY

We have seen (p.94) that even after fixation, an extractive process and embedding, sections can sometimes affect an emulsion layer chemically. This is even more likely when all the ions and reactive groups that were present *in vivo* are next to the emulsion through exposure. Some tissues are worse than others in this respect: we have found that brain, salivary gland and pancreas are particularly bad. It must be realised that chemography is quite likely with frozen sections, and that its influence on the final grain densities can be anatomical in distribution (Fig. 30). No autoradiograph of frozen sections can be interpreted without controls to exclude chemography.

For this artefact to occur, material from the section must diffuse into the emulsion and react there. From first principles, the removal of water (or rather, ice) from section and emulsion should reduce the chance of interaction, and exposure at very low temperatures should also help. These possibilities have been examined[12], and reductions in negative chemography were achieved by thorough drying of the emulsion layer before picking up the sections in the Appleton technique. Freeze-drying the section is even more effective, whether this is done in a deliberate and controlled fashion as in the Stumpf and Roth method, or by allowing the sections to stay for several hours in the cryostat before placing them on emulsion.

Exposure at the temperature of solid carbon dioxide ($-79°$) gives less

chemography than exposure at −20° (ref. 12). Appleton[20] has claimed that the
sensitivity of Kodak AR-10 stripping film falls rapidly with exposure temperatures below −20°, but it is important to note that his experiments were carried
out with constant development conditions. Our experience has been that the
efficiency of an autoradiograph exposed at −79° is very similar to that at −20°
or +4°, provided development is adjusted. It seems as if the latent images
formed at lower temperatures are smaller or more diffuse: they are still there,
however, and can be visualised with increased development.

Rogers and John[12] found an interesting effect on the severity of negative
chemography from the choice of developer. An Amidol developer, used in
conditions which gave reasonable development in the absence of negative
chemography, produced autoradiographs of salivary gland in which loss of
developed grains was very severe. By contrast, similar preparations developed
with Ilford 1D-19 (or Kodak D-19b) were hardly affected at all. They suggested
at the time that Amidol is only affecting latent images at the surface of the
crystal, the very ones most likely to be affected by chemography: the other
developer, with a considerable solvent action, could reach deep latent images
also. In the nuclear emulsions as a whole, such a high proportion of the latent
images are surface ones that this explanation may not be valid. Whatever the
reason for it, this effect exists, and if chemography is a problem in autoradiographs of frozen sections it may be wise to look at several developers. Gold
latensification may help to visualise latent images that have been severely eroded
by chemography (p.27).

If chemography does occur in spite of drying, low temperature exposure and
a suitable choice of developer, it is very difficult to know what to do about it. It
is not easy to place an impermeable layer, such as that described on p.118,

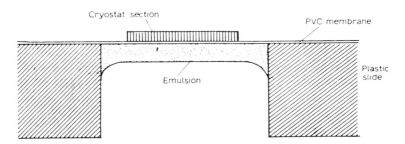

Fig.45. A diagram to illustrate the positions of cryostat section and emulsion relative to
the PVC membrane in the suggested method for the autoradiography of soluble isotopes in
the presence of chemographic artefacts.

between section and emulsion without preventing access of developer and fixer to the emulsion, or of stain to the section. Nor is it easy to get the final sandwich together with good contact between the various layers without the frozen section thawing. A possible but clumsy technique is to drill a hole about 1 cm diameter in a thin piece of plastic and cover it with an impermeable membrane (p.118). Liquid emulsion can be placed on one side of the membrane, and the frozen section picked up by the Appleton method on the other (Fig. 45).

It seems likely that most of the interaction between frozen section and emulsion affects the surface layer of silver halide crystals only. It may be that coating the emulsion with a very thin layer of gelatin by dipping the slide once in a dilute solution, such as 0.5%, before putting the section on the emulsion, would reduce the severity of this artefact.

ASSESSMENT OF THE VARIOUS AVAILABLE TECHNIQUES

It is notoriously difficult to compare different techniques. A procedure that works admirably in one laboratory may not be satisfactory in another, for reasons that are very difficult to sort out. Also, some labelled substances are more difficult to autoradiograph than others in this general group of diffusible materials, and tissues vary in the way in which they bind drugs or hormones and in their ease of sectioning and liability to chemography.

The methods for autoradiographing diffusible materials that involve embedding can only be used after very careful examination of isotope loss through the entire process, including bringing the section in contact with the emulsion. The careful work of Attramadal[6-8] suggests that for steroid hormones and their target tissues this method can be made to work. But the hormones oestradiol and testosterone are tightly bound to receptor molecules in their target cells, molecules that are fairly large proteins which must restrict the mobility of the labelled hormones very considerably. There is no guarantee that the same method will be universally suitable. Kinter's work with labelled sugars[9] showed that useful results can be obtained with much smaller molecules that do not appear to be bound in the tissue in the same way, but loss of radioactivity does occur even with this technique, and this loss is so severe with labelled sodium that the method as used is impracticable[10]. While embedding gives excellent histology, more reproducible section thickness and the possibility of extension to the electron microscope level in very favourable cases, it is not universally applicable and always leaves some measure of doubt in its validity. In a direct comparison of an embedding technique with the freeze-drying of frozen sections, Stumpf and Roth[21] found the former method to give slightly different distributions of [³H] oestradiol and [³H] mesobilirubinogen, suggesting preferential loss of radioactivity from some tissue compartments.

The frozen section techniques are, in general, preferable. A direct comparison of the Appleton and the Stumpf and Roth techniques in my laboratory in two experiments has failed to show any difference in the distribution of radioactivity, or any very obvious advantage of the one method over the other. One experiment examined the distribution of I-125 as iodide in the salivary glands of mice[22] (Fig. 43). This required very short exposure times, often of 24—48 h, and it was noticed that freeze-dried sections gave higher grain densities than the Appleton method; presumably self-absorption was less after drying. The other experiment studied the distribution of [³H] progesterone and [³H] megestrol acetate in the rat uterus, with exposure times of 2—6 weeks[23] : this time there was no demonstrable difference in efficiency, since the Appleton sections presumably freeze-dried during the first day or two of exposure.

Both methods, sensibly and carefully carried out, can give valid data, and one is left with a choice which may depend on the circumstances of the experiment. The Appleton method requires a cryostat in the darkroom, eliminating it as a possibility for those who have to work in a modified coffin. Chemography is in general more troublesome than after freeze-drying, so that it may not be sensible to use the Appleton approach for particularly difficult tissues. It is quick and simple, however, and fairly large blocks can be serially sectioned and autoradiographed without too much extra trouble. The Stumpf and Roth method is very time-consuming if many serial sections are needed, as each section must be freeze-dried in a separate labelled container.

With both methods, controls for chemography are essential. Statements will be found in the literature that some emulsions do not show chemography, or that freeze-drying the sections will prevent it altogether. These are not true.

THE RESOLUTION AND EFFICIENCY OF AUTORADIOGRAPHS OF DIFFUSIBLE SUBSTANCES

The resolution obtainable by methods for diffusible materials is determined by the factors discussed in Chapter 4: in addition, two other effects must be taken into account. The first is the possibility of diffusion of the radioactive compound in the tissue. This, whether it occurs in the interval between obtaining the specimen and freezing it, during transient thawing, or even in the frozen state during exposure, can only make the resolution worse by comparison with the best that can be done with the same autoradiographic system. Large molecules diffuse more slowly than small ones, and the resolution of frozen section autoradiographs may well vary with the molecule under study. The diffusion rate also depends critically on the medium through which the molecule is trying to move. A true solution of low viscosity will permit more rapid diffusion than cell cytoplasm, with its submicroscopic organisation. This may be clearly seen in different areas of the same autoradiograph. When iodine-125 in ionic form is examined in the salivary gland of the mouse, the cells of the convoluted granular tubules concentrate the iodide, giving autoradiographs which are often very precisely localised. In the lumen of the collecting ducts, the iodide often gives a clumpy distribution with poor resolution. So the influence of diffusion on the resolution of autoradiographs varies with the labelled molecule and with its immediate environment.

A second factor has been identified by Clarkson[24], working with frozen section autoradiographs of plant material. On freeze-drying, the vacuole in the centre of plant cells will dry down to a very thin layer of solute in contact with the emulsion, while the cellulose cell walls remain the original thickness of the section. While more obvious perhaps with plant material, this effect must occur with any frozen tissue section, giving geometry which varies from place to place in a very striking and non-random fashion. There have been no serious attempts to take this variation into account so far in the literature.

Measurements of resolution in the literature suggest that it is of the order of twice that of fixed and precipitated material. Appleton[20] found a resolution of $9-13\ \mu$ with sodium-22, compared with expected values of 4–5 microns: with tritium in the form of thymidine, he claimed $2-4\ \mu$, compared with an expected $1\ \mu$. Creese and Maclagan[25], working with [^{3}H] decamethonium in muscle, claimed a resolution of $1-1.5\ \mu$. For embedded material, Kinter's[10] demonstration of the concentration of [^{3}H] glucose in the eutectic bands of frozen plasma indicates that a resolution practically as good as that of non-diffusible material can be obtained (Fig. 40).

Efficiency should also be similar to that of conventional autoradiographs. Once again the variable geometry produced by freeze-drying described by Clarkson[24] must have quite an effect on the efficiency of recording from adjacent tissue compartments. The influence of this on grain counting has not so far been investigated in detail. The one great advantage of the "modified sandwich" technique (p.138) is that freeze-drying of the section during exposure is prevented. It would be interesting to compare the efficiencies in nucleus, cytoplasm and extracellular space of a tissue autoradiographed by this technique and by the Appleton method.

If care is taken to base the results on a sufficiently large series of sections to compensate for variation in thickness, autoradiographs based on frozen sections can give precise quantitative results. The technique can be combined with track autoradiography[26] .

EXTENSION OF FROZEN SECTION AUTORADIOGRAPHY TO THE ELECTRON MICROSCOPE LEVEL

This would open up a whole new field of study in the distribution of labelled compounds. Unfortunately, techniques do not exist at present to permit this type of work. Progress towards the cutting of ultrathin frozen sections for electron microscopy has been slow but steady over the past five years, and the apparatus and techniques that are evolving have been described by Appleton[27] , Christensen[28] and Hodson and Marshall[29] . Even when satisfactory sections are obtained, their handling and autoradiography will be a further problem. The analysis of autoradiographs at the electron microscope level is already a complicated affair (p.208). With frozen sections the movement of labelled material due to diffusion, to the process of freezing, and perhaps even during freeze-drying can only make the analysis less certain. Adequate techniques will come, but they are not here yet.

THE AUTORADIOGRAPHY OF DIFFUSIBLE MATERIAL IN CELL SUSPENSIONS

The previous sections have dealt with solid tissues that require sectioning before autoradiography and microscopy. How about specimens that are already thin enough, such as cell suspensions or bacterial preparations?

It is tempting to prepare an air-dried smear of suspended cells and then place it in contact with a preformed emulsion layer. But there are few diffusible substances that retain their *in vivo* position after this treatment. As drying proceeds, the fluid outside the cell becomes hypertonic and many intracellular materials will leak out. In fact the production of a halo of silver grains around such cells was used by Miller, Stone and Prescott[30] to differentiate diffusible material from radioactivity firmly incorporated into macromolecules in the cell. A similar criticism can be applied to touch preparations from solid tissues[31] .

One can of course rapidly freeze a small drop of the suspension and treat the block as if it were a solid tissue, sectioning it before autoradiography. Alternatively, a technique has been described by Darżynkiewicz and Komender[32] for spraying a cell suspension on to a Teflon slide, freezing it rapidly, freeze-drying, and then pressing it against a preformed emulsion layer. At the end of exposure the Teflon slide is separated from the emulsion leaving the cells on the emulsion.

With this technique they were able to achieve a very reasonable resolution with sodium-22: grain counts fell to 10% of the levels over the cytoplasm at a distance of 10 μ from the cell membrane.

REFERENCES

1 M.A. Williams, *Advan. Optical Electr. Microscop.*, 3 (1969) 219.
2 H.F. Steedman, *Section Cutting in Microscopy,* Blackwell, Oxford, 1960.
3 D. Branton and L. Jacobson, *Stain Technol.,* 37 (1962) 239.
4 K.R. Wilske and R. Ross, *J. Histochem. Cytochem.,* 13 (1965) 38.
5 N.J. Nadler, B. Benard, G. Fitzsimmons and C.P. Leblond, in L.J. Roth and W.E. Stumpf, (Eds.), *The Autoradiography of Diffusible Substances,* Academic Press, New York, 1969, pp. 121–130.
6 A. Attramadal, *Histochemie,* 19 (1969) 64.
7 A. Attramadal, *Histochemie,* 19 (1969) 75.
8 A. Attramadal, *Histochemie,* 19 (1969) 110.
9 C.E. Stirling and W.B. Kinter, *J. Cell Biol.,* 35 (1967) 585.
10 W.B. Kinter, personal communication.
11 L.J. Roth and W.E. Stumpf (Eds.), *The Autoradiography of Diffusible Substances,* Academic Press, New York, 1969.
12 A.W. Rogers and P.N. John, in L.J. Roth and W.E. Stumpf, (Eds.), *The Autoradiography of Diffusible Substances,* Academic Press, New York, 1969, pp. 51–68.
13 W.E. Stumpf and L.J. Roth, *Nature,* 205 (1965) 712.
14 O.L. Miller, G.E. Stone and D.M. Prescott, *J. Cell Biol.,* 23 (1964) 654.
15 T.C. Appleton, *J. Roy. Microscop. Soc.,* 83 (1964) 277.
16 W.B. Kinter and T.H. Wilson, *J. Cell Biol.,* 25 (1965) 19.
17 W.E. Stumpf and L.J. Roth, *Stain Technol.,* 39 (1964) 219.
18 W.E. Stumpf and L.J. Roth, *J. Histochem. Cytochem.,* 15 (1967) 243.
19 W.E. Stumpf, in *Introduction to Quantitative Cytochemistry,* Vol. 2, Academic Press, New York, 1970, 507–526.
20 T.C. Appleton, *J. Histochem. Cytochem.,* 14 (1966) 414.
21 W.E. Stumpf and L.J. Roth, *J. Histochem. Cytochem.,* 14 (1966) 274.
22 A.W. Rogers and K. Brown-Grant, *J. Anat.,* 109 (1971) 51.
23 P.N. John and A.W. Rogers, *J. Endocrinol.,* 53 (1972) 375.
24 D.T. Clarkson, personal communication.
25 R. Creese and J. Maclagan, *J. Physiol.,* 210 (1970) 363.
26 A.W. Rogers, G.H. Thomas and K.M. Yates, *Exptl. Cell Res.,* 40 (1965) 668.
27 T.C. Appleton, in L.J. Roth and W.E. Stumpf, (Eds.) *The Autoradiography of Diffusible Substances,* Academic Press, New York, 1969, pp. 301–319.
28 A.K. Christensen, in L.J. Roth and W.E. Stumpf, (Eds.), *The Autoradiography of Diffusible Substances,* Academic Press, New York, 1969, pp. 349–362.
29 S. Hodson and J. Marshall, *J. Microscop.,* 91 (1970) 105.
30 O.L. Miller, G.E. Stone and D.M. Prescott, in D.M. Prescott (Ed.), *Methods in Cell Physiology,* Vol. 1, Academic Press, New York, 1964, pp. 371–379.
31 W.E. Stumpf, *Acta Endocrinol.,* Suppl. 153 (1971) 205.
32 Z. Darżynkiewicz and J. Komender, *J. Histochem. Cytochem.,* 15 (1967) 605.
33 K. Brown-Grant and A.W. Rogers, *J. Endocrinol.,* 53 (1972) 355.

CHAPTER 9

The Microscopy and Photomicrography of Autoradiographs

CHOICE OF ILLUMINATION

In practically every technique of autoradiography in use at the present time, the emulsion remains in contact with the biological specimen throughout processing and subsequent viewing. In many instances, the examination of the autoradiograph raises no particular problem. If the specimen can be stained adequately, either before or after applying the emulsion, any reasonably good microscope fitted with conventional optics for transmitted light will suffice to show the presence of developed silver grains over the stained section or smear. Many staining methods can be used with autoradiographs, and these are discussed in more detail in Chapter 7 (p.114). But even with stained specimens, there are cases in which the use of transmitted light alone raises problems in observing and interpreting the autoradiograph; and these problems become much more serious with photomicrography.

Ideally, the presence of the emulsion layer should not interfere in any way with the microscopy of the specimen. The choice of staining method should not be limited, nor should the silver grains be so large or so closely packed as to hide important detail in the underlying tissue. At the same time, it should be possible to examine the distribution of silver grains at low magnification over large areas of the autoradiograph, in order to assess the overall patterns of labelling and its relation to background. This ideal situation is not easy to meet with transmitted light alone. If the tissue has been stained with haematoxylin, for instance, giving blue-black chromatin and nucleoli, and cytoplasmic staining as well in some cells, it may be extremely difficult to distinguish the silver grains at low magnifications from dark granules in the specimen. Fig. 46 shows a low power view of the developing cerebral cortex of the rat, after an injection of tritiated thymidine. It is extremely difficult to see the labelled cells, particularly in those parts of the section where the nuclei are very densely packed. One might get quite a mistaken impression about the distribution of silver grains, influenced by their relatively clearer visibility in areas where the staining is less heavy.

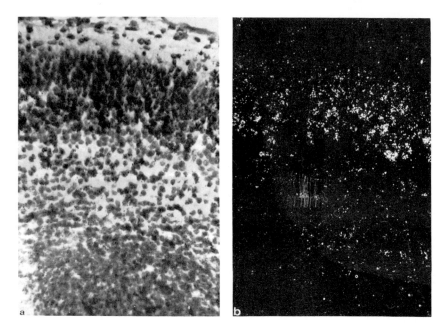

Fig.46 Photomicrographs of the same field of an autoradiograph, taken by (a) transmitted, and (b) incident dark-field illumination. The material is the cerebral cortex of a foetal rat, injected with [^{3}H] thymidine on the 16th day of pregnancy and sacrificed 4 days later. In (a), the silver grains are easily seen across the middle of the field, where the density of stained cells is low. In (b), these silver grains are clearly insignificant relative to the heavily labelled band of cells just above. Autoradiograph prepared with Ilford G5 emulsion, applied over a PVC membrane; section stained with Harris' haematoxylin before autoradiography. (× 176) (Material prepared in collaboration with Dr. M. Berry)

If the silver grains are made very large, by selecting an emulsion with large crystal diameter and developing it fairly strongly, they may become easier to see at low magnifications. Under oil immersion, however, they will be enormous, obscuring detail in the specimen, and incidentally reducing both the resolution and the efficiency by comparison with a fine-grained emulsion (see Chapters 4 and 5).

These may be very real problems, particularly in experiments that require detailed cytological observation of the labelled cells. One autoradiographer of several years' experience told me that she is unable to score the percentage of mitotic figures labelled with tritiated thymidine in her material, owing to this difficulty of distinguishing the clumped metaphase chromosomes from silver grains. Few would agree that this particular problem is insoluble, and such counts are often made in other laboratories. But in studying the correlation of

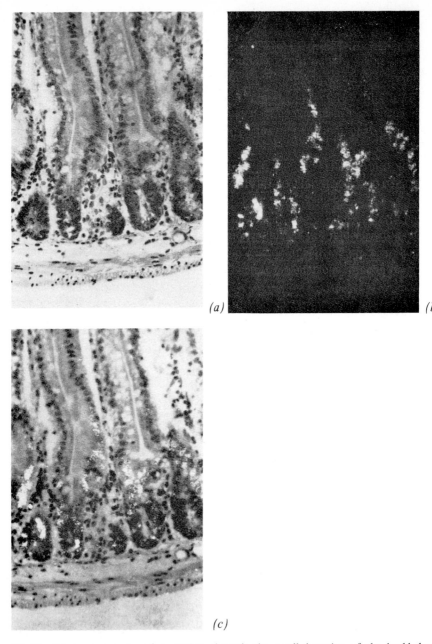

Fig.47. Photomicrographs of a section through the small intestine of the bushbaby (*Galago demidoffi*), 24 h after the injection of tritiated thymidine. (*a*) Section viewed by transmitted light alone: silver grains invisible. (*b*) Same field seen by incident dark-field lighting: silver grains clearly seen, but section invisible. (*c*) Same field by balanced transmitted and incident lighting. Autoradiograph with Ilford L4 emulsion. Leitz Ultropak × 22 objective. Stained with Harris' haematoxylin. (× 135) (From *Leitz Mitt. Wiss. u. Techn.*, 3 (1964) 43)

labelling with the various stages of meiotic prophase in the developing ovary, for example, where the fine structure of the chromosomes is of crucial importance, and their condensed or beaded appearance with haematoxylin stains produces dark specks the approximate size of silver grains, very real problems in interpretation can arise.

If it is sometimes difficult for the microscopist to observe detail in an autoradiograph, the problems of photomicrography will obviously be greater. Most published photomicrographs are in monochrome, and the sorting out of stained granules from silver grains at low magnifications can be almost impossible (Fig. 47). At high magnifications, a different problem arises. The silver grains are necessarily often at a different focal plane from the specimen, and it may be quite impossible to focus both of them sharply on the same photograph.

If anyone doubts that this problem exists, he has only to look through the pages of any journal of cytology. The photomicrographs of autoradiographs are hardly ever comparable in quality to those of histological preparation alone. Often, the silver grains are critically focused, and the specimen a blurred background. Sometimes, the section is photographed, and the position of the silver grains marked in by hand; or two photographs of the same field may be shown, with the section in focus in the one, the silver grains in the other. These photomicrographs may even be superimposed, though this is time-consuming enough to deter most authors.

It is possible to resolve many of these problems of observation and photography by making use of dark-field illumination, either separately or in conjunction with transmitted light. The principles involved, the choice of equipment, and the techniques of photography will be discussed in some detail, since the methods that will be used in microscopy have a considerable influence on the selection of the autoradiographic technique that is most suitable for a given experiment, and since only a partial description is available in the literature[1].

DARK-GROUND ILLUMINATION

Ideally, a method of microscopy is needed that distinguishes clearly between silver grains and stained material in the specimen. Developed grains are irregular, ribbon-like knots of metallic silver. They do not absorb light that falls on them, but reflect and scatter it. This is why they appear dark by transmitted light, just like stained objects, which do absorb the light passing through the specimen. But if they are illuminated by a beam of light so placed that it does not enter the objective, silver grains will scatter light from its original path into the optical axis of the microscope, resulting in a light signal from each grain. Stained objects in the tissue will still absorb light of the appropriate wavelength: this will not give any image that can be seen through the objective.

In short, dark-ground illumination can produce an unmistakeable signal from silver grains, distinguishing them from material in the specimen that absorbs light. Viewed in this lighting system, the silver grains will be bright specks on a dark background. Very few components of vertebrate tissue will scatter light in this way. Curiously enough, pigment granules often appear bright in dark-field illumination, and may be very difficult to distinguish from silver grains. Naturally, if the technique of staining has introduced metallic deposits, or anything that scatters light rather than absorbing it, these sites will also be bright against the generally dark background of the tissue.

In general, dark-field lighting does differentiate silver grains from tissue section. A further characteristic of this lighting system is that objects too small to be resolved in transmitted light by a given optical system may be seen clearly if they can be converted into sources of light on a dark background. In other words, silver grains at or even just below the limits of visibility by transmitted light can be seen, using dark-field illumination. In addition, this conversion of silver grains into light signals greatly simplifies the problems of automating the drudgery of grain counting. The use of dark-field lighting for photometric grain counting will be considered in Chapter 10 (p.165).

With dark-field illumination, then, it is possible to recognise even very small grains against a stained background. As can be seen in Fig. 47, the stained material, when viewed by transmitted light alone, can look like a normal histological preparation. The use of dark-field illumination alone gives a clear idea of the distribution of silver grains, without any interference from the stained section. With both systems of lighting in use simultaneously, the relation of grains to stained material is obvious.

Optical systems for dark-ground illumination

There are two main methods of illuminating the specimen to obtain a dark-field effect. The system in general use in bacteriology and cytology employs sub-stage illumination with a special condenser, which produces a cone of light converging on the specimen from below. The metallurgical illuminators, on the other hand, being designed for use. with solid, opaque materials, direct the light on to the specimen from above, *i.e.* through or around the objective lens itself. Both methods can give the required effect with silver grains, but the latter is far more convenient. It can be used not only in rapid alternation with direct transmitted light, but even simultaneously. However rapid the switchover from dark- to bright-field illumination, it is not easy to carry over the mental picture of

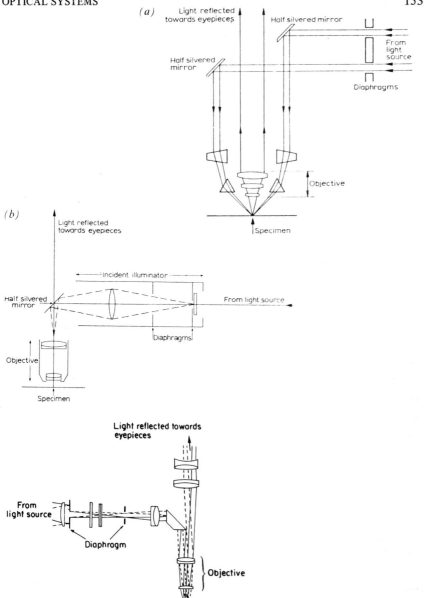

Fig.48. Diagrams to illustrate the light paths in the two methods of dark-field illumination from above the specimen that can be used in viewing autoradiographs. (*a*) The Leitz Ultro-pak system, in which a cone of light converges on the specimen from above. (*b*) The vertical-incident system, in which the illuminating beam travels through the objective itself to reach the specimen. (By courtesy of E. Leitz, G.m.b.H.).

References p. 164

grain distribution accurately, and the simultaneous use of both methods of lighting is a great advantage.

With illumination from above the specimen, there are again two choices of optical system available. The first projects a converging cone of light on to the specimen from around the objective lens, in a manner rather similar to the sub-stage dark-field system. In the second, or vertical, system, the illuminating beam is actually directed down the optical axis and through the objective itself. Fig. 48 illustrates these two systems diagrammatically.

Dealing first with the convergent cone system, many manufacturers produce suitable equipment, such as the Ultropak illuminator and lenses of E. Leitz, G.m.b.H. Since the equipment was produced for a very different optical task, not all the lenses available are suitable for autoradiographs. At very low magnification, lenses like the Ultropak X6.5 (N.A. 0.18) can give a satisfactory dark-field effect, but they have a considerable depth of focus, and scratches and imperfections on the upper surface of the coverglass will scatter light and interfere with the dark-field picture. This can be avoided by using an immersion cone with the objective. At higher magnifications, the X22 (N.A. 0.45) objective is very useful, and many of the illustrations in this book have been taken with it: at this level, no immersion cone is needed as the depth of focus is less. High dry objectives, such as the X50 (N.A. 0.65) should be avoided, as with increasing numerical aperture much more light is scattered from the upper surface of the coverglass, so that the background against which the silver grains are viewed is quite bright and hazy, instead of being black. With oil immersion objectives such as the X75 and X100 (N.A. 1.0) an excellent dark-field picture can again be seen.

These four Ultropak objectives X6.5, X22, X75 and X100 provide a very satisfactory series, with acceptable performance when used with transmitted light alone, as well as a good dark-field picture. This is the system of choice for observing autoradiographs, and also for photomicrography.

A surprising amount of light is reflected back through the specimen by the sub-stage condenser when the Ultropak illumination alone is being used. In many cases, this scattered light is enough to outline structural detail in the specimen, and there is no need to supplement it with transmitted lighting. If a really dark field is wanted, the top lens of the sub-stage condenser can be flipped out of the optical axis, or the sub-stage condenser itself racked down. Either manoeuvre will abolish the reflections from the upper surface of the condenser.

The second type of system for giving dark-field lighting from above the specimen is the vertical illuminator, in which the light is directed down on to the specimen through the objective lens itself. This is very different in use. I have never been able to get a satisfactory dark-field effect, except with oil-immersion objectives of high numerical aperture. This reduces the usefulness of this particular system for autoradiography. However, with an oil-immersion objective, one can obtain a finely focused beam of light which gives a higher ratio of light reflected per silver grain to light scattered from the various optical interfaces than is possible with the Ultropak type of lens. It is also possible to limit the area of emulsion illuminated to the precise area from which observations are required, by using the field diaphram of the illuminator. This, as will be discussed in Chapter 10, has practical advantages in the design of photometric devices for grain counting. In this particular application, therefore, the vertical illuminator is the system of choice. For routine viewing and for photomicrography, the convergent cone type of illuminator is preferable.

Let us summarise the advantages to be gained from using the Ultropak lenses for dark-field viewing of grain density autoradiographs. Provided staining methods which involve the deposition of metals in the tissues are avoided, and also certain histochemical reactions for enzymes, which produce a light-scattering precipitate in the specimen, it is possible to view the silver grains as bright specks on a dark background. This makes it feasible to keep the size of the developed grains relatively small, so that fine detail in a heavily labelled cell can still be recognised. At the same time, small, darkly stained granules in the specimen can be confidently identified, without confusing them with silver grains.

Even in autoradiographs in which the grains appear small under high magnification, it is still possible to observe the overall distribution of silver grains over a stained specimen at low magnifications, using dark-field illumination (cf. Figs. 4 a and b).

THE PHOTOMICROGRAPHY OF GRAIN DENSITY OF
AUTORADIOGRAPHS

If dark-field illumination with Ultropak lenses is useful in viewing autoradiographs, it is invaluable in their photomicrography.

As has been shown in Fig. 47, it is possible to photograph the section at relatively low magnification, and produce a print as good as with histological material alone. It is possible to photograph the silver grains without the section being visible. Finally, it is possible to produce a composite photograph, in which the silver grains, appearing as bright specks, can be clearly seen against the stained section. At low magnifications, the depth of focus of the objective is sufficient for both section and autoradiograph to appear sharp on the same exposure. This type of picture is best taken with transmitted and dark-field illuminating systems both on together. It will be found that the bright-field lighting has to be kept to a very low intensity, or it will flood out the dark-field effect, and the silver grains will be very difficult to see. The best method is to adjust the two lighting systems under direct visual control, and then take the photomicrograph when the best balance has been obtained.

With the increasing use of exposure meters and automatic cameras, this balancing process may not be easy. If one reduces the intensity of transmitted light in order to emphasise the silver grains, the camera will compensate by increasing the exposure time. It may be necessary to deceive the camera by providing it with false information. Most of the photomicrographs in this book were taken on Kodak High Contrast Copy Film, for which an ASA rating of 6 normally gives good results. If one sets an automatic camera for an ASA value of 12, this effectively shortens the exposure, resulting in a darker print. This is ideal for a photomicrograph at low magnification with both lighting systems balanced, as the bright silver grains show up well against the darker specimen.

At high magnifications, the biggest problem in obtaining clear photomicrographs is to focus section and silver grains sharply on the same negative. The solution to this is to employ a double exposure technique, superimposing a dark-field picture of the silver grains, critically focused, on a transmitted light picture of the specimen. Once again, the duration of the two exposures is extremely important, in order to see sufficient detail on the specimen without fading out the light signal from the silver grains.

If one considers first the dark-field picture of silver grains, the exposure should give as black a background as possible, with the grains contrasting brightly. The exposure time that achieves this is really independent of the number of silver grains present in the field of view: if one grain is correctly exposed, so will be one hundred. But all meters and automatic cameras relate the light output of the field to the exposure time, so that if the field with one hundred grains in it is correctly exposed, the one with only one grain will be exposed for a very much longer time, resulting in a background that is not quite so black.

The best solution is to standardise the conditions of illumination and of processing the negative as far as possible, and then to try various exposure times on a field with relatively few grains in it. When this gives a negative with clear black specks on a background that is really white, that exposure time should then be used for all subsequent pictures under those conditions of microscopy and of autoradiography. As a rough guide, the dark-field exposure I use for oil-immersion photomicrographs is 2 min: by contrast, the automatic camera

that is available may indicate exposure times from 1 up to over 20 min for
similar material, depending on the number of grains in the field. These long
exposure times for dark-field work require complete freedom from vibration.
The microscope should preferably be on a slate bench. Dust on the coverglass, in
the immersion oil, or on the emulsion, may prove embarrassingly obvious in

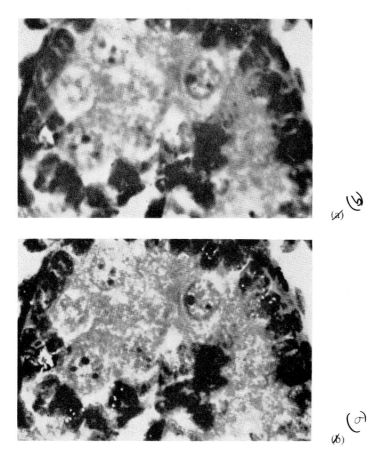

(a)

(b)

Fig.49. Section of the testis of a newborn rat, 24 h after the injection of tritiated thymidine. The section was stained with Harris' haematoxylin. *(a)* A photomicrograph of the
silver grains by incident dark-field illumination superimposed on a transmitted-light picture
of the section by the double-exposure technique described in the text. The small bright
grains can be clearly seen against the darkly stained nuclei, and both are sharply in focus.
(b) The same field photographed by transmitted light alone, with the silver grains critically
in focus. The very small grains are invisible against the darkly stained section, which is out
of focus. Autoradiograph prepared with Ilford K2 emulsion. Leitz Ultropak × 100 objective, with mirror condenser. (× 660) (From *Leitz Mitt. Wiss. u. Techn.*, 3 (1964) 43)

dark-field photographs, and dust or scratches on the negative will be very difficult to ignore when over 90% of the finished print is intended to be uniformly black.

For a double exposure photomicrograph, after the dark-field picture is taken, the film, of course, must be restrained from winding on. The dark-field illumination is then replaced by transmitted, bright-field lighting. The stained section is carefully focused and the second exposure made. For this exposure, the same comments apply as for the low power photomicrographs. The light intensity must not be such as to make the bright silver grains invisible on the finished photograph. I find that half the exposure that would normally be required for a simple photomicrograph of the histological specimen in transmitted light gives about the right picture. This can be achieved with automatic cameras by setting them for an ASA value twice that of the film.

Fig. 49 illustrates the advantages of this double exposure method. When photographed in transmitted light alone, focusing on the silver grains has put the tissue out of focus: even so, many of the grains are invisible against the stained background. The double exposure method has produced a much clearer picture of the tissue, with increased clarity of recognition of the silver grains.

Colour pictures and transparencies may be obtained by precisely the same methods that have been outlined above the monochrome. The trick of shortening the transmitted light exposure of a double-exposure picture to half its normal length will obviously result in some distortion of colour in the final picture. But, in an autoradiograph, the precise reproduction of colour in the specimen is normally of secondary importance to the clear demonstration of the distribution of silver grains. In colour pictures, it may be a help to make the silver grains some brightly contrasting colour. This can easily be done by putting a colour filter in the incident illuminator. This trick may be very helpful if many of the grains are over unstained areas of autoradiograph, and do not show up very clearly as bright specks.

THE IMPLICATIONS OF DARK-FIELD VIEWING FOR
AUTORADIOGRAPHIC TECHNIQUES

The use of dark-field illumination for viewing nuclear emulsions is not new. Walmsley and Makower[2], in 1914, published pictures of α tracks taken by this method. It has not achieved much popularity with autoradiographers, however, in spite of its obvious advantages for the design of photometric grain counters[3-5]. The reason for this is suggested in the discussion following Gullberg's paper[4].

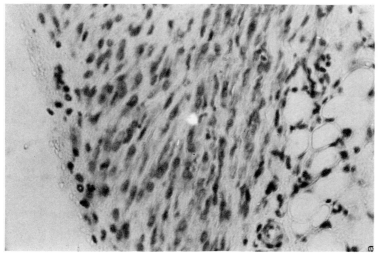

Fig. 50. A section through the site of repair of a severed tendon from a rat, 24 h after the administration of tritiated thymidine. *(a)* Photomicrograph taken with simultaneous use of transmitted and incident dark-field illumination, showing one heavily labelled cell in the centre of the field. *(b)* Same field viewed by incident light alone, to illustrate the very low background levels that can be obtained with correct development of the emulsion. Autoradiograph prepared with Ilford K2 emulsion. Leitz Utropak × 22 objective. (× 185) (Material prepared in collaboration with Dr. Chaplin)

If an autoradiograph, prepared for viewing by transmitted light alone, is examined by dark-field illumination, many tiny silver grains are often visible, constituting an embarrassingly high and hitherto unsuspected background.

The reason for this high background of tiny grains becomes clearer if one looks again at Fig. 4 (p.20). Here, identical autoradiographs were developed under constant conditions for increasing lengths of time. When viewed with dark-field illumination, the second picture is probably the best, with nice, clear grains and relatively low background. In the third picture, the small background grains characteristic of overdevelopment have begun to appear. Yet, seen by transmitted light, the silver grains are still too small for comfortable viewing in the second picture, and only just sufficiently developed in the third. Certainly, with transmitted light, there is no hint of gathering hordes of background grains in the latter photograph.

Objects too small to be seen with transmitted light may become visible in dark-field conditions. It follows that the optimum development time for a series of autoradiographs will be shorter if dark-field methods are to be used than if they will be viewed by transmitted light alone. Development must be stopped short before these tiny background grains begin to appear. Fig. 50 shows that, with correct development, the background levels with dark-field viewing can be very low indeed.

If, therefore, dark-field methods are to be used to view the finished auto-radiograph, the development schedule must be appropriate. In this sense, it is obviously important to match the autoradiographic technique to the system of microscopy available.

But I feel that the use of dark-field methods can and should have a greater impact on autoradiographic techniques than this. We have already seen that reducing the dimensions of the silver halide crystals in the emulsion layers of grain density autoradiographs can improve both the resolution and the efficiency considerably (p.55 and p.77). Dark-field microscopy enables one to take full advantage of this fact, for the small developed grains can still be adquately recognised. At the same time, it becomes possible to study fine cytological detail, even in a heavily labelled cell, for the grains are so small that they cover relatively little of the cell. Fig. 51 illustrates this point. This is an autoradiograph of the ovary of *Galago demidoffi*, after the injection of tritiated thymidine. The central cell is an oogonium in the prophase of mitosis. Even though there are many grains over the nucleus, the fine thread-like chromosomes can still be distinguished.

There are clear advantages to be gained from the intelligent use of dark-field methods of viewing, together with an emulsion with crystals of small diameter, such as the Ilford K or L series.

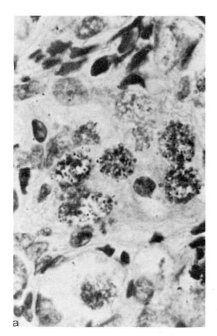

Fig.51. Photomicrographs of the same field of an autoradiograph taken by (a) transmitted, and (b) incident dark-field illumination. The material is a section of the ovary of the bushbaby (Galago demidoffi); 24 h after the injection of [³H] thymidine. The autoradiograph was prepared with Ilford K2 emulsion, and the grain size kept small by use of a short development time. In spite of the high grain densities over these 5 labelled oogonia, they can be seen to be in mitotic prophase. (× 720) (Material prepared in collaboration with Dr. J. Ioannou)

PHOTOMICROGRAPHY IN TRANSMITTED LIGHT

In spite of my obvious preference for dark-field methods of photomicrography, it is still quite possible to make a satisfactory record of many autoradiographs by the use of conventional optical systems and transmitted light.

Variations on this method have been described by several authors, to try and avoid some of the difficulties inherent in the technique. An effect rather similar to dark-field incident lighting combined with transmitted light can be obtained with phase contrast, if the tissue is accurately focused rather than the silver grains: the latter appear as an overfocused phase image, rather brighter than the underlying tissue[6].

The problem of the visibility of the underlying specimen is acute in squash preparations of chromosomes[7]. Several methods have been proposed to improve the chances of identifying the chromosomes below the silver grains. After photography of the autoradiograph, the silver grains may be removed with iodine and potassium iodide, followed by hypo treatment. After further staining, the same areas of specimen may be found, and the chromosomes alone photographed[8]. Alternatively, the Feulgen stained chromosomes may be photographed before autoradiography, and then again afterwards[9].

THE VIEWING AND PHOTOGRAPHY OF TRACK AUTORADIOGRAPHS

Dark-field techniques are difficult to use successfully with thick emulsions. So much of the incident light is scattered in the upper layers of the emulsion that silver grains more deeply placed do not appear bright, and the background against which they are viewed is not black. Occasionally, it may be possible to use dark-field methods with track autoradiographs of carbon-14 or sulphur-35 where the emulsion layer is about $20\,\mu$ thick (Fig. 52). Similarly, α tracks can be recorded satisfactorily in a relatively thin emulsion layer, and dark-field techniques can be used to photograph them (Figs. 5 and 6).

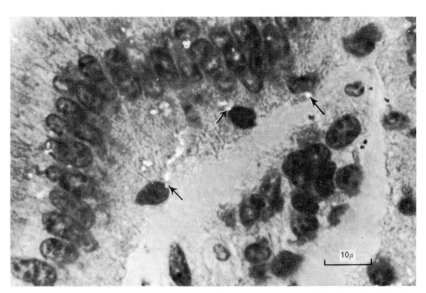

Fig.52. A section of the small intestine of a mouse, killed 1 h after the injection of [^{35}S] sulphate. The autoradiograph was prepared with a $25\,\mu$ layer of Ilford G5 emulsion. β Tracks can be seen entering the emulsion at the nuclear membranes of three adjacent epithelial lymphocytes (see arrows). Section stained with Harris' haematoxylin and photographed with a double-exposure technique, using a Leitz Ultropak × 100 objective. (× 1300) (From Darlington and Rogers, *J. Anat.,* 100 (1966) 813)

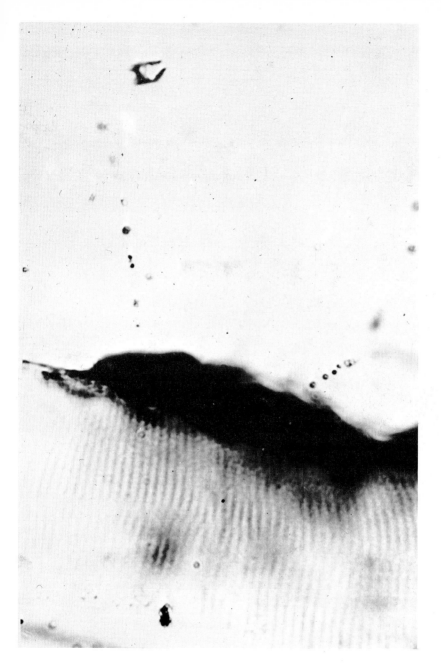

Fig.53. A photomicrograph of a darkly stained endplate on a single muscle fibre, obtained by microdissection from the sternomastoid muscle of a mouse. The endplate was treated with [^{32}P]DFP, and autoradiographed with a 60 μ layer of Ilford G5 emulsion. Two β tracks can be seen entering the emulsion from the endplate. Leitz KS × 100 objective. (× 1300) (From Rogers *et al., Nature,* 210 (1966) 1003)

References p. 164

With emulsion layers thicker than about 20 μ, however, it is virtually impossible to get a reasonable dark-field picture. Track autoradiographs are therefore usually viewed by transmitted light alone. This makes desirable the use of an emulsion with a fairly large crystal size. Since most of the quantitative data on the characteristics of β particle tracks in nuclear emulsion have been obtained from Ilford G5, this is probably the most convenient choice.

β Track autoradiographs remain extremely difficult to photograph. Fairly high magnifications are needed to see the silver grains clearly, and the tracks climb and dip in the emulsion in such a way that only short lengths of track can usually be seen in any one focal plane. This is particularly true if the emulsion has been reswollen prior to microscopy (p.322). It often pays to prepare special slides for microphotography. These should be exposed for longer than is usual, in order to collect a relatively high track density around the source. Instead of reswelling the emulsion in glycerol, it should be dehydrated prior to mounting under a coverglass in the normal way. In this way, the chances of finding several tracks in the same focal plane as the source will be increased. Even then, only relatively short lengths of track can usually be included in the photograph (Fig. 53).

For track autoradiographs that have been reswollen for microscopy to thicknesses of 60 μ or more, special objectives with a long working distance are usually needed, such as the Leitz KSX53 and KSX100 oil-immersion objectives. Most manufacturers produce objectives of this type.

REFERENCES

1   A.W. Rogers, *Sci. Tech. Inform.,* 1 (1965) 62.
2   H.P. Walmsley and W. Makower, *Proc. Phys. Soc. (London),* 26 (1914) 261.
3   J.E. Gullberg, *Exptl. Cell Res.,* Suppl. 4 (1959) 222.
4   P.P. Dendy, *Phys. Biol. Med.,* 5 (1960) 133.
5   A.W. Rogers, *Exptl. Cell Res.,* 24 (1961) 228.
6   D.E. Schlegel and G.A. de Zoeten, *J. Cell Biol.,* 33 (1967) 728.
7   D.M. Prescott and M.A. Bender, in D.M. Prescott (Ed.), *Methods in Cell Physiology,* Vol. 1, Academic Press, New York/London, 1964.
8   A. Fröland, *Stain Technol.,* 40 (1965) 41.
9   M. Callebaut and P. Demalsy, *Stain Technol.,* 42 (1967) 227.

CHAPTER 10

The Collection of Data from Autoradiographs

Most scientific experiments, whatever their initial aims, end up with some unfortunate sitting down to measure something. Autoradiography is no exception. In this chapter we will examine the various properties of nuclear emulsions that can conveniently be measured, and how they are related to the radiation dose to which the emulsion layer has been exposed. The methods available at the present time for collecting data from autoradiographs will then be discussed in detail. The problems of selecting appropriate areas for measurement and of interpretation of the data will be considered in Chapter 11.

THE RESPONSE OF NUCLEAR EMULSIONS TO RADIATION

When a volume of nuclear emulsion is exposed to β particles, a number of silver halide crystals form latent images which, on subseqent development, are converted into metallic silver grains. This basic response of the emulsion to radiation bears a defined relationship to the number of β particles entering it. The emulsion response can be looked at in many ways: the number of silver grains produced, the mass of developed silver per unit volume, the transparency or blackening of the emulsion are all examples of measurable parameters that will change as a result of exposure to radiation. Which parameters can be conveniently measured, and how are they related to radiation dose?

(a) Grain number

This is probably the most obvious and basic change in an emulsion exposed to radiation, and grain counting has for years been the most widely used method of assessing the radiation dose.

The relationship between radiation dose and number of grains per unit volume of emulsion has been investigated by Goldstein and Williams[1], amongst others. It is not a direct and linear relationship, but a logarithmic one. As the number of β particles entering the emulsion increases, the increase in grain number becomes less and less. Two factors are responsible for this. The first is that as the radiation dose increases the probability of silver halide crystals being hit more than once also increases, and a crystal hit three times by separate β particles can only produce one developed grain. The second factor is that the recognition and counting of silver grains become very difficult at high radiation doses, adjacent grains overlapping and even fusing during development.

If one plots the grain density produced in a given autoradiographic system against the density of radioactive disintegrations in the source, the first part of this logarithmic curve can be approximated to a straight line. In other words, up to a limiting grain density, grain density can be considered directly proportional to radioactivity. This limit is reached when the probability of multiple hits on single crystals becomes unacceptably high, or the developed grains are so closely packed that counting becomes impossible. Both of these factors are related to the size of the undeveloped crystals in the emulsion: the smaller the crystal diameter, the higher the grain densities that will still be proportional to radioactivity.

We have seen (p.79) that multiple hits on crystals can be ignored up to the point where 10% of the available crystals have already been hit. For practical purposes, only the monolayer of crystals nearest the source is "available" to the β particles of tritium. Although for isotopes of higher energy crystals in many layers above the first will be "available", at grain densities higher than one-tenth of the crystals in a packed monolayer, the chances of grains overlapping or fusing during development become so high that it is advisable to make this the upper limit of density for grain counting. So, with Ilford L4 emulsion, where a packed monolayer contains between 45 and 50 crystals per square micron, grain number can be considered proportional to radiation dose up to about 5 grains per square micron. With Ilford G5, the corresponding limit would be 1.5 grains per square micron.

There have been attempts to calculate or measure "coincidence coefficients" for grain density, which would enable one to correct for the non-linearity of grain number and radiation dose[2]. In practice, however, the problems of reproducible grain counting by direct visualisation in the microscope become so great at these high grain densities that it is better to choose some other emulsion response to measure.

As a means of measuring the density of β particles entering the emulsion, then, the grain density may be considered as directly proportional up to limits corresponding to one-tenth the density of undeveloped crystals in a packed monolayer of the emulsion. In this range, counting should not present great problems. Obviously, counting of individual grains can only be done at sufficiently high magnifications for the grains to be recognised. Each counting area will necessarily be rather small with the nuclear emulsions, and large areas can only be examined by repeated sampling. This is not a severe restriction in most histological experiments where sources of cellular dimensions are being studied, since the grain densities often vary abruptly within distances of $10-20\,\mu$, and small counting areas positioned over many cells of the selected type have to be examined in any case to sample a cell population. Where relatively extended uniform sources are being autoradiographed, however, the necessity to work at high magnification and make repeated samples may be avoided by choosing some other parameter of the emulsion response to measure.

(b) Track number

The grain density mentioned above may be proportional to the number of β particles entering the emulsion, but it is often extremely difficult to determine the number of β particles responsible for a given number of grains. Many factors can influence the efficiency of an autoradiograph (see Chapter 5), and it may not be possible to calculate the absolute efficiency of recording, or to prepare standard sources which correspond accurately enough with the experimental ones.

If an isotope of maximum energy equal to or higher than carbon-14 is used, a sufficient percentage of the β particles entering a thick emulsion layer will give rise to recognisable tracks for these to be made the basis of data collection.

There will be few applications for which track autoradiography offers clear advantages, and these are discussed in more detail in Chapter 17. The recognition and counting of tracks is slow relative to grain counting, and it becomes very difficult and inaccurate at high track densities. In fact, the range of radiation doses in which track counting is reliable is much shorter than for grain counting. The limits for carbon-14 and sulphur-35 are reached when 10 tracks or so start at one surface of the emulsion within an area of 500 square microns: for the longer, straighter tracks of phosphorus-32, the corresponding figure is about 15 tracks per 500 square microns.

Within these limits, track counting is a precise and reproducible method of measuring the number of β particles entering the emulsion. As with grain counting, the counting areas will be fairly small as the emulsion must be viewed at a high enough magnification to recognise individual grains.

(c) The reflectance of the emulsion layer

We have seen in Chapter 9 that if an emulsion layer is viewed by dark-field incident light the silver grains reflect and scatter the light, appearing as bright specks on a black background (Fig. 47). Obviously this method of illumination can be used as a basis for recognising and counting the individual silver grains, and everything that was said above about grain number applies directly to this procedure. But it is also possible to measure the total light reflected by a given area of emulsion and to relate this to the radiation dose there[3]. In fact, the reflectance of a thin layer of a given emulsion is directly proportional to the grain density, as has been demonstrated by a number of authors[3,4,1]. So, as with measurements of grain density, the reflectance is a logarithmic function of the radiation dose, but may be approximated to a linear response over the first part of the curve[1]. The direct correspondence of reflectance to grain density has been shown to extend up to 7 grains per square μ for Kodak AR-10 (ref.2), which is higher by far than the upper limit of linearity between grain density and radiation dose, and higher also than the reproducible upper limit for visual grain counting.

Reflectance measurements are at their best with oil immersion objectives, and, as with the counting of silver grains, would seem to be most useful for fairly small measuring areas[5].

(d) Optical density

The presence of developed grains in a thin layer of emulsion reduces its transparency. From the early days of photography, measurements of some function of the transparency of film have been related to the exposure of the emulsion[6]. The transparency (T) is defined as the ratio between the light transmitted by the film and the light incident on the film: this ratio is only valid when the area of film measured has been uniformly exposed to light and uniformly processed, and is large relative to the size of the silver grains. Hurter and Driffield[7] defined the density as $\log(1/T)$, and demonstrated that it was proportional to the mass of developed silver per unit area for a given emulsion. Plotted against the logarithm of the exposure to light, density produces a curve (known as the H and D curve) which contains a long central linear portion[6]. Over a specific range, then, the density of a film is directly proportional to the logarithm of the light exposure.

The response of nuclear emulsions to β particles differs from that of photographic emulsions to light. This is due to the fact that a single hit by an electron will have a high probability of producing a developable latent image, whereas multiple hits by light photons are needed. With β particles, the density is proportional to the exposure at low densities[1,8], rather than to the logarithm of the exposure. This proportionality extends to considerably higher radiation doses than the approximately linear relationship between grain number and radiation dose[1]. It follows that density measurements on the emulsion layer provide satisfactory data over a much wider range of radiation doses.

Density measurements are quick and simple to make. They impose certain restrictions on the autoradiographic material, however. The measurements must be made at a magnification low enough to avoid resolving individual silver grains. The areas of emulsion chosen for measurement must be uniformly irradiated, so that sources that vary abruptly in radioactivity over very small distances should be autoradiographed in a way that averages out the radiation dose to the film over areas that are big enough for sensible measurements. Finally, the specimen must either be transparent (i.e. unstained), or separated from the emulsion layer during measurement.

In general, density is a useful parameter to choose when fairly large, homogeneous areas of emulsion are to be compared. It tends to be a difficult measurement to apply to sources of cellular dimensions, where the problems of relating source to emulsion are much more critical, and where the variations of radioactivity between cell and extracellular space, nucleus and cytoplasm, have been resolved by the autoradiograph.

(e) Other possible parameters of the emulsion response

Back in the last century, it was realised that the mass of developed silver per unit volume of emulsion could be related to the exposure of the film[7]. This parameter has not been utilised on more than an experimental scale for measuring the radiation dose to the emulsion. I have heard of a laboratory in which conversion of the developed silver to iodide, using iodine-131 in controlled conditions, was followed by the measurement of radioactivity in selected volumes of emulsion with a Geiger counter. The adsorption of labelled thiosulphate to the surface of freshly developed silver grains has been used in investigations into the photographic process itself[9].

The only excuse for mentioning the mass of developed silver in this context is the interesting possibility of working out a system for the rapid collection of data from electron microscope autoradiographs, utilising X-ray microanalysis for measuring the mass of silver present over different regions of the specimen.

When one comes to consider television image analysis systems and their place in the collection of data from autoradiographs, other parameters of the silver grains in the emulsion will have to be considered; but this rather specialised topic will be deferred to p.186.

MEASUREMENTS OF EMULSION RESPONSE

It is obvious that several responses of the emulsion to radiation can be observed. What methods are available for measuring these responses, and what factors might lead one to choose one method rather than another for a particular experiment?

VISUAL GRAIN COUNTING

Basically, this is a very simple process. The observer records the number of developed grains visible in the volumes of emulsion selected for study. Two problems require consideration. The first is one of deciding what is to be accepted as a silver grain. The second concerns practical planning, so that the best possible conditions are provided for the observer.

"The definition of a silver grain" may sound unreasonably academic. It is usually easy to reject specks of dust, or granular deposits from the histological stain on the basis of their appearance. The precise definition of a grain is nevertheless important.

At the end of its track (see p.39), a β particle loses energy more rapidly than it did earlier, and the silver grains it produces lie closer together and tend to be larger. These grains may even make contact in the course of development (see, for instance, Fig. 8), and it may be very difficult to decide whether a given blob of silver represents one large grain, or several smaller ones fused together. In fact, blob counting has replaced grain counting in some of the analyses of particle tracks by physicists. The β particles of tritium are an example of this rapid rate of energy loss by particles of very low energy, and it is a common observation that the grains produced by tritium are usually larger than the background grains on the same autoradiograph. One observer may feel each blob represents one grain: another may estimate that, since the larger blobs are twice as big as the average background grain, they probably represent two grains fused during development. There is no simple way of deciding which interpretation is correct. If counts by different observers are to be compared, it is best to agree on one or other definition before counting starts.

There is no reason why dark-field conditions should not be used for grain counting, provided the development routine has been appropriate (see Fig. 51, p. 161). In such a case, every grain that can be seen should be counted. It is impossible to discriminate successfully against the smaller grains, and only count the larger ones, as the distribution in grain size is continuous, and this type of decision introduces an unacceptably high element of subjectivity.

In deciding whether to plan for dark- or bright-field conditions, it should be remembered that the former give much lower light intensities than are usual in a well-lit laboratory. During the period of accommodation to darkness, the eye's threshold of recognition for silver grains must be expected to alter, and any interruption in counting will produce another period of accommodation, if the lighting in the room is very bright. If constant, subdued ambient lighting is not available, it may well be better to count grains by bright-field illumination.

The conditions for visual grain counting

With most observers, the reproducibility of their grain counts begins to fall off after the first hour, though the precise time relations of this effect obviously vary with the experience of the microscopist. Beginners may feel actual nausea, particularly if the work involves much scanning of the slide, with frequent movements of the microscope stage. Even with the most experienced grain counter, the accuracy of the counts will decrease if they are attempted for more than a few hours each day.

Perhaps the most tiring aspect of grain counting is the necessity to hold the head in a constant position relative to the microscope. Even when sleeping, we are always shifting around, and the constraint imposed by the need to keep the eyes level and still at the eyepieces of the microscope is physically wearing. A comfortable and relaxed position is quite essential. Many systems have been suggested to free the observer from this constraint while grain counting. Micou and Goldstein[10] thought it worthwhile to publish an account of a projected system for throwing the field of view on to a screen. Closed-circuit television has been used in the same way. Sometimes, photomicrographs are taken of each field, and the grains counted on the developed print[11] . All these methods extend the period of counting before fatigue begins to affect the results, and make it easier to employ personnel who have no training or experience in microscopy.

Whatever system of counting is chosen, it takes a certain time to adjust to the conditions of work. Freedom from interruption will give more reproducible counts, so that a quiet room with subdued lighting is obviously better than a busy and well-lit laboratory. Extending this principle further, two people can usually work faster and more accurately than one. The microscopist concentrates on the specimen itself, and the assistant records the counts. The need to write down each count before going on to the next can break the rhythm of work significantly. In one laboratory where physicists are carrying out particle track analysis, each microscope has a tape-recorder beside it, so that measurements and comments can be recorded without the observer taking his eyes from the microscope.

References p. 192

Decision-making should be reduced to a minimum while counting. The appropriate volumes of emulsion to be scanned should be determined in advance and translated into practical instructions before counting starts. "All cells of type A on a line from X to Y", or "All cells in the field of view at such-and-such settings of the microscope stage" should be counted, and these instructions strictly adhered to. Quite apart from the time spent in deciding whether to count grains over this cell or that one in the absence of such precise instructions, the subjective element introduced opens the way to the choice of "typical cells" to count, and makes the results as a whole suspect.

Similarly, the shape and size of the volume of emulsion to be examined around each cell should be predetermined. If this area is large or contains many silver grains, it should be subdivided by a grid in the eye-piece into smaller squares, and each square counted in turn, as with blood cell counting in a haemocytometer. Small tally counters are very useful if the numbers to be counted are higher than about 20.

Once the influence of external conditions on the accuracy and reproducibility of visual grain counts is realised, it is possible to plan the procedure in such a way that reliable results can be obtained fairly rapidly. Perhaps the most important single step is to arrange that grain counting is done in relatively short periods, with breaks for other work. In this way, all the counts can be obtained during the period of $1-2$ h when the observer is fresh.

TRACK COUNTING

This is inevitably a slower and more difficult task than grain counting. Tracks are three-dimensional, and each field chosen for examination must be scanned at many focal levels. The tracks themselves must be followed for some distance, to try and determine the direction of travel of the β particles, and to record their points of entry into the emulsion as precisely as possible.

Track counting requires a certain amount of experience, and it is not a good idea to turn over the task of track counting to an untrained person, whereas grain counting can be delegated with the minimum of explanation to anyone who is competent to use a microscope. When this has been said, it must also be admitted that many autoradiographers are unnecessarily frightened by the difficulties of track recognition. On several occasions, I have asked students to count tracks on material prepared with carbon-14, sulphur-35 or phosphorus-32; after half-an-hour of explanation and demonstration, their counts have been reasonably accurate and reproducible.

The characteristics of β particle tracks are dealt with in detail in Chapter 3 (p.35). Briefly, their chief characteristic is their variability. The distance between successive grains, the changes in direction, and the grain size vary in a disconcerting way, so that any statement about them only reflects the statistically probable behaviour of an idealised particle. High energy β particles, such as those from about 400 keV and upwards, tend to run in approximately straight or gently curving lines for considerable distances. The grains lie, on the average, about $2\,\mu$ apart in Ilford G5 emulsion[12], though there will be gaps of $4-5\,\mu$, and other regions where several grains lie more closely spaced. The majority of grains will be rather small under normal conditions of development. Below about 75 keV, either in the terminal part of the track of a higher energy particle or in the case of one with a low initial energy, the grains lie on the average $1\,\mu$ apart. The chances of a gap of more than $3\,\mu$ are quite low, and the grains in the terminal few microns of track may even fuse together. The grains themselves are larger than those usually found at higher energies. The track usually changes direction many times in the last $25\,\mu$, whereas abrupt changes of course, due to deflection of the β particle by an atomic nucleus, are generally much more widely spaced at higher energies (Fig. 8, p.37).

It is usual to define a β particle track as 4 or more silver grains in a row. It is clearly possible to arrange any 4 background grains in some sort of linear array. A track of only 4 grains, however, represents the terminal 10–20 keV from a β particle, and these grains one would expect to be large, and very closely spaced. If the ends of undoubted β particle tracks are used as a basis for comparison, it will be found, in any reasonably prepared material, that the chance of observing 4 background grains of comparable size and similar spacing is very low indeed.

δ Tracks often prove confusing. These are the tracks left by electrons that have been ejected from orbit by the passage of a particle through their parent atom. Fig. 14 (p.45) shows such a track taking origin from the long, straight track of a high energy cosmic ray. The only difference between a δ track and that of a β particle is the mechanism of production of the particle itself. If a track that resembles that of a typical β particle starts from another track, it should be considered a δ track, and not a β particle. In this case, the original track forks, with an angle of approximately 90 degrees between the two branches, both of which have typical terminal portions, with large grains closely spaced (Fig. 9, p. 38).

It may be possible to recognise and reject background tracks caused by β particles that did not arise from the source being studied. If the specimen is mounted on a glass slide, with a thick layer of emulsion over it, it is evident that tracks entering the emulsion from its upper surface must be considered as due to background particles. Background tracks may also be recognised if their length or grain number is greater than expected from the known characteristics of the isotope being used. Unless the emulsion layer has been accurately reswollen after processing to its thickness during exposure (p.317), the track length is not such a reliable guide to the initial energy of the particle as the number of grains in it. The equations relating initial energy to track length and grain number are given on pp.40, 41, 42 and are illustrated graphically in Figs.10–12. To give an example, the mean number of grains produced by a β particle of initial energy 155 keV in Ilford G5 emulsion is 74. There is a statistical scatter of grain numbers in each track around this mean figure, and tracks of up to 90 grains may be encountered from carbon-14 (E_{max}, 155 keV), but the probability of finding a track with more than 90 grains in it from this isotope is extremely low. If, therefore, one finds a track of 105 grains in an autoradiograph of carbon-14, it is reasonable to conclude that it is a background track.

Track counting with β particles is just about impossible to automate, because of the wide variety of track lengths and patterns that can occur with one isotope. It is slower and requires more patience and experience than visual grain counting. It is not unduly difficult, however, and it can become very precise and reproducible.

The most important single step in the technique of preparing track autoradiographs for microscopy is probably the reswelling of the shrunken emulsion layer immediately prior to mounting it under a coverglass (p.317). There are often many scattered background grains at the upper surface of the emulsion, and these are separated clearly from the specimen beneath the emulsion, by the process of reswelling. Tracks which cross in a hopeless tangle before reswelling can often be seen to pass each other at an appreciable distance after this step. The task of recognising and recording the tracks of β particles is considerably eased by this simple procedure.

PHOTOMETRIC MEASUREMENTS IN REFLECTED LIGHT

Gullberg[13, 14] was the first to devise a semi-automatic method of measuring grain densities using dark-field conditions to view the silver grains, but his was a scanning system, counting the individual bright specks produced by the silver grains. Rogers[3] described the first apparatus for measuring the light reflected by the silver grains, and showed that this gave an integrated value for the mean number of grains in the measuring field. Since then, several descriptions of the technique have come from Dörmer and his associates[2,4,15], it has been examined by Goldstein and Williams[1], and a recent discussion of its characteristics and limitations has been presented by Rogers[5].

Briefly, the autoradiograph is illuminated with a fine, narrow beam of light directed vertically downward on the emulsion through the objective lens itself. The light reflected by the metallic silver grains back through the objective is collected on the photocathode of a photomultiplier, and the current flowing through the photomultiplier generates a reading. Since the light on which the reading is based enters and leaves the upper surface of the emulsion without passing through the underlying specimen, a stained section can be used in contact with the emulsion without, in many cases, affecting the reading at all. A rather similar method described by Dendy[16] was based on substage dark-field illumination, but this has fewer applications, since the light has to traverse the specimen to reach the emulsion, introducing the possibility of variations in reading due to light absorption by the specimen.

We have seen above (p.167) that the reflectance of an area of emulsion is directly proportional to the grain count, after subtraction of machine background. This method, then, gives a reading that can be directly related to the radiation dose received by the emulsion layer, provided the number of developed grains per square micron does not exceed one tenth the number of undeveloped crystals per square micron of a densely packed monolayer. The method gives its best results with oil immersion objectives in the range of magnifications × 60 to × 105, and with measuring areas of 10–200 square microns. It is not affected by grain densities immediately outside the measuring area, so the method can be used in autoradiographs where grain densities vary over structures of cellular dimensions.

The speed of operation is obviously determined by the time necessary to find the next object for measurement in the specimen. With biological specimens of reasonable complexity, 200 measurements per hour can be made without strain[5], representing a considerable mass of data in one working day. With suitably prepared material, this method of data collection offers many advantages over the much slower visual grain counting.

(a) The apparatus needed for photometric measurements

The most important single step in making reflectance measurements is to obtain the best possible conditions of dark-field illumination, with bright, clear silver grains on a black background (Fig. 54c). The two types of illuminating system available have been discussed in Chapter 9, and illustrated in Fig. 48. The first, providing a convergent cone of light entering the emulsion from a condenser system surrounding the objective lens itself, gives a good dark-field picture, but has the great disadvantage that it is not possible to limit the area illuminated by means of a field diaphragm. Silver grains are not plane mirrors,

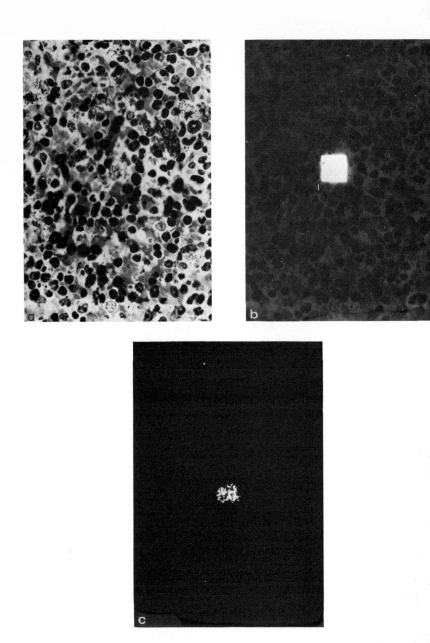

Fig.54. Three photomicrographs of the same field of an autoradiograph of mouse spleen following an injection of [^{3}H] uridine, to illustrate steps in the setting up of a photometric grain counter. (*a*) The section is viewed by transmitted light and the area selected for measurement is centred in the field. *(b)* The diaphragm defining the area from which light will be collected by the photocathode is matched in shape, size and position to the area illuminated by the incident beam. (*c*) Viewed by incident light only, an integrated measurement is taken of the light reflected by the measuring area. (× 820)

but coiled masses of filamentous silver (Fig. 2), and they scatter and reflect light in every direction, behaving as point sources of light in this dark-field illumination. Adjacent silver grains can thus illuminate each other with light scattered in the plane of the emulsion layer, and also, since the emulsion after processing is never completely clear optically, produce a certain amount of background glare from the surrounding gelatin. With the convergent cone method of lighting, reflectance measurements from small areas of emulsion without a single silver grain will vary considerably with the number of developed grains immediately outside the measuring area.

This light scattered from outside the measuring area can be avoided if the emulsion outside the measuring area is not illuminated, and this can only be done with the vertical incident system of lighting, which permits control of the diameter of the illuminating beam with a field stop. This system, in which the light travels to the specimen through the objective lens itself, is essential if reflectance measurements are to be made from chosen small areas of emulsion within a specimen of varying radioactivity. Obviously, the convergent cone system can be used for special situations where the grain densities surrounding each measuring area are always uniform: smears of cells, widely separated by emulsion with background grain densities only, might be examined in this way.

Most manufacturers of microscopes provide vertical incident illuminators that are suitable. It is important to ensure that the field stop can close far enough to produce an illuminated area the same size as the measuring area that will be required. The Leitz Pol-Opak illuminator has the most convenient diaphragm system I have seen from this point of view, giving rectangular or circular areas of illumination down to 1 μ diameter.

The light source must be well stabilised, so that variations in light output do not introduce errors into the measurements of light reflected. This can be cheaply and conveniently done by a constant voltage transformer and a stepped transformer providing current to the light source at reproducible levels. For measurements in reflected light, even with the simultaneous use of colour filters on the incident and reflected light paths, I have found a 30 W tungsten light source adequate. If polarised light is to be used[17] (p.182), it is better to go to a 100 W source. Since the light output and colour temperature of the source will vary for some time after first switching on, it is better to allow the light source a warm-up period of 20–30 min before starting to make measurements.

The area for measurement is identified and centred by the microscopist, who may need transmitted light to view the stained section. The transmitted light must be cut off, and the reflected light picture focused, before the reflected light is switched over to the photomultiplier. The microscope head should present all the light entering the objective lens either to the eyepieces or to the photomulti-plier tube. Systems that give a partial separation of light, permitting observation of the specimen during the act of measurement, should be avoided. The light intensities reflected by a few silver grains are very low, and it is a mistake to reduce them still further by diverting a fraction of the light to the eyepieces, while light entering the system through the eyepieces of the microscope may affect the measurement.

It is possible to use the objective lens as a simple projection device, throwing the light from the silver grains on the photocathode without an intervening lens system.[3] It is also possible to image the light on the photocathode by a lens system similar to an eyepiece, and introduce a diaphragm to define the measuring area accurately. In the first case, the measuring area can only be defined by the field diaphragm on the illuminator; in other words, the area of emulsion illuminated becomes the measuring area. With the second, more complicated system, it is necessary to match the shape, size and position of the field diaphragm (defining the area of emulsion illuminated) with that of the diaphragm in front of the photomultiplier (which defines the area of emulsion from which light is accepted by the photocathode). The second system does reduce the scattered light reaching the photocathode, improving the signal-to-noise ratio. If there is any doubt about the uniformity of response of the photocathode from one point on its surface to another, it is advisable to place a diffusing screen between the second diaphragm and the photocathode.

Many microphotometers are commercially available which can do the job required by reflectance measurements. The one in use in my laboratory at present is a Photovolt model 520-M (Photovolt Corp., New York), which has about the right sensitivity. A full scale deflection on the most sensitive range corresponds to 5×10^{-6} foot-candle, or 0.01 microlumen.

This, then, completes the list of the basic equipment needed for reflectance measurements: in my case, at present, it comprises a Lietz Ortholux microscope with a Pol-Opak illuminator, and a 30 W tugsten bulb, which is stabilised with a constant voltage transformer. An FS trinocular microscope head carries an MPV microphotometer attachment with Photovolt 520-M photometer. The apparatus is not expensive, costing less than £ 2,000 at present prices.

It is obviously possible to increase the sophistication of the apparatus in many ways. A higher intensity light source may be needed if polarised light is to be used (p.182)[17]. More elaborate stabilisation of the light source is possible. The Leitz Ploem illuminator for fluorescence work can be used instead of the Pol-Opak type[18]. More sophisticated photometers are available giving digital print-out facilities. Clarkson and Sanderson[19] use a stage drive to get traces of grain density across their specimens, with a pen-recorder output to the photometer. A stage drive has even been combined with an X–Y plotter and desk computer, to print out the co-ordinates and grain count of labelled cells[20]. There is no limit to the degree of elaboration possible on the basic design.

It is quite possible, incidentally, to make reflectance measurements with a phase-contrast objective in place of the usual objective for reflected light. This may be useful in permitting one to view the specimen unstained, by transmitted light phase contrast, before turning to incident dark-field lighting for the measurement of reflectance.

(b) The characteristics of a photometer measuring light reflected by silver grains

Goldstein and Williams[1] have estimated that silver grains reflect only about 3% of the light falling on them. The light intensities to be measured are low. It makes sense to instal the photometer in reasonably constant, low light levels, to reduce the chance of variations in ambient light affecting the readings. A suitably prepared autoradiograph (p.181) is placed on the microscope stage, and a heavily labelled area found. The transmitted light is switched off, the dark-field picture focused, and the reflected light directed to the photomultiplier. By adjusting the current to the light source and the high voltage supply to the photomultiplier, conditions of measurement are found which give a satisfactory reading, with a sufficient difference between the heavily labelled area and one with no silver grains. At the same time, the field diaphragm is adjusted to the size required for the measuring area for that particular set of readings, and the diaphragm in front of the photomultiplier is adjusted to correspond to the field diaphragm in size, shape and position. When these adjustments are completed, the photometer is left for a further 10 min or so to stabilise. With every series of measurements, it is essential to have a reference standard which can be examined before, after and at intervals during the series of measurements, to check that variations in operating conditions are not occurring. I use an autoradiograph of a section of labelled methacrylate for this purpose, but any standard which gives reproducible results can be used.

As with visual grain counting, decisions should be made about the choice of areas for measurement before starting the series. With the autoradiographs available, and the instructions about finding the next area to hand, the microscopist finds and centres the appropriate areas, switching off the transmitted light to focus the silver grains before sending the reflected light to the photometer (Fig. 54). The vertically incident light should be left on throughout the whole series of measurements.

In these conditions, the photometric readings are directly proportional to the number of silver grains in the measuring area (Fig. 55), above a level, the machine background, which is mainly due to light scattered by various optical interfaces in the system, and by the gelatin itself. This machine background can be found by making several measurements from areas with no visible silver grains in them, or simply summed with the autoradiographic background by taking measurements from suitably chosen areas in the autoradiograph.

Not only is the mean photometric reading proportional to the mean visual grain count, but the use of the photometer does not add to the variance of measurements about the mean. England and Rogers[21] have shown that the Poisson distribution, which describes the variability in the rate of radioactive disintegration within the source, is reflected in the visual grain counts and the photometric readings taken from over a uniformly labelled source (Fig.59).

Large silver grains reflect more light than small ones. In any series of measurements involving large numbers of grains, this variation evens out. Grains deep in the emulsion layer may reflect significantly less light than grains at the surface, particularly if the gelatin is not clear, or has been stained. With emulsion layers $3-4\,\mu$ thick during exposure, the developed grains after dehydrating the processed emulsion ought to lie within $1\,\mu$ of the section, and there is seldom a serious problem from the depth of the grains in the emulsion.

The observed reading varies with the focus of the microscope, but does not vary very abruptly (Fig. 56). At about the level where the majority of silver

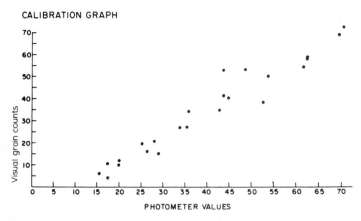

Fig.55. A graph relating the number of developed grains in the measuring area, determined by visual counting, to the photometer reading from the same area. Above a given value, the photometric measurement is directly related to visual count over a considerable range of grain densities.

Position	Reading	Position	Reading
1	8.8 units	6	9.4
2	9.0	7	9.7
3	9.0	8	10.1
4	9.4	9	9.8
5	9.4	10	10.0
		11	10.1

Fig.56. Photometric measurements of grain density taken from a single field of Ilford K2 emulsion over a cell labelled with tritiated thymidine. Each reading from 1 onwards was taken with the objective 1μ nearer the slide. All the silver grains were in focus visually between positions 5 and 6. It is clear that the effects of gross alterations in focus are relatively slight, and that all readings taken with one or more grains sharply in focus visually are likely to be the same. (From Rogers, 1961)

grains are in focus visually, the reading reaches a maximum. I have found readings to be very reproducible when taken with the grains in focus as judged visually: it is possible to alter the focus until a maximum reading is obtained, and record this, but it is slower to work this way and the readings have been no different to those obtained by visual focusing, in our experience.

(c) Preparing autoradiographs for photometry in reflected light

The specimen can scatter and reflect light, and every care should be taken to reduce this source of error to a minimum. Clean working is essential in preparing the sections for autoradiography, and the processed emulsion should never be allowed to dry out or to acquire dirt on its surface. The processed emulsion can scatter light also. Dichroic fog, due to active developer present in the fixing solutions, must be avoided at all cost by an adequate stop bath and rinse. Fine particulate deposits in the emulsion can also result from decomposition of sodium thiosulphate in the fixing solution. Fresh fixing solutions should be used, and a definite improvement in the clarity of the processed emulsions may result from making up the 30% thiosulphate used for fixing in a buffer of the following composition: dissolve 2.2 g sodium sulphite ($7 H_2O$) in 100 ml water, add 0.46 ml of a solution of sodium hydrogen sulphite (spec. gravity 1.34) to a further 210 ml, and mix the two solutions.

Many stains fluoresce: eosin is a particularly bad example, giving a coloured glow from the specimen and emulsion in incident dark-field lighting. We have found light staining with Harris' haematoxylin to be compatible with reflectance measurements, and to give very little trouble. If stain fluorescence is a problem, it may be reduced by illuminating and measuring in monochromatic light of a

Treatment	Mean photometric reading			
	Lumen	Glands	Stroma	Muscle
Ethyl oleate	1.09	0.81	0.35	1.87
Progesterone	0.74	−0.17	0.46	0.86
[³H] megestrol acetate	15.24	17.65	29.79	39.14

Fig.57. Photometric grain counts taken from sections of rat uterus that were non-radioactive, and similar sections from rats injected with [³H] megestrol acetate. Note the low values from the non-radioactive specimens, showing that light scattered by the sections, which were stained with Harris' haematoxylin, contributed very little indeed to the readings.

wavelength chosen to avoid the absorption and emission wavelengths of the stain involved.

In most experiments, there will be slight fluctuations in the machine background reading from slide to slide, and from place to place on a slide, but these should be so small relative to the readings from labelled areas that they can be ignored. Fig. 57 illustrates this point from a paper that relied heavily on photometric measurements[22].

Occasionally, there will be experiments where the light scattered in the absence of a silver grain varies significantly from area to area. Some tissue components, such as melanin granules, can be extremely troublesome. Goldstein and Williams[17] have shown that working with polarised light can reduce this source of background variation considerably.

(d) The development of autoradiographs for photometry in dark-field lighting

We have seen in Chapter 2 that the number of grains over a labelled source is not critically dependent on the conditions of development. Fig. 3 illustrates the plateau in grain density that is found with increasing times of development. Unfortunately, when one measures the light reflected by the emulsion rather than the grain number, no such plateau appears (Fig. 58). With increasing development, the grains have grown larger or more reflectile. This makes comparisons between batches of autoradiographs difficult by photometric measurements, as the ordinary, rather sloppy method of developing autoradiographs on the bench at room temperature does not give adequate control of development, or sufficiently reproducible reflectivity per silver grain from one day to the next.

A specially designed developing tank is available from John Varney and Co., Blidworth, Mansfield, Notts., which greatly improves the reproducibility of processing. Temperature is closely controlled in all the solutions, and nitrogen burst agitation is used in the developer. With standard sections of labelled methacrylate autoradiographed and developed in this tank in separate experiments, the reproducibility of photometric measurement is excellent. If a really close correlation of photometric readings between different batches of auto-

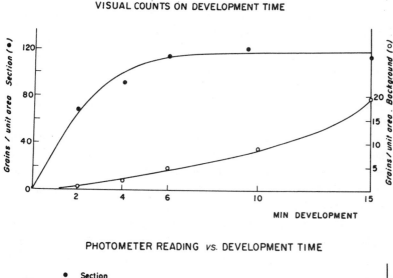

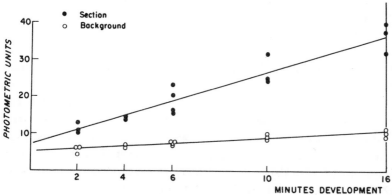

Fig.58. The effects of increasing development on visual grain density *(a)*, and on reflectance measurements in incident light *(b)*. The specimens were sections of [³H] methyl methacrylate, autoradiographed by dipping in Ilford L4 emulsion. (*a*) Note the long plateau in grain number that is found with visual grain counts. (*b*) Photometric readings, however, show no such plateau. With Ilford 1D-19 developer there appears to be a steady growth in size of the developed grains, and a consequential increase in their reflectivity, even though their number is constant. (From Rogers, 1972)

radiographs is essential, the exposure of some standard preparation on each occasion should provide a basis for accurate comparison.

Naturally, the development conditions chosen should be matched to the requirements of viewing the autoradiograph in dark-field lighting (see p.19 and Fig. 4). Overdevelopment causes the appearance of a second population of tiny silver grains through the emulsion, which can make measurements of reflectance quite meaningless.

(e) Summary of reflectance measurements as a means of data collection

The choice of reflectance as a parameter of emulsion response introduces technical difficulties which are not present when grain number is used — scattered light from specimen and emulsion, and the variation in grain size from batch to batch of autoradiographs, for instance. These difficulties can be overcome in the preparation and microscopy of the specimen in nearly every case.

For very low grain densities, below 5 per measuring area, visual grain counting is as rapid as photometry in incident light, and more accurate, since at this level variation in grain size and in the reflectance of the specimen can swamp the variations in grain density. For very irregular sources, it may be simpler to count visually, since the photometer's counting area can only be rectangular or circular, and it may be difficult to devise a large enough area of simple geometry to fit inside the source.

These are exclusions which affect only a very small percentage of experiments, however. Counting over nucleus and cytoplasm of many mammalian cell types is quite feasible. If a nuclear profile is about 7μ in diameter, a counting area 6μ in diameter placed within it can contain over 120 developed grains with Ilford L4 emulsion and still be on the linear part of the curve relating grain density to radioactivity. Given preparations with a grain density that is sufficiently high — higher by a factor of two at least than material designed for visual grain counting — photometric measurement provides reliable results at a speed far higher than is possible with visual grain counting. The apparatus is not excessively expensive, and the techniques have been worked out in some detail already. As a method of data collection from high resolution autoradiographs at the light microscope level, it has a great deal to recommend it.

MEASUREMENTS OF OPTICAL DENSITY OF THE EMULSION

We have seen (p.168) that exposing a layer of nuclear emulsion to β radiation reduces its ability to transmit light, and the density of the layer is directly proportional to the radiation dose over a considerable range[1,8]. Since measurements of optical density require the light to travel through the emulsion, the specimen must either be completely transparent, or separated from the emulsion before measurement. For a valid estimate of radiation dose, the optical density must be measured over an area of emulsion uniformly exposed to radiation, at a magnification that does not resolve individual silver grains. In short, density measurements are best suited to measuring areas rather larger than are customary for visual or reflectance measurements.

(a) Apparatus needed for density measurements

Goldstein and Williams[1] have examined the Joyce—Loebl microdensitometer and the Vickers flying-spot microscope, and we have extensively used a microscope fitted with a Photovolt 520-M photometer in this laboratory. As with ·reflectance measurements, the basic apparatus is simple, and capable of almost infinite elaboration to meet particular needs.

Silver grains both reflect and scatter light. If the light transmitted by the film in a direction perpendicular to its surface only is collected and measured, the density value calculated from this is known as the specular density. If all the light emerging from the surface of the film, regardless of its direction relative to the film, is collected, the diffuse density may be calculated[6]. In many cases, the measurement made in an autoradiograph will be a sort of hybrid between specular and diffuse: this does not affect the validity of the measurements, but it is important to use the identical conditions of microscopy if comparable results are to be obtained on some later occasion. Density measurements based on an objective of a given numerical aperture are not immediately comparable with those made with another objective of different aperture, since, out of the total light transmitted diffusely by the film, the proportion collected will be different in each case.

The conditions of illumination of the emulsion are also important, and the apparent density will be different if a wide angle of illuminating beam is used rather than a narrow, finely collimated pencil of light. Density measurements also vary somewhat with the wavelength of light used.

Any apparatus for this type of work must have the following features. The light source must be stabilised and of reproducible colour. The measuring area must be evenly illuminated by a beam of reproducible geometry. The light entering the measuring system should be specular, diffuse, or some fully reproducible combination of the two. The photometer should be of appropriate sensitivity, and preferably be calibrated directly in density units. (See also NOTES ADDED IN PROOF, p. 360)

(b) The apparatus in use

In any series of measurements, three types of standard are advisable. The first, a completely transparent emulsion layer, is used to calibrate the zero setting on the photometer scale. The second is an emulsion fully blackened by β radiation, used to calibrate the infinite density setting. The third is a standard preparation of intermediate density for reference purposes. When the size and shape of the measuring area have been determined, usually by a diaphragm just in front of the photomultiplier tube of the photometer, these three standards are examined, and the photometer is calibrated ready for use.

It is a good idea to make the measuring area smaller than the uniformly blackened area of emulsion over the source. If the measurement includes an element of diffuse light, the region immediately around the measuring area can contribute significantly to the reading.

If the biological source has local variations in radioactivity within the chosen measuring area, these can often be averaged out in terms of blackening of the overlying emulsion by choosing an autoradiographic technique of low resolution. If, for instance, one is interested in the rate of protein synthesis within a given part of the brain in animals treated with various drugs, it is clear that there will be differences within that area between neurones and glia, between cell bodies and fibres, between nucleus and cytoplasm. It is possible to obtain uniform blackening of the emulsion with sections labelled with carbon-14, autoradio-graphed against X-ray film, in spite of these local variations, and this type of material will favour rapid measurement and give a valid integrated reading for a fairly large area, which may be very difficult to extract from a high resolution autoradiograph with tritium.

Optical density measurements are quick and simple to make, and the results are proportional to radiation dose up to higher limits than with grain density or reflectance measurements[1]. They are best used with fairly large measuring areas, at least 50μ in diameter. They are applicable to whole-body autoradiographs, for instance, or to any other macroscopic specimen. At higher resolution, such measurements have been used in the study of amino acid incorporation in the brain in unstained sections viewed by phase contrast microscopy[23], and in the study of sugar absorption by the intestine[24]. Like photometric measurements of reflectance, optical density measurements provide a rapid and accurate means of collecting data from autoradiographs, in suitably prepared material.

IMAGE ANALYSIS BY TELEVISION SCANNING SYSTEMS

A television camera effectively scans the picture presented to it in a series of parallel lines, converting the variations in light intensity along each line into electrical signals. If such a scan line across a picture is broken down into a large number of individual points separated from their neighbours by small gaps in the line, the screen becomes a very large number of picture points, each of which generates a signal proportional to the light intensity there. Since these points are scanned in a regular sequence, we now have a series of electrical signals representing the picture, and these signals can be processed electronically in varied ways with great speed and precision. Television systems for analysing images are available from Metals Research, of Cambridge, who manufacture the Quantimet 720, and from E. Leitz, of Wetzlar, who market the Classimat. Both systems have the same basic design. The field of view of the microscope is converted into picture points, and the operator sets a level above which the signal from a picture point (that is, the light intensity at that place in the picture) becomes recognised by the computer circuitry of the system. At the very simplest level, the system can count all the picture points brighter than a given intensity: with more sophisticated circuitry, the points brighter than the preset level can be recombined into areas of brightness, and the number and size of these areas can be found. Obviously, once the initial data on the light intensity at each picture point are available as an electrical signal, many different computer functions can be designed to analyse various features of the initial image.

Clearly this approach has tremendous possibilities in data collection from autoradiographs. Little has been published on it to date, but work is proceeding

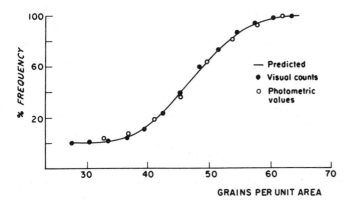

Fig.59.   The results of visual and photometric estimates of grain density from the layer of L4 emulsion over a section of uniformly labelled [³H] methyl methacrylate. A cumulative distribution curve built up from 200 counting areas over the section shows a close correlation with the curve predicted from the Poisson theory, whether visual or photometric grain counts are used. (From England and Rogers, 1970)

fast in several laboratories to explore the possible applications of this new system to autoradiography.

If one starts with transmitted light through an emulsion layer, viewed at relatively low magnification so that individual silver grains are not resolved, it is possible to use a machine like the Quantimet 720 as a sort of glorified densitometer[25] . It does not at present measure the light intensity at each picture point, and give an integrated "densitometric" value for the area scanned. It counts instead the number of picture points brighter than a preset level. If the preset level is adjusted so that all the points scanned are just counted in a background area of emulsion, then moving the emulsion to an area that is relatively blacker will result in fewer points being counted. We have found that the logarithm of the number of points counted in these circumstances is inversely proportional to the radiation dose to the emulsion, over a range of values that is long enough to be useful. At the simplest level, then, it is possible to use this machine as a glorified densitometer, although the parameter being measured is not strictly the same as optical density.

But this is really using a sledgehammer to crack a peanut. A higher magnifi-

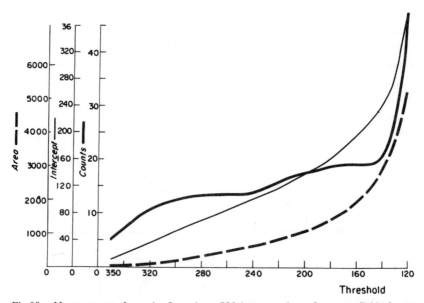

Fig.60. Measurements from the Quantimet 720 image analyser from one field of an autoradiograph containing few grains, with varying levels of detection threshold. The area of silver grains detected varies continuously with threshold level, as does the intercept, or vertical height of the detected images of the grains. The counts of silver grains show a plateau, however, at a value slightly lower than the visual grain count from the same area.

cations, it should be possible to measure the emulsion response precisely in much smaller areas. A good start on this problem has been made by Prensky[26], using the earlier Quantimet "B", and Rogers and Darrah[25], with the Quantimet 720. If one considers a field with a few silver grains in it, each separate and distinct, the Quantimet can be used to count the number of grains, to measure their area, or to measure their intercept (a factor related to their projected circumferences). But, owing to the imperfections of the optical system, each grain appears to the television camera as a dense spot surrounded by a halo of lower density, merging with the rest of the picture at its outer rim. The area occupied by silver grains will vary critically with the setting of the detection level of the machine, as will the intercept measurement. In fact, if one plots area and intercept against detection level for such a field, there is no obvious point on the curves at which measurements could be made (Fig. 60). On the other hand, a count of dense features plotted against detection level shows a reasonably long plateau which corresponds to the visual grain count. If one now examines a field with very many grains in it, the area and intercept measurements are still critically dependent on detection level, but now the counts are also. At low detection settings, only the densest silver grains will be recognised. At higher settings, progressively more and more of the grains will be recognised, but each grain will appear to the machine as a larger object, with a higher probability of touching or overlapping the image of an adjacent grain. When the images of two grains touch, the machine counts them as one feature. So, at high grain densities, a graph of grain count against detection level produces a simple peak.

The choice of an appropriate detection level becomes more difficult the higher the density of developed grains, and the bigger their size. Rogers and Darrah[25] examined a series of layers of Ilford G5 emulsion with increasing grain densities, and plotted the grain density estimated by photometry against the Quantimet count: for each grain density, the detection level was separately adjusted, either to the centre of the plateau of counts against detection level at low densities, or to the peak of counts at higher densities. Up to a limiting grain density, the count was directly proportional to the photometric measurement (Fig. 61): above this density, it proved impossible to relate the Quantimet count to the photometric density in any sensible way.

So, up to a limiting grain density, the Quantimet count is directly proportional to the number of silver grains in the counting area. In a series of visual and Quantimet counts from the same material, it was soon seen that the latter counts were always lower than the visual, presumably owing to clumping of grains into single features. It seemed, however, that a constant factor governed the relationship in this experiment: multiplying the Quantimet counts by 1.2, converted them to the appropriate visual counts.

References p. 192

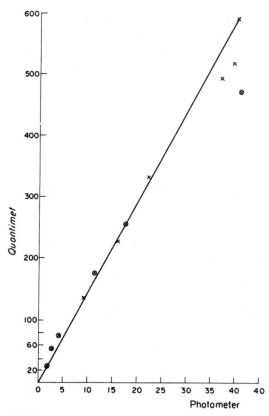

Fig.61. The reflectance of a series of autoradiographs, measured photometrically, is here compared to their grain density measured by the Quantimet 720 image analyser. A series of sections of [³H]methyl methacrylate was exposed to Ilford G5 emulsion for increasing lengths of time to produce a range of grain densities. Up to a limiting value, the Quantimet count is proportional to the photometric reading, and hence to the visual grain count. Above the limiting value, where the probability of grain images touching on the Quantimet screen becomes significant, the Quantimet count falls below the photometric reading.

The selection of an appropriate detection level is the major difficulty in using this machine at the present, and it is further complicated by the presence of a stained specimen, which provides varying densities across the screen against which the silver grains have to be detected. Prensky[26] worked with lightly stained smears of cells, viewed by transmitted light, and found the problems of detection level so severe that he devised a computer programme giving a visual readout next to the Quantimet screen for the calculated number of grains on the field, and adjusted the detection level until this number corresponded with a quick visual estimate of grain number. This problem is eased if one examines the autoradiograph in dark-field incident lighting, which effectively blacks out the stained section (Fig. 51). In a series of measurements of [³H] methionine uptake by areas of the brain,[27] we were able to avoid frequent changes of detection level by working with an Ultropak X75 oil immersion lens; and to demonstrate that each measurement was made at an appropriate setting by recording on three channels simultaneously, each working at a detection level 5 units higher than the channel below. In this situation, the count on each channel should be very nearly the same, if the middle channel is set at or near the optimum level (see Fig.60).

Since one is counting individual grains, the focusing of the field is critically important, and reproducibility of counting is favoured by having a flat upper surface to the section, and a thin emulsion layer. Since the count obtained is proportional to grain density only up to a rather low limiting figure, the exposure of the autoradiographs should be carefully controlled. Finally, since there is a certain amount of care required both in focusing and checking that the detection level is appropriate, the number of fields that can be measured in an hour is, in our hands, less than with the photometer. To get the best out of the system, the measuring area should be as large as possible, for, with low grain densities and small areas, visual counting is probably as quick. In the experiments mentioned above[27] , each area was 58 × 72 square microns, giving many grain counts of over 200 per field. In this situation, the use of the Quantimet enabled 10 days' work to accumulate data that would have taken over 2 months by visual counting.

These experiments represent only a beginning. As experience accumulates, the capabilities of this highly sophisticated machine will be exploited more and more fully for the collection of autoradiographic data. Mertz[28] has already shown that it is possible to differentiate between the larger silver grains caused by tritium and the rather smaller background ones, using the particle size analysis feature on the Quantimet. Television analysis systems are very expensive, perhaps ten times more so than photometers for reflectance measurements, but their potential is obviously very great, and is not yet being fully exploited in autoradiography.

To sum up, then, several options are open to the autoradiographer who wants quantitative data rapidly from his material, without the immense labour of protracted visual grain counting: reflectance measurements and optical densities, obtained either with a microdensitometer or a flying-spot microscope, are the main candidates. Together, they can cover most of the situations in which quantitative data are required. The ability to get accurate information more rapidly and more reproducibly than by visual counting has greatly extended the scope of experimentation possible in a single laboratory in a year, and permits one to carry out investigations at a speed that makes a significant contribution to the usefulness of autoradiography.

REFERENCES

1   D.J. Goldstein and M.A. Williams, *J. Microscopy*, 94 (1971) 215.
2   P. Dörmer, *Histochemie*, 8 (1967) 1.
3   A.W. Rogers, *Exptl. Cell Res.*, 24 (1961) 228.
4   P. Dörmer, W. Brinkmann, A. Stieber and W. Stich, *Klin. Wochenschr.*, 44 (1966) 477.
5   A.W. Rogers, *J. Microscopy*, 96 (1972) 141.
6   G.C. Farnell, in C.E.K. Mees and T.H. James (Eds.), *The Theory of the Photographic Process*, 3rd ed., Macmillan, New York, 1966.
7   F. Hurter and V.C. Driffield, *J. Soc. Chem. Ind. (London)*, 9 (1890) 455.
8   J.F. Hamilton, in C.E.K. Mees and T.H. James (Eds.), *The Theory of the Photographic Process*, 3rd ed., Macmillan, New York, 1966.
9   G.W.W. Stevens and P. Block, *J. Phot. Sci.*, 7 (1959) 111.
10 J. Micou and L. Goldstein, *Stain Technol.*, 34 (1959) 347.
11 K. Ostrowski and W. Sawicki, *Exptl. Cell Res.*, 24 (1961) 625.
12 H. Levi, A.W. Rogers, M.W. Bentzon and A. Nielsen, *Kgl. Danske Videnskab. Selskab, Mat.–Fys. Medd.*, 33 (1963) No. 11.
13 J.E. Gullberg, *Exptl. Cell Res., Suppl.*, 4 (1957) 222.
14 J.E. Gullberg, *Lab. Invest.*, 8 (1959) 94.
15 P. Dörmer and W. Brinkmann, *Acta Histochem., Suppl.* 8 (1968) 163.
16 P.P. Dendy, *Phys. Biol. Med.*, 5 (1960) 131.
17 D.J. Goldstein and M.A. Williams, *Proc. Roy. Microscop. Soc.*, 6 (1971) 142.
18 J. Combs, Personal communication.
19 D.T. Clarkson and J. Sanderson, *Proc. Roy, Microscop. Soc.*, 6 (1971) 136.
20 J. Bisconte, J. Fulcrand and R. Marty, *C.R. Soc. Biol.*, 162 (1968) 2178.
21 J.M. England and A.W. Rogers, *J. Microscopy*, 92 (1970) 159.
22 P.N. John and A.W. Rogers, *J. Endocrinol.*, 53 (1972) 375.
23 J. Altman, *J. Histochem. Cytochem.*, 11 (1963) 741.
24 W.B. Kinter and T.H. Wilson, *J. Cell Biol.*, 25 (1965) 19.
25 A.W. Rogers and H.K. Darrah, in preparation.
26 W. Prensky, *Exptl. Cell Res.*, 68 (1971) 388.
27 H.K. Darrah, P.C.B. MacKinnon and A.W. Rogers, in preparation.
28 M. Mertz, *Histochemie*, 17 (1969) 128.

CHAPTER 11

The Analysis of Autoradiographs

The analysis of an autoradiograph always involves measurement. The method of making the measurement may be relatively crude and insensitive, but even a statement like "The blackening over follicles of the thyroid gland is more intense than over skeletal muscle after an injection of radio-iodide" is based on a measurement of emulsion response in two areas, using the microscopist himself as a machine for estimating the degree of blackening. Clearly, the more carefully controlled the techniques employed, the smaller the differences in radioactivity that can be detected, and the more sensitive and precise the final measurement becomes.

The principles underlying these relative measurements are common to all the techniques of recording radioactivity. The samples to be compared must be presented to the recording device under identical conditions — in other words, the efficiency with which the isotope is measured must be the same for each sample. The observed counting rate must be corrected by subtracting the background count that would be found with an indentical but unlabelled source. The final counts from the samples will then be proportional to their radioactivity. With a Geiger tube or a scintillation counter, it may be fairly simple to ensure identical efficiencies for a series of samples and to find the background figure that is appropriate. Each sample in this case is usually considered to be homogeneous, and none of the samples can affect the recording device in any way except by its radioactivity, with the exception of quenching in liquid scintillation counting. But the preservation of inhomogeneity in the specimen is one of the most valuable attributes of autoradiographic techniques. A typical biological specimen contains sources that differ in size, in shape, and in geometrical relationship to the emulsion, so that it is often difficult, perhaps impossible, to record from different series of sources at the same efficiency. The very different efficiencies with which tritium may be recorded in cytoplasm, nucleus, and nucleolus of the same cell have already been referred to[1] (p.77).

Not only is it often necessary to compare sources which differ in their geometrical relationship to the emulsion, and hence in the efficiency with which their radioactivity is recorded, but each source may be able to affect the emulsion directly in a manner quite independent of its radioactivity. Figs. 30 (p.80) and 34 (p.97) illustrate the creation of artefactual silver grains over the source, and the failure to record latent images known to overlie the source, by the processes of positive and negative chemography respectively.

It is deceptively easy to count silver grains over a specimen. But if the grain density observed may reflect other factors than the radioactivity of the under-lying specimen, simple grain counts can only be usefully interpreted in the context of a suitably controlled experiment.

In short, there are many practical pitfalls in using nuclear emulsions to compare the radioactivity present in sources of cellular dimensions. The principal factors that control the efficiency of autoradiographic measurements have been dealt with at length in Chapter 5. Here, the problems that arise in making relative measurements will be discussed in a more practical fashion, in an attempt to indicate these pitfalls, and how they may be avoided.

FACTORS IN THE EMULSION THAT AFFECT RELATIVE
MEASUREMENTS

The emulsion variables that can affect the efficiency of an autoradiograph are discussed in Chapter 5. Some of them are briefly reviewed here, as a reminder that they can and do influence the observed emulsion response. They must therefore be controlled in the design of the experiment if differences in emulsion response are to be the basis of comparisons of radioactivity in the specimen.

(a) Variations in emulsion thickness
We have already seen (p.77) that in grain density autoradiographs, variations in emulsion thickness can produce considerable differences in efficiency. This effect has a profound influence on the selection of the technique to be used in an experiment that requires relative grain counts.

It is very difficult to produce a layer of liquid emulsion that is uniformly thick. Leblond, Messier and Kopriwa[2] have described attempts to do this, which, at best, seemed to give variations in thickness from 1−1.5 units. One has only to take several slides covered with liquid emulsion, and bring them out into the light, undeveloped, to become convinced of the lack of uniformity of their emulsion layers.

By contrast, the thickness of stripping film is very much more uniform, and, in some cases, this will be the technique of choice.

Two situations exist in which it is possible to exploit the many advantages of liquid emulsion techniques without this variation in emulsion thickness making it impossible to interpret the resulting grain counts. The first is when tritium is the isotope. In this case, it is quite simple to coat the specimen with a layer of emulsion thick enough to contain all the β particles emitted. $3\ \mu$ of emulsion during exposure are sufficient to do this. Provided that any variations in thickness are taking place above this depth, the effective thickness is determined by the maximum range of the β particles. The background count will still be roughly proportional to the emulsion thickness, but it should be possible to hold background to a low enough level for this source of error to be insignificant. A simple method for checking that the emulsion layer is thick enough is outlined on p. 304.

The second set of circumstances in which variations in emulsion thickness may be tolerated in making relative measurements occurs when small volumes of emulsion very close together are to be compared. The variations in thickness occur gradually with liquid emulsions that have been carefully applied, and there should be little difference between the thickness of two areas a few microns apart. Darlington and Rogers[3] took advantage of this in an experiment designed to test the ability of lymphocytes in the epithelium of the small intestine to incorporate sulphur-35. They found differences in absolute numbers of grains per 100 cells in slides from different animals: these were almost certainly due to variations in emulsion thickness from one slide to another, since the track counts, which were independent of this particular error, showed very similar absolute values for sulphur-35 incorporation from one animal to the next. But the ratios of grain counts over lymphocytes to those over control areas immediately adjacent to the cells fell into a relatively narrow range from 1.1 to 1.3, in spite of variations in emulsion thickness.

(b) Differences in development

It is very difficult indeed to develop several batches of autoradiographs in such a way that all have had identical treatment. Many factors can influence the kinetics of development (see Chapter 2), such as the composition of the developer, the temperature and time of development, and the amount of agitation that the slides receive. Although one aims to use conditions of development selected so that slight differences in these factors are not likely to cause dramatic changes in efficiency, it is as well to process together any material which will subsequently be compared.

It may be impossible to do this in some cases. The design of the experiment may require material to be prepared at different times, and comparison of grain counts then becomes rather more difficult. Obviously, big differences in labelling between the sources to be compared should still be easily demonstrable. If variation from batch to batch is sufficient to obscure experimental differences, two possibilities are open. The conditions of development can be more strictly controlled, by using a special developing tank, as was discussed on p.182 in connection with photometric grain counting. Alternatively, some reference standard can be exposed with each batch of autoradiographs, and the observed emulsion response over the standard can be made the basis for a correction factor applied to the experimental material. A convenient reference source is a section of uniformly labelled methacrylate labelled with tritium[4].

(c) Fading of the latent image

The conditions of exposure can produce considerable differences in efficiency between one batch of autoradiographs and another, and even, though this is less likely, between individual slides in the same batch. The presence of atmospheric oxygen, and failure to dry the emulsion sufficiently are the two most important factors in promoting latent image fading (p.14).

This source of variation will not be noticed unless suitable control slides are exposed with each batch. If slides fogged with light or radiation, and then exposed together with the experimental slides, are not uniformly black after development, the conditions of exposure should be examined carefully to remove this source of variation in the emulsion response.

It is probable that many of the quantitative differences between batches of autoradiographs can be traced to slight differences in drying and the conditions of exposure.

(d) Chemography

We have seen (p.94) that chemography may produce developed grains in the absence of radiation, or remove the latent images caused by radiation. Chemography is often variable from one part of a specimen to another, and these variations, having at times an anatomical origin, may produce effects in the emulsion which follow the patterns of the underlying tissue. Clearly, no comparison of grain counts over two series of sources can be claimed to reflect their relative radioactivities unless this source of error has been demonstrably excluded.

The control measures needed in order to do this are discussed more fully later (see p.263). One simple method is to autoradiograph two sections, identical in every respect to the experimental ones except for the absence of radioactivity, in the same batch with the latter. One of the two slides should be fogged by light or radiation before exposure with the other slides. When developed, this slide should show uniform blackening throughout the emulsion. Areas of fading over the section indicate negative chemography (Fig. 30, p.80). The other inactive slide is exposed and developed in the usual way, without fogging. If positive chemography occurs, it will produce grain densities higher than the background levels elsewhere on the same slide.

(e) The choice of exposure time

In Chapter 10 we saw that the grain densities in a thin layer of nuclear emulsion can only be approximated to the dose of radiation to which the film was exposed over a relatively limited range. When 10% of the crystals available in the lowest layer of the emulsion have already been hit by β particles, the upper limit of the approximately linear response between grain density and radiation has been reached. In experiments where the sources differ in their radioactivity by a factor of ten or more, it may be tempting to expose the emulsion until the weaker sources give a reasonably heavy grain density. The limit to exposure must be the grain density over the most radioactive source if grain counting is to be used to assess the emulsion response. It may be possible to extend the range over which emulsion response is proportional to radiation dose by using the optical density of the emulsion layer as the measured response, rather than the grain density (p.168).

To summarise so far, it is a waste of time to compare the emulsion response over different sources unless the emulsion is recording radiation in a reproducible and predictable fashion. No experiment can be adequately analysed without this firm baseline. Since control slides exposed with each batch of autoradiographs are needed to exclude latent image fading and chemography as possible sources of error, any experiment that omits these simple controls is suspect.

THE ANALYSIS OF AUTORADIOGRAPHS OF ISOLATED SOURCES

Let us assume that the emulsion is recording the incident radiation in a quantitative fashion: let us also assume that the radioactive material of interest has remained in the specimen through the steps of preparation for autoradiography, whether this material was macromolecular and precipitated by histological fixation (Chapter 7), or relatively diffusible (Chapter 8). What factors must be considered in assessing the emulsion response over isolated sources, that is, sources separated from each other by relatively large areas of non-radioactive specimen? Such conditions are to be found in many experiments where smears of cell suspensions are autoradiographed, or where labelling of DNA in the

nucleus by tritiated thymidine produces discrete autoradiographic images which
do not overlap.

(a) Differences in thickness in the sources to be compared

The ways in which the efficiency of an autoradiograph can be influenced by
the thickness of the source have been discussed in Chapter 5. With β-emitting
isotopes of low maximum energy, the thicker the source the lower the
efficiency, since self-absorption prevents a higher percentage of the β particles
produced from reaching the emulsion. In Chapter 4 we saw that a thicker source
has a poorer resolution; in other words, the area of emulsion over which the
silver grains are distributed will be greater, and hence, even if we ignore possible
changes in efficiency, the grain densities over the source will be lower, for the
same total grains produced by the source.

If smears are autoradiographed of two cell types with nuclei of different
mean diameter, these factors will combine to give lower grain counts over those
with larger nuclei, if the radioactivity per nucleus is identical in the two cell
types.

Cells which have incorporated tritiated thymidine into their DNA are sometimes examined at several later times to see if there has been any loss of radioactivity from their nuclei, loss which could perhaps be interpreted as evidence for
cell division or even for a metabolic turnover of DNA. If the cell nuclei in the
population have increased in diameter during the period under study, there will
clearly be an increase in thickness of nuclei on smears of whole cells, and a
corresponding reduction in grain density in the absence of any differences in the
amount of radioactive DNA per nucleus.

Differences in specimen thickness are a serious source of variability in autoradiographs of tissue sections. It is often assumed that sections cut at an
indicated $3\,\mu$ on a microtome will be uniformly $3\,\mu$ thick. This is just not true.
Serial sections cut under identical conditions vary from one another in thickness.
This may be easily demonstrated by preparing a block of embedding material
which is uniformly labelled, for instance by dissolving a tritiated steroid in
molten paraffin wax and casting from it a block which has parallel sides. Each
section in a series may then be dissolved in scintillation fluid for liquid scintillation counting. The variation in count rate from one section to the next
indicates the reproducibility with which the microtome is removing a constant
volume of wax at each stroke. A similar experiment can be run with a block of
uniformly labelled methacrylate cut on an ultramicrotome.

In experiments of this sort in my laboratory, the variance (the standard
deviation of the scintillation counts from individual sections expressed as a

percentage of the mean count) ranged from about 5% with the best available microtome and an experienced operator up to about 30% with one particular microtome. In general, the variance was fairly constant for one combination of operator and microtome at section thicknesses down to about $5\,\mu$, but then increased as the section thickness was further reduced. Attempts to cut similar series of methacrylate sections at $1\,\mu$ on ultramicrotomes produced even worse statistics, with variances that usually exceeded 50%. The reproducibility of section thickness in cryostat sectioning has not been tested yet, but is likely to be considerably worse.

This approach measures the ability of the microtome to remove a constant volume of section from a parallel-sided block at each stroke. Even when this is done, variations in section thickness have not been fully determined. As the indicated thickness of section is progressively reduced from $10\,\mu$ to $1\,\mu$, the area occupied by a single wax section, after floating out on the slide, decreases, particularly under about $3\,\mu$. The "thinner" sections become compressed on the knife, resulting in a final thickness of dewaxed tissue that may vary up to 1.5 times the nominal thickness. This compression is not uniform over the whole section, and may give rise to variations in grain density.

The whole problem of the reproducibility of section thickness was studied by Hallén[5], who investigated the optimal conditions of sectioning, and designed a simple but ingenious device for measuring the thickness of sections in the microscope. He concluded that, under the very best conditions, the variance of section thickness would be about 14%, with material embedded in paraffin wax and cut at $3\,\mu$ or thicker.

This source of variability in specimen thickness must be reckoned with. Grain counts over experimental and control sections can easily vary by 20% in the absence of any variation in radioactivity in the material itself, from chance variation in section thickness. Two choices are open. One can live with the variation in section thickness, and base one's counts on a large number of sections in each experimental group. Alternatively, some attempt must be made to measure the thickness of the sections, and either reject any that are not within a fairly close range of thickness, or make some correction to the observed grain counts on the basis of the measured section thickness. Unless one or other method is adopted, the autoradiographs will be unlikely to detect differences in radioactivity of less than 50% with any degree of certainty.

The measurement of section thickness is not easy. The apparatus described by Hallén[5] is not, so far as I know, available commercially, and measurements made by focusing on the upper and lower levels of the specimen in turn and reading the difference in height from the calibration of the fine focus control of the microscope are not accurate enough at mean thicknesses less than about 20 μ. Interference microscopy in reflected light is the best method available at present, providing accurate measurements of section thickness in the range below about 4 μ: this method has been used with considerable success by Dr. Salpeter[6].

If the sections are thicker than the maximum range of the β particle in the embedding medium, then variations in thickness from one section to another will not affect the observed grain densities.

The very serious variations of thickness within a cryostat section that can arise from freeze-drying have been mentioned elsewhere (p.145).

(b) Separation of source from emulsion

In smears of isolated cells, it is clear that the nucleus is always separated from the emulsion by a layer of cytoplasm, and the nucleolus by layers of nucleus and cytoplasm. The effects of this variation in source-detector geometry on attempts to estimate the radioactivities of these three cell compartments have already been mentioned (p.77): Perry and his co-workers[1] have calculated self-absorption corrections for this model based on the mean thickness of the intervening layer in the cell smears they were using. In addition, the density of the intervening layers should also have been taken into account[7,8].

A similar situation faces the autoradiographer if the labelled sources he is interested in are distributed at different depths in a section. It is a common observation that a nucleus labelled with tritiated thymidine will not produce an autoradiograph if it lies only in the lowest level of the section, separated from the emulsion by 4 or more μ of tissue.

Attempts to measure the relative radioactivities of nuclear and extranuclear compartments may thus be closely linked to section thickness, especially with tritium. As the section thickness increases, the probability of observing a bit of sectioned nucleus in a given area of section increases, without a corresponding increase in the observed grain density over that area.

If two sets of sources are to be compared, and they vary in their distance from the emulsion, it is important to decide whether this variation is random within both sets, or one set is consistently further from the emulsion than the other. If the variation is random, grain counts over a sufficient number of sources in each set will allow them to be compared statistically. If the variation in distance is non-random, it must either be calculated and corrected for, or an isotope of higher maximum energy used so that the difference in source—emulsion separation becomes less important in terms of β absorption in the separating layer.

(c) Differences in density of the sources being compared

Self-absorption is often investigated in terms of the thickness of the source (Fig. 28), and it may be overlooked that the density of the source in units such as milligrams per square millimetre is the parameter that really determines the degree of self-absorption. Maurer and Primbsch[8] have drawn attention to the differences in density between cytoplasm, nucleus and nucleolus. Let us consider an experiment to determine the number of cell divisions involved in the production of a mature frog erythrocyte from a precursor cell, based on labelling the DNA of the precursor with tritiated thymidine and observing the reducation in grain density over the nucleus with successive cell divisions, in autoradiographs of cell smears. The increase in cytoplasmic density with increasing haemoglobin concentration might well introduce a significant reduction in grain density over the cell nuclei unrelated to DNA labelling.

(d) Differences in size of the sources being compared

Let us look first at sources which differ in size, in which the disintegration rate per unit area is the same. An isolated circular source whose diameter is small relative to the range of the β particles emitted will produce a distribution of silver grains in the overlying emulsion (Fig. 62a), many of the grains lying outside the edges of the source itself. If the number of silver grains immediately above the source is counted, the volume of emulsion scanned has a given

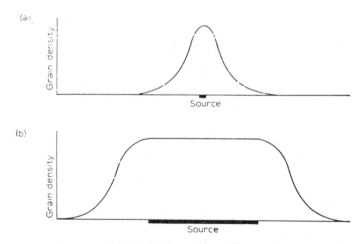

Fig.62. A diagram illustrating the grain densities on a line passing directly through: (*a*) a small source, giving a bell-shaped distribution of grain densities, highest over the source itself; and (*b*) an extended source, showing the higher grain densities over the source caused by crossfire effects from neighbouring areas of the source itself.

efficiency with which it records β particles from the source. It also records β particles originating from outside the source, though with lower efficiency; and the further away from the source that these β particles start their tracks, the lower the efficiency with which this particular volume of emulsion responds. If, therefore, one scans a similar volume of emulsion from the centre of a circular source of twice the diameter, but with the same concentration of isotope (Fig. 62b), the central part of that source, of diameter d, will give rise to exactly the same number of grains counted as the first source, whose total diameter was d. But, in addition, the rim of source around this central portion will also contribute grains to the volume of emulsion examined. In other words, the observed grain density will be higher over the larger source, even though both contain the same concentration of radioactivity. As the diameter of the source is further increased, the efficiency with which the central volume of emulsion records particles from the periphery of the source decreases, until, at their maximum range, it is zero. Above a certain source diameter, therefore, the small centrally placed volume of emulsion gives a record of the concentration of radioactivity that is independent of the size of the source. This critical diameter is governed mainly by the characteristics of the β particles emitted: the lower their energy, the smaller the diameter above which variations in the size of the source have no effect on the grain count over the central region of the source.

For the peripheral parts of a flat, circular source to have no effect at all on the emulsion directly over its centre, the diameter of the source should exceed that of the central measuring area by twice the track length of the highest energy particle emitted. Several factors combine to make this rather a counsel of perfection. Most isotopes emitting β particles have a relatively small percentage of particles at the high end of the energy spectrum (see Fig. 7, p.36). The track radius, or penetration, is always shorter than the point-to-point track length. The solid angle subtended to the central volume of emulsion by the periphery of the source is relatively small. In short, although the efficiency with which the central volume of emulsion records particles from the periphery does not fall to zero until the difference in diameters is twice the greatest track length, it approaches very close to zero at much smaller diameters. As a rough guide, if the resolution of a given autoradiograph (defined as the radius around a radioactive point which contains half the silver grains produced by it) is $R\mu$, the edges of the central volume of emulsion used for counting should be separated from the perimeter of the source by at least $2\ R\mu$. In these circumstances, grain counts over a series of sources should reflect their concentration of radioactivity, even if they differ in size.

These difficulties are illustrated in Fig. 63, in which Dr. Salpeter has calculated the percentage of the total grains produced in the emulsion that

Radius of source (in HD units)	% grains over source	% grains over and within 1 HD	Source diameter for HD = 1600 Å
16	90	95	6 μ
4	60	70	1.5 μ
1	25	55	3500 Å
0.25	2.5	35	800 Å

Fig.63. For solid radioactive discs of different diameters, the percentage of the silver grains produced that lie directly over the source, and that lie over and within a circle of 1 *HD* width outside the source, have been calculated. The source diameters in the last column are the measurements that would correspond in an electron microscope autoradiograph of *HD* 1600 Å. (Data provided by Dr. M.M. Salpeter)

directly overlie sources of different radii. In the same table, it can be seen that increasing the area of emulsion scanned to include a rim 1 *HD* wide around the edges of the source, while improving the percentage of grains counted over the smallest source by a factor of X14, still leaves a big difference between the percentage of grains counted over the smallest and largest sources.

If the total grains per source are to be used as a basis for comparing the radioactivities of sources of differing diameter, the grains should be counted in an area of emulsion overlying each source and extending for at least 2 *HD* on every side: if the size differences in the sources are very great, it may be necessary to extend this area of emulsion even further, to as much as 5 *HD* all round the source. The grain distributions around model sources from which this type of calculation can be derived are presented by Salpeter, Bachmann and Salpeter[9].

If grain densities (grains per unit area of emulsion) are to be the basis for comparing the radioacitvities of sources which differ in diameter, the grain density in a central part of the source, separated by 2 *HD* from the edge of the source on all sides, can be found. The grain density from over the whole source is not a very good indication of the total radioactivity, as can be seen from Fig. 64. Here, for sources corresponding in size to those in Fig. 63, are the densities observed by counting all the grains over the source and dividing by the source area. Here also are the densities obtained by counting all the grains within the emulsion over the source plus a rim of 1 *HD* around it, divided by the area of emulsion scanned. Although the percentage of all the grains emitted by the smallest source that are counted has been considerably increased by scanning the emulsion around as well as over the source, as seen in Fig. 63, the density of

Radius of source (in HD units)	Grains over source/ source area	Grains within 1 HD/ area within 1 HD	Grains within 1 HD/ source area	Source diameter for HD = 1600 Å
16	1.0	1.0	1.0	6 μ
4	0.7	0.5	0.7	1.5 μ
1	0.3	0.15	0.6	3500 Å
0.25	0.03	0.015	0.4	800 Å

Fig. 64. The relative grain densities over solid radioactive discs of different diameters are here presented, calculated in three ways: (*a*) grains over the source divided by area of source; (*b*) grains over and within 1 *HD* of the source, divided by the area lying within 1 *HD* of the source; (*c*) grains over and within 1 *HD* of the source, divided by the area of the source itself. (Data provided by Dr. M.M. Salpeter)

grains calculated in this way is in fact smaller, since the area of emulsion scanned has increased by an even larger factor. A better "density" figure can be obtained by counting the grains in the larger area of emulsion, but relating this to the actual area of the source itself (Fig. 64).

In summary, there are two approaches to the problem of sources that differ significantly in size. If the sources are large relative to the *HD* value of the autoradiograph, the emulsion response over central areas at least 2 *HD* within the edge of each source can be used as a basis for comparison. Alternatively, the emulsion over the source and outside it for a distance of at least 2 *HD* can be scanned if the sources are small relative to the *HD*. In either case, the observed grain counts can be related to the area of the source, if required. Note that the crucial measurement in each case is the *HD* for the autoradiographic system being used. It may be possible to simplify these problems of analysis by manipulating the *HD* values. By careful selection of the isotope and the conditions of autoradiography, an *HD* may be obtainable which minimises the effects of variation of source size on the emulsion response.

(e) Differences in shape of the sources to be compared
   This is really an extension of the situation discussed in the previous section. If one compares a disc to an extended, linear source, keeping their total content of radioactivity, their volume, and their isotope concentration equal, it is very difficult to select two equal volumes of emulsion that would contain the same

number of grains. The grain density in the emulsion directly over the linear source will be lower than it is over the radioactive disc.

Once again, if the sources are large relative to the resolving distance, counts from a small centrally placed volume of emulsion as far as possible from the edges of the sources will give a measure of the concentration of radioactivity within them. If the sources are small relative to the resolving distance, it may be possible to ignore the differences in shape, and treat each as a point source.

In dealing with irregular sources, it may be possible to select volumes of emulsion over each source which are sufficiently similar geometrically to permit the assumption that the efficiency of measurement in each case is the same.

Clearly, the selection of the volumes of emulsion on which a comparison of radioactivities is to be based is a matter of very considerable importance. It really takes very little skill or brilliance to count silver grains, whereas it takes a lot of care and some understanding of the basic processes of autoradiography to chose the areas of emulsion from which to count. Life is much simpler if the same type of source can be compared under a number of different experimental conditions, as all the sources will then be similar in size, shape, density and so on. Comparisons between unlike sources, however, test one's competence, often severely.

THE ANALYSIS OF AUTORADIOGRAPHS OF SOURCES WHICH
PRODUCE OVERLAPPING EFFECTS ON THE EMULSION

We now progress from sources which are separated from each other by a distance that is large relative to the HD of the autoradiograph to the next level of complexity. Here, the sources are close or maybe contiguous, and the emulsion over one source is registering radiation not only from the source itself, but from surrounding sources. Let us assume that the emulsion response is adequately controlled, and that variations in the thickness, density, size and shape of the sources to be compared have been remembered and corrected for. How can one select suitable volumes of emulsion for analysis when there are crossfire effects between sources?

This type of problem is illustrated diagramatically in Fig. 65.

The areas A are known to be heavily labelled: those marked B are presumed to be inactive. The experiment is designed to determine the relative radioactivities of the small structures C and D. The HD is indicated for the autoradiographic system being used. It is clear that the volumes of emulsion overlying the C's and D's near to the areas A will receive very significant irradiation from their heavily labelled neighbours. The grain counts in them will reflect their distance

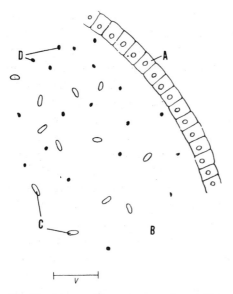

Fig.65. Diagram illustrating crossfire problems in a biological specimen. (*A*) An epithelial surface, assumed to be heavily labelled. (*B*) Unlabelled connective tissue. *C* and *D* are nuclei of two distinct cell types, randomly distributed relative to *A*, whose radioactivity is to be compared. *v* is the resolution of the autoradiograph.

from the nearest *A* far more accurately than they indicate the concentration of isotope in the underlying structures.

The simplest type of crossfire problem occurs when the two series of sources, *C* and *D*, are randomly scattered throughout the tissue section: in other words, both of them may be found at any distance from the highly radioactive *A*. In this case, it is possible to select volumes of emulsion to count on the basis of distance from *A*. For example, it may be decided to count grains over all the *C*'s and *D*'s that lie between 1 and 1.5 *HD* from the nearest *A*, and to count grains over a similar number of areas of the non-radioactive *B*. The *B* counts then represent the background in this position in the section, and the ratio $C-B/D-B$ should reflect the relative radioactivities of *C* and *D*.

But there are many experiments in which this assumption of the random distribution of *C* and *D* relative to the highly radioactive *A* does not hold. In Fig. 66, for example, *A* is the content of the follicle, *C* is the epithelium around the follicle, *D* is an epithelium some distance away from the follicles, and the rest of the tissue is presumed to be unlabelled. The appropriate grain count for *D* can be fairly simply found, by counting over specified areas of *D*, and subtracting the counts over predetermined areas of inactive tissue far enough from *A* and *D* to give a reasonable control value, as at *B*. The epithelium of the follicle (*C*) represents a real difficulty. Fortunately, it is the distance from the nearest *A* on the tissue section that determines the crossfire effect in the autoradiograph, not the distance *in vivo*. While a section that passes through the epithelium at *C* at right angles to it will produce a single layer of cells around the follicle, a tangential section may give a much wider rim of epithelium several cells thick. It may be possible, therefore, to select areas of *C* in tangential sections that lie many microns from *A*, and to find areas of inactive tissue a similar distance from *A* in follicles sectioned perpendicularly to the epithelium (as at B_2). In this case, $C-B_2/D-B$ will give the relative activities of *C* and *D*. It may even be possible to identify small areas of *C* cut so fortunately that none of the radioactive follicular contents (*A*) appears in that particular part of the section (as at C_2).

There are no hard and fast rules for treating these experiments in which crossfire may play a significant role. The central principle is the selection of areas of emulsion for analysis which are balanced with respect to the radiation they have received from surrounding structures. If it is not possible to find a large number of areas which are similar in the radiation they have received, one may have to

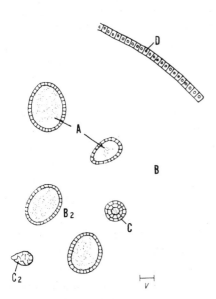

Fig.66. Diagram illustrating crossfire problems in a biological specimen. *D* is an epithelial surface, below which a number of follicles lie in connective tissue. The content of the follicles (*A*) is highly radioactive: the connective tissue is assumed to be unlabelled (*B*). The radioactivity of the follicular cells (*C*) is to be compared with that in the epithelial cells (*D*). C_2 represents a tangential section through follicular cells with no follicular contents visible. *v* is the resolution of the autoradiograph.

use a number of paired observations in which crossfire is similar in the two areas that are paired, though different from one pair to another.

Obviously, any alteration in the conditions of autoradiography that makes the resolution better (the *HD* smaller) will help to reduce the severity of crossfire effects.

THE ANALYSIS OF AUTORADIOGRAPHS AT THE ELECTRON MICROSCOPE LEVEL

The problems of analysing autoradiographs are basically the same, whatever the magnification at which the final preparations are viewed. The principles of analysis are no different with electron microscope autoradiography to those that have already been described above in relation to light microscope experiments. Operationally, however, the ability of the electron microscope to resolve structures in a biological specimen is so much greater than the autoradiographic resolution that one is always working with sources that are small relative to the scatter of silver grains around them, and this rather specialised situation has produced a group of analytical techniques which are seldom required at the light microscope level.

The factors governing the resolution of autoradiographs in the electron microscope have been discussed on pp. 62–68, and the reader will be assumed to be familiar with that material in the following section. Two definitions of resolution will be used, the *HD* and the *HR*. The *HD*, or half-distance, is the distance from a linear source of radioactivity to the lines parallel to it which enclose the area of emulsion containing the centres of half the silver grains produced by the source. The *HR*, or half-radius, is the circle around a point source of radioactivity which encloses the area of emulsion containing the centres of half the silver grains produced by the source.

In the following section, it will be assumed that the preparations to be analysed are technically adequate: the emulsion thickness and the photographic processing will be taken as comparable and controlled, latent image fading and chemography as absent, and the final grain densities as within the linear portion of the response curve of the emulsion layer to radiation.

Once again, we will consider first the assessment of autoradiographs of isolated sources, and the basis for comparing their relative radioactivities, and go on from there to the more complicated problem of closely packed or adjacent sources, which may differ in radioactivity while contributing to the grain densities seen over neighbouring structures.

COMPARISONS BETWEEN ISOLATED SOURCES OF RADIOACTIVITY: THEORETICAL CONSIDERATIONS

The starting point for the analysis of autoradiographs of sources that are separated from each other by distances large relative to the *HD* of the system being used can be found in a series of experiments by Salpeter, Bachmann and Salpeter[9]. They produced simple model sources, radioactive lines about 500 Å thick labelled with tritium, and autoradiographed them under a number of experimental conditions. They then measured the distance from the centre of every developed grain to the centre of the line source up to a distance of 2μ from the line, and prepared distribution histograms for each experiment. As expected, varying the section thickness, the diameter of the silver halide crystal or the diameter of the developed silver grain all influenced the *HD*, and they were able to derive a table of *HD* values for different autoradiographic systems (Fig. 26). In the course of this experiment, they made an observation which opened the way to a considerable advance in the methods of analysing auto-radiographs. Although the observed *HD* value differed for each set of experimental variables, the *shape* of the distribution histogram was the same for every case studied. In short, it is possible to take a distribution of silver grains about a line source and recalibrate it in units of *HD* instead of in Ångstom units (Fig. 18), and the resulting curve is generally applicable to all the combinations of autoradiographic variables which they examined at the electron microscope level, and even to several which they have since examined with the light microscope[10].

Given this universal curve for the distribution of silver grains around a linear source, it is possible to calculate the expected distribution of grains around a point source, or a disc of known radius, or a radioactive band, or any one of a number of simple geometrical shapes, the distribution always measured in units of the *HD* of the autoradiographic system in use. Salpeter *et al.*[9] have presented distribution curves for hollow and solid circular and band sources of various sizes, some of which are shown in Fig. 19.

If one is using a combination of autoradiographic variables for which the *HD* value has already been found (Fig. 26), one can immediately translate this family of distributions into distances in Å, and a whole series of predicted grain distributions around sources of different sizes and shapes becomes available. If a different isotope or emulsion is used, the *HD* value will have to be determined using a radioactive line source before the universal curves can be applied to the analysis of those particular experiments. In either case, it is relatively easy to obtain predicted grain distributions about any sources that can be approximated to simple goemetrical shapes of known size.

The impact of this data on the analysis of electron microscope autoradio-graphs is difficult to overestimate. It is possible to compare observed with predicted grain distributions around particular structures to confirm whether or not they are the only source of radioactivity in the specimen. It is possible to attribute to a labelled structure silver grains lying at a considerable distance from it with confidence, if the observed and predicted distributions match. It may be possible to differentiate between a solid structure which is uniformly labelled and a similar structure labelled only at its rim by comparing the grain distribu-tion observed with those predicted for solid or hollow circles. The predicted distributions, in addition, provide a firm basis on which to decide which areas of emulsion to examine if sources which differ in size or shape are to be compared.

Many factors were identified on pp.194—197 as potential causes of variability in observed grain counts, which must be taken into account before the grain counts can be regarded as measurements of radioactivity in the sources under study. Some of these are relatively easy to control in electron microsope auto-radiography. The thickness of the specimen, which is usually a thin section, can be determined by its interference colour with a moderate degree of accuracy[11] . Source—emulsion separation is seldom a serious variable with thin sections in contact with an emulsion layer, though, if a layer of evaporated carbon is used to separate sections from emulsion (p.337), care should be taken to standardise its thickness. Sections of plastic-embedded material have a density which is near enough uniform to be ignored as a serious source of error. By contrast, variations in the size and shape of sources pose very considerable difficulties in deciding the precise area of emulsion from which to derive grain counts.

From the universal distribution curves, Dr. Salpeter has derived some inter-esting figures which illustrate this problem (Fig. 63). As the radius of a radio-active disc is reduced from 16 HD to 0.25 HD, the percentage of the total grains produced that lies directly over the source drops from 90% to 2.5%. It is obvious that if one counts the grains overlying two sets of sources that differ in size, the smaller sources will be recorded at a lower efficiency than the larger ones. Dividing the number of grains overlying each source by the area of the source to give a grain density makes no difference to this error.

Obviously, if one counts developed grains not only over the source but in a rim of emulsion around the source, a higher percentage of the grains from the small source in particular will be registered. Fig. 63 shows that counting the grains over the source in a rim 1 HD wide all around the source improves the situation. Now, 95% of all the grains produced by a source 16 HD in radius will be counted, and 35% of those for the source 0.25 HD. If grain densities are required, it is no use dividing the observed number of grains by the area of emulsion scanned. This is even less fair to the small source than counting the grains immediately over it, since although more grains are now being registered they are found in an area of emulsion very much larger than the area of the small source itself. Grain densities are better expressed as the number of grains in the emulsion within 1 *HD* of the source, divided by the area of the source itself, as seen in Fig. 64.

It will be seen from Fig. 64 that counting within 1 *HD* of the source may be quite adequate if the two sets of sources to be compared do not differ greatly in size. Even sources of radius 4 and 1 *HD* can be compared in this way with a certain degree of accuracy: the grain density estimated will be 1.2 times higher for the larger source if the initial radioactivity is the same for both sets of sources. As the difference in size increases, so does the error introduced by the higher percentage of grains from the smaller source that fall outside the counting area. The universal distribution curves, however, provide a basis for predicting the precise percentage of the total grains produced that lies within a stated distance of the source, and the autoradiographer must either select areas of emulsion around his sets of sources which contain similar fractions of the total grains, or else apply a correction to his observed counts from the smaller sources.

Sources that vary in shape can also be dealt with on the basis of the universal curves. If one compares a radioactive disc with a solid band source (Fig. 67), the fraction of the total grains produced that lies directly over the source is higher for a band source of a given width than for a disc of the same diameter, and this difference becomes greater as the size of the sources is reduced. Here again, areas of emulsion around each type of source can be chosen so that both are counted at the same efficiency, or a standard area around both types can be scanned, and

Radius or half thick-ness of source (in HD units)	% of total grains over source		Source diameter or thickness for 1 HD = 1600 Å
	Disc	*Band*	
16	90	95	6 μ
4	60	80	1.5 μ
1	25	45	3500 Å
0.25	2.5	15	800 Å

Fig.67. The percentage of the total grains produced in the emulsion that lies directly over the source varies not only with the size of the source but also with its shape. Here solid disc sources of different radius are compared to solid band sources of different thickness. (Data provided by Dr. M.M. Salpeter)

the counts corrected to allow for the difference in efficiency due to the difference in shape. Whatever the counting area, grain densities should always be referred to the area of the source, not to the area of emulsion examined.

PRACTICAL STEPS IN COMPARING THE RADIOACTIVITIES OF ISOLATED SOURCES

What, then, should one do if one wishes to compare the radioactivity of one set of sources with another by electron microscope autoradiography? As with any other type of autoradiograph, the response of the recording layer of emulsion must be reproducible. The emulsion should be applied as a densely packed monolayer of crystals (p.340), and micrographs of test specimens should confirm this. The reproducibility of response of the emulsion layers to β particles should be demonstrated by exposure to standard sections, such as tritiated methacrylate, and a suitable development procedure worked out. Latent image stability over exposure periods as long as will be needed experimentally can be demonstrated by irradiating emulsion layers with β particles, and comparing layers developed immediately with ones developed after exposure with experimental material. Chemography should be excluded by exposing emulsion to sections of tissue similar in all respects to the experimental except that they should not be radioactive: emulsion layers previously irradiated with β particles should also be exposed in contact with non-radioactive sections to exclude negative chemography. Grain densities over the most radioactive sources should not exceed one-tenth the density of silver halide crystals in the emulsion monolayer. Source thickness should be controlled, by interferometry preferably, and the thickness of any barrier layer of evaporated carbon should be made as reproducible as possible. At this stage, any autoradiographs produced should be suitable for analysis.

The *HD* value for the autoradiographic system should be found, either from the literature (Fig. 26) or by preparing a radioactive line source and determining the distribution of grains around it[9]. Each type of source should be approximated to a simple geometrical shape and its dimensions found in units of *HD*. On the basis of the sizes and shapes of the sources to be compared, the areas of emulsion in which grains are to be counted can be calculated, following the principles outlined in the preceding section (pp.197–205). Then, using some predetermined method of scanning the autoradiograph, micrographs should be taken of a sufficient number of sources of each type. Each micrograph should ideally include the whole area of emulsion to be counted in relation to the source, and every source encountered should be photographed until the required number is complete: selection of the source to photograph, or of the area relative to the source introduces the possibility of subjective bias. The choice of the number of sources to photograph depends entirely on the number of grains observed in the emulsion, the difference in labelling between the sources to be compared, and the accuracy required in the comparison. The number of sources or of photographs has no bearing on the validity of the statistics, only the number of grains (p.216 and Fig. 69).

The assumption that the two sets of labelled sources are isolated from other radioactive structures in the specimen can be tested, if necessary, by preparing distribution histograms of silver grains around the two types of source. This is done by marking the centre of the smallest possible circle that contains each grain, and measuring the distance from this point to the nearest edge of a source. These distances are accumulated into a histogram, which should agree closely with the distribution predicted for the model source.

Finally, the grains are counted in the selected emulsion area around and over each source. If the radioactivity per unit area of source is to be compared, the relative areas of each type of source on the micrographs that produced the grain counts should be estimated: methods for the estimation of relative area on sections are discussed by Weibel[12].

Examples of this type of analysis applied to sources that are widely separated from each other are provided by Salpeter[13, 14], who examined motor endplates labelled with [^{3}H]DFP, and Budd and Salpeter[15], who studied [^{3}H]norepinephrine in the terminals of sympathetic nerves.

THE ANALYSIS OF ELECTRON MICROSCOPE AUTORADIOGRAPHS OF SOURCES WHOSE EFFECTS ON THE EMULSION OVERLAP

In tracer experiments, the administration of a labelled precursor, such as an amino acid, is often followed by the incorporation of radioactivity into many cell types, and into many structures within each cell. Far from having isolated sources, we are dealing with closely packed cellular constituents which may all be labelled to some extent, many of them contributing silver grains to the emulsion over their neighbours.

In this situation, it may be difficult to determine by observation alone which components are in fact labelled, or which are more heavily labelled than others. Counting the silver grains over various cell components is clearly inadequate: some components may occupy a greater fractional area of section than others. Even if the counts are corrected for the relative areas of each component[16], there is still the problem of crossfire, with components next to heavily labelled sources registering high counts due to scattered grains from their neighbours.

This situation has been dealt with by Williams[17] , who has devised a technique which is effective, and simpler in use than might at first appear. Williams' method is based on the *HR* concept, which defines an area of emulsion around a point source which contains half the silver grains produced by it. But the autoradiographer has to start from the silver grains, and may not know the likely source of the β particles which caused them. If one places a circle of radius *HR* around the centre of a developed grain, it will obviously have a 50% probability of including in it the source of the β particle. The analysis starts by placing a circle of radius *HR* around every silver grain on the series of micrographs, and recording the components lying in each circle. This produces a table of frequencies with which grains occur over various components. Next, a number of circles of radius *HR* are scattered randomly over the same micrographs, and the frequencies with which cell components occur in these random circles are recorded. If the labelling is indeed random, the frequencies in the two columns will be approximately equal. A chi-squared test will indicate at once which components are more or less heavily labelled than their frequency in the random circles would lead one to expect.

The information that can be derived from this approach is largely determined by the selection of components to be registered (Fig. 68). Some components will fill some circles completely — nucleus, mitochondrion or phagosome, for instance. Other circles will include more than one component in them, falling on the junctions between nucleus and cytoplasm, or mitochondrion and ribosomes: these Williams terms "junctional items". Some structures are so small that they may never fill a circle completely, such as the cell membrane or pinocytotic

Single items	Junctional items	Compound items
Nucleus	Dense bodies/ribosomes	Ribosomes/plasma membrane
Phagosome	Phagosomes/ribosomes	Mitochondrion/plasma membrane/ribosomes
Mitochondrion	Nucleus/ribosomes	
Ribosomes	Mitochondrion/ribosomes	
Dense body	Mitochondrion/dense bodies	Smooth vesticles/ribosomes
	Mitochondrion/phagosomes	
	Mitochondrion/ribosomes/nucleus	
	Mitochondrion/ribosomes/dense bodies	

Fig.68. Examples of the listing of cell components as single, junctional and compound items in the method for analysing electron microscope autoradiographs devised by Dr. M.A. Williams.

vesicles: these always occur in the company of other components, forming "compound items". By comparing the grain frequencies over junctional items with those that would be predicted from the frequencies with which grains occur over the component each side of the junction when it occurs as a single item, it is possible to test the hypothesis that the junctional region is specifically labelled. In the same way, one can compare the grain frequencies over compound items with those over the components in them that occur as single items elsewhere in the list, and determine whether or not the small components, such as small vesicles, which only occur in the compound item, are significantly labelled.

The choice of items for analysis is determined only by the needs of the experiment, and the overall frequency of developed grains. If only four grains occur over compound items that include cell membrane in a set of micrographs, further subdivision of these items is obviously a waste of time. If, however, many grains are available for analysis, one might wish to list as separate items those which include apical, basal and lateral cell membranes in an epithelium. By this approach, structures smaller than the HR may be identified as radioactive, and morphologically similar structures in different positions in the cell or tissue may be differentiated with regard to their degree of labelling.

This type of analysis can indicate with considerable precision which components in a complex specimen are more heavily labelled than is consistent with a random spread of radioactivity throughout the specimen. If similar specimens are to be compared under different experimental conditions – for instance, at different times after the administration of a labelled precursor – it may be sufficient to analyse the autoradiographs in this way: the sequence in which cell organelles become labelled will indicate the passage of the precursor through the synthetic mechanisms of the cell. If, however, a strict comparison of the radioactivity present in one organelle with that in another is needed, the tables of observed and predicted grain frequencies may not provide a sufficient basis, since they are based entirely on the grains which overlie the organelles. As was discussed earlier in relation to light microscope autoradiography (pp.201–204), the analysis of grain densities when the sources are small relative to the HD of the autoradiograph calls for considerable judgement. It may be possible to select areas of emulsion in relation to each type of source to be compared which have a similar surrounding radiation field. Alternatively, if some indifferent structure can be found with no significant radioactivity, as judged by the tables of predicted and observed grain densities, paired observations can be made, relating the grain density over each source examined to that over an indifferent structure in a similar position in the tissue. Clearly, accurate comparison between the radioactivities of mitochondria and lysosomes in cells in which all components of the cytoplasm are labelled to some extent, to quote an example, may involve a great deal of care and measurement, and the result may not be very precise.

If, on the other hand, only a few cell components appear to be labelled from the table of observed and predicted grain frequencies, it may be possible to treat them on particular sections as isolated sources, and study the grain counts in areas of emulsion around them, selected on the basis of the grain distributions predicted by the universal curves of Salpeter et al.[9] (See also NOTES ADDED IN PROOF, p.360).

The analysis of electron microscope autoradiographs is not quick or simple. The methods that have been outlined above may seem extremely tedious, in fact. In many cases, however, autoradiography at this level is an extension of a series of investigations by other techniques, which permit quite precise hypotheses to be formulated. The testing of a specific hypothesis may dictate the pattern of analysis to be adopted, and render unnecessary many of the steps required to establish the quantitative distribution of radioactivity between all the components in the tissue.

THE STATISTICAL ANALYSIS OF AUTORADIOGRAPHS
(Written in collaboration with J.M. England)

Statistical techniques are of wide applicability, and are not in general restricted to any one experimental approach in biology. The inclusion of a section on statistics in a book of this nature may seem at first a little difficult to justify. However, in the course of several years' autoradiography, some problems in statistics have recurred frequently enough to make it worth while outlining them and possible methods of tackling them.

Autoradiographers are often dealing with relatively low numbers of observed events – usually silver grains. The levels of radioactivity in biological specimens for autoradiography are often low, the methods of data collection slow and tedious. Experiments may be based on counts of 500 or 1000 grains over each group of sources: with pulse counting techniques and larger biological samples, counts of 10 000 or more per sample are, in contrast, easy enough to obtain. Working with low total counts of silver grains, corrections for radioactive background assume far greater importance, and the level of radioactivity in the source, estimated from the mean grain density, becomes less accurate than with larger numbers of observed events.

THE POISSON DISTRIBUTION

Poisson[18] derived a formula which describes the probability of occurrence of
rare events, when a large number of individuals is at risk. This formula has been
shown to predict accurately the statistical variations in disintegration rate on
repeatedly sampling a population of atoms of a particular radioisotope, for
instance. If λ d.p.m. is the mean disintegration rate for the whole population,
and λA d.p.m. the mean disintegration rate for repeated samples containing A
atoms, the frequency with which a counting rate of i d.p.m. will be observed in
samples of size A is given by:

$$\frac{(\lambda A)^i \cdot e^{-\lambda A}}{i!}$$

The standard deviation (S.D.) of repeated samples of size A will be $\sqrt{\lambda A}$, the
square root of the mean value. If the standard deviation is expressed as a percentage of the mean, this is known as the coefficient of variation (C.V.).

It can be seen from Fig. 69 that as the mean number of events counted per
sample rises, the C.V. gets smaller: in short, the accuracy with which the true
disintegration rate for the whole population of radioactive atoms is estimated by
one sampling increases.

If one takes a large, uniformly labelled source, such as a section of tritiated
methylmethacrylate, the number of β particles per hour leaving small areas of
equal size on the upper surface of the section will vary according to the Poisson
distribution. If a technically satisfactory autoradiograph, free from artefact, is

Grains/unit area due to source	Sample to background ratio	Coefficient of variation of sample grain density, corrected for background
10	1	55%
20	2	32%
50	5	17%
100	10	11%
200	20	7%
500	50	4.6%

Fig.69. The variability in grain counts over uniform sources of different levels of radioactivity, assuming the background to be 10 grains per unit area. It is assumed that counts have
been made of 1 unit area of background and 1 unit area of emulsion over the source.

prepared from such a section, the observed grain counts over small areas of section also have a Poisson distribution[4]. The autoradiograph faithfully reflects the radioactive events taking place in the source. If our "source" now becomes a population of cell nuclei, scattered through a tissue, the grain counts in repeated samples will be comparable to the counting areas over the labelled methacrylate. In other words, if the population is really homogeneous and uniform in terms of the number of radioactive atoms per cell nucleus, the observed grain counts will have a Poisson distribution. The accuracy of our estimate of the radioactivity per nucleus will depend, not on the number of nuclei counted, nor on the total area of emulsion scanned, but on the total number of silver grains counted in our sampling of the population.

THE DETERMINATION OF BACKGROUND

The grain counts taken from over the source include a contribution from a variety of factors other than source radioactivity (Chapter 6). Background (B) must be estimated separately, and subtracted from the observed counts of source plus background to give a value for the source alone (S). But repeated counts of background show that this, too, has a Poisson distribution[4]. The observed count, $S_o + B_o$, therefore, consists of estimates of the "true" values S and B, each of which is likely to be in error, and these errors are additive when $(S_o + B_o) - B_o$ is used to measure S. The S.D. of estimates of S obtained in this way is given by:

$$\sqrt{[\text{S.D.}(S_o + B_o)^2]} + [\text{S.D.}(B_o)^2]$$

There is a limit to the number of B_o and $S_o + B_o$ silver grains one is prepared to count, and the optimal allocation of counting effort between these two in order to reach an accurate estimate of S is obviously of considerable interest. Many workers count equal areas of emulsion to estimate B_o and $S_o + B_o$: in doing so, their estimates of B are clearly less accurate than of $S + B$. At very high ratios of S to B, the inaccuracy of estimating B matters little: the lower the ratio of S to B, the more important it becomes to count large numbers of background grains. In general terms, the grain density due to the source should be at least five times higher than that due to background if the requirement to scan very large areas of background is to be avoided.

England and Miller[19] have examined the optimal allocation of counting effort between source and background for given levels of accuracy. Their treatment requires that the number of different types of source to be studied in the specimen should be known, and that preliminary counts should give a rough estimate of the ratio in labelling between sources and background. Then, for a chosen level of accuracy, the required number of grains to be accumulated over each type of source and over background areas can be read off from a chart (see Appendix, (p.357). By noting the area of emulsion that needs scanning to reach this total of grains in each case, the appropriate grain density for each type of source plus background can be found, together with the estimated background density.

When photometric measurements of grain density are used instead of grain counts, it has been shown that a well-adjusted photometer does not introduce added variability to the results[4]. The photometer records in arbitrary units, however. One should not substitute the readings in these units for grain numbers in calculations of the accuracy and distribution of observations. It is possible to adjust the photometer to give ı very high numerical reading from a field with few grains in it, and quite a spurious idea of the accuracy of the estimation may result. It is the number of events in the emulsion, usually silver grains, that has been observed that governs the accuracy of the sampling. To use the chart on p. 357, then, one should convert the photometric values to the number of silver grains responsible for those observed readings in order to calculate the optimal allocation of counting effort[4].

THE RADIOACTIVITY OF BIOLOGICAL SOURCES

We have seen that a model source can be sufficiently uniform for grain counts over it to have a Poisson distribution[4]. Unfortunately, biological sources are seldom as uniform as this, and there are many reports in the literature of grain counts which fail to conform to the expected Poisson model[20-22]. It may well be that cells or organelles of a particular appearance are not a homogeneous population: perhaps old cells may not incorporate as much radioactive precursor as younger ones of the same tissue, or position in the organ relative to a blood-vessel may affect labelling. Any one of a hundred possible reasons may be responsible for the source, defined in histological terms, having a wider variability of radioactivity than a uniform model source. In this case, the emulsion will accurately mirror events in the population of structures making up the source, and the grain counts will have a wider scatter about the mean value than predicted.

In addition to variability in the biological material, technical factors can also introduce added variability into the grain counts. We have seen (p.198) the variability that inevitably occurs in the thickness of sections cut under comparable conditions. Similarly, variations in emulsion thickness or in the degree of development may increase the variance of grain counts over a homogeneous source.

In short, in most experiments with biological material, the S.D. of the grain counts will be greater than the square root of the mean grain count. That the variance is greater than predicted from a Poisson distribution does not rule out sensible analysis of results, though it may mean that certain procedures and tests are preferable to others. Many of the so-called parametric tests require that the observations from sources that are to be compared have distributions of a particular type, or even that they have S.D.'s that are equal. In particular, most parametric tests assume that the grain counts for each source are normally distributed about the mean.

The non-parametric statistical tests, which make few or no assumptions about the distributions of the initial data, are well described in an invaluable book by Siegel[23] . Since they are in general less powerful at discriminating between different levels of labelling than their parametric equivalents, they should not be used if the data meet the rigid criteria of the latter. The use of parametric tests on unsuitable data, however, may well suggest the presence of differences where none exist.

THE PAIRED t-TEST

If two sets of sources are to be compared, the selection of which individuals in each set are to be counted should not be left to the whim of the microscopist at the time of counting. We have already seen that it is better to work out criteria for selecting the areas of emulsion to be examined before starting counting (p.172), so that the complete population of sources can be sampled in as thorough a way as possible. There is a lot to be said for applying the same selection criteria to each set of sources, so that each observation on one set is balanced by an observation from the other, made as far as possible under identical conditions. This pairing during grain counting reduces some at least of the variability due to position within the specimen. It also provides data which are suitable for use with the paired t-test, which combines considerable power with relative freedom from restrictive assumptions about the distributions of the original grain counts about the mean[24] . Basically, even if the shapes of two distributions differ from each other or from the normal pattern, the differences between paired observations from the two series are often normally distributed.

The calculations are simple. If the grain counts, corrected for background, from two sets of sources are x_1, x_2, x_3 .... x_n, and y_1, y_2, y_3 .... y_n, for each pair of counts the difference is found, retaining the sign.

$$x_1 - y_2 = d_1$$
$$x_2 - y_2 = d_2$$
$$x_3 - y_3 = d_3$$
$$\cdots\cdots\cdots$$
$$x_n - y_n = d_n$$

The number of pairs is n, the degrees of freedom $(n-1)$. The S.D. of the differences (S_d) is given by

$$\sqrt{\frac{n\Sigma d^2 - (\Sigma d)^2}{n(n-1)}}$$

and the statistic t by $\dfrac{\bar{d}}{S_d}\sqrt{n}$ where $\bar{d}$ is the mean of the differences.

The probability associated with the value found for t can be looked up in the appropriate book of statistical tables; it indicates the probability that d_1, d_2, d_3 .... d_n do not differ significantly from zero. If a reasonably high number of paired observations is made, such as thirty or more, this test provides a sensitive and powerful way of comparing grain counts, and it is applicable to a great many autoradiographic experiments.

Sometimes, it may not be possible to collect data that are paired in any way that is significant biologically. This does not rule out the use of the paired *t*-test. The results from the two sets of sources can be randomly allocated to pairs, and the test still used. It becomes less powerful when used in this way, however, because random pairing is less effective at reducing the variability of the differences between pairs than pairing based on some genuine similarity between the members of each pair.

ESTIMATIONS OF THE PERCENTAGE OF A POPULATION OF SOURCES
THAT ARE RADIOACTIVE

This has already been mentioned in connection with background estimation (p.103). Many autoradiographic experiments set out to find the percentage of a given population of sources that are radioactive in given circumstances – the proportion of cells synthesizing DNA in a population, for instance. Often, a rule-of-thumb is applied, that every cell with four or more grains over its nucleus will be considered labelled. This type of rule inevitably introduces errors into the experiment. If the cut-off figure is placed low, the upper end of the Poisson distribution of background grain counts will produce false positives: if the figure is high, the lower end of the Poisson distribution from radioactive nuclei will not be recognized. Often, these two distributions overlap, and no arbitrary level can be found which separates background from radioactive successfully. Several treatments of this problem are available in the literature, with different basic assumptions and of varying complexity[19, 25-28]. The treatment presented here is based on work by England and Miller[29].

The only assumptions made are that background, measured over a similar but non-radioactive population of sources to the ones under investigation, has a Poisson distribution, and that grain counts over the radioactive sources also conform to this predication. To make use of the method, four measurements must be made. The proportion of sources with one or more grains over it and the mean grain count per source are determined for both radioactive and non-radioactive populations. In estimating the mean grain counts, sources with no grains at all over them should be included. The proportion of sources that are actually labelled in the radioactive population (P_s) can be found from

$$\frac{(P_{S+B} - P_B)}{(X_{S+B} - X_B)(1 - P_B)} = \frac{\left[1 - e^{\dfrac{-(X_{S+B} - X_B)}{P_S}}\right]P_S}{(X_{S+B} - X_B)}$$

where P_{S+B} is the proportion of sources in the radioactive population with one or more grains, P_B is the corresponding proportion in the non-radioactive population, X_{S+B} is the mean grain count over sources in the radioactive population, and X_B is the corresponding mean from the non-radioactive population. The ratio

$$\frac{(P_{S+B} - P_B)}{(X_{S+B} - X_B)(1 - P_B)}$$

can be calculated from the measurements made on the specimens. Using the graph (Fig. 70), this value is located on the vertical scale, and the corresponding value of $\dfrac{(X_{S+B} - X_B)}{P_S}$ is read off directly. The value for P_S can be found by dividing $(X_{S+B} - X_B)$, which is known, by the value that has been determined from Fig. 70.

To take an example, let P_{S+B} be 0.25 and P_B be 0.20: let $(X_{S+B} - X_B)$ be 0.10. The first half of the equation becomes $\dfrac{0.05}{0.10 \times 0.80} = 0.63$

Locating this on the vertical axis of Fig. 70, the corresponding figure on the horizontal axis becomes 1.0, and P_S is $\dfrac{0.1}{1.0} = 0.1$. So 10% of the radioactive population of sources in fact contain radioactive material.

This method of analysis is quick and simple, and gives accurate estimates even when the levels of grain density over the radioactive sources are so low that some "labelled" cells give rise to no silver grains at all. Earlier treatments of the problem are less accurate at levels of labelling near to background: the formula of Stillström[25], for instance, would only recognise 4% of the population as radioactive in the above example, a substantial underestimate. Where the grain densities over radioactive cells are much higher than background, the results given by the various formulae quoted tend to converge.

STATISTICAL ANALYSIS AND EXPERIMENTAL DESIGN

An experiment should be designed to test a particular hypothesis. Since grains are often in short supply over biological specimens, and grain counting is slow and tedious, the collection of data should always be purposeful and economic. If, instead, many different structures in the specimen are sampled by collecting a few score grains from over each of them, and all are compared to each other in a shotgun series of tests, the chances are high that little useful information will result. To begin with, even if labelling is uniform over every structure, the statistical tests will indicate a probability of better than 0.05 once in every 20 tests. If genuine differences in radioactivity exist between different structures, the small numbers of grains counted will make them difficult to recognise unless the differences are very big.

Naturally, every effort must be made to exclude technical causes of variability in the observed grain counts – the choice of littermate animals, the selection of sections of a given thickness, the control of emulsion thickness and development, and so on. The question is often asked: "Is it better to count from many sections and a few animals, or from fewer sections and more animals?" The answer depends on the experiment. Whichever stage in preparing the sources for counting introduces the greatest variability into the final counts, that is the step

References p. 225

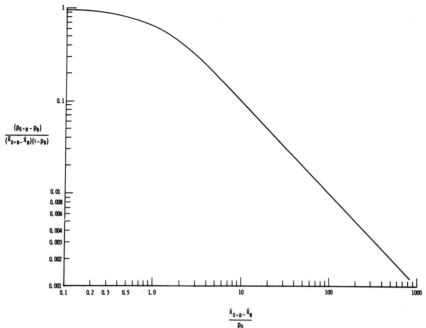

Fig. 70. A graph to assist in the determination of the percentage of sources which are radioactive in a large population. P_{S+B} is the proportion of sources in the population which have one or more developed grains over them; P_B is the corresponding proportion in a control non-radioactive specimen; X_{S+B} is the mean grain count over sources in the population which includes radioactive members: X_B is the mean count from the control, non-radioactive population. From the observed value of $\dfrac{(P_{S+B} - P_B)}{(X_{S+B} - X_B)(1 - P_B)}$, the corresponding value of $\dfrac{(X_{S+B} - X_B)}{P_S}$ can be read off on the graph, and the value of P_S (the proportion of sources that are radioactive in the experimental population) can be calculated. For the full treatment of this method, see p.222.

that should receive the greatest investment in terms of the number of observations made. If variation between animals is small, but section thickness poorly controlled, or variation from place to place within an organ or tissue considerable, many sections will be needed from each animal, but relatively few animals. An insatiable curiosity about the reproducibility of one's techniques helps to build up experience, which enables one to allocate effort between animals, slides, sections and counting areas without too much waste. An analysis of variance may assist in indicating the point in the collection of data at which the addition of more material will have the most effect on the precision of the final grain counts. It is precisely at this point where the variance is greatest that the most benefit can be obtained from some system of pairing between the observations.

The more controlled the preparation of the autoradiograph and the more thorough and careful the collection of observations, the more sensitive will be the final statistical analysis in determining whether or not significant differences in radioactivity exist between sources. In general, it is often possible to identify differences in labelling where they are of the order of 20% of the mean grain density: there are occasional examples in the literature where a difference in labelling as small as 10% has been shown to be significant. In view of the many causes of variability, both technical and biological, this represents a considerable achievement.

REFERENCES

1   R. Perry, M. Errera, A. Hell and H. Durwald, *J. Biophys. Biochem. Cytol.*, 11 (1961) 1.
2   C.P. Leblond, B. Messier and B.M. Kopriwa, in R. Wegmann (Ed.), *Histochemistry and Cytochemistry*, Pergamon, London, 1963.
3   D. Darlington and A.W. Rogers, *J. Anat.*, 100 (1966) 813.
4   J.M. England and A.W. Rogers, *J. Microscopy*, 92 (1970) 159.
5   O. Hallén, *Acta Anat., Suppl.* 25 (1956).
6   M.M. Salpeter, in M.A. Hyatt (Ed.), *Principles and Techniques of Electron Microscopy*, Vol. 2, Nostrand/Reinhold, New York, 1972.
7   R.P. Perry, in D.M. Prescott (Ed.), *Methods in Cell Physiology*, Vol. I, Academic Press, New York/London, 1964.
8   W. Maurer and E. Primbsch, *Exptl. Cell Res.*, 33 (1964) 8.
9   M.M. Salpeter, L. Bachmann and E.E. Salpeter, *J. Cell Biol.*, 41 (1969) 1.
10 M.M. Salpeter, personal communication.
11 L. Bachmann and P. Sitte, *Mikroscopie*, 13 (1958) 289.
12 E.R. Weibel, *Int. Rev. Cytol.*, 26 (1969) 235.
13 M.M. Salpeter, *J. Cell. Biol.*, 32 (1967) 379.
14 M.M. Salpeter, *J. Cell Biol.*, 42 (1969) 122.
15 G.C. Budd and M.M. Salpeter, *J. Cell Biol.*, 41 (1969) 21.
16 R. Ross and E.P. Benditt, *J. Cell Biol.*, 27 (1965) 83.
17 M.A. Williams, *Advan. Opt. Elect. Microsc.*, 3 (1969) 219.
18 S.D. Poisson, *Recherches sur la Probabilité des Jugements en Matières Criminelles et en Matières Civiles Précédées des Règles Générales du Calcul de Probabilité*, Paris, 1837.
19 J.M. England and R.G. Miller, *J. Microscopy*, 92 (1970) 167.
20 F. Forro, *Exptl. Cell Res.*, 12 (1957) 363.
21 L.G. Lajtha, R. Oliver, R.J. Berry and E. Hell, *Nature*, 187 (1960) 919.
22 B. Chernick and A. Evans, *Exptl. Cell Res.*, 53 (1968) 94.
23 S. Siegel, *Non-parametric Statistics*, McGraw-Hill, New York, 1956.
24 J.E. Freund, P.E. Livermore and I. Miller, *Manual of Experimental Statistics*, Prentice Hall, Englewood Cliffs, 1960.
25 J. Stillström, *Intern. J. Appl. Radiation Isotopes*, 14 (1963) 113.
26 F. Bresciani and K. Thompson, *Rept. Brookhaven Natl. Lab.*, BNL-8360, 1963.
27 W. Sawicki, O. Blaton and J. Rowinski, *J. Histochemie*, 26 (1971) 67.
28 D.J. Moffatt, S.P. Youngberg and W.K. Metcalf, *Cell Tissue Kinet.*, 4 (1971) 293.
29 J.M. England, A.W. Rogers and R.G. Miller, *Nature*, in the press.

CHAPTER 12

Absolute Measurements of Radioactivity

THE NEED FOR ABSOLUTE MEASUREMENTS

The basic requirements for relative measurements of radioactivity by means of autoradiographs have already been discussed in Chapter 11, and they make a sobering list. Is it possible to extend these techniques so that the number of radioactive disintegrations taking place in the source during exposure can be found?

In most autoradiographic experiments, such absolute measurements are not necessary. In the usual sort of tracer experiment, where a labelled compound is injected into an animal, and its subsequent distribution between different tissues and cell types studied, the absolute disintegration rate within one cell is not very meaningful, without a great deal of information about the size and turnover rate of precursor pools, which is seldom available. There are situations in which such measurements are of value, however.

One of these is the rapidly growing field of isotope cytochemistry. Labelled reagents can be applied to a tissue, either *in vivo* or *in vitro,* in conditions in which they combine with a specific active group. Subsequent measurement of the amount of isotope in a cell or other histological structure can, in controlled circumstances, indicate the number of such reactive groups present. Examples of this approach are the measurement of the total number of groups reacting with tritiated acetic anhydride in red blood cells[1], the estimation of the number of receptor sites for acetylcholine in endplates of mouse diaphragm[2], and the later work of Barnard and his collaborators on the number of acetylcholinesterase molecules in motor endplates[3]. With the increasing availability of highly specific enzyme inhibitors and alkylating agents, it is likely that this approach will find wider application. Here, clearly, the ability to determine the absolute number of reactive sites within a structure from its autoradiograph is extremely valuable.

In microbiology, the elegant work of Levinthal and Thomas[4] illustrates a further application for absolute quantitation. They were able to calculate the number of phosphorus atoms in single bacteriophage viruses by means of β-track counts, a technique they called "molecular autoradiography". In many small organisms which can be cultured in controlled conditions, it should be possible to label one particular constituent to a known specific activity by regulating the radioactivity of its precursor in the medium. Subsequent determination of the disintegration rate within the organism would then give a measure of the total number of molecules of that species present.

In radiobiology, the study of the dose rates resulting from internally absorbed radioisotopes and their effects on the tissues depend on a detailed knowledge of the distribution of radioactivity, and of the amounts of isotope present in each target organ. Here, too, the ability to infer the disintegration rate in a structure from its autoradiograph would be extremely valuable.

Absolute measurements of any sort require very high standards of technique. In making relative measurements of radioactivity, comparing the activity of one source with another, it is often enough to assume that the conditions under which the two sources are studied are identical, without investigating them in great detail. Thus the self-absorption need not be known, provided it is similar in the sources being compared. The same is true of many other factors, such as the thickness of the emulsion, its sensitivity, and the possibility of loss of isotope in preparing the sources for autoradiography. In absolute measurements of radio-activity, however, each of the factors that is capable of influencing the efficiency of measurement must be known and corrected for, if the final response of the emulsion is to serve as a basis for calculating the disintegration rate in the source.

It is often said that autoradiographic techniques are fundamentally so unreli-able that absolute quantitation is out of the question. This is really a statement of technical failure. One has only to read the use made of nuclear emulsions by particle physicists to see that they have potentialities as a medium for recording the passage of charged particles which biologists have hardly begun to realise. It is possible, with good techniques, to deduce the mass, charge, and initial energy of a particle from its track in nuclear emulsion. In fact, Powell, Fowler and Perkins[5] list the fundamental particles which were first identified in nuclear emulsion. As far as β particles are concerned, Ross and her co-workers[6,7] have used the criteria of track length and grain yield in nuclear emulsion to calculate the energies of the β particles emitted by certain radioactive isotopes. In view of the precision with which emulsions can be used, it seems reasonable to expect that the number of β particles emitted by a source can be accurately measured — a problem far simpler than any of these listed here.

In many instances, autoradiography offers the only means of measuring the disintegration rate in a small source. Nuclear emulsions have a high efficiency for low energy β particles. The record they give is cumulative, and since counting can be limited to extremely small volumes of emulsion in direct contact with the source, the period of counting can be very long indeed, relative to the other methods of detecting charged particles, before the background becomes unacceptably high. For biological sources of cellular dimensions, a disintegration rate as low as 1 per day may be accurately recorded in favourable circumstances.

In this chapter, some of the attempts that have been made at absolute measurements of radioactivity will be discussed, and the technical requirements that must be met will be indicated. To do this without repeating too much of the material that has already been dealt with elsewhere, certain assumptions will be made about the conditions of autoradiography. It will be taken for granted that there is no loss or translocation of isotope in preparing the source for exposure, or that if there is any such loss it will be accurately measured and corrected for. The size and shape of the source should be known. The source must be presented to the emulsion in such a way that self-absorption can be ignored, or else calculated and allowed for. It will be assumed that chemography, either positive or negative, has been demonstrably controlled. As far as the emulsion itself is concerned, a suitable exposure time and development routine must be selected to avoid the pitfalls of emulsion saturation or inadequate development. Not until all these conditions have been met can one begin to discuss the possibility of determining the disintegration rate within the source. It is obvious that absolute measurements of radioactivity demand a high level of technical competence, and a number of preliminary control experiments, if they are to be taken seriously.

One further prerequisite to accurate measurement requires consideration in rather more detail – the control of fading of the latent image.

THE CONTROL OF LATENT IMAGE FADING

The creation of a latent image within a crystal of silver halide is a reversible process. The passage of an ionising particle through the crystal results in the deposition of minute amounts of un-ionised silver at preformed sensitivity specks. If these atoms of silver are not too few or too disperse, they can act as a catalyst for the conversion of the entire crystal to metallic silver in the process of chemical development (see p.15). But the silver deposited at the sensitivity specks may become ionised to silver bromide once again before the end of exposure, wiping out the latent image (p.14). High temperatures favour this instability of the latent image, as do the presence of oxidising agents, such as atmospheric oxygen, or of water in the emulsion.

Emulsions differ in their liability to latent image fading. It is usually more

severe in emulsions with a smaller grain size, and in emulsions of higher sensitivity.

The duration of exposure clearly influences the severity of fading. Conditions
which give quantitative results at 2–3 days may produce very serious fading in
an exposure of 2–3 months. The steps that can be taken to reduce this loss of
latent images are mainly concerned with controlling the conditions of exposure.
In the first place, the autoradiographs are usually stored in the cold: 4° is
recommended, though the emulsions in general use can be cooled to –40°
without damage after thorough drying. Adequate drying of the emulsion is
important: Ilford recommend drying to a relative humidity (R.H.) of 45–50%
and this seems quite adequate in my experience. Messier and Leblond[8] are
insistent that the Eastman Kodak NTB emulsions need complete drying to 0%
R.H. to ensure freedom from fading. As for the exclusion of atmospheric
oxygen, Herz[9] has suggested a very simple method for exposure in carbon
dioxide. This seems satisfactory, though there is no direct evidence on the effect
of the very low pH that might result from the presence of water in the emulsion.
Other inert gases may be used, such as nitrogen, helium, or argon, depending on
their availability.

How may latent image fading be recognised in a thin emulsion layer, where
the presence of radioactivity is indicated by an increased density of silver grains?
A series of slides can be given a uniform exposure either to light or to radiation,
and then developed after varying periods of time. If the blackening, measured by

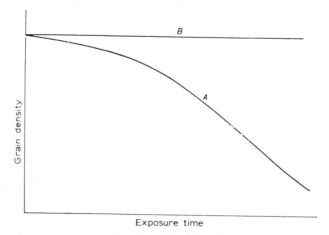

Fig. 71.   A graph illustrating the effect of latent image fading on an emulsion layer deliberately fogged before the start of exposure (Line *A*). The observed densities of silver grains
will decrease with increasing exposure. Line *B* shows the unaltered grain density in a similar
slide exposed in the absence of latent image fading.

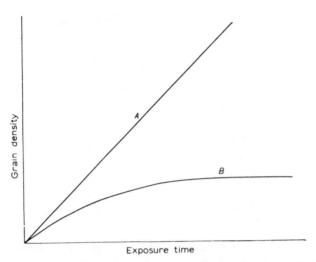

Fig. 72.   A graph illustrating the increase in developable silver grains over a labelled source with increasing exposure time. In *A*, a linear relation between grain density and exposure time exists, showing that there is no latent image fading. In *B*, the rate of increase of grain density falls with increasing exposure times, until a plateau is reached, when the rate of latent image fading has reached an equilibrium with the rate of latent image formation over the source.

grain counting or by microdensitometry, remains constant at all exposure times, there is no loss of the latent images formed by the initial irradiation(Fig. 71). If the grain density falls off with increasing time, fading is present. This is probably the most convenient way of conducting experiments into the optimal conditions of exposure.

As a check with each batch of autoradiographs, to ensure that latent image fading is satisfactorily controlled, grain counts should be taken over similar structures after exposures lasting different lengths of time (Fig. 72). After correcting for radioactive decay, where appropriate, the increase in grain count with time should be strictly linear. Loss of latent images shows itself by the failure of the grain count to maintain its initial rate of increase. In conditions where fading is severe, the graph may flatten off to a plateau, when the rate of latent image formation is balanced by the rate of fading.

In grain density autoradiographs, as mentioned in Chapter 6 (p.102), latent image fading is often tolerated in an attempt to keep the background as low as possible. With most techniques, the process of applying the emulsion to the specimen and the subsequent drying create a number of background grains. A long exposure with a certain amount of latent image fading results in these grains, present at the start of exposure, being wiped out: in these conditions, the background is likely to consist only of grains due to environmental radiation. Where techniques have evolved with the aim of producing clear autoradiographs with as low a background as possible, it is usually the case that latent image fading is present, even though the autoradiographer may not be aware of the fact. Stringent control of the conditions of exposure may therefore result in higher background levels than are customary, since the emulsion is preserved for viewing with all the grains which were present at the start of exposure, as well as those acquired from environmental radiation during exposure.

In view of the very common occurrence of latent image fading in autoradiographs that are otherwise excellent and of the difficulty in recognising fading by simple examination of the emulsion, it cannot be emphasised too strongly that no measurement of the disintegration rate within a source can be accepted as valid unless the linear response of the emulsion with increasing exposure times has been clearly shown.

In considering track autoradiographs, the position is slightly different. The units being counted are tracks, not individual silver grains, and even if latent image fading has reduced by one third the number of grains in a track, the latter may still remain recognisable. With a little experience, the limits of variation in grain size and spacing in tracks of a given length can be recognised under constant conditions of development. Latent image fading will tend to wipe out the smaller grains, and reduce the size of the larger ones. In effect, in a slide affected by fading, a track that has been formed early during exposure will have larger gaps between the grains, and the grains that are present will be smaller, by comparison with a track produced towards the end of the exposure period. So minor degrees of fading may be recognised by examining a single autoradiograph, and yet may not make any appreciable difference to the track count.

Obviously, if fading proceeds further, the spaces between surviving latent images may become so great that it is impossible to follow the course of the track: all that remains of tracks formed early in exposure in this case is a few short runs of small grains, which cannot be satisfactorily linked together. Fig. 31 illustrates this type of appearance. Severe fading like this will vitiate attempts to make absolute measurements, and will be clearly demonstrated by the technique of exposing slides from the same batch for increasing periods, as was the case in grain density autoradiographs.

Whether tracks or silver grains are the units to be measured, it is more valuable to have counts available for a series of exposure times than to have the same number of observations for one exposure alone, if absolute values are required. In the former case, the absence of latent image fading can be clearly demonstrated: in the latter, it has to be assumed, or inferred from separate control experiments.

ABSOLUTE MEASUREMENTS FROM GRAIN DENSITY AUTORADIOGRAPHS

Let us assume that the many technical problems of preparing an acceptable autoradiograph have all been dealt with, that there is no loss of isotope, no chemography, no latent image fading, and so on. The radioactive source is covered with a thin layer of nuclear emulsion, and the developed grains over it can be clearly counted. Is it possible to relate the observed number of grains to the number of radioactive disintegrations that have taken place in the source during exposure?

Two basically different approaches have been adopted towards this problem. The first is the rigorous, mathematical attempt to predict the grain yield from a given source from basic principles. The second approach is empirical, and involves the preparation of reference sources of known activity, and observation of their grain yield under reproducible conditions. Each of these will be considered in turn.

(a) Calculations of grain yield

β Particles have very irregular tracks, so that any prediction based on the distribution in space of their trajectories must be a statistic with very wide limits of variation. The mathematical treatment for the scattering of a collimated beam of monoenergetic electrons passing through a homogeneous medium of known characteristics is already fairly complicated. But, with a radioactive isotope, the β particles have a spectrum of initial energies, and may leave the source in any direction. In addition, the situation represented by Fig. 15c (p.48), where the typical grain density autoradiograph is illustrated, involves four different media – the glass of the slide, the source itself, which is usually a tissue section, the nuclear emulsion, and the air or inert gas in which exposure takes place.

Taking all these factors into account, it is, I believe, true to say that accurate prediction of grain densities from sources of known activity is not possible at present from first principles. Not enough is known about the scattering of electrons at interfaces between media of different densities to make the very considerable burden of computation worthwhile. In consequence, any attempt to calculate grain densities has to start from a number of simplifying assumptions.

The most thoroughgoing attempt to date to calculate expected grain densities from known autoradiographic situations is the work of Odeblad[10-12]. It is worth considering it in some detail, if only to illustrate the difficulties of this approach. This is a very interesting attempt to apply matrix theory to the evaluation of grain density autoradiographs. Certain simplifying assumptions are made to begin with. It is assumed that the distribution of radioactive isotope within a tissue section will correspond with the observed pattern of histological structures, and that, within each structure — for example, within the nucleus of a cell — the distribution of radioactivity will be homogeneous. It is assumed that the effects of a large number of β particles on the emulsion can be observed, so that statistical statements based on the characteristics of the entire spectrum of energies of the isotope under study are likely to hold good. It is further assumed that precise data are available for the shape and size of the histological structures under study, for the thickness of section, of emulsion, and of intervening material, if any.

Odeblad then introduces a system of co-ordinates, the X and Y axes in the plane of the specimen, the Z axis a vertical one, at right angles to this plane. Using these co-ordinates, it is possible to describe the relationship between a given histological structure and a defined volume of emulsion in accurate terms. Finally, it is assumed that the transmission of β particles from specimen to emulsion in the conditions of the experiment can be described by a dimensionless transmission coefficient $T(C)$.

The grains observed in any given volume of emulsion are caused by radiation from the immediately adjacent structure in the specimen, plus a contribution from other nearby structures that reflects both their distance from the observed volume of emulsion and their total content of radioactivity. By examining a large number of volumes of emulsion in this way, it is possible to set up a series of simultaneous equations relating the observed densities of silver grains to the geometrical factors between the chosen volumes of emulsion and each histological structure, to the volume of each structure, and to the concentration of isotope within it.

In order to solve these equations, the transmission function $T(C)$ for the particular isotope must be separately determined. The matrix elements needed for their solution must be either calculated or found by experiment. Finally, a proportionality factor must be determined experimentally for the autoradiographic conditions used, preferably using point or planar sources of known activity, of which the matrix elements are easily calculated.

It is clear that there is a great deal of work involved in the preliminary determination of these factors, and in the many measurements needed for the assembly of the equations. The mathematics involved is also pretty complex. It is nevertheless true that, once these necessary factors have been found for a given autoradiographic situation, it is possible to calculate the amount of radioactivity present in any structure in a biological specimen from observed grain densities.

There is one limitation on the applicability of this mathematical approach which Odeblad himself has pointed out. With isotopes of low maximum energies, the use of the transmission coefficient $T(C)$ becomes more difficult to justify. With tritium, the extreme example, self-absorption in the specimen becomes such an important factor that this generalised coefficient can no longer be used. Odeblad sees his computations as valid and useful only for isotopes of considerably higher maximum energy such as phosphorus-32.

Even with the simplifying assumptions made in these calculations, at least two factors have to be determined empirically before the necessary equations can be set up – the transmission coefficient and the proportionality factor. Odeblad's analysis illustrates very forcibly the difficulties involved in calculating the radioactivity of a source within a complex specimen from the pattern of silver grains in the overlying emulsion.

It is not surprising that most attempts at making absolute determinations of radioactivity have been based entirely on the empirical approach, on the preparation of standard reference sources of known activity, and their comparison under controlled conditions with the unknown sources under study.

(b) Comparisons with standard reference sources

There are many examples of this method of measuring radioactivity, at varying levels of sophistication. Mamul[13] prepared gelatin sources with a known content of sulphur-35 for comparison with his experimental material. Waser and Lüthi[2] used rather similar standard sources containing carbon-14 in their measurements of the uptake of labelled curare by the motor endplates of mouse diaphragm. Probably the most careful attempt to measure radioactivity within the specimen from observed grain densities is the work of Andresen and his co-workers[14, 15], who studied the amoeba *Chaos chaos* after feeding it with ^{14}C-labelled material. Possible loss of radioactivity in preparing the autoradiograph, latent image fading, and the reproducibility of grain counts, were all investigated in a most thorough way. The observed grain densities over sectioned amoebae were correlated with the results of geiger counting from the same amoebae prior to embedding them, and from the sections prior to autoradiography. In addition, standard sources of a solution of labelled glucose were prepared and autoradiographed.

Certain basic principles must be observed in any attempt to estimate the amount of a radioisotope in an experimental source from a comparison of its autoradiograph with that of a known reference source — principles that emerge from the discussion on relative measurements of radioactivity in Chapter 11 (p.194). Ideally, the reference source should resemble the experimental source as closely as possible. Barnard and Marbrook[1] have suggested the acetylation of frog red blood cells with tritiated acetic anhydride under controlled conditions as one way of producing uniformly labelled reference sources of cellular dimensions. Cells or bacteria grown in culture in the presence of labelled amino acids also might provide suitable sources. Caro and Schnös[16] have described labelled phage-infected bacteria which could serve as reference sources for electron microscope autoradiography.

Cells or organisms that can be obtained in bulk and labelled uniformly are probably the best reference sources. Suspensions of such cells can be readily prepared for counting in a haemocytometer, and known numbers of cells taken for estimates of radioactivity by scintillation counting, for example. Smears of these reference sources can then be exposed alongside the experimental sources. Provided the criteria necessary for accurate relative quantitation listed in Chapter 11 are met, the ratio of grain counts over reference and experimental sources can be converted directly into terms of radioactivity.

In situations in which radioactive sources are very closely packed, as in many autoradiographs of tissue sections, crossfire effects will complicate the comparison between experimental and reference sources. Grain counts over the experimental sources will include contributions from adjacent parts of the tissue, and these must be corrected for before valid comparisons with the reference sources can be made. This may be very difficult. In some cases, it may be possible to distribute reference sources randomly between the experimental sources, and to try and select sources of both types for grain counting from positions where the crossfire effects are likely to be the same. This is almost impossible to achieve with tissue sections, however. One can then only hope to estimate the contribution of neighbouring structures to the grain count over the experimental source by trying to find unlabelled areas of tissue which have a similar relationship to surrounding structures, and counting in these positions.

Absolute measurements of radioactivity by means of grain density autoradiographs are difficult to make with any precision. It is of course always possible to count the silver grains lying directly over a source, and to convert this number into the number of disintegrations taking place within the source during exposure, by using one of the figures for grain yield available in the literature[9]. This may be valid if all that is needed is a rough estimate of the radioactivity within the source, and a factor of 3 or 4 in the answer makes little difference. It is clearly not a method of getting a precise measurement, however.

References p. 244

(c) Absolute measurements by electron microscope autoradiography

The main problem in analysing electron microscope autoradiographs is the great disparity between the dimensions of many of the structures observed, and the relatively wide scatter of silver grains around them. In Chapter 11 (p.208–216), the methods that can be used to define the grain distributions about labelled sources of various sizes and shapes have been discussed already[17]. Provided only that the *HD* value for the autoradiograph is known, it should be possible to approximate the radioactive structure of interest to a simple geometrical shape of standard size, and to calculate the predicted distribution of silver grains over and around it. If the observed distribution matches the predicted ones, the next step is to count all the developed grains within a defined distance from the source, and calculate from the distribution curve the fraction of the total grains produced by the source that they represent. It is an easy step then to calculate the total number of grains attributable to the source, even though many of them will lie over adjacent structures.

To derive from this grain number the disintegration rate in the source, the efficiency of the autoradiograph must be known. Fig. 23 presents a series of efficiency determinations for various combinations of emulsion and developer: in view of the considerable influence of the precise conditions of exposure and development on efficiency, it may be better to determine the efficiency of one's own system directly with a model source of known radioactivity.

These steps in the measurement of radioactivity by electron microscope autoradiography may be clearer with a practical example. Reference has already been made to radioisotope cytochemistry, in which a labelled reagent is titrated against a compound in the tissue, and to the use which has been made of this technique in measuring acetylcholinesterase in motor endplates by reaction with the enzyme inhibitor, DFP[3]. Working with sternomastoid endplates of the mouse, Dr. Salpeter[18] first plotted the distribution of silver grains relative to the pre-synaptic membrane, and compared this with the distribution predicted around a radioactive line: as can be seen from Fig. 73, these did not agree. Next, the same grains were analysed for their distribution relative to the post-synaptic membrane (Fig. 74), and a satisfactory fit obtained. The possibility remained that both pre- and post-synaptic membranes were labelled. This has now been tested on external ocular muscle endplates in which foldings of post-synaptic membranes are much reduced by comparison with the sternomastoid endplates. The membrane profiles on the autoradiographs were divided into two zones: one in which pre- and post-synaptic membranes ran parallel, the other in which folds of post-synaptic membrane were present. A simple comparison of the length of pre-synaptic, post-synaptic, and total membranes in these two zones with the numbers of silver grains in each showed reasonable support for the hypothesis that both the membranes had equal densities of acetylcholinesterase (Fig. 75)[19].

On the basis that pre- and post-synaptic membranes were equally rich in the enzyme, the total membrane length was measured on a series of autoradiographs of endplates, and the total number of developed grains attributable to them

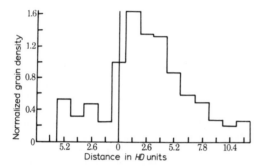

Fig. 73. The distribution of silver grains relative to the pre-synaptic membrane of motor endplates of mouse sternomastoid muscle labelled with [³H]DFP. The line at zero represents the membrane: values to the left lie over the nerve terminal, to the right over the post-synaptic region. The hypothesis that all the radioactivity is on the pre-synaptic membrane is clearly untenable. (Data derived from Salpeter, 1967)

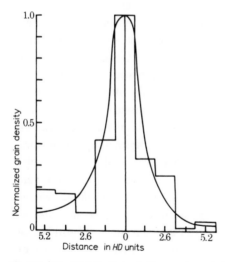

Fig. 74. The distribution of silver grains relative to the post-synaptic membrane of motor endplates of mouse sternomastoid muscle, labelled with [³H]DFP. The smooth curve represents the distribution predicted for a linear source following the course of this membrane: the histogram shows the observed distribution. These data are consistent with labelling confined to the post-synaptic membrane. (Data derived from Salpeter, 1967)

	Zone I (no junctional folds)	Zone II (junctional folds)	Ratio II/I
Developed grains	102	170	1.67
Relative areas			
Pre-synaptic membrane	825	752	0.91
Post-synaptic membrane	390	2447	2.76
Total membrane	1715	3199	1.86
Cleft	291	685	2.35

Fig. 75. The analysis of the distribution of silver grains relative to the pre- and post-synaptic membranes of the motor endplates of extraocular muscles of the mouse, after labelling with [³H]DFP. In these endplates, post-synaptic folds are infrequent, and the endplate can be divided into zones in which both membranes run parallel (Zone I), and zones in which there are junctional folds (Zone II). An analysis of the relative areas of pre-synaptic, post-synaptic and total membrane and of synaptic cleft, in these two zones shows that the observed grain densities in these zones are compatible with uniform labelling of both membranes, but not with uniform labelling of any other structure. (Data provided by Dr. M.M. Salpeter)

counted. Since the section thickness was known, the total area of membrane responsible for these grains was known. From the efficiency of the autoradiograph, measured with a standard radioactive section, the disintegration rate in the source was obtained, and, from this, a statement of the density of molecules of acetylcholinesterase on the pre- and post-synaptic membranes[18].

In these admirably precise experiments, Dr. Salpeter not only demonstrated that quantitative measurements are possible by electron microscope autoradiography: she also showed that, with ingenuity and patience, it is possible to identify as labelled two structures which are much smaller than the resolution. The values she obtained for mouse sternomastoid endplates agreed well with those of β-track autoradiography and liquid scintillation counting[20].

The results obtained from autoradiographing a standard radioactive line source permit one not only to calculate the efficiency of the technique used, but also to measure the *HD*, and to construct a model source of the same size and shape as the suspected structure in the biological specimen[17]. From this, grain distributions and densities in defined areas of emulsion relative to the source can be predicted, and compared with those over the biological structure. Although the special conditions of electron microscope autoradiography have produced this approach, there is no reason why it may not be applied equally to grain density autoradiographs at the light microscope level, instead of attempting to label reference sources of the same approximate shape and size as the biological structures of interest.

ABSOLUTE DETERMINATIONS OF RADIOACTIVITY FROM TRACK AUTORADIOGRAPHS

Many of the uncertainties that arise in attempting absolute measurements by grain density techniques stem from the difficulty of relating the observed silver grains in the emulsion to the disintegrations taking place in the specimen. In a track autoradiograph, this problem is very much simplified. One track represents one β particle.

As long ago as 1957, Levinthal and Thomas[4] published a description of absolute measurements carried out with track techniques. They labelled bacteriophage virus with phosphorus-32, and prepared a suspension of virus particles in molten Ilford G5 emulsion. This was gelled in a thick layer, and, after suitable exposure and development, was scanned for β tracks. The viruses could not be seen, but their positions in the emulsion could be inferred because each one was the centre of a star of β tracks, radiating out into the emulsion from a common origin. The number of tracks forming each star gave an immediate and direct figure for the number of disintegrations taking place within the virus during exposure. This very elegant experiment is the only one I know in which the absolute radioactivity of the source was calculated directly from its autoradiograph, without any simplifying assumptions or empirical factors, as are needed in the interpretation of the conventional grain density autoradiograph.

In some ways, this experiment was a special case. There was no self-absorption in the sources. They could be suspended in emulsion, giving the best and simplest geometry possible between source and emulsion. The isotope, phosphorus-32, gave long tracks, most of them straight at their start, simplifying the problems of track recognition and counting.

The fact remains, however, that the type of measurement made by Levinthal and Thomas could not have been carried out by any other technique at present available, and it is rather surprising that the sensitivity and simplicity offered by β-track autoradiography have not been widely exploited.

Two complicating factors arise in many of the experiments in which one would like to use track autoradiography for absolute measurements – both of them absent in Levinthal's case. The first concerns the proportion of β particles in the energy spectrum of the isotope that would be expected to give rise to a recognisable track. The second arises when the source cannot be suspended in emulsion, but has to be mounted on a slide, and covered only on one side by the recording medium. Each of these introduces uncertainty into the otherwise simple relationship between observed tracks and β particles, and each will be discussed in turn.

(a) The problem of unrecognised β particles

A β track is usually considered as four or more silver grains, arranged in a linear fashion. The characteristic way in which they are arranged is described fully elsewhere (p.173). It is necessary to specify a minimum number of grains in order to distinguish tracks from a random arrangement of single background grains in the emulsion. The energy spectrum of all β-emitting isotopes is continuous from the maximum energy right down to zero, and it is clear that, below a certain energy level, the particles will have very little chance of producing four grains in a row. With phosphorus-32, the proportion of these unrecognisable β particles is likely to be a fraction of 1%, since the maximum energy is high (1.4 MeV), and the curve of energy distribution rather bell-shaped. With carbon-14, however, the maximum energy is only 155 keV, and the shape of the energy spectrum (Fig. 7, p.36) indicates that a high proportion of the particles have initial energies less than 40 keV. What percentage of these particles will fail to cause four grains in a row?

This problem has been investigated in some detail by Levi et al.[21] They took the isotopes carbon-14, calcium-45 and chlorine-36 and prepared track autoradiographs with each one using Ilford G5 emulsion. After processing, the emulsions were carefully reswollen to their thickness during exposure. In this way, a large number of tracks was available for study, arranged three dimensionally in the emulsion in the original patterns produced by the β' particles. The grain-to-grain track length was measured, and the number of grains counted, for many tracks. The initial energy of each particle was not known, but could be calculated from the track length. In this way, the relationship between initial particle energy and the mean number of grains produced by the particle in G5 emulsion was arrived at (Fig. 12, p.42). The variation coefficient about this mean value appeared to be about 20%.

From these relations, it is possible to calculate the percentage of β particles in any known energy spectrum which will give rise to less than 4 grains per track. Levi et al.[21] calculated that 14% of all the β particles emitted by carbon-14 would give rise to less than 4 grains. For calcium-45, the percentage of unrecognised β particles was 10%.

Using the convention that 4 or more grains constitute a β track, it is possible, with any isotope with a maximum energy of 150 keV or higher, to calculate the percentage of particles that might be expected to go unrecognised through failure to produce 4 developed grains. The observed track counts can therefore be corrected to take account of this factor. At maximum energies below 150 keV, the percentage of unrecognised particles becomes rather high, and the certainty with which it can be calculated falls off, so that this correction factor becomes both less accurate and more significant.

(b) The effect of different geometrical relations between source and emulsion

In the experiment of Levinthal and Thomas[4] which was described above, a point source of phosphorus-32 was suspended in emulsion. All the β particles leaving the source were therefore recorded. This very favourable situation cannot always be achieved. How can one relate the number of tracks observed to the number of β particles when the source is mounted on a glass slide, and covered on one side only by emulsion?

Fig. 27 (p.68) illustrates this situation, which is frequently encountered. Let us assume that the source is very small, and is isolated from other sources. It is reasonable to believe that 50% of the β particles will be initially directed upwards into the emulsion, and the other 50% downwards into the slide. Some of those entering the emulsion will be scattered back into the slide at some point along their trajectory. Similarly, some that initially enter the slide will be reflected back into the emulsion at a variable distance from the source.

The mean distance between adjacent silver grains at the commencement of a track at the high energy end of the spectrum for the isotope concerned can readily be estimated from data given by Levi *et al.*[21] For carbon-14, the mean figure is about 1.6 μ: for chlorine-36, it is 2.0 μ, and it is not likely to be more than 2.5 μ for any isotope of higher energy. Gaps as big as twice the mean figure may occur, but are unlikely to be exceeded. It follows that the first silver grain in a track has a very high probability of lying within 3.2 μ of the source with carbon-14, 4.0 μ with chlorine-36, and 5.0 μ with particles at minimum ionisation. If one views the source from above, in the usual way, a circle of this diameter around the source will contain all but a negligible fraction of the first silver grains in the tracks of the particles that enter the emulsion directly.

When examining such a source, it is reasonable to count any track that can be traced back to within this radius of the source. It is reasonable also to assume that these tracks represent all the particles that left the source to enter the emulsion directly. In other words, the observed track count within this radius of the source, multiplied by two, will give the number of disintegrations taking place in the source. Clearly, since the initial direction of the β particles leaving the source is randomly determined, there will be a statistical uncertainty associated with this factor of two, which will become less significant as more tracks are counted.

There is up to the present very little detailed work on the scattering of β particles between the emulsion and its glass support. Preliminary counts with phosphorus-32 in this laboratory suggest that fewer than 20% of the particles emitted by a source cross the glass—emulsion interface at any point in their trajectory, and that these points of entry or exit are distributed over a very large area. In considering a small source of phosphorus-32 mounted on a glass slide, over 75% of all the tracks produced by it in the emulsion can be traced back to within 5 μ of the source, while the remaining tracks are distributed over an area several hundred microns in radius.

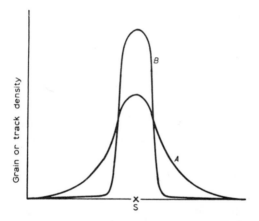

Fig. 76. A graph illustrating the differences between the distribution of silver grains around a source in a grain-density autoradiograph, and the distribution of points of entry around a source in a β-track autoradiograph. The source (S) is presumed to be labelled with phosphorus-32. The grain densities in a thin emulsion layer (line *A*) fall off relatively slowly with increasing distance from the source. By contrast, the points of entry of tracks into a thick emulsion layer (line *B*) fall very sharply to a low figure at 4-5μ from the source.

The curve of distribution of the points at which tracks enter the emulsion from a point source labelled with phosphorus-32 has therefore the form shown in Fig. 76. It is far from a bell-shaped curve. It has, rather, a high peak over the source, falling very rapidly to low levels at distances greater than 5 μ. It is therefore relatively simple to recognise and count the tracks that enter the emulsion directly from the source. This distribution tends also to simplify problems due to crossfire, since the probability of finding a point of entry of a particle that has been scattered back into the emulsion from the glass slide is uniformly low over wide areas around the source.

(c) Experimental validation of β-track measurements

Two experiments will illustrate the application of β-track measurements to biological specimens, and show the very close agreement that can be obtained between these techniques and the results of liquid scintillation counting. In the first experiment, leucine labelled with carbon-14 was injected into a newborn rat, and portions of the liver embedded and sectioned. Protein synthesis was proceeding so fast in this tissue that practically every cell was labelled, and the labelling was reasonably uniform from one part of the liver to another. Serial sections were cut at 5 μ: some were coated with Ilford G5 emulsion for track autoradiography, some were mounted and stained for measurement of the area of each section, and some were deparaffinised in xylene and suspended in scintillating fluid for counting in a liquid scintillation counter.

The scintillation counting gave a mean figure of 245.9 c.p.m. from samples of 5 sections each, after subtracting background. There was no measurable quenching and the efficiency of counting, estimated with a weighed amount of carbon-14 labelled toluene of known activity, was 74.5%. This represented 330 disintegrations per minute per 5 sections.

Track counts from autoradiographs with 3 different exposure times showed no latent image fading. The tracks from the areas counted were multiplied up to give a figure for an area equal to 5 sections, and this was converted into tracks per minute per 5 sections. This figure was then corrected for the 14% of carbon-14 β particles which would have failed to give rise to recognisable tracks of 4 or more grains (see p.240). Finally, the corrected track count was multiplied by 2, on the assumption that 50% of the particles entered the emulsion. This method of estimating the radioactivity of the liver gave an answer of 325 disintegrations per minute per 5 sections.

The agreement between these two answers is very encouraging. It is interesting to compare the simplicity and directness of this method, using track autoradiography, with the very complex and uncertain attempts to calculate the number of disintegrations in a source from grain density autoradiographs.

Further confirmation of the validity of estimates of radioactivity based on the tracks entering the emulsion directly form a source is provided by Rogers et al.[22] They measured the number of molecules of diisopropylfluorophosphate (DFP) labelled with phosphorus-32 that were bound to the enzyme acetylcholinesterase in motor endplates of the sternomastoid muscle of the mouse. β-Track autoradiographs were prepared with Ilford G5 emulsion from single, microdissected endplates (Fig. 53, p.163). The number of tracks entering the emulsion directly from the endplate was taken to be half the number of disintegrations taking place in the endplate during exposure. In this way, a value was obtained for the number of molecules of acetylcholinesterase present at these motor endplates.

Using a method of labelling that was basically similar, employing tritiated DFP, measurements were obtained by liquid scintillation counting which were in very close agreement with the results of β-track counts[23], and also of quantitative electron-microscope autoradiographs of the same material[20].

The possibilities of making absolute measurements of radioactivity with nuclear emulsions may be summarised in the following way. For carbon-14 and all isotopes of higher maximum energy, the rather neglected technique of β-track autoradiography offers the best approach. The correlation between the number of tracks entering the emulsion from the source and the disintegrations taking place within the source is simple and direct.

For tritium, iodine-125, and other low energy isotopes, absolute measurements of radioactivity are best made by preparing sources of known radioactivity, which should resemble the experimental sources as closely as possible. Exposure of both types of source together to a thin emulsion layer and comparison of the grain densities in selected volumes of emulsion over them, permit the concentration or the amount of radioactivity present in the experimental sources to be calculated.

For the electron microscope, where one is restricted to the use of a thin emulsion layer, the method of comparing grain densities with those of standard reference sources is the only satisfactory one, whatever the isotope used. The standard sources will usually be model ones, whose grain distributions will have been calculated from the observed distributions about a radioactive line source.

Given a reasonable standard of technical competence, and careful control of the many factors that can influence the accuracy of absolute measurements, it is undoubtedly possible to measure the disintegration rate taking place in biological sources of cellular and even subcellular dimensions.

REFERENCES

1 E.A. Barnard and J. Marbrook, *Nature*, 189 (1961) 412.
2 P.C. Waser and U. Lüthi, *Helv. Physiol. Pharmacol. Acta*, 20 (1962) 237.
3 E.A. Barnard, *Intern. Rev. Cytol.*, 29 (1970) 213.
4 C. Levinthal and C.A. Thomas, *Biochim. Biophys. Acta*, 23 (1957) 453.
5 C.F. Powell, P.H. Fowler and D.H. Perkins, *The Study of Elementary Particles by the Photographic Method*, Pergamon, London, 1959.
6 B. Zajac and M.A.S. Ross, *Nature*, 164 (1949) 311.
7 W. Stanners and M.A.S. Ross, *Proc. Phys. Soc., London*, A69 (1956) 836.
8 B. Messier and C.P. Leblond, *Proc. Soc. Exptl. Biol. Med.*, 96 (1957) 7.
9 R.H. Herz, *Lab. Invest.*, 8 (1959) 71.

10 E. Odeblad, *Acta Radiol.*, 45 (1956) 323.
11 E. Odeblad, *Acta Radiol.*, 48 (1957) 289.
12 E. Odeblad, *Lab. Invest.*, 8 (1959) 113.
13 Y.V. Mamul, *Intern. J. Appl. Radiation Isotopes*, 1 (1956) 178.
14 N. Andresen, C. Chapman-Andresen and H. Holter, *Compt. Rend. Trav. Lab. Carlsberg*, 28 (1953) 189.
15 N. Andresen, C. Chapman-Andresen, H. Holter and C.V. Robinson, *Compt. Rend. Lab. Carlsberg*, 28 (1953) 499.
16 L.G. Caro and M. Schnös, *Science*, 149 (1965) 60.
17 M.M. Salpeter, L. Bachmann and E.E. Salpeter, *J. Cell Biol.*, 41 (1969) 1.
18 M.M. Salpeter, *J. Cell Biol.*, 32 (1967) 379.
19 F. Machenry, A.W. Rogers and M.M. Salpeter, in preparation.
20 A.W. Rogers, Z. Darzynkiewicz, M.M. Salpeter and E.A. Barnard, *Nature*, 210 (1966) 1003.
21 H. Levi, A.W. Rogers, M.W. Bentzon and A. Nielsen, *Kgl. Danske Videnskab. Selskab. Mat.–Fys. Medd.*, 33 (1963) No. 11.
22 A.W. Rogers, Z. Darzynkiewicz, K. Ostrowski, E.A. Barnard and M.M. Salpeter, *J. Cell Biol.*, 41 (1969) 665.
23 A.W. Rogers and E.A. Barnard, *J. Cell Biol.*, 41 (1969) 686.

PART 3: DESCRIPTIONS OF AUTORADIOGRAPHIC TECHNIQUES

CHAPTER 13

The Planning of Autoradiographic Experiments

A cat may be killed by choking it with cream, but only a few enthusiasts would insist that this is the only available method. Similarly, most autoradiographic experiments can be carried out by several different techniques, all of them producing valid results. There is no "right technique", in many cases. All too often, unfortunately, a research worker who wishes to use autoradiography for the first time "learns the technique" from some other laboratory, without any clear idea of the range of techniques that are available, or of their relevance to particular types of experiment. In this way, a technique that was perhaps ideal for the work of the first is applied in the second to a problem for which it is quite inappropriate.

It is the aim of this chapter to give an overall survey of the techniques at present available for autoradiography, and to indicate, in general terms, the type of problem to which each is relevant. Inevitably, this will involve a certain amount of repetition of material to be found elsewhere in this book, but there appear to be advantages to this type of arrangement for the biologist who wishes to select a method of carrying out an experiment without necessarily reading the whole book first.

Autoradiographic experiments may be broadly classified on the basis of the way in which the finished autoradiograph will be viewed. Macroscopic observation covers the autoradiography of chromatograms, of large and often irregular objects such as complete skulls, or of hemisections of experimental animals. It can give a rapid, roughly quantitative survey of the distribution of radioactivity between areas that are relatively large. Autoradiographs intended for viewing through the light microscope are usually sections or smears of biological material. The need to correlate the distribution of radioactivity with the range of structures visible microscopically makes quite different demands on the techniques to be employed. Electron microscope autoradiography again has a different spectrum of requirements, and the techniques are here heavily biased towards obtaining the highest possible resolution. While the underlying principles governing the detection of ionising radiations by photographic emulsions are the same for the three methods of viewing, the techniques required obviously differ considerably.

Within this classification, the information that is sought from an experiment also influences greatly the choice of technique. At the simplest level, autoradiography can be used to demonstrate the distribution of radioactivity. "Is the isotope present in a given structure or not?" Techniques that may be sufficient to answer this type of problem are often rather inadequate for accurate quantitative work, where the radioactivity in one cell or structure is to be compared with that in another, or in similar cells after different experimental treatment — the process of relative quantitation. A further step in technical complexity has to be taken if the radioactivity within a structure has to be measured in absolute terms.

Finally, a miscellaneous group of factors influences the selection of technique. The energy and half-life of the isotope; the characteristics of the labelled compound, which may be soluble or insoluble in any or every one of the solvents used in the usual techniques of preparing an autoradiograph; the physical nature of the specimen, which may be a fine particulate suspension, fibres, solid tissue, and so on; the availability of emulsions, and the physical conditions which will be met in the darkroom and during exposure: all these may have a bearing on the final choice of technique.

THE SELECTION OF AN APPROPRIATE TECHNIQUE

(a) Autoradiographs for macroscopic viewing

The majority of experiments for which this type of autoradiography is needed are simple studies of the localisation of radioactivity, and quantitative data is seldom required. In autoradiographs of chromatograms, for instance, the aim is to determine which spots are radioactive and which are not. Gross differences in the amount of isotope present in each active spot can be judged by eye, while accurate measurements are usually better referred to some other detector, such as a Geiger or scintillation counter. The same considerations apply to hemisections of small animals in studies of the distribution of radioactivity through the various organs and tissues. The autoradiograph provides a rapid method of scanning a large number of possible sites for radioactivity: accurate measurements from any particular tissue are more conveniently made by Geiger or scintillation counter.

High resolving power is generally not so important as the unmistakable recognition of sites of radioactivity. Heavy blackening in active areas in the shortest possible time, combined with a low and uniform level of background is the ideal. This situation is best met by using X-ray films, which have a high sensitivity, a large grain size, and the advantages of reproducibility and simplicity of handling. Provided the source can be prepared as a flat, regular surface, there is little point in looking at alternative techniques.

Irregular surfaces cause difficulties, and may have to be dealt with by dipping in or spraying with a liquid emulsion. Here again the larger the grain size, the more intense the blackening for a given level of radioactivity.

Densitometry can be carried out on the developed X-ray film if necessary, but, as mentioned above, with large sources and the fairly high activities that are usually present, pulse-counting techniques can give more accurate and rapid quantitative data in most instances than measurements made on the autoradiograph itself.

(b) Autoradiographs for the light microscope

Higher resolution and clearer visibility of the underlying specimen are needed when the autoradiograph is to be viewed with the light microscope. The smaller grain size of the nuclear emulsions makes them obviously preferable to the X-ray emulsions for this type of work.

There are two main groups of techniques available for studies with the light microscope — grain density autoradiographs and track autoradiographs. In the former, the specimen is covered with a relatively thin layer of emulsion, in which the β particles record their passage by the production of individual silver grains. The presence of radioactivity is recognised by an increase in grain density over background levels. In track autoradiographs, a thicker emulsion layer is used, and the passage of a particle through it is recognised by the characteristic arrangement of silver grains to form a particle track. Track autoradiographs are more difficult to prepare, and it is much more tedious to extract information from them.

For studying the distribution of radioactivity within a specimen, grain density methods are clearly preferable to track autoradiographs. Apart from their simplicity, the resolution obtainable is in most cases better than with track autoradiographs, and viewing and photography of the specimen are much easier when it is not covered with a thick layer of emulsion.

If the radioactivity in one site is to be compared with that elsewhere, situations can arise in which track autoradiographs are preferable to grain density methods, though the latter will usually be the technique of choice. Grain density autoradiographs are easy to prepare, and have good resolution, particularly for isotopes with a low maximum energy. Measurements of grain density can be made rapidly, either by visual grain counting or by means of a photometric device, as described in Chapter 10 (p.174). Track autoradiographs are more difficult to prepare, and track counting requires more patience and skill than grain counting, nor can it be easily automated. Track autoradiographs are only possible with isotopes of the energy of carbon-14 (E_{max} = 155 keV) or sulphur-35 (E_{max} = 167 keV) or higher. In most situations, then, comparisons of grain density will be the basis for relative measurements of radioactivity. In a few cases, particularly when self-absorption with tritium makes it very difficult to relate the grain densities over two types of source, it may be better to go to an isotope, such as phosphorus-32, with which self-absorption becomes negligible, and to record the β particles emitted in a thick emulsion layer.

The real advantages of track autoradiography become evident in measurements of radioactivity in absolute terms. The simple relation of one track to the passage of one β particle through the emulsion makes it comparatively easy to determine the number of disintegrations taking place in the source during exposure. By contrast, absolute determinations of radioactivity with grain density autoradiographs are at best extremely difficult. Track autoradiography, then, is a necessary technique if absolute measurements are to be made with isotopes of the energy of carbon-14 or higher. It is a very precise and elegant method, but it is likely to remain a rather specialised one.

For most autoradiography for the light microscope, then, grain density techniques are the appropriate ones to use. The resolution obtainable ranges from 0.3 μ for tritium to perhaps 10 μ for the highest energies likely to be needed in biological studies. It is possible to observe a great deal of histological detail in the underlying specimen, and the comparison of grain densities over different structures is, in controlled cases, a valid measure of their relative content of radioisotope.

Two main groups of grain density techniques exist: the use of stripping film, and of liquid emulsion. Most experiments can be carried out quite adequately by either method, and the selection will often be made on secondary factors, such as the availability of emulsion, or previous familiarity with one or other technique. Stripping film is a compromise product, giving adequate sensitivity and resolving power, and the benefits of reproducibility that come from a factory-made emulsion layer. It can be used for studying the localisation of radioactivity, and for relative quantitation. It can be applied to any isotope that emits α or β particles, and techniques have been worked out for its use with soluble isotopes. It has a long shelf-life before the build-up of background makes it useless, sometimes proving adequate after 6 months. The one product, Kodak AR-10, and the one basic technique can cover the great majority of autoradiographic experiments quite adequately.

In my experience, however, nearly everything that can be done with
stripping film can also be done with liquid emulsions, in many cases somewhat
better. Many liquid emulsions are available, in a range of sensitivities and of grain
sizes, and simple modifications to the technique of applying the emulsion can
give controlled differences in emulsion thickness, from a monolayer of silver
halide crystals upwards. With a little bit of experience, then, it is possible to
select the sensitivity, grain size, and thickness of the emulsion layer to give the
optimal results for the experiment in hand. For detailed cytological work, where
unimpeded visibility of the specimen at very high magnifications is essential, a
thin layer of a fine grained emulsion can be used. For observation at low magnifications, larger sizes are available. In much the same way, the sensitivity of the
emulsion can be matched to the isotope being studied. Phosphorus-32 (E_{max} =
1.4 MeV) requires the highest possible sensitivity to record the initial part of the
tracks of the particles emitted with reasonable efficiency. Tritium (E_{max} = 18
keV) can be detected at high efficiency by an emulsion of considerably lower
sensitivity, which is likely to mean lower background levels.

In short, with the liquid emulsion techniques, it is possible to adapt the
autoradiograph to the experimental situation more accurately. But liquid emul
sion techniques also have their shortcomings, as will be seen from the following
comparison of their performance with that of stripping film in the various types
of autoradiographic experiment.

For studies of the localisation of radioactivity within tissues, my own
experience is that liquid emulsions are capable of giving better results. By
matching the grain size and sensitivity of the emulsion to the needs of the
experiment, and by using emulsion layers thinner than that provided by stripping film, it is usually possible to obtain better resolution, without any significant decrease in efficiency. Technically the process of dipping in liquid emulsion
is very quick and simple, and adhesion of emulsion to specimen is better. In
addition, the absence of the overlying layer of gelatin which is present in stripping film simplifies the staining of the specimen, and makes the use of dark field
illumination for viewing and photomicrography much easier.

When one considers relative quantitation, the user of liquid emulsions faces
the hitherto unsolved problem of producing an emulsion layer that is uniform in
thickness. Many modifications to the simple process of dipping the slide in liquid
emulsion have been tried, but I know of no way to produce a consistent and
uniform emulsion thickness on a series of slides, particularly if they carry
histological sections, which usually have a very irregular upper profile. In these
circumstances, variations in emulsion thickness from one section to another will
introduce a source of error into comparisons of grain counts that is quite

unacceptable. By contrast, stripping film is far more uniform in thickness, even over the irregularities of a tissue section, and variations in grain density over the specimen will not in general be complicated by fluctuations in the thickness of the emulsion.

Isotopes of very low maximum energy, such as tritium or iodine-125, provide an important exception to the difficulties of relative quantitation with liquid emulsions. It is very unlikely that a particle from either of these isotopes would travel more than $2\,\mu$ through a nuclear emulsion. It is relatively simple to produce an emulsion the thickness of which during exposure will not be less than $3\,\mu$. Any variations in thickness of such a layer, whether on or between slides, will not affect the efficiency with which radioactivity is recorded, since this is a function of only the lower $2\,\mu$ of the emulsion. In these circumstances, it is only the density of background grains that will vary with emulsion thickness, and, since this should be a very low figure anyhow, it is perfectly reasonable to use this type of preparation for relative quantitation.

Leblond, Kopriwa and Messier[1] have produced interesting figures illustrating this point, using as sources sections labelled with iodine-131, carbon-14, and tritium. With the two former isotopes, fluctuations in grain density of $\pm 10\%$ were observed from one part of the slide to another, after dipping in liquid emulsion. With tritium, the results were remarkably consistent, in spite of comparable variations in emulsion thickness on these slides.

To sum up the position with relative measurements of grain density, therefore, liquid emulsions can be used to give satisfactory grain density autoradiographs with tritium and iodine-125, but not with isotopes of higher energy. Stripping film, on the other hand, can give good results with any isotope.

Absolute measurements of radioactivity will often require track autoradiography. If suitable standardised reference sources are available, however, the problem simplifies itself to relating the grain densities over experimental and reference sources, and the conclusions of the previous paragraph are again applicable.

When, then, is the final verdict? When should one choose stripping film techniques, and when liquid emulsions?

If the volume and variety of autoradiographs expected in a laboratory are not large, and if, as is usually the case, absolute measurements are not required, stripping film techniques are probably the best. The one product, Kodak AR-10, and the one basic technique can be adopted to practically every experiment that suggests itself. In many laboratories, autoradiography is not the principal technique in use, but it is required from time to time to provide supplementary information. In these circumstances, it is unreasonable to use a selection of emulsions and techniques, and it is unlikely that sufficient experience will be built up to exploit the full potentialities of liquid emulsions.

If, however, the amount of autoradiography justifies the time spent in working out suitable methods for several emulsions, and the expense of keeping up regular deliveries of each product, better results can be expected with liquid emulsions than with stripping film. Grain density autoradiography can be used for studies of the localisation of radioactivity for isotopes of any energy, and for relative measurements with tritium and iodine-125. Track techniques can give relative and absolute quantitation with isotopes of higher energy. The experience gained with liquid emulsions will provide a firm basis for autoradiography with the electron microscope.

It is, of course, quite possible to use liquid emulsion and stripping film – the former for localisation, and for relative quantitation with tritium and iodine-125, the latter for relative quantitation with isotopes of higher energy. This is not a common choice, however, as most workers prefer to limit the time they spend on acquiring technical proficiency, to leave more time and effort available for their principal investigation.

(c) Autoradiographs for the electron microscope

There are two principal reasons for attempting autoradiography at the electron microscope level. The first is the need to correlate the distribution of radioactivity with the range of structures that can only be visualised with the electron microsope. The second, related to it, is the wish for the highest possible resolution.

In practice, the available techniques are based on two groups of emulsion. Ilford L4, with a mean crystal diameter of around 1400 Å, is more frequently used at the electron microscope level than any other emulsion. Its developed grains can readily be seen in the light microscope, which makes it easier to control the preparation of suitable material. The resolving power, however, is limited by the crystal diameter, and is unlikely to be better than about 1500 Å, though better results can probably be obtained in optimal conditions, with extremely thin sources labelled with tritium or iodine-125.

Two very fine-grained emulsions form the second group. These are the Gevaert NUC 307, with a mean crystal diameter of 700 Å, and the Eastman Kodak NTE, where the corresponding figure is around 500 Å. These offer the theoretical possibility of reducing the resolution to within the range of 500–1000 Å, depending on the nature and thickness of the source.

It is important to realise what a technical achievement these latter emulsions represent. When the crystal diameter is around 500–700 Å, the degree of sensitisation necessary to record the passage of β particles is approaching the theoretical limit, with a correspondingly high probability of spontaneous formation of background grains. At the same time, latent image fading is a far worse problem than with the emulsions used for light microscope work, since the severity of fading is related to crystal size. It is consequently unreasonable to expect the same high sensitivity and reliability from these two emulsions that one finds with Ilford L4.

Any improvement in resolution involves two related variables – the thickness of the specimen and the thickness of the emulsion layer. The best resolution results from a very thin specimen, and a monolayer of the smallest crystals of silver halide available. But both these factors operate to reduce the number of developed grains produced by the source in a given exposure. Reducing the specimen thickness decreases the number of radioactive disintegrations per unit area of emulsion, while the chances of a β particle traversing the monolayer of crystals without creating a latent image increase as the crystal diameter is reduced. So attempts to get very high resolution may fail to give an acceptably high yield of silver grains without exposures of many months. These may in turn prove abortive if spontaneous formation of background, or fading of the latent image, occur to any significant extent.

It is important to stress these limitations to high resolution autoradiography in the electron microscope at the outset. It is generally speaking not difficult to achieve a resolution of 1500 Å for tritium with Ilford L4, provided sufficient radioactivity can be concentrated within the source to give an adequate trace at the light microscope level. This emulsion has a long shelf-life, is easy to handle, and can be exposed for very long periods before the build-up of background or the fading of latent images limits its effectiveness. It will also record β particles of all energies, so that electron microscope autoradiographs can be obtained, though with poorer resolution, with carbon-14 or even phosphorus-32.

With the Gevaert NUC 307 or Eastman Kodak NTE emulsions, it is possible to bring the resolution down below 1000 Å for tritium or iodine-125. Their sensitivity is lower, however, so that isotopes of higher energy will only be recorded at extremely low efficiencies. The sensitivity may vary from one batch of emulsion to the next. The exposures that are possible are limited by the build-up of background, which is much faster than in Ilford L4.

It seems reasonable at the present time to make Ilford L4 emulsion the basis for the majority of autoradiographic experiments at the electron microscope level. The NUC 307 or NTE emulsions should be reserved for situations in which the highest possible resolution is essential, and previous autoradiographs with Ilford L4 have demonstrated that there is sufficient radioactivity in the source to give a reasonable number of silver grains in the limited exposure time that is possible with these emulsions.

Many techniques have been suggested for applying emulsions to a specimen as a monolayer of silver halide crystals. The techniques that will be described in Chapter 18 (p.348) are based on two methods: that of Bachmann and Salpeter[2,3], which involves dipping the specimen in liquid emulsion, and that of Caro and Van Tubergen[4], in which an emulsion layer is formed in a wire loop, and then placed in contact with the specimen. Both methods are capable of giving satisfactory monolayers of emulsion.

THE SELECTION OF EMULSION

This topic will be considered in more detail under the separate sections devoted to the various techniques, but a few introductory remarks here may draw attention to the general principles involved.

The choice of a large grained X-ray emulsion for macroscopic specimens has already been referred to, and the relative merits of Ilford L4 and Gevaert 307 or Eastman Kodak NTE emulsions for electron microscope autoradiography have also been discussed.

It is when one considers the emulsions available for light microscope auto-radiography that there is a wide choice of products commercially available. Even here, however, selection of a particular technique may virtually imply selection of one emulsion. With the stripping film technique, there is only one reasonable choice — Kodak AR-10. Other stripping films are obtainable and these are mentioned briefly in Chapter 15 (p.285), but AR-10 is such a widely used product, and so much data is available in the literature on various aspects of its handling and performance, that it is in most instances the emulsion of choice.

With track autoradiography, Ilford G5 emulsion is probably the best emulsion to use. Its sensitivity is as high as that of any other emulsion available, and its relatively large grain size makes the viewing of tracks through thick emulsion layers relatively simple. But perhaps the most powerful reason for its selection in this context is the detailed information available on many aspects of the recording of β particle tracks in G5. From this data, one can calculate the appropriate correction factor for β particles of too low an initial energy to give rise to a recognisable track (p.240), for instance, in any experiment to measure the radioactivity of a source in absolute terms. Long and tedious calibration experiments would be required before this type of calculation could be made for another emulsion.

It is with the use of liquid emulsions for grain density autoradiography that there is a really wide selection of possible emulsions. The widest range of products is provided by Ilford Ltd., of Ilford, Essex, England. Their materials that are of interest to the autoradiographer come in a range of sensitivities from 0–5: emulsions with the number code 0 will record α particles, but not β particles: those labelled 2 will record β particles up to about 50 keV in energy, as well as α particles; while those labelled 5 will record β particles at minimum ionisation (*i.e.* at energies above about 1 MeV) as a continuous track, as well, of course, as less energetic β particles. Ilford emulsions are also produced in three grain sizes – the G emulsions, with a mean crystal diameter of 0.27 μ, the K emulsions, at 0.20 μ, and the L emulsions, at 0.15 μ. Undeveloped crystals from each of these emulsion types are illustrated in Fig. 1(p.12). Each emulsion therefore has a letter and number, which identify it. G5 will record β particles at minimum ionisation, and has large silver halide crystals; K2 is sensitive only to β particles of low energy, and to α particles, and has a smaller crystal size; L4 is nearly as sensitive as G5, but has the smallest crystal size that Ilford provide.

Eastman Kodak, of Rochester, N.Y., produce the NTB series, with a mean crystal diameter of about 0.20 μ. NTB emulsion will record α particles, and low energy β particles, such as those from tritium and iodine-125. NTB-2 is more highly sensitised, and can be used for β particles up to about 200 keV, though the grain spacing in tracks at this sort of energy is fairly sparse. NTB-3 will record β particles at minimum ionisation.

Other manufacturers make emulsions suitable for autoradiography, for instance Gevaert; and the fine grained NIKFI emulsions have been used both in cosmic ray research and in autoradiography in the Soviet Union, but since I have no personal experience with these emulsions and they have not been widely reported on in the Western literature, they will not be discussed further. Their characteristics are listed by Barkas[6]. Several emulsions have recently also been produced by Japanese manufacturers.

There are several important differences between the Ilford and Eastman Kodak emulsions, and techniques evolved for the one will not be suitable for the other without modification. For instance, the Ilford emulsions are less sensitive to visible light, and it is possible to work with lighter safelighting than is needed for Eastman Kodak products. This does not matter much with a simple dipping procedure, but if cryostat sections are to be cut in the darkroom, as in the autoradiography of soluble isotopes, the whole process becomes much quicker and easier with Ilford emulsions, due to this one factor. The physical consistency of the emulsions is notably different, Ilford products requiring dilution to give a layer of 30 μ or so, while the Eastman Kodak emulsions give a thin layer of around 5 μ when used undiluted. The Ilford emulsions should be exposed at a relative humidity of about 45%, and they show little latent image fading under these conditions. Eastman Kodak emulsions should be much more rigorously dried[7] to preserve the latent image, to conditions which would produce a high background from stress artefacts (see p.91) in the corresponding Ilford products. The developing schedules suitable for the one are not necessarily optimal for the other.

It is probably advisable to use either the NTB emulsions, or the Ilford products. So many points of technique are different in the two cases that it complicates the smooth running of the darkroom unnecessarily to use both types. My own choice is for the Ilford emulsions, with their greater range of characteristics, but this decision must depend a little on geographical position. Nuclear emulsions are best stored at a constant temperature of around 4°, which is difficult to ensure during shipment overseas. Even when packaged in ice, transportation by air may cause a significant increase in background, perhaps due to the cosmic ray intensity at high altitudes. It may therefore be better to use a locally produced emulsion, which can be obtained in good condition, than an overseas product which may have a variable shelf-life and background level on arrival. Certainly, in my own experience, the Ilford emulsions had lower and more reproducible levels of background in Birmingham and Oxford, England, than in New York State, though they were still quite usable in the latter place.

How does one select the correct level of sensitivity for a given experiment? It should be realised that a high degree of sensitisation produces an emulsion with a higher rate of production of spontaneous background grains, and a higher sensitivity to all the extraneous factors, such as pressure or environmental radiation, which can produce latent images. Clearly, if a less sensitive emulsion will still record the radiation under study satisfactorily, there will be benefits gained from its use in terms of lower levels of background. NTB and the Ilford 0 emulsions should be used for α particles. NTB2 and the Ilford level 2 of sensitisation give excellent results with tritium and iodine-125, but both may fail to record the β particles from the high energy end of the spectrum with carbon-14 and sulphur-35. Ilford level 4 should cope well with carbon-14 and sulphur-35. NTB3 and Ilford level 5 will record β particles of any energy.

When one considers the selection of an appropriate grain size, the method of viewing that will be employed is of paramount importance. If a stained section is to be viewed at low magnifications by transmitted light, a relatively large developed silver grain is needed, such as that provided by the NTB series, or the Ilford G series. High magnification work with transmitted light and stained sections is probably more satisfactory with the Ilford K series. At the highest magnifications, the Ilford L series can be seen satisfactorily by transmitted light.

If, however, dark-field illumination is used to view the autoradiograph, the fine grained Ilford K and L series can be used much more extensively (see Chapter 9, p.158). The advantages of this system are that, even at high magnifications, the silver grains can be held to such a small size that they do not interfere with the microscopy of the underlying tissue. They nevertheless give an unmistakeable light signal, even in the presence of heavily stained biological material.

The choice of grain size, then, depends on the final effect that is required. While it may be practicable to produce a small developed grain from a large silver halide crystal by selecting the correct conditions of development, one should not attempt to produce a grain that is larger than usual by increased development, as this will inevitably give a higher background than is necessary.

EXPERIMENTS WITH TWO ISOTOPES

It is sometimes desirable to autoradiograph material that is labelled simultaneously with two different radioactive isotopes. In this way, the relationship between patterns of synthesis of DNA and RNA, or of RNA and protein can be studied in the same cell population, using precursors labelled with tritium and with carbon-14, for example. It would be extremely useful if the microscopist could determine very simply which cells are labelled with one or the other isotope, or with both at once.

Unfortunately, the basic physics of the situation makes this simple differentiation between two different isotopes almost unobtainable. In the case of tritium and carbon-14, for instance, the β particles from tritium have initial energies from 18 keV down to zero; those from carbon-14 are from 155 keV down to zero. In the range from 18 keV to zero, then, β particles will be given off by both isotopes, and no technique exists to differentiate between the two at these energies. This energy range includes about 15% of the β particles emitted by carbon-14. Any attempt to differentiate between these two isotopes must take account of this overlap in energies. The presence of carbon-14 can readily be inferred by a number of techniques which indicate the presence of particles of higher energy than 18 keV. The presence of tritium can only be established by showing that the number of particles of less than 18 keV coming from a source is significantly greater than the figure predicted for labelling with carbon-14 alone.

It is quite possible to autoradiograph the specimen with a single layer of Ilford G5 emulsion about 30 μ thick (p.321). In this situation, tritium will produce many single developed grains over the source, with decreasing probabilities of finding two, three, or more grains per β particle, up to the maximum of about 7 grains, which would be a highly improbable finding[8]. All these grains would lie within 3 μ of the source, the majority of them within 1 μ. Carbon-14 will give rise to tracks of up to 80 or so grains, at the improbable upper limit, and these grains may occur up to 40 μ from the source, though most of them will lie within 10 μ of the source[5]. It is possible, then, to scan the emulsion for tracks of more than 10 grains, extending more than 5 μ through the emulsion. These can only come from carbon-14. All the cells are then examined for grains lying within 3 μ. Those with grains within 3 μ that are not labelled with carbon-14 tracks are sites of localisation of tritium. All those identified as sites of carbon-14 activity will also contain silver grains within the smaller emulsion volume. Tritium will only be confidently recognised in these cells if the proportion of silver grains in the smaller volume is obviously greater than would be expected from the known yield of carbon-14 tracks. This can simply be determined by comparison with reference cells labelled with carbon-14 alone.

This sounds a difficult procedure, but in fact it can be greatly simplified by controlling the ratio of tritium to carbon-14 in the specimen. If this ratio is deliberately kept high, any cell significantly labelled with tritium will have a higher grain density in the small volume of emulsion over it than would be expected from the heaviest labelling with carbon-14.

Several attempts have been made to devise methods of autoradiography that would simplify still further this differentiation between tritium and isotopes of higher energy. Baserga[9,10] suggested a double exposure method. He dipped his slides in Eastman Kodak Emulsion (NTB-2 or NTB-3), giving a presumed thickness of about 5 μ during exposure, and developed this layer after exposure in the usual way. The section was then stained, and a layer of nitrocellulose applied over the autoradiograph. The slide was then dipped a second time in emulsion and exposed and developed once more: this time, only the second emulsion layer could record the passage of β particles. It has sometimes been assumed that silver grains in the first emulsion layer are caused by tritium, those in the second layer being due to carbon-14, an assumption unfortunately strengthened by the diagram that has been used to illustrate the technique[10]. Obviously, tritium cannot affect the second emulsion layer: it should be equally obvious that carbon-14 can affect the first, as well as tritium.

The principle of two exposures is useful, however, as it enables one to exploit to the full the effect of a high ratio of tritium to carbon-14 in the source. The first exposure can be made relatively short: the very high tritium activities in the source can cause sufficient blackening in this time, while the much lower activity of carbon-14 will hardly produce a significant number of silver grains in the first emulsion layer. The second exposure can be made much longer, to collect a reasonable grain density from the low activity carbon-14.

It is possible to use two layers of stripping film for the two exposures, the gelatin support for the first layer providing an effective separation in focal level between the two emulsions. This has the advantage that the various layers of this sandwich are of defined and reproducible thickness. The final thickness of two complete layers of stripping film makes microscopy rather difficult, however, and an unsupported emulsion layer is sometimes used for the second exposure (p.285).

Some means of isolating the second emulsion layer from the first during exposure and processing is necessary. But given that fact, many variations are possible to try to improve the ease with which silver grains in the two layers may be differentiated from each other during observation of the completed autoradiograph. Kesse, Harriss and Gyftaki[11] have used Gevaert NUC 715 for the first layer, and Eastman Kodak NTB-2 for the second, producing differences in the size of developed grains as a distinguishing feature of the two layers. Field, Dawson and Gibbs[12] have suggested the development of coloured grains in the first layer as an aid to discrimination.

The sensitivity of the two emulsion layers might also be varied to improve the discrimination between tritium and carbon-14. An emulsion such as Ilford K2 records tritium at relatively high efficiencies, while its sensitivity is not enough to record the initial part of the track of particles from the high energy end of the spectrum from carbon-14, except as sporadic grains. This emulsion could be used for a first exposure, and the size of developed silver grain held down by the method of development. The second emulsion layer could then be Ilford G5, which has a larger crystal diameter and a higher sensitivity. Full development of this second layer would give a clear difference in grain size between the two layers.

However simple the differentiation of the silver grains in the two emulsion layers becomes, the problem of sorting out the relative contributions of tritium and carbon-14 to the first layer remains. This is essentially a statistical problem. The determination of the percentage of cells labelled in a population may require a certain amount of care, even if one isotope only is used: on pp.221–224 a technique for doing this is presented, which enables radioactive cells which have not produced a silver grain during exposure to be recognised. With two isotopes, the same problem exists, but in more complex form. Cells containing carbon-14 may give rise to grains in the lower emulsion only, forming the lower end of the Poisson distribution of grain numbers per cell when one looks at the upper emulsion alone. Some of the problems inherent in this type of analysis have been discussed by Harriss[13] . Clearly, a high standard of technical competence is essential for accurate work with two isotopes. If the thickness of the first emulsion layer varies, or that of the inert layer between the emulsions, the efficiency of each emulsion for carbon-14 will also vary, introducing a greater uncertainty in the attempt to decide whether or not grains in the lower layer are due to carbon-14.

The simultaneous use of tritium and carbon-14 has been discussed at considerable length, as this is the combination of isotopes that has been most studied to date. Clearly, tritium can be paired in the same way with sulphur-35, or any other β emitting isotope of similar or higher energy. There is no reason why iodine-125 could not be used as the less energetic isotope in place of tritium.

Provided there is sufficient difference between the maximum energies of the two isotopes, it is always possible to differentiate between them. If carbon-14 or sulphur-35, for instance, has to be examined in the same material as phosphorus-32, this can be done by a technique similar to the single emulsion technique described above (p.257). An emulsion layer 60 μ thick would serve to demonstrate the presence of tracks with more grains in them than could be due to carbon-14: a comparison of the ratio of short to long tracks from each source could determine whether there were significantly more short tracks than would be expected from phosphorus-32 alone. In this case, track analysis of this sort would provide the only basis for differentiating the two isotopes: it would be very difficult to devise techniques with two emulsion layers like those that have been proposed where tritium is one of the two isotopes.

SETTING UP A NEW TECHNIQUE

There are a few experiments which should be done before any biological investigation is started on with a new autoradiographic technique. It may in some cases be possible to get the required information from the literature, or from another laboratory, but, in the majority of instances, there is no real alternative to doing these preliminary experiments oneself. Two factors require investigation – the possibility of loss or displacement of radioactive material in the process of autoradiography, and the optimal conditions of development.

(a) Loss or displacement of radioactive material

In some experiments, such as the incorporation of labelled thymidine into DNA, there is sufficient evidence available in the literature to assure that there will be no significant loss of label on preparation of tissues for autoradiography.

In many other cases, however, this type of documentation will not be available. The techniques of histology and of autoradiography that are necessary for labelled material that is soluble in aqueous or organic solutions are described in Chapter 8 (p.123). They are very different from the routine methods of paraffin embedding and dipping in molten emulsion, for instance.

Conventional histological and autoradiographic methods give a finished product which can and should be of a very high standard when viewed under the microscope. The methods of dry autoradiography inevitably give a poorer histological preparation. It is preferable to reserve the latter techniques for experiments which really require them.

If the distribution of a labelled compound, such as a drug or hormone, is to be studied in a tissue, it should be shown that the methods of tissue preparation and autoradiography do not involve loss of radioactivity at any stage. The biological material can be sampled by pulse counting techniques before, during and after histological processing, or the processing fluids themselves can be examined for radioactivity which has leached out of the tissue. Alternatively, autoradiographs can be prepared by conventional histological methods, and also by cryostat sectioning and dry autoradiography: a comparison of the final grain distributions should indicate if substantial removal or displacement of radioactive material has taken place in embedding and dipping in liquid emulsion. It is worth emphasising that the production of a reproducible pattern of labelling by conventional methods of histology and autoradiography is no guarantee that loss of radioactivity has not occurred[14].

Experiments involving the incorporation of a precursor molecule into some tissue component are rather more difficult to assess. Here, one relies on the histological processing to extract all the unincorporated precursor, so that the presence of radioactivity in the solutions through which the tissue has passed is to be expected. The chemical analysis of the radioactive molecules extracted and those retained in the tissue may be needed before a given routine can be accepted as satisfactory. These problems are discussed in greater detail in Chapter 7.

(b) Development

Many of the factors that must be examined in setting up a technique are described in the particular section that deals with that technique later. The one factor that is common to all methods of autoradiography is the development of the exposed emulsion. As was seen in Chapter 2 (p.15), development is a form of amplification, increasing the deposit of metallic silver present at each latent image speck until it reaches the threshold of visibility. This threshold is a function of the methods that will be used to view the finished autoradiograph. High or low magnification, transmitted bright field or incident dark field illumination, the intensity and colour of staining which will provide a background against which the grains must be visualised, all these will influence the size to which grains must be developed in order to be recognised. The amount of silver at the original latent image specks themselves determines the time required for the grains to grow up to this threshold, under constant conditions of development.

It is thus rather naive to imagine that the conditions of development for a given emulsion can be specified in a final and definitive way. The ideal conditions should be determined in the context of the particular experiment. The simplest way in which to do this is to take a series of slides with the type of labelled biological specimen on them that will be used experimentally. Cover them with emulsion and expose them, and then separate the slides into perhaps six different groups, each containing at least three slides. With the developer that will be used subsequently, these slides should then be processed, holding constant the dilution of the developer, its temperature, and the amount of agitation given to the slides, but varying the time of development. If, for instance, the data sheet from the manufacturer recommends a time of 4 min, it would be reasonable to develop for 1, 2, 4, 6, 8 and 10 min. After fixation, staining, and mounting for microscopy, the autoradiographs should be viewed under the conditions chosen for examining the later experimental material, and the most suitable development time selected. This series of autoradiographs can be kept for future reference, and the best development time for subsequent experiments that may require different conditions of microscpy can be found simply by examining the slides from this time series under the new conditions of viewing. Such a series is illustrated in Fig. 4 (p.20).

The study of development time is an essential prelude to reliable autoradiography. If the best time appears to be very short, either 1 or 2 min in the above example, it may be a good idea either to dilute the developer further, or to work at a slightly lower temperature, so that the inevitable small deviations from accurate timing that are bound to occur occasionally in the darkroom do not have too dramatic an effect on the end product. Similarly, there is no point in using times much in excess of 10 min with thin emulsion layers, if the process of development can be conveniently speeded up by using a higher temperature, or a more concentrated developer. It is not easy to achieve absolutely reproducible conditions of development. It would be a mistake, therefore, to choose a development time that is only just short of producing an unacceptably high number of background grains, since slight variations in the amount of agitation given to the slides in developer may be sufficient to produce this high background in occasional batches of slides. One should select a time that appears to give a little latitude for slight errors in technique without damaging the experiment.

Each emulsion will require its own time study. In my experience, Ilford G5 and K2 emulsions, for instance, need quite different conditions of development.

It is possible, though not necessary, to place the results of such a study of development time on a quantitative basis (Fig. 3, p.18), by plotting the observed density of grains in labelled areas against time, and also the increase in background against time. In most instances, the density of grains in labelled areas will rise to a certain figure, and then level off. The density of background grains will remain at a fairly low level at first, rising rapidly at longer development times. With such a plot available, the choice of the best development time becomes more precise, as it is relatively easy to select a point on the plateau of grain density well short of the rapid climb in density of background grains.

CONTROL PROCEDURES NECESSARY FOR EACH EXPERIMENT

It cannot be emphasised too strongly that autoradiography is not a simple staining technique, but a method for carrying out experiments with radioactive isotopes[15]. There is no valid deduction that can be made from looking at a single autoradiograph. The situation is similar to liquid scintillation counting where the counts observed from a single sample are quite impossible to interpret. In both cases, specific controls are needed in each experiment to exclude the presence of spurious counts, and the possible loss of counts through some process reducing the efficiency of the recording medium.

Silver grains can be produced in the emulsion by chemography (the chemical interaction of specimen and emulsion), by heat, by light, or by pressure. The most reasonable control against these false positives is to expose, with every batch of autoradiographs, identical specimens which are not radioactive. It is not sufficient to do this control experiment only once, as the conditions of working may change slowly over a period of weeks without the autoradiographer being aware of the relevance of the change. It takes very little planning and work to have one slide which is not radioactive available for inclusion in every batch of autoradiographs.

The occurrence of silver grains from causes other than radioactivity in the specimen is usually fairly easy to detect. By contrast, the loss of silver grains from areas in which they should be found is very easy to miss. The comparable phenomenon in liquid scintillation counting is quenching, the process whereby the energy lost by the β particles is transformed, not into a pulse of light, but into other forms of energy, or into light of inappropriate wavelengths. No results with liquid scintillation counting are acceptable unless some control step to indicate the presence and extent of quenching has been carried out. In the same way, no attempt to interpret an autoradiograph should be accepted unless it can be demonstrated that the emulsion was truly recording the presence of radioactivity as developed silver grains. The common causes of false negatives of this sort are chemography, and fading of the latent image during exposure: the latter is fully discussed on p.228.

The best control against such false negatives is to take one experimental slide from each batch of autoradiographs and to expose it to light, or to a standard dose of external radiation. This control slide is then returned to the container holding the rest of the slides, so that exposure and development can proceed under identical conditions. The result of this simple control procedure is often surprising. Fig.33 (p.95) illustrates an instance where gross loss of emulsion response took place with a block of tissue, where the rest of the biological material being autoradiographed in the same experiment did not show any fading effect on the emulsion. If these blocks had represented the results of some experimental procedure carried out *in vivo*, this unexpected artefact might have been misinterpreted in terms of the abolition of the uptake of radioactivity, if adequate controls had not been available.

These two control steps – the specimen that is known to be non-radioactive, and the experimental specimen that has been exposed to light – should form just as vital a part of any autoradiographic experiment as the measurement of background and of quenching in liquid scintillation counting. If you go to the trouble of taking these steps, it is only reasonable to say so in any published account of your work.

If chemography has been found to occur occasionally in a series of specimens, it is possible to cover one section from each block with an impermeable film (these are discussed further in Chapter 7). If there is no significant difference in the distribution of silver grains between this control section and the sections without an impermeable film, it is reasonable to assume that there has been no chemography, and to base one's findings on the material without the film.

There is no technical difficulty in applying the necessary controls to most autoradiographic experiments. The only barrier to their routine use is a failure to realise that they are necessary.

THE STATISTICAL DESIGN OF AUTORADIOGRAPHIC EXPERIMENTS

Unless only the crudest correlations between grain density and radioactivity of the specimen are needed, every experiment is an exercise in statistical methods. Even the question "Is this structure labelled or not?" involves comparing the grain densities over the structure with those over and around neighbouring structures, and those seen on the control slides.

It is certainly not true that an experienced observer can "interpret" an autoradiograph satisfactorily. Many of my own confident predictions on first looking at a slide have had to be considerably modified when the analysis of the grain counts was available. This might merely indicate that I am a poor observer, had I not seen the same process affect others with more experience. There is no alternative to the careful collection and analysis of quantitative data, except the method of recording the presence of radioactivity under the headings of "Heavy trace", "Light trace", and "Absent". Even at this crude level, differences in the depth of staining of the underlying specimen can influence one's estimates of grain density to a surprising extent.

The statistical design and analysis of autoradiographic experiments are discussed briefly on p.216–225. It can be seen from that section that the decisions made on the methods of analysing the data are often restricted by the earlier decisions that have determined the conduct of the experiment. The benefits in statistical accuracy to be gained from careful pairing of observations at points where the experimental material is particularly variable are very considerable: the decisions on the number of animals in each group, the number of slides per animal, and so on, can also affect the precision of the experiment greatly. There is a lot to be said for a pilot experiment with few animals and sections, to provide some clue about the differences in grain density that have to be detected. In consultation with the statistician, if possible, the plan of the final experiment can then be worked out. The accumulation of autoradiographic data is slow and expensive, if costed to include the time of the microscopist. A deliberate and careful pilot experiment is usually a good investment, permitting the design of the major experiment to achieve the best possible precision with minimum effort.

Probably the most critical stage in the evaluation of any experiment is the actual collection of grain or track counts. The selection of the volumes of emulsion from which counts are to be taken is discussed at length in Chapter 11 (p.193). Once the decision has been made as to the precise volumes of emulsion to be examined, their position, size, and shape should be translated into practical directions to the microscopist, so that he will collect counts from a randomised series of selected volumes. In this way, the chances of the selection of a particular volume of emulsion for counting being influenced, even subconsciously, by the grain density within it can be kept to a minimum. I find it valuable to hide the identity of each slide from the microscopist by giving the entire series of autoradiographs code numbers. In this way, none of the decisions taken at the time of counting can be influenced either by the microscopist's expectations about the result of the experiment, or by his determination *not* to be biased by his expectations.

It is always better to count from different areas of specimen on many autoradiographs than to count exhaustively from one small area on a single slide. There is less chance for a local factor, such as pressure or inadequate drying, to influence the whole experiment.

THE DESIGN AND EQUIPMENT OF THE DARKROOM

Since the darkroom is an essential part of any autoradiographic experiment, a few words about its design are probably in place here. It is the laboratory in which many of the important steps of the experiment are carried out, and a bit of care and thought in its design and equipment will pay dividends.

Ideally, it should be kept for autoradiography. The requirements of a photographic unit are very different. In particular, temperature and humidity can affect the preparation of autoradiographs critically, while normal photographic procedures can tolerate a wide range of conditions. The standards of cleanliness are necessarily far higher in a room where nuclear emulsions for subsequent viewing under the microscope are handled. It is seldom satisfactory to prepare autoradiographs in a darkroom that is routinely used by a photographic unit.

Several workers I know have darkrooms that resemble converted broom cupboards. While this may be necessary if more space is not available, it is not satisfactory. Many of the techniques of autoradiography are more simply and conveniently carried out by two people working together, and some techniques require relatively bulky pieces of apparatus, such as a cryostat, to function in the darkroom. A light trap, enabling people to enter and leave the darkroom without admitting light, is essential, particularly if track autoradiographs are to be prepared, as these may take many hours to process.

Ideally, the temperature and the humidity in the darkroom should be controlled. For Kodak AR-10 stripping film, the ideal conditions are $15°-18°$, and 60–65% relative humidity, and considerable deviations from these conditions can make the technique almost impossible (see Chapter 15, p.289). For the

Ilford emulsions, the temperature should not be much over 20°, and the relative humidity 45—50%. Stable specified conditions like these are easier to obtain if the darkroom has no wall common with the outside of the building, and hence is little influenced by changes in the weather. By the time a darkroom is lightproof, it is usually also poorly ventilated so that an exhaust fan is a good idea. The air intake should be easily accessible: this makes it a simple matter to alter the humidity inside the darkroom by passing the entering air through water, or through a drying agent. Obviously, a thermometer and humidity gauge are needed.

In general, builders have no idea how dark a darkroom ought to be and they will frequently hand over a room into which the sun sends shafts of light. The user must be prepared to complete its light proofing himself, after a full 20 min in darkness to give full dark adaptation. It is easy to miss thin, horizontal beams of light at other than head height. If they occur at or about the height of the working surface, they may elude detection, unless specifically looked for, and cause a high level of background.

Safelight and ceiling light should be on separate switches, so that absolute darkness is possible, and preferably the switches should be well apart, so there is no danger of confusing them. It is usually a good idea to have a small bench safelight, in addition to the central one, for special techniques such as cryostat sectioning, and for working with the light reflected from surfaces, as with stripping film. The bulbs in the safelights should be 15 W or less.

Adequate working surfaces are essential. It is a good idea, if possible, to designate one area for preparing autoradiographs, and another for developing and fixing them. In Dr. Leblond's department at McGill University, separate darkrooms are used for these purposes[16]. It is useful to have a plentiful supply of electric points, so that driers, stirrers, waterbaths, and so on can be used as required without elaborate tangles of wires.

A refrigerator is essential, both to store the emulsion prior to use, and to expose autoradiographs. Once again, this should be kept for autoradiography. It is a good idea to place some lead or steel shielding, either inside the refrigerator or around it, to reduce the level of extrinsic radiation. Naturally the darkroom should be situated well away from any known source of radiation. As far as cosmic rays are concerned, a large building will provide a certain amount of screening: given the choice, the basement of a multistorey building is a better place for a darkroom than the roof, or a single-storey structure.

A sink with water supply is necessary in the darkroom, preferably in the area chosen for developing and fixing.

Cleanliness is extremely important. Wet nuclear emulsion will collect dust very fast, so that any step taken to make the darkroom easy to clean and dust is a good idea. Any shelves or cupboards should have doors, and apparatus not in use should be put away.

As far as equipment is concerned, the items needed for each technique will be indicated in the appropriate chapter. One general point that requires emphasis is that all electrical apparatus, including the switches on the light circuits, should not emit flashes of light. Many items of equipment that are perfectly satisfactory in normal laboratory use can be seen to emit showers of sparks when used in absolute darkness.

REFERENCES

1　C.P. Leblond, B.M. Kopriwa and B. Messier, in R. Wegmann (Ed.), *Histochemistry and Cytochemistry,* Pergamon, London, 1963.
2　M.M. Salpeter and L. Bachmann, *J. Cell Biol.,* 22 (1964) 469.
3　L. Bachmann and M.M. Salpeter, *Lab. Invest.,* 14 (1965) 1041.
4　L.G. Caro and R.P. van Tubergen, *J. Cell Biol.,* 15 (1962) 173.
5　H. Levi, A.W. Rogers, M.W. Bentzon and A. Nielsen, *Kgl. Danske Videnskab. Selskab. Mat.–Fys. Medd.,* 33 (1963) No. 11.
6　W.H. Barkas, *Nuclear Research Emulsions,* Part 1, Academic Press, New York, 1963.
7　B. Messier and C.P. Leblond, *Proc. Soc. Exptl. Biol. Med.,* 96 (1957) 7.
8　H. Levi, *Scand. J. Haematol.,* 1 (1964) 138.
9　R. Baserga, *J. Histochem. Cytochem.,* 9 (1961) 586.
10　R. Baserga, *J. Cell Biol.,* 12 (1962) 633.
11　M. Kesse, E.B. Harriss and E. Gyftaki, in *Radio-isotope Sample Measurement Techniques in Medicine and Biology,* IAEA, Vienna, 1965.
12　E.O. Field, K.B. Dawson and J.E. Gibbs, *Stain Technol.,* 40 (1965) 295.
13　E.B. Harriss and D. Hoelzer, *Proc. Roy. Microscop. Soc.,* 6 (1971) 143.
14　W.E. Stumpf and L.J. Roth, *J. Histochem. Cytochem.,* 14 (1966) 274.
15　A.W. Rogers, *Ann. Chir. Gynaecol. Fenniae,* 58 (1969) 269.
16　B.M. Kopriwa, *J. Histochem. Cytochem.,* 11 (1963) 553.

CHAPTER 14

The Autoradiography of Macroscopic Specimens

Autoradiography is not limited to microscopic specimens. Whole animals that have been sectioned, whole bones, or large and complex structures such as the brain may require scanning to find the distribution within them of radioactive material. In addition, many methods of chemical analysis produce specimens in which compounds which may be radioactive are separated in space from other related compounds. In fact, the autoradiography of chromatograms is so widely practised that it probably produces a greater volume of autoradiographs annually than does the study of sectioned biological material. Not only chromatograms may be autoradiographed: electrophoresis gels, precipitin reactions, in fact any method of analysis that gives spatial separation of the compounds studied may be combined with exposure to photographic emulsion.

There is no fundamental difference between an autoradiograph produced for viewing naked-eye and one for examination under the microscope. The geometrical factors influencing efficiency and resolution are common to both, as are the causes of background and the sources of artefact. The differences that arise in the autoradiography of large specimens are practical ones. The resolution that is required is usually measured in millimetres rather than microns. The presence of radioactivity in the source is now recognised by blackening of the film, not by a higher density of individual silver grains. Quantitative measurements of radioactivity are technically much simpler by electronic pulse-counting methods than is the case with sources of cellular dimensions: it may be possible, for instance, to use a Geiger counter with a small aperture directly over the surface of the specimen, to elute the radioactive area from a chromatogram for scintillation counting, or to dissect out the labelled organ for counting from the animal that has been examined by whole-body autoradiography.

Macroscopic autoradiographs, then, are usually required to give a quick, simple indication of the distribution of radioactivity between relatively large areas. In this situation, the emulsions produced commercially for X-ray films have several important advantages over the nuclear research emulsions used for

References p. 282

autoradiography for the light and electron microscopes. These nuclear emulsions have a small crystal size, and hence a small developed silver grain. Although their efficiency is high in terms of the number of developed grains per incident β particle, a very high density of developed grains is needed to produce blackening of the emulsion visible to the unaided eye. X-ray emulsions have mean crystal diameters an order of magnitude larger than the nuclear research emulsions. Fewer developed grains per unit area are therefore needed to give recognisable blackening. If one defines the efficiency of a macroscopic autoradiograph as the blackening, or optical density, of a layer of emulsion of constant thickness produced by a given exposure to radiation, X-ray emulsions are many times more efficient than nuclear emulsions.

The choice of X-ray film for this type of autoradiograph has many advantages. The films available commercially are very uniform in thickness and in emulsion response, they have a reasonably long shelf-life before the build-up of background reduces their usefulness appreciably, and the optimal conditions for development are usually stated by the manufacturer.

The preparation of large samples for autoradiography should therefore be designed with the use of X-ray film in mind. In other words, wherever possible, the specimen should present a flat surface to the film. In the case of chromatograms this is easily managed. Solid specimens can often be sectioned, ground, or otherwise flattened to achieve the same end. Irregular surfaces that cannot be reduced to a convenient shape may require coating with molten emulsion.

Specimens labelled with tritium are a special case. The specimen itself is almost always much thicker than the maximum range of the β particles from tritium, there may be a small air gap between specimen and film, and X-ray film itself is always coated with a layer of gelatin $0.5-1.0 \mu$ thick to protect the emulsion from abrasion during handling. These three factors combine to produce an extremely low efficiency for tritium. The several methods that have been proposed to get around this problem will be discussed later in the chapter.

WHOLE-BODY AUTORADIOGRAPHY

This technique is associated with the name of Dr. Sven Ullberg,[1-3] who pioneered the method for studying the distributions of drugs and hormones throughout the tissues of an experimental animal. His technique has the advantage that many tissues throughout the body can be scanned for the presence of the labelled compound rapidly and cheaply. It would be quite possible to prepare samples for pulse counting from a wide range of tissues from an experimental animal, but difficult to ensure that concentration by a totally unexpected organ had not been missed in selecting the tissues for counting. The technique of whole-body autoradiography has the further advantage that freely diffusible material is retained *in situ* during specimen preparation.

The specimen, which may be a whole mouse, is rapidly frozen, ideally in some sort of restraining structure to keep its final shape fairly reproducible. It is then mounted on the stage of a large sledge microtome, and kept frozen at about $-10°$. The body is best supported on the stage by packing it around with a slurry made of carboxymethylcellulose in water: this freezes rapidly, and can be built up into a satisfactory block around the body, without increasing the difficulties of sectioning or affecting the emulsion during exposure. The block is then trimmed down to approximately the right region. Sections are usually cut at about 20 μ thickness, though complete sections through a mouse have been cut as thin as 2 μ. Naturally enough, these thin sections covering a very large area are fragile. Their handling is simplified by applying adhesive tape (No. 810, Minnesota Mining and Manufacturing Co.) to the surface of the block before cutting the section, After cutting, the tape, with section attached, is lifted off the block. Difficulties have been experienced with the behaviour of different batches of adhesive tape at low temperatures.

As with cryostat sections of fresh frozen tissue (Chapter 8), these whole body sections may cause chemography if applied directly to the emulsion. Dr. Ullberg has found that leaving the section in the cryostat for 3–4 days produces sufficient freeze-drying to reduce chemography to negligible levels. It is as well to be aware of this possible artefact, and to expose the usual control, nonradioactive, sections to normal and fogged emulsion layers to exclude chemography (p.263).

After drying, the sections, still attached to the tape, are exposed by sticking the tape on to the emulsion. With all isotopes of maximum energies equal to or higher than carbon-14 and sulphur-35, an X-ray film should be used. Kodak Royal Blue Medical X-ray film has often been used in the past. This product is now no longer available: Kodak RP Royal X-Omat film is a suitable replacement. Eastman Kodak Company has suggested[4] that Kodak single-coated medical X-ray film – blue sensitive – has a higher sensitivity for low-energy β emitters. This film is only manufactured by Kodak in Rochester, N.Y., but should be available from suppliers of Kodak X-ray Products outside the U.S.A. Alternatively, Ilford Industrex C may be used. For tritium and isotopes such as iodine-125 that produce a low energy electron by internal conversion, Dr. Ullberg exposes against a plate coated with Ilford G5 emulsion. The nuclear emulsion is less efficient in terms of blackening than an X-ray film, but this is compensated for to some extent by the lack of an anti-abrasion coating of

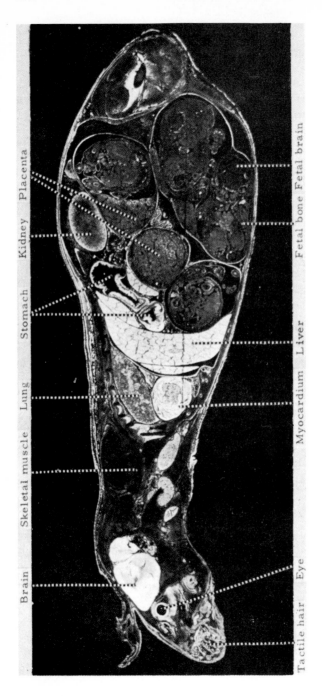

gelatin on the G5 plates. To date, there has been little attempt to exploit the phenomenon of β-radioluminescence in whole-body autoradiography, in spite of its wide and successful use in radiochromatography (p.276).

After exposure, the section is separated from the film, and may then be fixed and stained. The detail in the resultant autoradiograph is often quite clear (Fig. 77).

It is possible to use a similar technique on other large blocks, such as the brain, in which a rapid survey through the whole organ is required. Although the technique has usually been used in the context of localising diffusible drugs and hormones, one can also fix the tissue or organ first, and extract soluble precursors before autoradiographing sites of incorporation, or cut frozen sections through the whole body and then fix the sections, and extract labelled precursors in this way.

Very hard specimens, such as bones or teeth, may have to be sawn or ground to provide a flat surface for autoradiography. If an isotope of maximum energy similar to carbon-14 or lower is used, the resolution from the cut surface of a block will not be too bad: with β emitters of higher energy, the advantages of a section become increasingly significant.

THE AUTORADIOGRAPHY OF CHROMATOGRAMS

Chromatograms present few geometrical problems, as they are planar already. A few points arise in connection with their preparation, however. In most cases, 10 mg of compound is needed to enable a spot to be identified by staining or by spectrophotometry: at high specific activities, much less than this can give significant blackening on an autoradiograph. Tsuk, Castro, Laufer and Schwarz[5] have discussed the implications of this for the autoradiography of chromatograms. When microgram samples are chromatographed, artefacts may arise from such causes as the complexing of compounds with components on the paper, or even with trace metals. The precise method of drying the spot may influence the chromatogram. It is obviously a good idea to select the conditions of chromatography that will give the most concentrated spot: for the same total radioactivity, the blackening over it will be more intense.

Fig. 77. A whole-body autoradiograph of a section through a pregnant mouse, killed 5 min after the injection of carbon-14 labelled glucose. The autoradiograph was prepared by apposition of the frozen section to a fast X-ray film. White areas correspond to high grain densities. Note the accumulation of radioactivity in the brain of the mother, but not of the foetuses. Concentrations above blood level are seen in the myocardium and liver of the mother: there is also specific uptake of radioactivity in the foetal bones. (Photograph provided by Dr. Ullberg)

Thin film chromatograms, with either silica or alumina as the stationary phase, are very powdery, and it is easy to damage them in the darkroom manipulations of preparing an autoradiograph. A light spraying with one of the commercially available materials such as Quelspray (polyvinyl chloride in an aerosol) will make the chromatogram much more robust without increasing self-absorption significantly. Care should be taken to allow the solvent to evaporate completely before autoradiography, as it is possible to desensitise the emulsion if this step is omitted.

With all isotopes that emit β particles with a maximum energy above about 100 keV, such as carbon-14, sulphur-35, phosphorus-32, apposition to an X-ray film is the method of choice. X-ray films consist usually of a supporting layer, coated on both sides with emulsion. With carbon-14 and sulphur-35, the β particles can barely reach the layer of emulsion away from the specimen, and the autoradiograph is restricted to the nearer emulsion. In this case, it makes sense to use a film coated on one side only, such as Kodak Single-Coated Medical X-ray Film – Blue Sensitive (Code SB 54), which has been found to have the highest sensitivity for low energy β particles in a recent study at the Eastman Kodak Laboratories[4]. Alternatively, Kodak RP Royal X-Omat or Ilford Industrex-C film can be used, and the emulsion removed from the side of the film furthest from the specimen when development and fixation are over (p.282). With isotopes of higher maximum energy, such as chlorine-36 or phosphorus-32, the double-sided Royal Blue film gives more blackening for a given amount of radioactivity. Any separation of specimen from film will reduce both overall efficiency and the resolving power, so that it is best to place the film in direct contact with the specimen, if chemography is demonstrably absent. Efficiency can often be slightly increased by placing a layer of material of high density, and hence good back-scattering characteristics, on the side of the film away from the specimen. Direct pressure on the film, in order to keep it in close contact with the specimen, will not damage the film, unless it is excessive or combined with an uneven specimen surface, giving an uneven distribution of pressure. Sliding pressures should be avoided, as these cause scratches on the emulsion. Richardson et al.[6] have described a very simple exposure box for maintaining a gentle, evenly distributed pressure during exposure.

The X-ray film will have to be separated from the specimen for development and fixation. Usually, realignment of film and specimen to identify the position of the labelled areas presents few problems. If this proves difficult, marking the specimen with radioactive ink prior to exposure may help. Development and fixation should follow the recommendations of the manufacturer. These steps are often handled more easily if the films are placed in the special holders used in all hospital radiography departments.

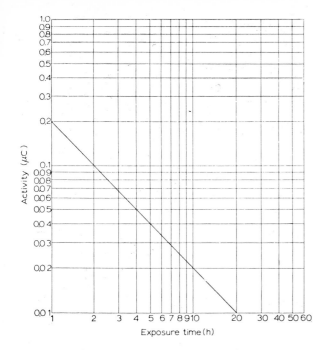

Fig. 78. A graph relating the activity of carbon-14 in μC applied to a paper chromatogram to the approximate exposure time in h needed to give a clearly discernible image on an apposed X-ray film. (From Tsuk *et al.*, 1964)

Tsuk *et al.*[5] have published a guide to exposure times for carbon-14 on paper chromatograms, which is reproduced as Fig. 78. The size of the spot will clearly have some modifying effect on the minimum exposure time needed to give a positive autoradiograph. It is sometimes possible to recognise blackening that would otherwise be too weak to distinguish from background by tilting the film, viewing it at an oblique angle. This in effect superimposes the blackening in adjacent areas, and may reinforce slight degrees of signal above noise to the level at which it can be confidently recognised.

It is possible to hazard a guess about the relative activities of two sources from just looking at the films under standard conditions, and, with experience, this visual quantitation can become surprisingly accurate[5]. It is possible to measure the blackening of the film with a microdensitometer, but is probably better to measure the radioactivity of the source itself if accurate quantitation is needed.

Artefacts due to chemography (see p.94) can occur with large specimens in contact with X-ray film just as in histological material covered with nuclear emulsion. Fig. 34 (p.97) illustrates a case of positive and negative chemography produced by a section of human femur. Even with relatively pure materials on chromatograms, Richardson et al.[6] and Chamberlain et al.[7] have drawn attention to this type of artefact. Chemography should always be looked for and if possible excluded, by exposing unlabelled but otherwise similar specimens to normal and to fogged emulsion (p.263). If chemography is found, it is usually sufficient to insert a thin layer of inert material, such as Saran, between specimen and film. Alternatively, the specimen can be coated with a thin layer of polyvinyl chloride (p.118) or nitrocellulose before exposure. Chemography may be reduced in severity by exposure at low temperatures.

THE AUTORADIOGRAPHY OF TRITIUM ON CHROMATOGRAMS

Tritium has become such an important radioisotope to biologists that the purification of labelled compounds by the manufacturer, and their separation and identification by the research worker have produced a considerable literature on the detection of tritium on chromatograms. A bibliography covering the period up to 1968 is given in a supplement to the Journal of Chromatography[8]; more recent papers are listed in the bibliographies published in current numbers of the same journal.

It is possible to autoradiograph tritium on a paper or thin layer chromatogram by placing it in contact with an X-ray film. The efficiency is very low, however. Chamberlain et al.[7] have calculated that $0.3 \ \mu Ci/cm^2$ for 24 h is needed to give blackening at the very limit of detection above background: a study from Eastman Kodak Company found an optical density in the developed film of 0.10 after $8.0 \ \mu Ci/cm^2$ in 24 h exposure[4]. The reasons for this low efficiency are the high self-absorption within the chromatogram, and the anti-abrasion coating of gelatin over the emulsion, which provides a very effective barrier to those betas that do leave the surface of the specimen. No X-ray film is available from the major suppliers without this coating.

Several approaches have been tried to improve efficiency. If the chromatogram could be actually impregnated with emulsion, the improved geometry would result in higher efficiencies. Rogers[9] tried dipping paper chromatograms in molten Ilford K2 emulsion, but the small grain size relative to X-ray film removed most of the advantage gained by better geometry. Markman[10] modified the method by spraying molten emulsion on to the chromatogram, which carries less risk of eluting compounds from the paper or the thin layer. Chamberlain et al.[7] obtained an X-ray emulsion in gel form, Ilford XK, and impregnated the chromatogram with that. They found an improvement in efficiency of about 10 times by comparison with contact exposure to an X-ray film.

This impregnation technique has never been satisfactory, and XK emulsion is no longer commercially available. The chromatogram cannot be recovered for a second exposure, or for elution and scintillation counting, after impregnation with emulsion. Spreading of the spots on the chromatogram is almost inevitable, even with spray application of emulsion, and chemographic artefacts are common with the very close contact of emulsion and specimen. It is also difficult to coat a chromatogram evenly, and high and variable backgrounds combine with efficiencies that often vary within one experiment by a factor of 5.

A much more satisfactory procedure has developed from a method proposed by Wilson[11] . He suggested immersing the chromatogram in a liquid scintillator, converting the β particles into light emission, and detecting this on an X-ray film attached to the chromatogram. As originally proposed, this method also had several major disadvantages. Compounds soluble in the organic solvents in which scintillators are dissolved were eluted from the chromatogram, while the efficiency that was claimed was not dramatically better than that achieved by apposition to X-ray film alone. Parups, Hoffman and Jackson[12] suggested dipping the chromatogram in a saturated solution of anthracene in benzene, and evaporating off the benzene, thus impregnating the paper with anthracene microcrystals, before exposing against X-ray film. Again, the improvement in efficiency was not remarkable.

The advance which permitted this approach to be useful was the discovery that efficiencies could be greatly improved by exposing the chromatogram, scintillator and film at low temperatures. Lüthi and Waser[13] , for instance, made thin layer chromatograms from a mixture of equal parts of silica gel G and finely divided anthracene. For tritium exposed by contact to X-ray film, reducing the temperature from $+4°$ to $-30°$ doubled the efficiency: reducing the temperature to $-70°$ increased the efficiency 30 times. Randerath[14] worked with cellulose or PE1-cellulose sheets. These were dipped in a 7% solution of the scintillator PPO in diethyl ether, which was then evaporated off. On exposure to X-ray film at $-79°$, $0.006-0.008$ $\mu Ci/cm^2$ could be detected in 24 h, while $15-20$ times as much was needed at room temperature to give a comparable autoradiograph.

The whole technique has been thoroughly investigated in a series of papers by Prydz and his co-workers in Oslo[15-18] . They have suggested the designation "β-radioluminescence" for the process by which β particles are converted to light photons for the purposes of detection. Several important observations emerge from their work.

In the first place, it was possible to incorporate up to 50% anthracene in the form of small crystals in thin layer chromatograms made of kieselguhr, silica-gel or cellulose without appreciably affecting the R_F values of a range of compounds tested[17] . If the light output of the chromatogram was measured with a photomultiplier tube instead of an X-ray film, a number of scintillators examined all showed an increase in light output down to −190°. While anthracene showed the best light output for a given radioactivity at −80°, benzene was better at −190°. Many scintillators gave different curves of light output against temperature on rewarming than were found on cooling: thermoluminescence peaks were often seen on rewarming at between −60° and −80° (ref. 15). However, the improvements in light output on cooling were nowhere near as dramatic with anthracene as scintillator, for instance, as were expected from the previous reports in which X-ray film was used as a detector[13, 14] . Cooling produced an improvement in light output from a scintillator incorporated in a tritium radiochromatogram by a factor of 2−5 times, depending on the precise conditions.

The possibility remained that the much greater improvements in sensitivity found with X-ray film were due to some effect of cooling on the photographic process. This was then investigated, using a controlled light source rather than a scintillator-radioisotope mixture[16] . Low temperatures produced very significant improvements in blackening on X-ray film, even with this standard source of photons. It appears that trapping of single electrons in the silver halide crystal in response to photons often proves transient at room temperature, but can be stabilised at very low temperatures, with a greatly increased probability of forming a developable latent image.

There are thus two components contributing to the high efficiency of detection of tritium on chromatograms, when β-radioluminescence and X-ray films are used at low temperatures. The first is a small but significant improvement in light output by the scintillator: the second is a dramatic increase in the sensitivity of the X-ray film for the photons emitted. These combine to lower the threshold of detection for tritium by factors of 15−30 times, depending on the conditions of chromatography and exposure.

It would seem natural to try this detection system with other β emitting isotopes, but a number of experiments with carbon-14 on chromatograms have all shown that the efficiency of detection is not significantly improved, either by the presence of the scintillator or the additional step of exposure at low temperature[13−15] . One can conclude from this that the detection of β particles by X-ray film is more efficient than the detection of the photons of β-radio-luminescence, and that the latent images produced by single β particles are so large that the stabilisation of trapping of single electrons by lowering the temperature contributes nothing to the overall efficiency of detection.

In summary, then, β-radioluminescence has nothing to offer to the autoradiography of chromatograms labelled with carbon-14 or other isotopes of similar or higher maximum energies. For tritium and other isotopes of similar energies, where the majority of the β particles never reach the emulsion layer, the conversion of the energy of the particles into light photons by a scintillator enables their presence to be detected. The efficiency of detection can be greatly improved by exposure at temperatures of $-70°$ or below. Half a loaf is better than no bread.

There is not as yet a large literature on this method. The scintillator may be incorporated in thin layers before chromatography, or applied after chromatography by dipping and evaporating off the solvent, or the chromatogram and X-ray film may be actually immersed in the scintillator and solvent. The choice of procedure must depend to a considerable extent on the compounds under study, and their solubility in the various possible solvents. The choice of the stationary phase for the chromatograms may have a very significant effect on overall sensitivity[15]. It is worth spending a little time on trying various combinations of stationary phase, scintillator and method of work before standardising any procedure that is likely to remain in use for any length of time.

There is, of course, no necessity to use X-ray film as the final detector for β-radioluminescence. Scanning devices based on photomultiplier tubes have been described[19, 20]. They give a quantitative, two-dimensional picture of the distribution of tritium over a chromatogram. They are at present expensive and complex, however, and there will for many years be a place for the much simpler method of exposure to an X-ray film.

THE AUTORADIOGRAPHY OF IRREGULAR SPECIMENS

It is sometimes necessary to autoradiograph specimens which cannot be reduced to a flat surface, such as whole skulls in the study of bone deposition during growth. In these circumstances, the choice lies between dipping the specimen in molten emulsion, or spraying emulsion on to it. Personally, I am very reluctant to spray: the fine aerosol of emulsion produced in the confined space of a darkroom is most unpleasant, and probably the grey hairs on the autoradiographer's head that result from it are the least damaging of its effects.

Once again, there is a gain in overall efficiency from the use of a large-grained emulsion. Now that Ilford XK in gel form is no longer available, Ilford G5 or one of the Kodak NTB series would seem to be the emulsion of choice. In addition to the possibility of chemography, an irregular specimen may produce stress artefacts, particularly at abrupt changes in surface contour, such as the fissures of the skull. These can only be guarded against by the autoradiography of non-radioactive controls. Techniques for applying the emulsion, both by spraying and dipping, are described at the end of this chapter.

FUTURE DEVELOPMENTS IN THE AUTORADIOGRAPHY OF CHEMICAL SPECIMENS

The biologist is very apt to associate autoradiography with the localisation of radioactivity in tissue sections. To the biochemist, on the other hand, it is a method of detecting radioactivity on chromatograms, a method that can often be replaced by chromatogram-scanning devices of one sort or another. It seems to me that the characteristics which make nuclear emulsions so valuable for the detection and measurement of radioactivity in single cells also open up very interesting possibilities in the field of microchemical determinations.

Most existing techniques of detecting and measuring compounds of biological interest require the presence of 10^{14} or more molecules in the sample. But, to the cytologist interested in the physiology of a single cell or group of cells, this may be an impossibly high lower limit. Autoradiographic measurements have already been made on biological structures in the range of 10^6-10^7 molecules[21, 22]. There is no reason whatever why the same measurements could not be made on purified chemical samples.

Specimens giving as little as 1 disintegration per day can be detected in ideal circumstances by autoradiography, provided only that they are sufficiently small for their effects to be registered by a minute volume of emulsion. Separative techniques that produce a spacing of 20 μ or more between bands that are less than 5 μ wide should give suitable specimens for autoradiography. This is not too ridiculous when one considers the elegant microchemical techniques of Edström[23], who has been able to separate the RNA bases from single nerve cells by electrophoresis along a cellulose fibre.

Many possibilities await exploration in this particular field. Ficq[24] has suggested that nuclear emulsion itself might be the matrix in which separation of related compounds could be effected, and Lambiotte[25] has described a technique for the electrophoretic separation of compounds in an X-ray emulsion.

Prophecy is always a risky business. It seems fair to guess, however, that the high resolution and sensitivity of nuclear emulsions for isotopes that emit β

particles, the long exposures and low background levels that can be achieved, and the precision with which absolute measurements of radioactivity can be made, will make autoradiography an attractive prospect to the biochemist interested in developing techniques for the separation and measurement of compounds from single cells or subcellular structures.

DESCRIPTION OF TECHNIQUES

(a) Impregnation by dipping in Ilford G5 emulsion

Ilford G5 emulsion in gel form should be stored at 4°. Like other emulsions in gel form, it should never be frozen. Its shelf-life is at least one month. The safelight should be a 15 W bulb behind an Ilford S 902 filter, at a distance of at least 3 feet.

(i) Equipment needed. Thermostatically controlled water-bath at 43°. 2 50-ml graduated cylinders. 1 dipping dish, the size and shape dependent on specimen — large and shallow for paper chromatograms, smaller and deeper for small irregular specimens. 1 pair of plastic print forceps. 1 glass stirring rod.

(ii) Procedure. Following the general procedure on p.310 for liquid emulsion work, prepare a molten, diluted emulsion in the dipping dish. The final volume will depend on the size of the specimen to be impregnated. The emulsion should be diluted 1 part to 3 parts distilled water, to which glycerol should be added to make 1% by volume of the final solution.

Dip the specimen gently in the diluted emulsion, and allow it to dry with as little handling as possible. Drying should be slow and gentle. The darkroom temperature should be $18-21°$, and the relative humidity around 50%. Circulation of air should be slow, and a direct blast from a fan is not recommended.

After $1.5-2$ h, the emulsion should be dry, and the specimen can be placed in a lightproof box for exposure. Dried silica gel can be placed in the box during the first 24 h of exposure, provided the specimen does not produce stress artefacts in the emulsion. Over-enthusiastic drying can lead to emulsion separating from the specimen.

(iii) Development. Place the specimen in Ilford Phen-X developer, diluted with an equal volume of distilled water, at 20° for 5 min, without agitation. Transfer to a 1% acetic acid stopbath for 2 min. Fix in 30% sodium thiosulphate for 15 min. Wash in gently running tapwater for 20 min and allow to dry.

If difficulties are experienced with emulsion separating from the specimen during exposure or processing, it may help to dip the specimen first in a dilute solution of gelatin (p.108), which is allowed to dry completely before dipping the specimen in emulsion. A thicker emulsion layer is best achieved by dipping the specimen a second time, after about 30 min drying: attempts to increase the viscosity of the emulsion by reducing the concentration of distilled water in the dipping bath usually make for very uneven final coating with emulsion.

(b) Impregnation by spraying with Ilford G5 emulsion

(i) Equipment needed. The equipment needed is the same as for impregnation by dipping, except that the dipping dish is replaced by an all glass chromatogram spray with large orifice, and a 500-ml conical flask with ground glass joint to fit the spray. A small nitrogen cylinder is also needed, connected to the spray.

(ii) Procedure. The molten, diluted emulsion is this time prepared in the conical flask. The emulsion should be diluted 1 part to 7 parts distilled water, with glycerol added to 1% of the final volume.

When the emulsion is prepared, allow it to cool to room temperature in the conical flask before spraying, swirling the flask at frequent intervals to keep the emulsion well mixed. When the emulsion is cool, attach the spray head, apply gentle pressure from the nitrogen cylinder, and spray the specimen with steady, even strokes from a distance of about 9 inches.

Drying should be complete in about 1.5 h at 18–21° and 50% relative humidity.

Exposure and development are as for impregnation by dipping in G5 emulsion.

(c) Removal of emulsion from one side of a processed X-ray film

Take a large, flat dish big enough to hold the X-ray film. Place 6 layers of filter paper on the bottom of the dish, and pour on enough 10% sodium hydroxide to wet the paper thoroughly without producing puddles over it. Place the film carefully on the filter paper, unwanted emulsion layer downwards, taking care to avoid trapping air bubbles between film and paper. After a few minutes at room temperature, the emulsion layer will disintegrate: this can be easily recognised by the appearance of a reticulated pattern beneath the film. Remove the film, and wash it thoroughly in rapidly running tapwater for 20 min.

At no stage should the sodium hydroxide be allowed to wet the upper surface of the film.

REFERENCES

1   S. Ullberg, *Acta Radiol., Suppl.* 118 (1954).
2   S. Ullberg, *Biochem. Pharmacol.,* 9 (1962) 29.

3 S. Ullberg, in L.J. Roth (Ed.), *Isotopes in Experimental Pharmacology*, University of Chicago Press, Chicago, 1965.
4 Eastman Kodak Company Research Laboratories, personal communication.
5 R.G. Tsuk, T. Castro, L. Laufer and D.R. Schwartz, in J. Sirchis (Ed.), *Proc. Conf. Methods of Preparing and Storing Marked Molecules*, Euratom (EUR 1625 e), Brussels, 1964.
6 G.S. Richardson, I. Weliky, W. Batchelder, M. Griffith and L.L. Engel, *J. Chromatography*, 12 (1963) 115.
7 J. Chamberlain, A. Hughes, A.W. Rogers and G.H. Thomas, *Nature*, 201 (1964) 774.
8 Bibliography of Chromatography, *J. Chromatography Suppl.* (1968) 700.
9 A.W. Rogers, *Nature*, 184 (1961) 721.
10 B. Markman, *J. Chromatography*, 11 (1963) 118.
11 A.T. Wilson, *Biochim. Biophys. Acta.*, 40 (1960) 522.
12 E.V. Parups, I. Hoffman and H.R. Jackson, *Talanta*, 5 (1960) 75.
13 U. Lüthi and P.G. Waser, *Nature*, 205 (1965) 1190.
14 K. Randerath, *Analyt. Chem.*, 41 (1969) 991.
15 S. Prydz, T.B. Melö, J.F. Koren and E.L. Eriksen, *Analyt. Chem.*, 42 (1970) 156.
16 J.F. Koren, T.B. Melö and S. Prydz, *I. Chromatography*, 46 (1970) 129.
17 L.H. Landmark, A.K. Hognestad and S. Prydz, *J. Chromatography*, 46 (1970) 267.
18 S. Prydz, T.B. Melö, E.L. Eriksen and J.F. Koren, *J. Chromatography*, 47 (1970) 157.
19 S. Prydz, T.B. Melö, and J.F. Koren, *J. Chromatography*, 59 (1971) 99.
20 E.B. Chain, A.E. Lowe and K.R.L. Mansford, *J. Chromatography*, 53 (1970) 293.
21 A.W. Rogers, Z. Darżynkiewicz, K. Ostrowski, E.A. Barnard and M.M. Salpeter, *J. Cell Biol.*, 41 (1969) 665.
22 Z. Darżynkiewicz, A.W. Rogers and E.A. Barnard, *J. Histochem., Cytochem.*, 14 (1966) 379.
23 J.-E. Edström, *Biochim. Biophys. Acta*, 22 (1956) 378.
24 A. Ficq, in J. Brachet and A.E. Mirsky (Eds.), *The Cell*, Vol. 1, Academic Press, New York, 1959.
25 M. Lambiotte, *Compt. Rend.*, 260 (1965) 1799.

CHAPTER 15

The Stripping-Film Technique

The stripping-film technique as used at present was developed by Berriman, Herz and Stevens[1], of Kodak Ltd., England in close association with Pelc[2]. The product, Kodak AR-10 stripping film, and the technique that they evolved have been very widely used ever since, and have probably been the basis for more investigations at the histological level than any other autoradiographic method.

The technique is described by Pelc[2,3], and is also summarised in two descriptive leaflets issued by Kodak, Ltd. (Nos. Pl. 1157 and SC-10).

Briefly, AR-10 stripping film consists of a thin layer of nuclear emulsion carried on a layer of plain gelatin. These arrive from the factory mounted on a glass support, with the gelatin layer in contact with the glass. When it is required for use, an appropriate area of emulsion plus gelatin is cut around with a scalpel or sharp knife, and gently stripped off the glass support on to the surface of water. Here it floats for a minute or two, emulsion side downwards, while it imbibes water, spreading as it does so. When it has reached its fullest dimensions, the stripped film is picked up on the specimen — usually histological material on a microscope slide — by dipping the slide in the water under the film and lifting it out with the film draped over it. As the film dries, it makes very close contact with the specimen. The layer of plain gelatin makes it easier to handle the very thin layer of emulsion in the stripping stage, and protects the emulsion from scratches during drying and exposure. Both emulsion and gelatin remain in contact with the specimen throughout development and preparation for microscopy.

EMULSIONS AVAILABLE

Several stripping films are available from Kodak, Ltd. (obtainable in the U.S.A. through Eastman Kodak) and from Ilford, Ltd.

Kodak AR-10 is far and away the most commonly used product. This arrives from the factory as a 5-μ layer of emulsion on a 10-μ gelatin base. The silver halide crystals have a mean diameter of about 0.2 μ. The emulsion is not fully sensitive to electrons at minimum ionisation: in other words, it would record the passage of β particles of say, 200 keV and over as an occasional developed grain rather than a complete track, if it were to be used in thick layers. On the Ilford scale of sensitivity (Fig. 82, p.298), this is roughly equivalent to the third level of sensitisation. This will be the only stripping film discussed in detail.

Kodak has also provided 2 other products in the past, which have been described in the literature, but which are now no longer available. Kodak Experimental Stripping Plates V1062 had the same basic emulsion as AR-10 in a layer 4 μ thick, unsupported by the layer of gelatin. They were originally produced for two-emulsion autoradiography for material containing both tritium and carbon-14 (see p.257). If two separate layers of AR-10 stripping film are used in this technique, the total thickness of the emulsion and gelatin becomes sufficiently great to make staining, mounting and viewing the specimen rather difficult. The intention was to use V1062 for one of the two emulsion layers, as described by Dawson, Field and Stevens[4]. Some autoradiographers found it a useful product in place of AR-10 for experiments with one isotope alone: the advantage lies in the better staining and visibility of the specimen. The film was more fragile and difficult to handle than AR-10, however.

Kodak's Special Autoradiographic Stripping Plates were designed to give better resolution than AR-10. They had the same emulsion as AR-10, but in a layer only 1–2 μ thick: this was on a gelatin base 5 μ thick. They have been used, for instance, in high-resolution studies of chromosome replication.

Ilford, Ltd., will provide any of their nuclear emulsions as a stripping film on request with a 5-μ layer of emulsion on 10 μ of gelatin. They have never been widely enough used to evaluate their potential. The limited experience I have had with them suggests that the optimal conditions of temperature and stripping for Kodak AR-10 may not be ideal for the Ilford products. Though the latter have been used with success[5], there is little information in the literature on their handling and characteristics.

I shall therefore limit myself to a consideration of Kodak AR-10 in the remainder of this chapter.

THE ADVANTAGE OF THE STRIPPING-FILM TECHNIQUE

The relative merits of stripping-film and of liquid emulsion techniques have been discussed in some detail in Chapter 13, p.249. To summarise the main advantage of stripping film briefly, it is an excellent compromise designed to meet all the main requirements of autoradiography at the light microscope level adequately. The emulsion layer and the crystal size give reasonably good resolution in the range of $0.5–5\ \mu$, depending on the energy spectrum of the isotope used. It can therefore give satisfactory results in any study of the distribution of radioactivity at the cellular level, and will also, in favourable conditions, distinguish between major cell compartments, such as nucleus and cytoplasm. The uniformity of the emulsion layer, which is claimed by Kodak to be within the range of $\pm 10\%$ of the stated $5\ \mu$, is better than can be obtained by liquid emulsion techniques. Valid comparisons of the radioactivity of different structures can be based on the grain counts observed over them in controlled conditions, even with isotopes of high maximum energy.

In short, this one technique can give acceptable results in the majority of autoradiographic experiments. The technique is not difficult, and the shelf-life of the film is of the order of 6 months under reasonable conditions. The laboratory in which an autoradiographic experiment is only needed occasionally would clearly do well to standardise its procedures around this reproducible technique, for which a great deal of data is already available in the literature.

THE LIMITATIONS OF THE STRIPPING-FILM TECHNIQUE

A single compromise technique like stripping-film autoradiography, which gives satisfactory results in a number of experimental situations, will often be inferior to a more specialised technique, designed for one particular application. If, for instance, the highest possible resolving power in the light microscope is required, a very thin layer of a fine-grained emulsion such as Ilford L4 will be superior to the thicker emulsion and larger crystal size of AR-10 stripping film. If high efficiency is particularly important, with very low levels of labelling or a very short isotopic half-life, a thicker layer of a more sensitive emulsion, such as Ilford K5, will give better results. If quantitative precision is important, the more specialised techniques of β-track autoradiography will be preferable. Inevitably, the single sensitivity, the one diameter of halide crystal, and the one emulsion thickness available places stripping film at a disadvantage with respect to the wide range of products and of techniques possible with liquid emulsions.

In addition, there are a number of drawbacks inherent in the stripping-film technique itself which should be mentioned. The process of stripping the film from the glass support inevitably involves more handling, with the chance of creating a higher initial background, than the relatively mild methods of liquid emulsion work. In inappropriate conditions of temperature and humidity in the darkroom, stripping can cause visible flashes of static discharge between film and glass support, resulting in a very high background. It is, in addition, almost impossible to keep the water surface of the stripping bath completely free of dust, and this is the very surface that becomes trapped between emulsion and specimen. The time required for the emulsion to swell on the surface of the water places a limit on the speed of preparation of autoradiographs. If batches of 30–50 slides have to be covered with emulsion, dipping in liquid emulsion is quicker than using stripping film.

When one considers development, fixation and washing, stripping film adheres to slide and specimen less firmly than a layer of liquid emulsion applied by dipping. It is possible for the film to slip relative to the specimen, particularly in the final stage of washing after fixation: it may even be lost altogether if it is carelessly handled. These problems are far more acute if the specimen has been covered with an inert layer of, for instance, polyvinyl chloride (p.118) before applying the film. In these conditions, it is difficult to keep the film in place, even if the PVC membrane has been coated with dilute gelatin. This tendency of the film to move in processing can be minimised. The film is permitted to spread fully before applying it to the slide by floating on water at 25° for a full 3 minutes, while the temperature of all processing solutions is kept to 18° or below. The film can be wrapped around 3 sides of the slide when it is picked up from the stripping bath. Finally, the very considerable swelling of the emulsion that occurs in the usual stopbath of distilled water can be reduced by controlling the salt concentration of the stopbath, following a suggestion by Stevens[6].

In preparing stripping-film autoradiographs for microscopy, it sometimes happens that small pockets form under the film in and around the specimen, with a different refractive index to the rest of the preparation. These are probably due to a failure of the mounting medium to penetrate the film completely. Many remedies have been suggested for this: the use of polyvinyl alcohol is quite effective[7], and will be described later (p.294).

Finally, the presence of the layer of gelatin above the emulsion may have, as noted above, an unfortunate effect on the appearance of the specimen under the microscope. Many stains applied through the emulsion after development and fixation are taken up to some extent by gelatin. This will be a much more noticeable effect in the presence of the relatively thick layer of plain gelatin of stripping film than with a single layer of liquid emulsion. Nor is this disadvantage purely cosmetic. It may be severe enough to rule out the use of dark-field incident illumination (p.151) to view or photograph the autoradiograph, and the light scattering caused by stain in this gelatin layer may make it impossible to automate the estimation of grain densities with dark-field incident illumination.

Many of these limitations of stripping-film autoradiography can be minimised by appropriate techniques. They are all, however, relevant to the selection of the most suitable method for any proposed autoradiographic experiment. In spite of its drawbacks, stripping film remains the only basic technique that is applicable to almost the entire range of observations that one might wish to make at the light microscope level.

USEFUL FACTS AND FIGURES ABOUT AR-10

In a series of tests with stripping film on the surface of water at $25°$, the area of the film was found to increase by a factor of 1.38. This seemed to be reached in 2–3 min, and no further increase followed over 15–20 min. This implies that the thickness of the emulsion layer during exposure is approximately 3.6μ.

The uniformity of the emulsion layer appears to be well within the tolerance quoted by Kodak, Ltd., in a series of experiments in which AR-10 was applied to a plane surface on a microscope slide. Emulsion thickness probably varies slightly more when the film is applied to a specimen with an irregular upper profile, such as a paraffin-embedded section after dewaxing.

The grain yield of stripping film, i.e., the number of developed grains per incident β particle, has been calculated by a number of authors for different isotopes[8]. The values range from around 1 for tritium down to about 0.7 for phosphorus-32. Naturally, the efficiency of stripping film, defined as the number of developed grains per disintegration in the source, varies widely with the nature of the specimen. The efficiency is a function of the autoradiograph as a whole, and includes factors such as self-absorption. Hughes, Bond et al. give a figure of 1 developed grain per 20 disintegrations in smears of white blood cells labelled with tritium[9]. The figure of 1 silver grain per 100–200 disintegrations is sometimes quoted for the efficiency of a $3-\mu$ section labelled with tritium[10]. There are technical grounds for doubting the validity of this measurement[5], which is inconsistent with several other values in the literature similar to that of Hughes et al.[9] quoted above.

It is possible to increase the sensitivity of AR-10 emulsion by hypersensitisation prior to exposure, following the recommendations of Herz[8]. I know of no subsequent experiment in which this has been attempted, so it is difficult to assess how reproducible this improved emulsion response would be.

Stripping film, as used in the normal way, is clearly unsuited to the autoradiography of soluble materials. Attempts have been made to float the stripped film on the surface of mercury, to avoid the necessity of immersing the slide in water while picking up the film. This technique has little to recommend it. It is possible to use stripping film in the Appleton[11] or Stumpf and Roth[12] techniques for diffusible material by covering the slide with film, gelatin layer in contact with the glass, and drying the film thoroughly, before placing the section in contact with the emulsion layer (see Chapter 8).

Stubblefield[13] has exploited the relatively poor adhesion between stripping film and slide in an ingenious technique to improve the statistics of grain counting over small sources. If the grain densities over such sources are kept low to avoid a high probability of adjacent crystals receiving double or multiple hits, it will never be possible in a single exposure to collect more than 1 or 2 grains per source. In his technique, a relatively short exposure is made, the autoradiographs are developed and photographed, and the film floated off the specimen. A second layer of film is then put on the slide, which is exposed for the second time. By serial short exposures in this way it is possible to build up quite high grain counts over sources as small as mammalian chromosomes.

O'Callaghan, Stevens and Wood[14] have drawn attention to the leaching of bromide ions out of the stripping film while it is floating on the water prior to picking up, and to the increased rate of build-up of background that may result during long exposures. They have shown that floating the film on a solution of potassium bromide and glucose can significantly improve the signal-to-noise ratio and the reproducibility of autoradiographs. This step should be incorporated in the technique whenever exposure times of more than 2 or 3 weeks are anticipated. It is described in detail later (p.290).

Some papers have given the unfortunate impression that latent image fading and negative chemography are unlikely to occur with AR-10 stripping film (see, for instance, Pelc, Appleton and Welton[15], and the reference to their work by Dörmer[16]). These effects are common to all emulsions and are inherent in the very nature of the photographic process. There is no reason to expect that this one product should somehow be exempt, and no excuse for neglecting the basic controls (p.263) which should be part of every autoradiographic experiment. I have several times encountered clear evidence of generalised latent image regression and of negative chemography in AR-10 autoradiographs, prepared by other laboratories as well as my own.

DETAILED DESCRIPTION OF TECHNIQUE

The shelf-life of AR-10 is about 6 months. It is best kept at about 4°, in the plastic bags inside the box in which it comes.

The conditions within the darkroom are very important to successful autoradiography. The temperature should be 18–21°, the relative humidity ideally between 60 and 65%. If it is too dry, spontaneous stripping of the film away from its glass support may occur, and static discharge between film and glass will give high levels of background. If it is too humid, it may be difficult to strip the film at all. There should be no violent air currents, such as are created by a powerful exhaust fan. The emulsion should be handled and processed at least 1–2 m (4 feet) from a safelight fitted with a 25-W bulb and a Kodak safelight filter No. 1 (red). The best position for the safelight is above bench height, so that the light can be seen reflected in the waterbath while one is standing in the spot most convenient for working. As always, the darkroom should be clean: a dusty room will make it impossible to keep the surface of the water free from specks, which will be trapped between emulsion and specimen.

The stripping film should be brought out of the refrigerator an hour to two before it is needed, to allow it to come to room temperature.

(i) Equipment needed. A dish containing distilled water at 25° will be needed: for exposures which may last more then 2–3 weeks, the water should be replaced with a solution of potassium bromide (10 mg/litre) with glucose (5%)[14] . The size of the dish is not very critical, but a bigger dish will hold more pieces of film while they are imbibing water and spreading. The water should be at least 1.5 inches deep, and its surface should be near the top of the dish, so that there is no awkward rim around the water to interfere with picking up the film. It is easier to see the film clearly if one is working against a black background: I use a glass dish standing on a piece of black paper.

A clean, sharp knife or scalpel and a pair of forceps (not rat-toothed) will also be required. It is useful to have a pair of straight scissors available. The surface of the slide must, of course, be gelatinised to get good adhesion between emulsion and slide (p.108).

(ii) Packaging the emulsion. Stripping-film plates come in boxes of 12: each box contains 3 plastic bags of 4 plates each. Fig. 79 illustrates the way in which the 4 plates are stacked: the innermost pair of plates are in direct contact, back to back, and their emulsion-coated surfaces face the emulsion of the outer

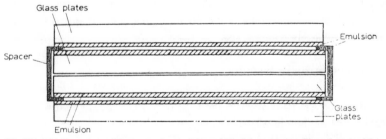

Fig. 79. A diagram to illustrate the packing of Kodak stripping-film plates, with cardboard spacers to prevent the emulsion surfaces from coming into contact.

two plates, from which they are separated by small cardboard spacers. It is important to prevent the emulsion from being scratched when returning unused plates to their plastic containers. It is often a good idea to reconstitute the stack of 4 plates just as they were received, before putting them away again, even if one or two of the plates have had all their emulsion removed, as these used plates can still protect the emulsion on the other ones.

(iii) Stripping the emulsion from its glass support. If there is any doubt which side of the glass is covered with film, gentle scratching with a fingernail at the very corner of the plate will at once give the answer. The film is firmly attached to the glass for a distance of about 0.5 cm from the edge of the plate. With the knife, cut around an oblong area of film at one corner of the plate, starting about 1 cm in from the edge: the size of the piece of film depends on the specimen to be covered. Remembering that the film will spread on the surface of the water, it should be big enough to lap over 3 sides of the microscope slide, or whatever the specimen is mounted on, and to cover the specimen with film extending at least 1 cm from it on all sides. Given this minimum size, nothing is gained by cutting pieces of film any bigger.

Usually, the cut piece of film will lift slightly from the glass at its edges, so that it can be held gently at one corner with the forceps. If it does not do this, one corner can be detached from the glass with the edge of the knife or scalpel. The piece of film should be grasped in the forceps by the corner nearest the centre of the plate, and stripped from the glass with a steady, slow movement. Always strip away from the film that is left on the plate, to avoid scratching it (Fig. 80). If the film crackles on stripping, or minute flashes of light due to static electricity are seen, it often helps to breathe gently on it.

During stripping, hold the plate vertically, near the surface of the water, and strip the piece of film off downwards towards the water. In this way, as the film separates from the glass, it will be facing the water surface, emulsion side downwards. As the film parts company with the glass, it should be placed on the surface of the water. It is a good idea to practice this in the light before attempting it for the first time. With very little effort, one gets the knack of floating the film in an unwrinkled condition on the water. If the film is very wrinkled or curled up, remove it from the waterbath and strip another piece: it is a waste of time to try and straighten it out.

Difficulties with this stage of stripping are usually due to incorrect conditions of temperature and humidity in the darkroom. Occasionally, large areas of film strip spontaneously from the glass, particularly after a few pieces have already been taken off. It is almost impossible to cut this peeling film with a knife or scalpel, but this can be done with scissors, and suitable bits of film salvaged for

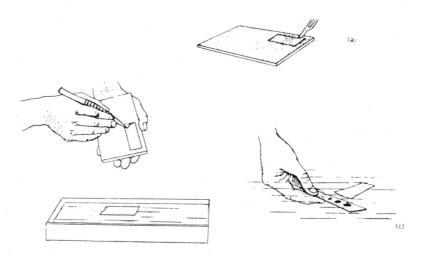

Fig.80. Three diagrams to illustrate the preparation of stripping-film autoradiographs. (*a*) An area of film is cut with a sharp scalpel, taking care to leave a margin of 0.5 cm around the edge of the plate. (*b*) Holding the plate vertical near the surface of the water, a corner of the cut square of film is taken with forceps, and the square stripped off the plate on to the water, emulsion surface downwards. Care should be taken to strip away from the rest of the film on the plate. (*c*) After the cut square of film has imbibed water for 3 min it is picked up on the surface of the slide that has the specimens on it. The emulsion thus achieves very close contact with the specimen.

use. Avoid holding the plate up at face level during stripping: it will probably be too near the safelight at this height, and the shorter the distance the stripped film has to travel to the water surface, the less chance there is of it curling up in transit.

Experts in the use of stripping film claim that its appearance changes while it is on the water, and that it becomes "granulated" when spreading is complete and it is ready for picking up. I must admit I have never been convinced of this change, and I prefer to leave the film floating for 3 min by the darkroom clock before going on to the next stage.

The forceps should be carefully dried before stripping the next piece of film, otherwise it will stick to them instead of floating free on the water.

(iv) Picking up the film. Holding the slide at the end furthest from the specimen, place it in the water and move it under the piece of film, at an angle of about 30° to the horizontal. Then lift the film out of the water on the slide. One edge of the film should attach itself to the slide first, the rest folding neatly around the slide as the latter comes out of the water. If there are wrinkles, or the film is not covering the specimen properly, do not attempt to move the film

along the slide while it is out of the water, but try to refloat the film and pick it up again. If things get too complicated at this stage, reject the piece of film and start again.

Around the edge of the strip of film, the background may be higher, due to the act of cutting and the grasp of the forceps. It is important to get a reasonable margin of film around the specimen, so that it lies under an area of low background.

(v) Drying and exposure. The slide with film on it should stand vertically to dry in a gentle stream of cool air for 20—ɔʋ min. Sawicki and Pawinska[17] have drawn attention to the lower background levels that result from very slow, and possibly even incomplete, drying of the emulsion. A certain amount of moisture left in the film would favour fading of the latent image. Since an appreciable background is usually present at the start of exposure from the process of stripping, this fading would result in an initial decrease in background (p.102).

Yet the drying must be complete if latent image fading is to be avoided. A suitable compromise is to allow the slides to remain in the darkroom for a further 1 h, and then to transfer them to a desiccator at room temperature over dried silica gel for 18—24 h. After this, they can be put away in light-proof boxes to expose. This drying routine appears to be somewhat more reproducible than exposure in the presence of a few crystals of drying agent, which may on occasions become saturated. If long exposures or latent image regression from any cause are anticipated, exposure should take place in an atmosphere of carbon dioxide or an inert gas[8], at a temperature of $-20°$ or lower. Otherwise, exposure in air at $4°$, or even at room temperature[18], are usually satisfactory.

Very low background levels can be achieved with stripping film with experience (Fig. 81).

(vi) Development and fixation. These stages should all be carried out at a temperature of $18°$. At this temperature, the emulsion will not swell to the same extent as it did at $25°$, thus reducing the chances that it will part company with the slide.

The recommended developer is Kodak developer	D19
"Elon"	2.0 g
Sodium sulphite (anhydrous)	40.0 g
Hydroquinone	9.0 g
Sodium carbonate (anhydrous)	38.0 g
Citric acid	0.7 g
Potassium metasulphite	1.5 g
Distilled water to	1000 ml

References p. 295

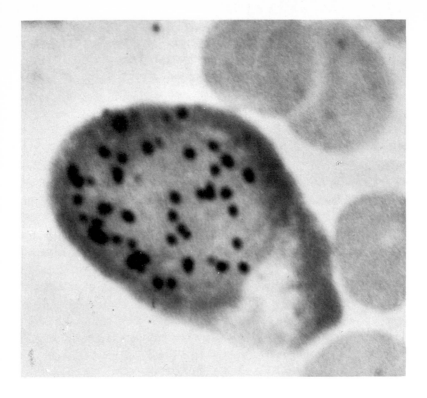

Fig.81. A photomicrograph of a smear of bone marrow cells, showing an early normoblast labelled after incorporation of tritiated thymidine. Autoradiograph prepared with Kodak AR-10 stripping film. (× 2000) (From Lajtha, 1961)

The chemicals should be dissolved in the order listed, and the developer used without further dilution.

Development should take about 5 min at 18°.

Rinse for 30–60 sec in distilled water.

Fix in 30% w/v solution of sodium thiosulphate for 10 min.

Alternatively, Kodak Acid Fixer may be used.

Wash in gently running tapwater for 5 min.

After staining, the slides can be allowed to dry in air, and viewed dry or with immersion oil applied directly. Alternatively, they can be dehydrated, cleared in xylene and mounted under a coverglass for microscopy in the usual way. If the latter process produces opaque areas around the specimen under the film, the slides can be treated with polyvinyl alcohol during dehydration[7]. After rinsing the slide in 50% alcohol, it is transferred to a 2% solution of polyvinyl alcohol ("Elvanol", Dupont 51-05) in 50% alcohol for 1–2 h: it is advisable for the slide to be lying horizontal during this time. After drying in the air, the slide can be dipped in absolute alcohol, followed by xylene, and mounted under a coverglass in one of the conventional histological mounting media.

Swelling of the emulsion in the stopbath, with possible displacement of the image, can be minimised by substituting a rinse in Kodak SB-4 stopbath for the more usual distilled water[6]. This stopbath has the following formula:

Potassium chrome alum	30 g
Sodium sulphate (anhydrous)	60 g
(Alternatively, crystalline sodium sulphate	140 g)
Distilled water to	1 litre

Agitate the slides for 30–45 sec in the stopbath, and then leave them for 3 min. Discard the stopbath after use.

REFERENCES

1 R.W. Berriman, R.H. Herz and G.W.W. Stevens, *Brit. J. Radiol.*, 23 (1950) 472.
2 I. Doniach and S.R. Pelc, *Brit. J. Radiol.*, 23 (1950) 184.
3 S.R. Pelc, *Intern. J. Appl. Radiation Isotopes*, 1 (1956) 172.
4 K.B. Dawson, E.O. Field and G.W.W. Stevens, *Nature*, 195 (1962) 510.
5 H.K. Oja, S.S. Oja and J. Hasan, *Exptl. Cell Res.*, 45 (1967) 1.
6 G.W.W. Stevens, *Microphotography*, 2nd ed., Chapman and Hall, London, 1968.
7 M.J. Schlesinger, H. Levi and R. Weyant, *Rev. Sci. Instruments*, 27 (1956) 969.
8 R.H. Herz, *Lab. Invest.*, 8 (1959) 71.
9 W.L. Hughes, V.P. Bond, G. Brecher, E.P. Cronkite, R.B. Painter, H. Quastler and F.G. Sherman, *Proc. Natl. Acad. Sci. (U.S.)*, 44 (1958) 476.
10 W.E. Kisieleski, R. Baserga and J. Vaupotic, *Radiation Res.*, 15 (1961) 341.
11 T.C. Appleton, *J. Roy. Microscop. Soc.*, 83 (1964) 277.
12 W.E. Stumpf and L.J. Roth, *Stain Technol.*, 39 (1964) 219.
13 E. Stubblefield, *Federation Proc.*, 23 (1964) 332.
14 C. O'Callaghan, G.W.W. Stevens and J.F. Wood, *Brit. J. Radiol.*, 42 (1969) 862.
15 S.R. Pelc, T.C. Appleton and M.E. Welton, in C.P. Leblond and K.B. Warren (Eds.) *The Use of Radioautography in Investigating Protein Synthesis*, Academic Press, New York, 1965.
16 P. Dörmer, *Histochemie*, 8 (1967) 1.
17 W. Sawicki and M. Pawinska, *Stain Technol.*, 40 (1965) 67.
18 W. Sawicki, K. Ostrowski and J. Rowkinski, *Stain Technol.*, 43 (1968) 35.
19 L.C. Lajtha, *The Use of Isotopes in Haematology*, Blackwell, Oxford, 1961.

CHAPTER 16

Liquid Emulsion Techniques for Grain Density Autoradiographs

Bélanger and Leblond[1] pioneered the use of liquid emulsions in order to achieve very close apposition between specimen and emulsion. Their original technique involved melting the emulsion, and applying it to the specimen by means of a paintbrush. In 1955, Joftes and Warren[2] published a method in which the slide, with specimen on it, was dipped bodily in molten emulsion. This technique was described again, in slightly modified form, by Joftes[3]. Messier and Leblond[4] adapted this basic procedure of dipping the slide in liquid emulsion to their own requirements, and further modifications to the technique were described by Kopriwa and Leblond[5]. With the possible exception of the stripping film technique, this process of dipping in liquid emulsion is the most widely used autoradiographic method in biological laboratories at the present time.

Before going further into descriptions of techniques it would be well, at the risk of repeating statements made in Chapter 13, to discuss briefly the value and the very real limitations of autoradiographs prepared in this way.

THE ADVANTAGES AND LIMITATIONS OF DIPPING TECHNIQUES

After dipping, the biological specimen is covered, and even to some extent perhaps impregnated, with emulsion. No other method of applying the emulsion gives such close contact between emulsion and specimen. It is possible, by regulating the dilution of the molten emulsion, to produce a very thin layer over the specimen. Emulsions are available for autoradiography with crystal diameters significantly smaller than that of Kodak AR-10 stripping film. If one takes advantage of all these possibilities, the resulting autoradiograph will have a significantly better resolution with many isotopes than can be achieved with stripping film. If high resolving power is needed in an autoradiograph for the light microscope, a technique based on dipping in liquid emulsion offers the best possibilities.

The dipping technique has other advantages. It is very quick and simple to prepare the autoradiographs, and the layer of gelatin that remains after processing is so thin that staining, mounting under a coverglass, viewing and photomicrography are all improved relative to stripping film. The emulsion layer adheres to specimen and slide much more firmly than with stripping film, making it simpler to modify the basic technique for use with impermeable layers of plastic (see p.118). There is a wide range of emulsions available, differing in sensitivity and in crystal diameters.

The one great limitation to this type of autoradiograph is that it is all but impossible to produce an emulsion layer of constant and reproducible thickness. Leblond, Kopriwa and Messier[6] have investigated this in considerable detail. Even with their experience of this technique, the best they can achieve is a fairly uniform thickness over an area of perhaps one-half of the microscope slide. They present no data on the variations of emulsion thickness from one slide to the next.

If variations of emulsion thickness can occur within one series of autoradiographs, comparisons of the radioactivity within different structures become very difficult. It must be shown that the observed variations in grain density are not consequences of the differences in emulsion thickness. It is in this situation, where comparisons of grain density must be made, that stripping film has greater precision.

There are special circumstances, however, in which comparisons of grain density are valid with the dipping technique. With tritium and iodine-125, the energies of the emitted particles are so low that few, if any, might be expected to travel more than 2μ through emulsion. If the emulsion is nowhere less than 2μ thick, the grain densities due to these two isotopes will be independent of variations in thickness. The thickness of the recording layer is in effect determined by the maximum range of the particle in this case. It is quite acceptable to use a dipping technique for quantitative work with tritium and iodine-125, provided the emulsion layer is sufficiently thick.

It is sometimes possible to base comparisons of radioactivity on grain densities in liquid emulsion autoradiographs, even with isotopes of higher energy. Variations in emulsion thickness occur over relatively large distances, and it is unlikely that significant differences will be found over two sources separated by only a few microns. In experiments with sulphur-35 and emulsion layers about 3μ thick, paired observations were made over experimental and control areas about 5μ apart. Although it was clear from the grain counts that considerable differences in emulsion thickness were occurring from one section to another, the statistical treatment of these paired observations produced valid and useful results, which were independent of this variation[7].

References p. 312

To sum up, liquid emulsion techniques can provide grain density autoradiographs of high resolution. Comparisons of radioactivity between one site and another are possible, provided it can be shown that variations in emulsion thickness are not affecting the grain counts. With a thin emulsion layer and very small developed grains, the best possible conditions for viewing the underlying specimen can be realised.

THE CHOICE OF EMULSION

Some of the emulsions available commercially are listed in Fig. 82, with a note of their major characteristics. Most of the published work has involved the Eastman Kodak NTB-2 and NTB-3, or the Ilford emulsions, so that detailed discussion will be limited to these.

It is seldom appreciated that the Eastman Kodak and the Ilford emulsions differ considerably in many respects. To take only one example, a slide dipped in Kodak NTB-3 may be covered by an emulsion layer $4\,\mu$ thick, while using identical conditions, Ilford G5 will give a layer $25-30\,\mu$ thick. Not only does the physical consistency of the emulsions from the two sources vary, but also the

Manufacturer	Crystal diameter (μ)	Sensitivity					
		0	1	2	3	4	5
Ilford	0.27[abc]						G5
Ilford	0.20[abc]	K0	K1	K2			K5
Ilford	0.14[abc]					L4	
Eastman–Kodak	0.34[ab]						NTB-3
Eastman–Kodak	0.29[ab]			NTB			
Eastman–Kodak	0.26[ab]				NTB-2		
Eastman–Kodak	0.22[ab]		NTA				
Eastman–Kodak	0.06[a]			NTE			
Agfa–Gevaert	0.15[a]						NUC-715
Agfa–Gevaert	0.07[a]				NUC-307		
Kodak (England)	0.20[c]			AR-10			

a Available as liquid emulsion
b Available as coated plates
c Available as stripping-film plates

Fig.82. The nuclear emulsions in common use in autoradiography, presented on the scale of sensitivity used by Ilford, Ltd. Level 0 records α but not β particles. Level 2 is suitable for tritium: 3 for carbon-14 and sulphur-35: 5 for β particles at minimum ionisation.

sensitivity to latent image fading, the safelighting requirements, and the extent of formation of background fog on extreme drying.

The techniques that have been described in the literature for Eastman Kodak emulsions do not give optimal results with Ilford products, and *vice versa*. It follows that one must select a technique appropriate to the source from which emulsions will be normally obtained.

(a) Eastman Kodak emulsions

The two emulsions generally used for grain density autoradiographs in light microscopy are NTB-2 and NTB-3. The former is less sensitive, being suitable for tritium, iodine-125, and perhaps even carbon-14 and sulphur-35: the latter should be used for isotopes of higher energy. The less sensitive NTB-2 has a slightly lower background, as would be expected.

Both emulsions have the same physical characteristics, differing only so far as one can judge, in the degree of sensitisation. It follows that procedures devised for the one are fully applicable to the other. Both are reproducible in use, and have a low level of background.

NTB emulsions can be stored for up to 2 months, preferably at about $4°$. Nuclear emulsions in bulk should never be frozen.

The emulsion is usually melted in the glass or plastic container in which it was received. The same batch of emulsion may be melted and used several times without deterioration. It is usually not diluted, although dilution with distilled water is possible without altering the properties of the dried emulsion. From the data presented by Leblond and his co-workers, it appears that NTB emulsions are very liable to latent image fading. Careful drying, together with exposure in the presence of a drying agent, are recommended. These emulsions require strict safelighting conditions.

(b) Ilford emulsions

There are three series of emulsions produced by Ilford, designated G, K, and L respectively. They differ from each other in the crystal diameter, and in other characteristics (Fig. 82). The development routine that is optimal, the liability to latent image fading, and so on, are not identical in the three series.

Within each series, emulsions of different sensitivities may be obtained. The levels of sensitisation are indicated by a number after the series letter: thus level 5 is the highest normally produced, and G5 and K5, while differing in crystal diameter, have the same sensitivity. The emulsions that are in general use are G5 and K5, for isotopes of high energy, and K2, which is excellent for tritium and iodine-125. In the L series, the highest level of sensitisation available is L4.

Ilford emulsions should not be stored longer than 2 months: 4° is the optimal temperature for the bulk emulsion. As with the NTB emulsions, the bulk emulsion should never be frozen.

The Ilford emulsions should not be heated more than once, as this produces a high background. On each occasion that slides are to be dipped, a known amount of emulsion should be taken from the stock jar: this may be done by weighing the emulsion, or, more conveniently, by measuring it in a graduated cylinder. The emulsion is then melted, and added to a known volume of distilled water. This dilution is essential to obtain an emulsion layer thin enough for grain density autoradiography. The precise dilution required will be discussed later.

Rigorous drying, such as that recommended by Messier and Leblond[4] for NTB emulsions, is unnecessary and even harmful in the case of the Ilford emulsions. The Ilford Research Laboratory recommend exposure at 0–4°, and a relative humidity of 40–50%, and, in these conditions, latent image fading is not serious. Attempts to dry the emulsion too much will result in a high background, due to stressing of the silver halide crystals by the gelatin. This tendency to the formation of stress background can be considerably reduced by incorporating glycerol in the molten diluted emulsion, to a concentration of 1% of the final volume.

The Ilford emulsions can be used in lighter safelight conditions than the NTB emulsions, without producing a significantly increased background. This has considerable advantages in special circumstances, such as the autoradiography of soluble isotopes, where complicated procedures have to be carried out under safelighting, but probably makes no great difference with the very simple routine of dipping slides.

FACTORS AFFECTING THE THICKNESS OF THE EMULSION LAYER

A number of factors influence the thickness of the layer that covers the specimen when a slide is dipped in liquid emulsion. Some idea of their relative importance is essential if the full potentialities of the technique are to be realised. Some of these factors can be varied deliberately to give variations in emulsion thickness; others require stating only so that they may be controlled in the interests of consistency and reproducibility.

(a) The dilution of the emulsion
It is clear that dipping a slide in undiluted emulsion will result in a thicker layer than dipping in a mixture of 1 part emulsion to 3 parts distilled water. It is quite reasonable to dilute bulk emulsions in gel form in this way. During drying

of the slide, the excess water evaporates, and the composition of the emulsion during exposure returns to that of undiluted emulsion. There is no reason to expect changes in the composition or behaviour of the emulsion with dilutions up to 1 part in 10 parts of distilled water, which is far more dilute than will be normally required. The diluent should be glass-distilled or ion-free water. Small traces of metallic ions may cause fogging of the emulsion.

This is the variable that will normally be altered, if the emulsion thickness needs to be changed. A known and easily controllable change in dilution will produce a predictable change in emulsion thickness, if all the other factors affecting thickness remain constant.

(b) The temperature of the emulsion

The hotter the molten emulsion is, the less viscous it will be, and the thinner the layer that results when a slide is dipped and allowed to drain dry.

This parameter is only of limited usefulness, however. At temperatures above 50°, emulsions tend to develop high levels of background, while at the lower end of the temperature range at which emulsions are molten, a very slight change in temperature produces a large change in viscosity.

Caro and Van Tubergen[8] have suggested the use of liquid emulsion at a temperature near the gel point, to prevent redistribution of silver halide crystals during the process of drying. It is certainly true that a very thin emulsion layer at a temperature of around 50° will dry extremely fast, with a rather uneven distribution of silver grains. It is possible to avoid this artefact by careful attention to the conditions of drying, however. In the techniques that will be described, their suggestion is not adopted, as it is felt to be more convenient and reproducible to hold the emulsion throughout at a temperature of 42–43°.

(c) The temperature and wetness of the slide

If the slide to be dipped is warmed to 40°, the emulsion picked up will drain off more rapidly than off a cold slide, resulting in a thinner emulsion layer. Similarly, a thinner layer will result if the slide is thoroughly wetted before dipping. These are not particularly useful parameters to vary in order to achieve a given emulsion thickness, but they should be controlled in the interests of reproducibility. It is useful to establish a set routine for the handling of the slides prior to dipping, so that they always reach the emulsion in the same condition. If they require dewaxing before autoradiography, it may for instance be convenient to keep them in the darkroom in a dish of distilled water until a few minutes before dipping, and then to allow excess water to drain off them.

(d) The temperature and humidity during drying

Ideally, the molten emulsion should gel before it begins to dry, to prevent the redistribution of silver halide crystals mentioned above. This is most conveniently achieved by placing the slides on a cool surface as soon as possible after dipping. But the emulsion will dry more rapidly and thoroughly at a higher temperature, and this is not harmful once the emulsion has gelled. I have a metal plate, which is cooled beforehand by placing containers filled with ice on it, on which the slides are placed lying flat after dipping (Fig. 83). After 15 to 20 minutes on this plate, the slides are placed, still lying flat, on the bench top for a further hour or so: the darkroom conditions are about 20° and 45–50% R.H.

If the temperature or humidity of the darkroom are very variable, and no attempt is made to cool the slides immediately after dipping, an uncontrolled variable will be introduced which may affect the draining of emulsion from the slides, and thus its final thickness.

The effects of several combinations of temperature and humidity during drying on the thickness and uniformity of the emulsion layer have been studied

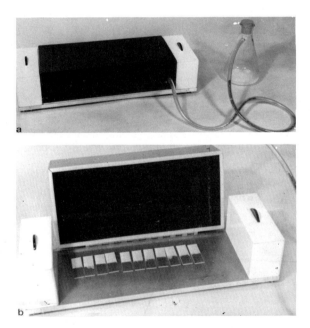

Fig.83. A levelled metal plate to facilitate the drying of autoradiographs: there are removable containers in each end compartment, which can be filled with ice or with water at any desired temperature. The closely fitting black plastic lid permits drying in an atmosphere of dried CO_2 if required.

by Leblond, Kopriwa and Messier[6]. They have suggested that high temperatures during drying help to give uniform layers, since excess emulsion can drain off the slide without gelling. But, as we have seen, high temperatures during drying result in very rapid drying, with high stress backgrounds in the emulsion. This can be prevented by maintaining a high relative humidity at the same time, which effectively slows down the rate of drying, and helps to keep the emulsion fluid while draining from the slide. They found that a temperature of 28° and a relative humidity between 60 and 80% gave reasonably uniform emulsion layers with a low background. The emulsion was "dry" in 30 min in these conditions, in the sense that the slides were ready for exposure to begin. Exposure took place in the presence of a drying agent, so it is certain that drying continued during the early stages of exposure. This is an interesting suggestion, and worth following up if the uniformity and reproducibility of the emulsion layer become of critical importance.

(e) The technique of dipping
    Even if all the factors mentioned above are kept constant, it is still possible to introduce differences into the thickness of the emulsion layer by varying the sequence and timing of events on withdrawing the slide from the emulsion. The slide may be withdrawn slowly or fast: it may be kept vertical, standing up against a support to drain, or it may be held immediately in a horizontal position, and laid flat for drying to start. In order to get a uniform emulsion coat, the slide must be withdrawn steadily from the dipping jar. Dr. Kopriwa has a simple little winch for doing this, steadily and at a chosen, reproducible speed. Each autoradiographer tends to develop his or her own technique of dipping, so that the slides produced by one person should have a fairly reproducible emulsion thickness. But different people, working with apparently the same conditions of dilution, temperature, and so on, can have very different emulsion layers on their slides.
    My own procedure is to keep the dipping jar vertical, and to withdraw the slide fairly slowly, holding it upright to drain for several seconds. The back of the slide is then wiped clean with a paper tissue, and it is placed on the cold metal plate, described above, lying emulsion side upwards. The thicknesses quoted below have resulted from this procedure in my hands, and will only provide an approximate guide to the emulsion layers others will produce if they try to follow this procedure.

References p. 312

SELECTING AN APPROPRIATE EMULSION THICKNESS

Generally speaking, there are two situations in which one wishes to dip slides in molten emulsion. The first is to produce an autoradiograph with the highest possible resolving power for viewing in the light microscope. In this case, the emulsion layer should be as thin as practicable, let us say between 1 and 2 μ during exposure. The second situation involves the preparation of autoradiographs for quantitative work with tritium or iodine-125, when as we have seen (p.251), the emulsion layer must never be less than about 2.5 μ during exposure, implying a mean thickness of between 3 and 4 μ to be on the safe side.

How can one accurately estimate the emulsion thickness during exposure? One very simple method is to take advantage of the limited range of β particles from tritium through nuclear emulsion. One can take as test objects slides with sections labelled with, for instance, tritiated thymidine. After development and fixation, they should be mounted in an aqueous mounting medium such as glycerin jelly, which leaves the emulsion in a swollen state. If labelled nuclei are then examined under the highest power objective available, it should be clear whether or not the silver grains over them extend all the way up to the upper surface of the emulsion, or are separated from it by a layer of emulsion that contains only a few scattered background grains (Fig. 84). If the emulsion is consistently thicker than the maximum range of the β particles, suitable conditions have been established for quantitative work with tritium or iodine-125. If

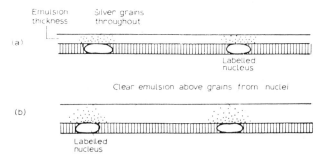

Fig.84. Two diagrams to illustrate a simple method of checking that a thin emulsion layer is sufficiently thick for the quantitative autoradiography of tritium. Heavily labelled structures, such as cell nuclei that have incorporated tritiated thymidine, are examined with an emulsion layer that has been swollen prior to microscopy. (*a*) The silver grains over the nuclei extend right up to the upper surface of the emulsion. This emulsion is too thin for quantitative work: slight variations in emulsion thickness will alter the autoradiographic efficiency significantly. (*b*) The emulsion layer is thicker than the maximum range of β particle. Variations in thickness at this level will not affect the efficiency of the system.

a layer between 1 and $2\,\mu$ thick has been obtained, it will be quite clear that the grains over labelled nuclei extend to the upper surface of the emulsion.

In making a thin emulsion layer for high resolution work, it is very easy to go too far, producing a layer that is too thin. Generally speaking, it is not advisable to try to dip to less than about $1.5\,\mu$, unless steps are taken to prevent the emulsion drying very rapidly, with consequent chances for redistribution of silver grains during drying, and a higher stress background. A very thin layer also has a considerably lower efficiency as a recording medium, resulting in longer exposure periods for the same grain density. It is useful to take a coated slide into the light after drying, and to examine the emulsion under the microscope. Over the section, there should be no gaps and no areas where the emulsion appears to be only one or two silver halide crystals deep. The emulsion layer should look reasonably uniform, and perhaps 5 crystals deep, though this may be difficult to determine accurately.

It is always a useful step to bring one slide of each batch out into the light, to check that gross variations in emulsion thickness are not occurring.

In view of what has been said in the previous section, even if the techniques outlined at the end of this chapter are carefully followed, it is necessary to check that the emulsion layers are of the correct thickness. It should not be a surprise to find that they are not, as slight differences in the timing and sequence of events after dipping can introduce relatively large variations into the emulsion thickness. The dilution of the emulsion should then be adjusted on future occasions, so that, with the routine that is most convenient to the autoradiographer concerned, the desired thickness will be obtained.

CONDITIONS OF DRYING AND EXPOSURE

These have been mentioned already, insofar as they influence the thickness of the emulsion layer. In general, the emulsion should gel before significant drying has time to take place. Once it has gelled, drying should be slow and gentle.

Placing the slides on a cool metal plate immediately after dipping helps the emulsion to gel fast. It also helps to ensure that the initial rate of drying will be fairly slow.

The work of Leblond and his collaborators[5,6], which has already been referred to, illustrates the way in which the temperature and humidity of the atmosphere in which the slides are dried can be varied. Their results show that the lowest background levels are produced by very slow drying, which may even extend into the early stages of exposure itself. Sawicki and Pawinska[9] have similarly demonstrated lower background levels from very slow drying with Kodak AR-10 stripping film.

Low background levels can also be produced by failure to dry the emulsion adequately before the start of exposure (p.102). If fading of latent images from this cause continues throughout exposure, the low background will also be accompanied by low grain yields over labelled structures. But if incompletely dried emulsion is exposed in the presence of a drying agent, such as dried silica gel, latent image fading can be limited to the first part of exposure. This can result in low background levels, since all the latent images present in the emulsion before exposure will have been lost, while the grain yields can remain high, because the emulsion is fully dry and free from fading for most of the exposure time. It should always be remembered that prolongation of drying into exposure in this way makes it very difficult to estimate the true duration of exposure accurately. This may not matter, if the distribution of radioactivity within a specimen is being studied. A more reproducible drying technique is preferable in quantitative work, however. The routine we use at present is to cool the slides for 15–20 minutes on the metal plate after dipping, then place them on the bench in the darkroom still lying flat, for a further 1 hour or so, at about 20° and 45–50% R.H. After this, the slides are placed in their exposure boxes, with the lids off, in a desiccator over dried silica gel overnight at room temperature. The next morning, the boxes are closed, and placed in the refrigerator to expose. This method gives slow but complete drying, with no evidence of latent image fading in exposures of up to two months, in experiments with Ilford emulsions in our laboratory. Drying has been more reproducible in this way than with silica gel in the exposure box. There have been occasions when the silica gel has been found saturated at the end of exposure, and the emulsion not completely dry: perhaps the slides were wetter than usual on putting them into the boxes, or the amount or dryness of the silica gel itself less than adequate.

From what has been said above, it should be quite clear that directing a blast of hot air from a hairdryer on to the slides immediately after dipping them is not an ideal method of drying (Fig. 32). There is latitude for considerable variation, and need for more careful documentation, in the techniques of drying autoradiographic emulsions. Enough is already known to indicate that gentle but thorough drying is the ideal to aim at.

If latent image fading must be prevented – as, for instance, in the case of a very low level of labelling requiring an exposure of many weeks to give a trace – it may be necessary to expose the slides in an atmosphere that does not contain oxygen[10] . This can be done with nitrogen, argon, or any inert gas, but is probably most convenient with carbon dioxide. When the slides are placed in the desiccator over dried silica gel, a small lump of solid carbon dioxide is put at the bottom, where it sublimes, filling the desiccator by displacement. When the exposure boxes are closed next morning, care is taken to put their lids on under the dry carbon dioxide layer in the desiccator. If the boxes are impermeable, such as the plastic slide boxes usually used for this purpose, the slides will remain in this atmosphere throughout exposure. If permeable boxes made of cardboard are used, it will be necessary to store them during exposure in a larger vessel with the same filling gas.

Caro and Van Tubergen[8] found it satisfactory to expose very thin layers of Ilford L4 at room temperature. This is not the usual practice, however, and other workers who have examined the conditions of exposure agree with the recommendations of the manufacturers that exposure should normally take place at 0–4°. Exposure can be made at considerably lower temperatures without significant loss of sensitivity, but this is seldom necessary or convenient, except in the autoradiography of soluble material (see Chapter 8), and as a measure to reduce the severity of chemography (p.98).

ESTIMATES OF RESOLUTION AND EFFICIENCY

There are very few published observations on the resolution and efficiency to be expected from liquid emulsions applied in thin layers. The difficulty of achieving a uniform and reproducible emulsion thickness makes detailed measurements rather pointless. The best that can be done is to equate the performance of these emulsions to that of Kodak AR-10 in rather general terms, making certain assumptions as to the emulsion thickness.

If one looks first at the emulsion layers of $1.5–2\,\mu$ that are desirable for high resolving power, it is clear on theoretical grounds (see Chapter 4, p.55) that a higher resolution should be obtained for isotopes of the energy of carbon-14 or higher than with the $3.8\,\mu$ layer of AR-10 during exposure. Emulsions such as Ilford G5 and the NTB series of Eastman Kodak have a crystal size similar to that of AR-10: when applied in a thinner layer, they should give a slight but significant improvement in resolution, similar to that obtainable with Kodak's Special Autoradiographic Stripping Plates (p.285). Ilford K5 and L4 have progressively smaller crystal diameters, so that layers $1.5–2\,\mu$ thick of these emulsions will give even better resolution still. There is little point in reducing the emulsion thickness further in an attempt to achieve very high resolution if the specimen is a tissue section $5\,\mu$ thick. At this level, reduction in the thickness of the specimen becomes the limiting factor. The highest resolution obtainable in light microscope autoradiography is given by a monolayer of Ilford L4 crystals over a source that is extremely thin, such as a tissue section $1\,\mu$ or less, cut from material embedded as for electron microscopy.

References p. 312

Is it possible to improve significantly on the resolution given by AR-10 stripping film for tritium and iodine-125, by using thin layers of liquid emulsion? At these low energies, the short maximum range of the β particle limits the effective thickness of the AR-10 to about $2\,\mu$. It would be unrealistic to expect improved resolution from the use of Ilford G5 or the NTB series in a 2-μ layer. An emulsion layer $1\,\mu$ thick of Ilford L4 should give better resolution for these isotopes, however.

When one considers efficiency, the situation is rather complex. Clearly, a thinner emulsion layer is likely to have a lower efficiency for isotopes of the energy of carbon-14, sulphur-35, or higher. In the cases of Ilford G5, K5 and L4, and of Eastman Kodak NTB3, this effect is offset by the higher sensitivities of these emulsions relative to AR-10 stripping film. The overall efficiency of a 1-μ layer of K5 should be much the same as that of AR-10 for phosphorus-32, for instance. The same emulsion, applied as a layer 3.5–$4\,\mu$ thick would give similar resolution to AR-10, but a significantly higher efficiency.

With tritium and iodine-125, efficiency is little affected by increasing the emulsion thickness above $2\,\mu$. Below this, reductions in thickness will clearly result in loss of efficiency. There is no gain in efficiency from using a highly sensitised emulsion: similar layers of K5 and K2 emulsions would have very similar efficiencies at these low particle energies. A layer of K2 that is $2\,\mu$ thick should have an efficiency practically the same as that of AR-10. An emulsion layer $1\,\mu$ thick of Ilford L4, which would give higher resolution than AR-10, will have a lower efficiency, giving perhaps 60–75% the grain yield of the latter. The same L4 emulsion, as a layer $2\,\mu$ thick, will have a higher efficiency than AR-10, since the smaller crystal size of the former provides a higher probability of one β particle activating more than one crystal.

Leblond[11] has reported briefly on some results of Kopriwa on the relative sensitivities of Eastman Kodak NTB-2, NTB, and Kodak AR-10, to tritium in tissue sections. Under comparable conditions of exposure, the relative grain densities found were 1.0, 0.4 and 0.5. Hence NTB-2 can be expected to have twice the efficiency for tritium of either of the other two emulsions.

By the selection of a suitable emulsion, and careful control of its thickness, it is possible to achieve optimal conditions for nearly every type of autoradiographic experiment. If only a technique were available which could give uniform and reproducible layers of liquid emulsions, stripping film would be replaced completely.

DETAILED DESCRIPTION OF TECHNIQUES

In view of the many differences between Eastman Kodak and Ilford emulsions, their use will be described separately, starting with the Eastman Kodak NTB series. Detailed descriptions of techniques of applying these emulsions have been given by Joftes[2, 3], and by Leblond and his co-workers[4-6].

1. *Emulsions:*   Eastman Kodak NTB-2 and NTB-3
   Safelight: Wratten No. 2
   Darkroom conditions: Temperature, 18–20°, relatively humidity, 40–50%
   Equipment required: Thermostatically controlled waterbath at 43°:
a suitable dipping jar, such as a 50-ml graduated cylinder cut short at the 40-ml mark, or a 100-ml beaker, depending on the size of the slides; a levelled metal plate with provision for placing containers of ice at each end (Fig. 83).

Preparing the autoradiographs: The NTB emulsion arrives in a plastic jar. Under safelighting, the jar should be placed in the waterbath at 43°, and allowed to stand there for 30 min (This 30-min period can be in absolute darkness). By this time it will have become molten, and most of the bubbles in the emulsion will have risen to the surface.

Pour the emulsion gently into the dipping jar to the required level. Stand the dipping jar once more in the waterbath.

Dip a clean slide into the emulsion, and take it up to the safelight to check that the emulsion is uniform and free from bubbles. If many bubbles are present, wait 2 min and dip another clean slide.

Take the experimental sides, and dip them individually into the emulsion. Keep the slide vertical in the emulsion, and withdraw it slowly and steadily. Holding the slide in a vertical position for several seconds, allow excess emulsion to drain into a paper tissue.

Wipe the back of the slide with a paper tissue, and place the slide, face up, on the cooled metal plate.

When all the slides have been dipped, leave them on the metal plate, in complete darkness, for 15–20 min. Transfer them, still lying flat, to the bench top for a further one hour. Then place them in their exposure boxes, with lids off, in a desiccator over dried silica gel overnight at room temperature. In the morning, close the boxes, and place them in a refrigerator at 4° to expose. A teaspoonful of dried silica gel wrapped in a paper tissue may be included in the exposure box with the slides if desired.

Processing.   Under safelighting, transfer the slides to stainless steel or glass slide racks. All solutions should be at the same temperature: the development times stated should be suitable for a developer temperature of 17°, and for subsequent viewing of the slides by transmitted light.

Eastman Kodak Dektol developer, 1 part stock solution diluted with 2 parts distilled water, for 2 min.

Rinse in distilled water.

30% sodium thiosulphate solution for 8 min.

Wash in running tapwater for 15 min.

This technique should give an emulsion layer of 3–4 μ, suitable for quantitative studies with tritium or iodine-125.

For emulsion layers 1–2 μ thick, for high resolution studies, dilute the emulsion in the dipping jar 2 parts to 1 part of distilled water.

If uniformity of the emulsion layer is not good enough by this technique, it may be possible to improve the method in this respect by varying the temperature and humidity at which the slides are initially dried[5,6] (see p.302).

If latent image fading occurs during exposure, in spite of the presence of a drying agent, it may be necessary to expose the slides in an atmosphere of dry carbon dioxide, or of nitrogen (p.228).

The development conditions are only approximate, and will require examination in the light of the needs of the particular experiment.

Eastman Kodak NTB emulsions should be stored at 4°. It is possible to melt the same batch of emulsion several times without significant increase in background levels.

2. *Emulsion:*   Ilford K2

   Safelight: Ilford 'F 904' or Wratten 'OC'

   Darkroom conditions: Temperature, 18–20°, relative humidity, 40–50%

   Equipment required.   Thermostatically controlled waterbath at 43°, 1 50-ml graduated measuring cylinder; 1 dipping jar; 1 25-ml graduated measuring cylinder; 1 pair plastic print forceps; 1 glass stirring rod; a levelled metal plate with provision for placing containers of ice at each end (Fig. 83).

   Preparing the autoradiographs.   With a black grease pencil, make a mark on the 25-ml measuring cylinder at 12 ml. Place 11.76 ml distilled water and 0.24 ml glycerol in the dipping jar. Stand the dipping jar and the two measuring cylinders in the waterbath at 43°.

   Under safelighting, transfer emulsion from the stock bottle to the 50-ml cylinder, using the print forceps. Shake the emulsion down gently, and continue until it reaches 20–25 ml. Stand this cylinder again in the waterbath for 10 min, stirring the emulsion very gently with the glass rod. Vigorous stirring will whip up a froth of bubbles: one revolution per second is adequate.

Take the 50-ml and 25-ml measuring cylinders out of the waterbath, wiping their sides with a paper tissue to remove water. Pour molten emulsion from the large cylinder to the small one, until the level reaches the black grease pencil mark at 12 ml.

Pour the molten emulsion from the 25-ml cylinder into the dipping jar. With the dipping jar standing in the waterbath, stir the emulsion gently for a minute or so to ensure complete mixing. Then leave the emulsion standing in the waterbath a further 2 min to allow bubbles to disperse.

Dip a clean slide into the emulsion, and take it up to the safelight to check that the emulsion is uniform and free from bubbles. If the emulsion is not uniform, it will appear thicker at the bottom of the slide: gentle stirring with a clean slide, moving it in a rotary, vertical direction will help. If bubbles are present, leave the emulsion a further 2 min, then dip another clean slide.

Take the experimental slides, and dip them individually in the emulsion. Keep the slide vertical in the emulsion, and withdraw it slowly and steadily. Holding the slide vertical for a few seconds, allow excess emulsion to drain into a paper tissue.

Wipe the back of the slide with a paper tissue, and place the slide, face up, on the cooled metal plate, from which the ice should now be removed.

When all the slides have been dipped, leave them on the metal plate, in complete darkness, for 15–20 min. Transfer them, still lying flat, to the bench top for a further one hour. Then place them in their exposure boxes, with the lids off, in a desiccator over dried silica gel overnight at room temperature. In the morning, close the boxes and put them in a refrigerator at 4° to expose.

Processing.   Under safelighting, transfer the slides to stainless steel or glass slide racks. All solutions should be at the same temperature: the times stated should be suitable for a developer temperature of 20°, and for subsequent viewing of the slides with transmitted light.

Ilford Phen-X developer, diluted with an equal volume of distilled water for 8 min.

Rinse in distilled water.

30% sodium thiosulphate solution for 8 min.

Wash in running tapwater for 15 min.

This technique should give an emulsion layer of 3–4 μ, suitable for quantitative studies with tritium or iodine-125.

For emulsion layers 1–2 μ thick, for high resolution studies, dilute the emulsion in the dipping jar 3 parts to 5 parts distilled water.

The description given here will produce 25 ml of molten, diluted emulsion, which is sufficient to cover about two-thirds of a 3″ x 1″ microscope slide when placed in a suitable dipping jar. It is simple to scale the volumes of water, glycerol and emulsion up or down according to the needs of the experiment.

If latent image fading is occurring, exposure can take place in an atmosphere of dry carbon dioxide or nitrogen (p.228).

Once again, the development conditions are only approximate, and should be altered, if necessary, to meet the needs of the experiment. Ilford G5 emulsion in general requires more gentle development than either the K or the L series: it may be convenient with G5 to dilute the developer with 2 parts of distilled water, instead of an equal volume.

Ilford emulsions should be stored at 4°. They should never be heated a second time. Emulsion left in the dipping jar should therefore be discarded.

REFERENCES

1   L.F. Bélanger and C.P. Leblond, *Endocrinology*, 39 (1946) 8.
2   D.L. Joftes and S. Warren, *J. Biol. Phot. Assoc.*, 23 (1955) 145.
3   D.L. Joftes, *Lab. Invest.*, 8 (1959) 131.
4   B. Messier and C.P. Leblond, *Proc. Soc. Exptl. Biol. Med.*, 96 (1957) 7.
5   B.M. Kopriwa and C.P. Leblond, *J. Histochem. Cytochem.*, 10 (1962) 269.
6   C.P. Leblond, B.M. Kopriwa and B. Messier, in R. Wegmann (Ed.), *Histochemistry and Cytochemistry*, Pergamon, London, 1963 .
7   D. Darlington and A.W. Rogers, *J. Anat.*, 100 (1966) 813.
8   L.G. Caro and R.P. van Tubergen, *J. Cell Biol.*, 15 (1962) 173.
9   W. Sawicki and M. Pawinska, *Stain Technol.*, 40 (1965) 67.
10 R.H. Herz, *Lab. Invest.*, 8 (1959) 71.
11 C.P. Leblond, in R.J.C. Harris (Ed.), *The Use of Autoradiography in the Investigation of Protein Synthesis*, Academic Press, New York, 1965, p.21.

CHAPTER 17

Liquid Emulsion Techniques for Track Autoradiography

Nuclear emulsions owe their existence to the physicists who wished to study the behaviour of ionising particles. The emulsions now available were developed to record the passage of ionising particles as discrete tracks, and a great deal of information on the interaction of these particles with matter has been obtained from studying the characteristics of their tracks in thick layers of emulsion.

It is surprising how seldom biological research has been carried out with thick emulsion layers giving track records, when one remembers this historical evolution of the nuclear emulsions and the techniques of their use. In the early days of autoradiography, the emphasis lay heavily on identifying the site at which radioactivity was localised within a tissue, and the techniques based on thick emulsion layers were difficult and time-consuming by comparison with the grain density methods which relied on thin layers of liquid emulsion or stripping film. Certainly, track recording techniques are more difficult, but, as has been pointed out in Chapter 13 (p.249), the advantages of track autoradiography are substantial when measurements of radioactivity are needed. The information on grain spacing and scattering angles required from a track record by a particle physicist represents a higher level of technical achievement than the straightforward recording of recognisable tracks, which is sufficient for quantitative autoradiography. There is thus no real doubt that the emulsions and methods developed for the former task should be quite adequate for the latter.

The recording and recognition of the tracks of α particles present no great problem. Quantitative studies based on counting α tracks have been described by several workers[1-3]. The short range and high rate of energy loss characteristic of the α particle combine to make a thin layer of a relatively insensitive emulsion the method of choice. In fact, either Kodak AR-10 stripping film or the technique employing Ilford K2 emulsion for work with tritium (described in Chapters 15 and 16 respectively) are suitable.

The recording of the tracks of β particles is made difficult by their long range and relatively slow rate of energy loss, as well as by their very irregular trajectory. The emulsion layers used must be considerably thicker, and the emulsion must have a sufficiently high sensitivity to give a close spacing of developed silver grains, if these tortuous tracks are to be recognised clearly. The technical problems of β-track autoradiography all stem from the need for a thick layer of emulsion of high sensitivity.

Dr. Hilde Levi, of Copenhagen, has been associated with much of the basic work on β-track autoradiography[4-6]. In 1954, she published a careful description of the technique developed in her laboratory for preparing 60-μ layers of Ilford G5 emulsion[7]. Levi, Rogers, Bentzon and Nielsen[8] presented further detailed descriptions of techniques for handling 60- and 120-μ layers of Ilford G5, together with the correlations between initial particle energy, track length, grain number and spacing and track radius, for β particles in the energy range of 20–400 keV.

Ficq[9-11], at Brussels, has also made extensive use of β-track recording, though this has usually been for purposes of localisation rather than quantitation. Her techniques are described in detail in a chapter in *The Cell* (1961), edited by Brachet and Mirsky[12].

The first attempt to realise the quantitative potentialities of this approach was the work of Levinthal[13] (1956) and Levinthal and Thomas[14] (1957), who measured the absolute disintegration rate of bacteriophage virus labelled with phosphorus-32. Their techniques are described in the latter paper. Phage particles were suspended in thick layers of Ilford G5 emulsion, and their position subsequently recognised by the star of β tracks radiating out from a common origin. The number of tracks per star formed the basic data for calculating the disintegration rate, and thus the number of atoms of phosphorus per virus.

Similar techniques have been applied to measurements of the phosphorylation of acetylcholinesterase by diisopropylfluorophosphate (DFP) in motor endplates[15], and in megakaryocytes[16]. From these values has been calculated, in absolute terms, the number of molecules of the enzyme acetylcholinesterase in these two sites. This work is interesting for the correlation obtained between track counts from DFP labelled with phosphorus-32, and liquid scintillation counting from DFP labelled with tritium[15,17].

BASIC CHARACTERISTICS OF β-TRACK AUTORADIOGRAPHS

Many facets of β-track autoradiography have been dealt with already in earlier chapters of this book. Here, the important facts will only be briefly summarised.

The use of a thick layer of emulsion to record the passage of β particles as tracks of developed silver grains is really only justified if accurate determinations of the disintegration rates of labelled sources are required. The localisation of radioactivity is more conveniently studied with thin emulsion layers, and, in most cases, the relative concentrations of isotope in different structures can also be compared more simply by comparing grain densities in thin emulsion layers. The measurement of disintegration rates in absolute terms, however, requires the use of track methods in most instances.

It is usually convenient, when preparing a track autoradiograph, to mount the biological material on a microscope slide, and cover it on one side only with nuclear emulsion. The technique of suspending the source in the emulsion, while it provides a record of tracks over the full space angle, is not essential for quantitative studies.

The basic concepts of autoradiography, such as efficiency, resolution, and background, require restating in terms unfamiliar to those accustomed to working with grain-density autoradiographs. They will therefore be briefly recalled.

(a) Efficiency

This is discussed in detail in Chapter 5 (p.85). In a track autoradiograph, the efficiency may be defined as the percentage of disintegrations taking place in the source during exposure which give rise to recognisable tracks. With no self-absorption, high initial particle energies, and emulsion completely surrounding the source, the efficiency of a track autoradiograph should be 100%: this is the sort of situation Levinthal[13, 14] achieved, with viruses labelled with phosphorus-32 and suspended in emulsion.

Efficiency may be reduced by three factors. The first is self-absorption, which becomes increasingly important at lower particle energies, and with increasing dimensions and mass of the source. For tissue sections of 5μ or less, and for smears of cell suspensions, self-absorption can be ignored with phosphorus-32, but may be considerable with carbon-14. The second factor concerns the ability of particles of low initial energy to give rise to a recognisable track – usually defined as 4 or more developed grains. With carbon-14, for instance, 14% of the total particles emitted will not produce as many as 4 grains in their trajectory[8].

The third factor tending to reduce the efficiency of track autoradiographs from the theoretical maximum of 100% is the geometrical relationship between source and emulsion. If the source is mounted on a glass slide, and covered by emulsion on one side only, the β particles that leave to enter the slide will not produce a recognisable track. In this situation (see Fig. 27, p.68), it is reasonable to assume that 50% of the particles leaving the source will enter the emulsion directly. Some of these will subsequently be scattered back into the glass, and some that enter the glass initially will be scattered into the emulsion, but, at a first approximation, the tracks that enter the emulsion directly over a source of cellular dimensions represent half the tracks that would have been observed if the source were completely suspended in emulsion.

If one assumes reasonable care in preparing the autoradiograph, so that factors like fading of the latent image and loss of activity in histological processing may be ignored, these three factors are all that need to be considered in relating the observed track count to the disintegration rate within the source.

(b) Resolution

This is discussed in Chapter 4 (p.68). Briefly, one cannot specify the point at which a β particle is emitted, unless one is dealing with a small source suspended in emulsion: one can only observe the point at which the particle enters the recording emulsion. With a tissue section mounted on a glass slide (see Fig. 27, p.68), we have seen that 50% of the emitted particles enter the emulsion directly from the source. The number of particles that are scattered subsequently across the glass-emulsion interface is difficult to determine accurately, but seems to be in the order of 10% of the total β flux from the source, from preliminary observations made in this laboratory with phosphorus-32.

If one defines the resolution of a track autoradiograph as the minimum radius around a point source that contains the points of entry of 50% of all the tracks produced by particles from that source, a resolution of about 2μ should be achieved, even with phosphorus-32.

(c) Background

One of the great advantages of track autoradiographs is their low background. In Chapter 6 (p.106), we saw that many factors apart from ionising particles can produce developed grains in nuclear emulsions – heat, light, pressure, and chemical agents, for example. One cannot distinguish between these silver grains and the ones produced by radiation in a thin emulsion layer. None of these agents gives rise to a β track, however, so that all the causes of random background grains can be discriminated against, in a track autoradiograph.

Background β tracks do occur. They arise from potassium-40 in the glassware, carbon-14 in the gelatin of the emulsion, and secondary electrons caused by cosmic rays. They should be rare, and their nature will often be obvious. A track of less than 70 grains, starting in the emulsion itself without any obvious event or structure at its origin, is probably carbon-14 in the gelatin: while secondary electrons usually start from the track of some other charged particle through the emulsion.

(d) Latent image fading

Fading of the latent image has been discussed in Chapter 12 (p.228). Particularly in the presence of oxidising agents and of moisture, latent images formed early in exposure are liable to regress. This shows itself in track auto-radiographs in a decrease in the number of grains per unit length of track, and, if this process goes far enough, it will be impossible to determine the trajectory of the β particle from the few grains that remain.

Levi et al.[8] have investigated the grain spacing in β tracks up to about 400 keV in Ilford G5, and this seldom drops below 10 grains per 25 μ, even at the start of tracks at the upper end of the energy range they examined. Even for phosphorus-32, it is unlikely to fall below 7 grains per 25 μ.

If therefore, tracks are observed which have a grain spacing below that predicted, latent image fading should be suspected. Such "faded" tracks will co-exist with tracks with a normal grain spacing, which were produced late in exposure. The presence of a normal track thus cannot be taken as evidence for lack of fading: the latter can only be assumed if no "faded" tracks are seen. Normal and "faded" tracks are illustrated in Fig. 31.

It is possible for lesser degrees of fading to occur without altering the observed track count, if all the "faded" tracks are still recognisable; but, if clear evidence for the existence of fading is found, it is dangerous to assume that tracks have not been lost, without additional supporting evidence.

(e) Problems of track recognition

These have already been discussed in some detail (p.172). In material that is technically good, with a suitable density of β tracks, a low background of random silver grains, and correct conditions for microscopy, it is very easy to recognise and to count β tracks. On several occasions, I have had track counts checked by microscopists who have had no previous experience of track auto-radiography, and statistical analysis has failed to show a difference between the two sets of counts. Even in good autoradiographs there will always be patterns of silver grains that can be interpreted in more than one way, but these should form only a small percentage of the total.

Levi and Hogben[18] showed that the variance of track counts increased with increasing track density, illustrating how the percentage of patterns capable of several interpretations increases as the tracks cross with greater frequency. As a rough guide, the exposure time and specific activity should be adjusted so that no more than 8–10 tracks per 500 μ^2 for carbon-14 or sulphur-35, and 12–16 tracks per 500 μ^2 for phosphorus-32, are produced.

The process of reswelling the emulsion prior to microscopy greatly assists in the interpretation of track patterns. After photographic fixation, dehydration, and mounting in one of the routine non-aqueous histological media, the emulsion layer is much thinner than it was during exposure. Tracks which in fact crossed at different levels in the emulsion appear to run into one another. Swelling the emulsion back to its original thickness restores the distance separating the tracks, and simplifies their recognition[8].

In any thick emulsion layer, the upper few microns will be rather unpleasant after processing, with a higher density of random background grains, and occasional scratches, bits of dust, and crystals of various sorts. It is an additional merit of reswelling prior to microscopy that this layer which is so full of artefacts is lifted away from the biological material deep in the emulsion, making observation easier.

(f) The choice of emulsion

The emulsion selected for β-track autoradiography must have a high sensitivity in order to give sufficient grains along the trajectory of the β particle to form a recognisable track. In the Ilford range of nuclear emulsions, only G5, K5, and L4 come into this category. Eastman-Kodak NTB-3 is also sensitive enough.

It is impossible to view emulsion layers more than about $20\,\mu$ thick with dark-field incident lighting, as light scattering in the emulsion interferes with the reflection of the incident beam by silver grains more than a few microns below the surface. The developed silver grains must therefore be large enough to be seen clearly by transmitted light, in conditions which are not ideal for microscopy. A large grain size is therefore preferable.

The descriptions of techniques in the literature are almost without exception based on Ilford G5 emulsion, and the comprehensive data assembled by Levi et al.[8] on the characteristics of β tracks are again based on this emulsion. Therefore, while it is clearly possible to make track autoradiographs with K5 or NTB-3, G5 would seem to be the emulsion of choice.

THE PREPARATION OF THICK EMULSION LAYERS

It will be seen, in the discussion on the processing of thick emulsion layers, that the difficulties of track autoradiography increase rapidly with increasing emulsion thickness. There is every incentive to keep the emulsion as thin as possible, without sacrificing the basic advantages of the technique.

The precise thickness of the emulsion layer will vary somewhat with the experimental material, and with the energy of isotope. As an example, if the material is a section or smear mounted on a glass slide, and labelled with carbon-14 or sulphur-35, the emulsion should be $15-20\,\mu$ thick. This is sufficient to contain all but a small percentage of the tracks. For phosphorus-32 in a similar geometrical situation, $60\,\mu$ is thick enough. If one wishes to suspend the sources in emulsion, as, for instance, one might with labelled bacteria or algae, $20\,\mu$ of emulsion should lie above and below the highest and lowest sources respectively with carbon-14 or sulphur-35, and $60\,\mu$ with phosphorus-32.

A layer of emulsion $20\,\mu$ thick may be very simply applied by a modified dipping technique[19] . For the thicker layers, it is more convenient to pipette the warmed, diluted emulsion on to the microscope slide. If suspended sources are to be studied, the first layer of emulsion is applied and allowed to dry. Then a few drops of liquid emulsion, in which the labelled sources have been previously suspended, are placed in the centre of the slide, and allowed to dry. Finally, a second thick layer of emulsion is pipetted on to the slide, making a kind of sandwich, with the sources in the thin middle layer.

The drying of these thick emulsions is of crucial importance. Unless it is complete and thorough, latent image fading will be severe in the deeper levels, precisely where the biological material lies. Unless it is slow and gentle, a high background of random silver grains may be produced by stress within the gelatin.

Exposure is usually very short by comparison with grain density autoradiographs. Seldom will more than 48 h be needed.

THE PROCESSING OF THICK EMULSION LAYERS

With thick emulsion layers, it may take an appreciable time for solutions to diffuse in as far as the lower levels of the emulsion. Similarly, the removal of the products of fixation will take much longer than with thin layers. In the case of the development of a $60\,\mu$ layer, for instance, if it were to be immersed in developer at 20° in the usual way for thin emulsion layers, the upper surface would be completely developed before developer had even penetrated to the lower surface. For emulsions not more than about $30\,\mu$ thick, it is usually sufficient to increase the time of development relative to the time of penetration, by lowering the temperature of the developer. For thicker layers, it is better to allow developer to penetrate completely into the emulsion at 5°, at which temperature very little development takes place, and then to warm the emulsion to permit development to proceed[20] . If this warming up is done by transferring the slides to developer at, say, 20°, there may still be an appreciable gradient of development, as the upper layers warm up faster than those next to the glass slide. Hauser[21] has suggested a useful method of avoiding this, by diluting the developer used at 20°. Thus, in effect, the upper surface will have had a longer period of development than the lower surface, but in a more dilute solution. Developers based on Amidol are usually recommended for thicker emulsion layers, as their rate of penetration into the emulsion appears to be higher than with other developers.

It would take a long time to wash the developer out of the emulsion with a distilled water rinse, as is common in thin emulsion work. It is preferable to use an acid stopbath to halt development.

Fixation presents problems also. At a rough .approximation, the time needed for fixation increases as the square of the emulsion thickness. Material which should have needed 4-h fixation was recently prepared twice as thick as intended. This error meant fixation lasting 16 h, which was rather tedious. Unfortunately, acid fixers, which act more rapidly than plain thiosulphate, should not be used with thick emulsion layers. Their presence in the emulsion for long periods etches and finally dissolves away many of the developed silver grains. Plain sodium thiosulphate is probably the best fixative. Its concentration is not critical, as it has a broad peak of efficiency between 25 and 35%. A large volume of fixative which is mechanically stirred, and replaced with fresh if necessary, will give the best results.

Washing after fixation must also be long and thorough.

It is a good idea to carry out all the stages of processing with the slides horizontal, and to keep the temperatures of all solutions below about 22°. If these precautions are not observed, lateral distortions of the emulsion may take place, particularly in the fixation and subsequent washing.

THE MICROSCOPY OF THICK EMULSION LAYERS

The value of reswelling the processed emulsion has already been mentioned.

It is necessary to use transmitted light and relatively high magnifications to view these thick emulsions. Unfortunately, the objectives designed for conventional microscopy seldom have a sufficiently long working distance to permit the scanning of the lower layers of reswollen emulsions. Most manufacturers of microscopes make special nuclear-track objectives for this purpose, such as the Leitz KS X53 and X100, both immersion lenses.

Many artefacts will be found at the surface of the emulsion, which often has small cracks and fissures produced during drying as well. These should not interfere with the examination of the rest of the emulsion, particularly if reswelling has been carried out.

The photography of β tracks is extremely difficult. A high magnfication is usually needed to see the grains clearly, but the three-dimensional nature of the tracks makes it difficult to get more than a few adjacent grains in focus at any one time. It may be necessary to scan many slides before a convincing track pattern is found, lying in one focal plane. It may be a good idea to expose a slide deliberately for longer than the optimum period for track counting, and to dehydrate and mount it histologically in the usual way, without reswelling the emulsion, to increase the probability of seeing several tracks at the one focal plane. Figs. 52 and 53 (p.162–163) illustrate the sort of picture that can be obtained with sulphur-35 and with phosphorus-32.

The problems of recognition of β tracks have already been discussed (p.172).

DETAILED DESCRIPTION OF TECHNIQUES

The preparation and processing of track autoradiographs for carbon-14 and sulphur-35

(a) *Preparing the autoradiographs*

Emulsion: Ilford G5 in gel form

Safelight: Ilford 'F 904' or Eastman-Kodak 'OC'

Darkroom conditions: Temperature 16–22°; relative humidity, 45–50%.

Material: Sections or smears on gelatinised slides.

Equipment needed: a thermostatically controlled waterbath; 1 50-ml graduated measuring cylinder, cut short at the 40-ml mark (the dipping jar); 1 50-ml graduated cylinder; 1 25-ml graduated cylinder; 1 glass rod; 1 pair of plastic print forceps; a levelled metal plate with provision for cooling by placing ice on it (Fig. 83).

1. Make a mark on the 25-ml cylinder at 15 ml with a black marking pencil.

2. Measure into the dipping jar 4.8 ml distilled water and 0.2 ml glycerol.

3. Stand these two measuring cylinders in the waterbath at 43°.

4. Under safelighting, transfer G5 emulsion from the stock bottle to the 50-ml cylinder, using the print forceps, until, after gentle shaking down, the emulsion fills it to between 25 and 30 ml.

5. With the 50-ml cylinder now in the waterbath, allow the emulsion to melt for 10 min, stirring gently with the glass rod. This stirring must be slow and gentle: one revolution per second is quite fast enough.

6. Holding the 25-ml cylinder so that the black mark at 15 ml can be clearly seen, pour molten emulsion into it from the 50-ml cylinder, up to the black mark.

7. Pour this 15 ml of molten emulsion into the dipping jar which already contains the diluting water and glycerol.

8. Return the dipping jar to the waterbath for 2 min, stirring gently to ensure complete mixing.

9. Place the dipping jar in a beaker of distilled water at room temperature. Dip into the emulsion a clean slide, and place it close to the safelight to check that mixing has been complete, and there are no bubbles. If the emulsion contains many bubbles, leave it to stand for 1 min, and dip in another clean slide.

10. When the emulsion appears satisfactorily mixed and free from bubbles, dip in the slides with biological material on them. On withdrawing each one from the dipping jar, hold it horizontal, with the section facing upwards, wipe the emulsion off the lower surface with a paper tissue, and place the slide flat on the cooled metal plate to dry. When all the slides are on the plate, and their emulsion has gelled, remove the ice, allowing the plate to come slowly up to room temperature.

11. Ideal drying conditions are provided by an ambient temperature of 18–20°, a relative humidity of 40–45%, and a gentle current of air. The emulsion should be hard, and present a shiny surface, after about 45 min. During drying, the safelight should be off.

12. Continue drying for a further period of at least 4 h in a desiccator over dried silica gel, at room temperature.

13. Expose in lightproof boxes at 4°.

(b) Processing the autoradiographs

1. Make up the Amidol developer, following the procedure given on p.327. Dilute it 1 part with 2 parts distilled water, and place it in a developing dish in a thermostatically controlled waterbath at 17°.

2. Under safelighting, place the slides, preferably lying horizontally, in the developer for 12–15 min. They should be shielded from safelight while in the developer.

3. Transfer the slides to a 1% solution of acetic acid for 2 min.

4. Transfer the slides to a 30% solution of sodium thiosulphate for 20 min, with mechanical stirring. They should clear completely at this stage.

5. Transfer the slides to a 10% solution of sodium thiosulphate for 20 min, with mechanical stirring.

6. Wash the slides in gently running tap water for 40–60 min.

Staining of the biological material may then be carried out.

After staining, soak the slides in a 20% solution of glycerol in a petri dish for 20 min. After removing excess fluid from the surface of the emulsion, mount in glycerine jelly or in Farrant's medium.

To prepare autoradiographs of suspended sources labelled with carbon-14 or sulphur-35, prepare an emulsion layer on a gelatinised slide, as outlined above, and, after drying, pipette a few drops of a suspension of the sources in dilute, molten emulsion on to the slide. When this layer has dried, pipette a further 0.5 ml of dilute, molten emulsion on top, following a modified version of the procedure outlined below. Processing should then follow the routine outlined below for emulsion layers 60 μ thick.

If Eastman Kodak NTB-3 emulsion is to be used instead of Ilford G5, this technique will have to be modified. Dipping in molten but undiluted NTB-3 does not appear to produce a thick enough layer of emulsion during exposure. The method of choice is a modification of the one that follows, for 60 μ thick layers of G5. The slides should lie flat on the level plate, and have molten but un-diluted emulsion pipetted on them. If 4 slides 3″ × 1″ are uniformly coated over most of their surface with a total of 2.5 to 3.0 ml emulsion, this should give an emulsion layer during exposure comparable to the method above for G5, suit-able for tracks from carbon-14 or sulphur-35. Drying, exposure and development should follow the routine given above.

The preparation and processing of track autoradiographs for phosphorus-32

(a) Preparing the autoradiographs
Emulsion: Ilford G5 in gel form.
Safelight: Ilford 'F 904' or Eastman-Kodak 'OC'.
Material: Sections or smears on gelatinised slides.
Darkroom conditions: Temperature, 16–22°; relative humidity, 45–50%.
Equipment needed: A thermostatically controlled waterbath; 1 50-ml graduated cylinder, cut short at the 40-ml mark (the dipping jar); 1 50-ml grad-uated cylinder; 1 25-ml graduated cylinder; 1 glass rod; 1 pair of plastic print forceps; 2 250-ml beakers; several Pasteur pipettes; 1 fine paintbrush; about 18 inches of rubber tubing, with a short length of glass tubing at one end; 1 large desiccator.

In addition some device will be needed to provide a current of dry carbon dioxide, and a level surface the temperature of which can be varied between about 5° and 30°. A suitable device is illustrated in Fig.83 (p.302). It consists of a metal plate, fitted with levelling screws, and measuring 24″ × 7″. At each end, a small container of rigid plastic is attached. The remaining, central portion of the plate has a removable cover, also of rigid plastic, with a small tubular open-ing at one end, and a small vent, situated near the roof of the cover at the other end. This cover can be connected by tubing to a drying flask filled with dry silica gel, and thence to a closed flask of solid carbon dioxide. The cover should fit well on the plate, so that when solid carbon dioxide is allowed to sublime in the first flask, it will flow through the drying flask into the cover, filling it, and providing an appreciable current of carbon dioxide at the outlet vent.

1. Level the drying plate with a spirit level, and place the slides on it, with the sections or smears facing upwards. Warm the plate and slides by placing copper troughs filled with hot water in the plastic containers at each end of the plate. 25–30° is sufficient.

2. With a black marking pencil, make a mark at 1 ml on each of the Pasteur pipettes, and attach one of them to the length of tubing. Fill the beakers with distilled water, place the pipettes in the first beaker, and put both beakers into the waterbath at 43°.

3. The emulsion should be diluted 3 parts to 1 part of water for use, with glycerol making up 1% of the final mixture. The total needed will depend on the number of slides to be covered; allow 1 ml diluted emulsion per slide, with 5 ml in addition. The figures given would be suitable for 15 slides.

4. Follow steps 1–8 of the technique for track autoradiographs for carbon-14 and sulphur-35 described above, with the volumes given in step 3 (above).

5. Leaving the dipping jar with molten diluted emulsion in it, in the waterbath, take the Pasteur pipette with the tube and mouthpiece attached, and fill it to the 1-ml mark with emulsion by gently sucking at the mouthpiece.

6. Allow the pipette to empty on the first slide. It is important to have warmed the pipette with distilled water at 43° before filling it, and not to delay too long before covering the slide, or the emulsion may gel in the pipette. Once the pipette is running freely, pressure should not be applied to empty it, except with great caution: otherwise bubbles will be blown over the slide. With a little practice, it is possible to pipette emulsion very accurately in this way, without making bubbles.

7. With the paint brush, spread the emulsion to cover the whole slide. If any bubbles have been produced, they can often be guided away from the smear or section. If only half the slide is covered with emulsion, it will be far too thick, making the fixation times unreasonably long.

8. Rinse the pipette several times in the second beaker of distilled water in the waterbath. This cleans it and warms it before it is filled with emulsion again to cover the next slide.

9. When all the slides have been covered, remove the copper troughs of hot water from the plastic containers, and replace them filled with ice. Allow the slides to stand on the cooled plate for 20 min, for the emulsion to gel.

10. Replace the troughs of ice with warm water once more, so that the temperature of the plate rises again to room temperature. Allow the slides to dry in a gentle current of air. Ideal conditions are provided by an ambient temperature of 18–20° and a relative humidity of 40–45%. The emulsion should be hard, and present a shiny surface, after 1.5–2 h. During drying, the safelight should be off.

11. When the emulsion appears to be dry, place the cover on the plate, and allow a gentle current of dry carbon dioxide to flow over the slides for a further 1 h.

12. Place the slides in lightproof boxes for exposure, and put the boxes open, with their lids beside them, in a desiccator with dry silica gel and a few pieces of solid carbon dioxide. After 2–3 h put the lids on the boxes without removing them from the desiccator, thus filling them with dry carbon dioxide.

13. Expose at 4°.

(b) Processing the autoradiographs

1. Make up the Amidol developer, following the procedure given on p.327.

2. Place a shallow dish full of concentrated, fresh developer in the refrigerator in the darkroom, so that it reaches a temperature of 6° or less.

3. Dilute the rest of the developer 1 part to 2 parts of distilled water, and place it in a developing dish in the waterbath at 20°.

4. Under safelighting, place the slides, lying horizontally, in the dish of concentrated developer in the refrigerator for 15 min.

5. Transfer the slides to the dish of developer at 20° for 20 min. The slides should be shielded from safelighting while in developer.

6. Transfer the slides to a 1% solution of acetic acid for 15 min. While here, wipe the surface of each slide gently several times with a paper tissue soaked in the acetic acid.

7. Transfer the slides to a 30% solution of sodium thiosulphate for 1 h, with mechanical stirring.

8. Transfer the slides to a second change of 30% sodium thiosulphate for 1.5 h, with mechanical stirring. They should clear completely during this time.

9. Transfer the slides to a 10% solution of sodium thiosulphate for 1.5 h, with mechanical stirring.

10. Wash the slides in gently running tapwater for 2 h.

Staining, reswelling in 20% glycerol solution, and mounting follow the procedure outlined on p.322 above.

Relatively large volumes of solution are necessary in steps 5–9 above: 1 1 per 6 slides would be reasonable. The slides should be kept lying horizontally throughout development, fixation, and washing.

Mechanical stirring during fixation should be gentle, and care must be taken not to raise the temperature of the solution above 25°.

To prepare autoradiographs of suspended sources labelled with phosphorus-32, pipette 1 ml of emulsion on to a gelatinised slide, as outlined above. When this has dried, pipette on a few drops of a suspension of the labelled sources in molten, diluted emulsion. Subsequently, cover this by pipetting on a further 1 ml of emulsion. The drying plate will have to be kept cool during the pipetting of the second and third layers.

Processing should follow the procedure outlined above, except that step 6 should last for 20 min, and considerably longer times will be needed in fixer. Either larger volumes of fixer in steps 7 or 8, or two changes at each step, should be allowed. Steps 7 and 8 together should take 6–6.5 h. Step 9 should take 2–3 h, and step 10, 4 h.

Even with such thick layers, there is no need to extend the period in developer. With G5 and the Amidol developer recommended here, there is a long plateau of development, so that times in stage 5 above can be varied from 15–40 min without a significant change in the grain densities in the β

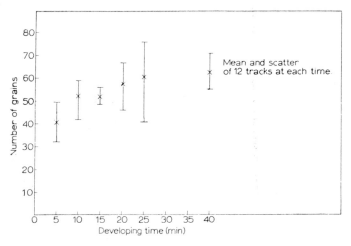

Fig.85. A graph to illustrate the increase in number of silver grains in the terminal 75 μ of β-particle tracks with increasing developing time. The tracks were recorded in Ilford G5 emulsion, which was developed with Amidol. The number of grains in the tracks increased rapidly at first, levelling off to a plateau after about 25 min. The grains in the tracks continued to grow in size after this, and the number of background grains outside the tracks was noticeably higher at 40 min than at 25 min. (From Levi *et al.*, 1963)

tracks (Fig. 85). The size of the developed grains in the tracks, and the density of random background grains, will increase with longer times; the development time should be selected on the basis of the ease of recognition of the tracks under the conditions of the experiment.

If Eastman Kodak NTB-3 emulsion is to be used, follow the same technique, but pipette 1–2 ml of molten, diluted emulsion on each slide. Drying, exposure and processing should follow the same routine outlined above, except that the 1% acetic acid stopbath should be replaced by a hardening stopbath p.295), otherwise the emulsion layer will be lost in the stopbath and subsequent fix.

Sometimes the processed emulsion contains very many fine, dust-like particles which interfere with microscopy. This can be avoided by buffering the 30% sodium thiosulphate used for fixation. The sodium sulphite: sodium hydrogen sulphite buffer used in making up the Amidol developer (see below) is satisfactory for this purpose.

Amidol developer

Dissolve 2.2 g sodium sulphite ($7 H_2 0$) in 100 ml water. To a further 210 ml water, add 0.46 ml of a solution of sodium hydrogen sulphite (spec. gravity 1.34). Mix the two solutions. Add 1 g Amidol, filter, and use immediately. Amidol is photosensitive and should be stored in darkness.

REFERENCES

1   H. Levi, *Biochim. Biophys. Acta.* 7 (1951) 198.
2   B.L. Miller and F.E. Hoecker, *Nucleonics,* 8 (1951) No. 5, 44.
3   T.F. Dougherty (Ed.), *Some Aspects of Internal Irradiation,* Pergamon, London, 1962.
4   G.A. Boyd and H. Levi, *Science* 111 (1950) 58.
5   H. Levi, *Exptl. Cell Res.. Suppl.* 4 (1957) 207.
6   H. Levi and A. Nielsen, *Lab. Invest.,* 8 (1959) 82.
7   H. Levi, *Exptl. Cell Res.,* 7 (1954) 44.
8   H. Levi, A.W. Rogers, M.W. Bentzon and A. Nielsen, *Kgl. Danske Videnskab. Selskab, Mat.–Fys. Medd.,* 33 (1963) No. 11.
9   A. Ficq, *Exptl. Cell Res.,* 9 (1955) 286.
10 A. Ficq, *Lab. Invest.,* 8 (1959) 237.
11 J. Brachet and A. Ficq, *Exptl. Cell Res.,* 38 (1965) 153.
12 A. Ficq, in J. Brachet and A.E. Mirksy (Eds.), *The Cell,* Vol. 1, Academic Press, New York, 1959.
13 C. Levinthal, *Proc. Natl. Acad. Sci. (U.S.),* 42 (1956) 394.
14 C. Levinthal and C.A. Thomas, *Biochim. Biophys Acta,* 23 (1957) 453.

15   A.W. Rogers, Z. Darżynkiewicz, K. Ostrowski, E.A. Barnard and M.M. Salpeter, *J. Cell Biol.*, 41 (1969) 665.
16   Z. Darżynkiewicz, A.W. Rogers and E.A. Barnard, *J. Histochem. Cytochem.*, 14 (1967) 915.
17   A.W. Rogers and E.A. Barnard, *J. Cell Biol.*, 41 (1969) 686
18   H. Levi and A.S. Hogben, *Kgl. Danske Videnskab. Selskab, Mat.–Fys. Medd.*, 30 (1955) No. 1.
19   D. Darlington and A.W. Rogers, *J. Anat.*, 100 (1966) 813.
20   C.C. Dilworth, C.P.S. Occhialini and R.M. Payne, *Nature*, 162 (1948) 102.
21   J. Hauser, *Photographie Corpusculaire*, 2 (1959) 207.

CHAPTER 18

Autoradiography with the Electron Microscope

The development of the electron microscope has greatly extended the scope of cytology, enabling biologists to visualise structures down to the molecular level in favourable conditions. It is inevitable that attempts to link the technique of autoradiography to electron microscopy should have been made — attempts to exploit the spatial precision and high efficiency characteristic of nuclear emulsions so that the pattern of the tracer experiment could be applied to the whole range of subcellular structures. Unfortunately, there are physical limitations to the resolution that can be obtained with autoradiographic techniques. These limitations are imposed partly by the ranges of the β particles themselves, which, even with isotopes of low maximum energy such as tritium, are very great relative to the smallest distances that can be resolved by the electron microscope.

The other limiting factor on the resolution of electron microscope autoradiography is the nature of the photographic process. The latent image that forms in a silver halide crystal hit by a β particle does not correspond necessarily with the path of the particle through the crystal, but lies at a preformed sensitivity speck. In a crystal of very small diameter, the latent image must lie very close to the actual trajectory of the β particle. The search for high resolution therefore demands a nuclear emulsion with a small crystal size. But this process of latent image formation requires the transfer of a certain amount of energy from the particle to the electrons within the crystal. If the crystal is reduced in size below a critical diameter, it becomes highly improbable that a β particle will lose sufficient energy in its short path through the crystal to create a latent image.

There is a great disparity between the resolving power of the electron microscope, which may be of the order of 10 Å, and that of electron microscope autoradiography, which, with the best techniques at present available, is around 700 Å. Nor is it likely that future improvements in technique will ever bring this figure below about 100 Å. Problems requiring a higher resolution than this will almost certainly need a different approach altogether, and will remain outside the scope of nuclear emulsions. Malmon[1], for instance, has suggested the use of very thin metal films to detect heavy, charged particles produced by neutron irradiation of biological specimens.

Within these limitations, autoradiography with the electron microscope is still a very valuable technique. A resolution of 500 Å is already 10–20 times better than that normally obtained with the light microscope, and this, it must be remembered, is not the same as the size of the smallest structure which can be identified as labelled.

Liquier-Milward[2], working at Birmingham University, was probably the first to couple autoradiography with electron microscopy. She used β-track techniques, and the lower magnifications of the electron microscope to observe the specimen. Her results look very strange beside the best preparations available today, and it comes as a surprise to learn that her first publication on this work was as recent as 1956.

Since that time, improvements both in the nuclear emulsions themselves and in the techniques of using them have been rapid. In 1961, Pelc, Coombes and Budd reported a technique which involved mounting ultra-microtome sections on a formvar film, which was stretched over a hole in a plastic slide. A thin layer of liquid emulsion was then pipetted over the sections. Ilford L4 emulsion, with a mean crystal diameter of about 1 400 Å, was found to be the best then available[3].

In 1962, Caro and Van Tubergen, also working with L4, evolved a method in which a thin film or bubble of emulsion was picked up on a wire loop. This was allowed to gel, and then placed over the sections, which were already mounted on their grids[4]. At the same time Caro published an excellent analysis of the factors influencing resolution in electron microscope autoradiography[5].

Koehler, Mühlethaler and Frey Wyssling[6] suggested the use of a centrifuge in order to obtain suitable monolayers of emulsion, an idea extended by Dohlman et al.[7]

Meanwhile, new emulsions with smaller crystal sizes were being developed, and, in 1963, Granboulan[8] described autoradiography with the Gevaert NUC 307, which had a mean crystal diameter of 700 Å. The latest reduction in crystal size was reported by Salpeter and Bachmann[9]: Eastman Kodak NTE emulsion, with crystal diameters in the range of 300–500 Å.

This is by no means a complete list of the many contributions made to the developing technique. They serve to show that several emulsions and many techniques of applying them are now available. Recent reviews of electron microscope autoradiography have been published by Williams[10] and by Salpeter[11].

THE USES AND LIMITATIONS OF ELECTRON MICROSCOPE
AUTORADIOGRAPHY

Before discussing the preparation of autoradiographs for viewing in the electron microscope in detail, it is worth reviewing briefly the value of the technique, and its very real limitations. The latter are seldom appreciated by those who have not tried the method for themselves.

To start with the disadvantages, it is at present not possible to prepare frozen sections for electron microscopy. The range of experiments available is therefore limited to the study of material that can be fixed and preserved in position by the conventional embedding techniques using araldite or Epon. Several laboratories are working on cryostats for ultrathin sections[12-14], but the method is not a successful, routine procedure yet.

The factors that limit the resolution in electron microscope autoradiography were fully discussed in Chapter 4, where it was concluded that a resolution of 500–700 Å is the very best that can be got in present circumstances. This resolution requires the thinnest possible sections, and a monolayer of crystals of the smallest possible diameter. It is difficult at times to get sufficient radioactivity into an experimental animal for a 500 Å section to have a significant disintegration rate, while the efficiency of the emulsion layer is not very high if the emulsion with the smallest available crystals is used. The latter emulsion, Eastman Kodak NTE, tends to produce very high backgrounds if exposure is prolonged beyond about 6 months. In many cases, it may not be possible to prepare satisfactory autoradiographs at the highest resolution, as the final grain densities may be too low for analysis, and the experimenter is forced to compromise, accepting thicker sections and a larger crystal diameter in order to carry through the experiment at all.

The efficiency of autoradiographs was discussed fully in Chapter 5, and the problems of analysis in Chapter 11. Faced with a biological specimen in which structures down to 50 Å can be visualised, a resolution which places 50% of the developed grains further from their origin than 500 Å at the very best, and often further than 1 800 Å, and relatively few developed grains at that, the analysis of the final autoradiograph becomes a statistical exercise which may involve months of work. The cost–effectiveness of any proposed experiment should be weighed very carefully, and any part of it that can be carried out by other techniques that are less time-consuming should be eliminated. This aspect of the technique is discussed elsewhere in a recent article[15]. As a rough guide, it is unlikely that an experiment with this technique will be carried through to completion in less than two years from the planning stage.

Having looked at the disadvantages, one might wonder what could persuade anyone to use the technique at all. The answer is that it is capable of giving information which is often not obtainable by any other technique. The methods of cell fractionation may indicate the presence of radioactivity in one or other cell compartment, but information on the distribution of the labelled elements of that group within a cell or between adjacent cells cannot be inferred from any method that begins by homogenising tissue. Autoradiography at the light micro- scope level may well identify cells that are radioactive, but the distribution of radioactivity between organelles within cells is, in general, out of the question As a climax to a series of experiments by light microscope autoradiography anc biochemical techniques, which have defined a problem with considerable pre cision, electron microscope autoradiography can provide answers not availabl by any other technique; but as a method of having a quick look to see what is happening in a poorly defined experimental situation, it is a dismal failure.

THE SELECTION OF AN APPROPRIATE TECHNIQUE

In effect, the techniques available fall into two groups. The first of these is based on the use of Ilford L4 emulsion. This has excellent working character- istics, and gives reproducible results from one batch of emulsion to the next. Bachmann and Salpeter[16] have drawn attention to its relative freedom from latent image fading and chemography. With a mean crystal diameter of 1200–1400 Å, a monolayer that is reasonably well packed will give one silver grain for every 12 electrons of 10 keV incident on it. It is possible to observe the same emulsion over 1-μ sections in the light microscope, in order to check the level and distribution of labelling obtained. The techniques for using L4 for electron microscopy are reasonably simple, and the emulsion is stable over very long exposure periods. In short it is possible to devise a technique for L4 that is both simple and reliable. Unfortunately, the large crystal size means that the resolution is likely to be within the range of 1200–1800 Å. The sort of auto- radiograph that can be obtained by this technique is illustrated in Fig. 86.

The second group of techniques uses the Gevaert NUC 307 and Eastman Kodak NTE emulsions. With optimal conditions and the latter emulsion[16], a resolution of 700–900 Å is obtainable. Both of these very fine-grained emul- sions have a reputation for being fickle. The sensitivity varies from one batch to the next, and is likely to be lower than that of L4, unless special steps, such as gold latensification, are taken during development. These emulsions are more prone to latent image fading and to chemography. With NTE, the length of exposure is limited by the fact that spontaneous background builds up rapidly

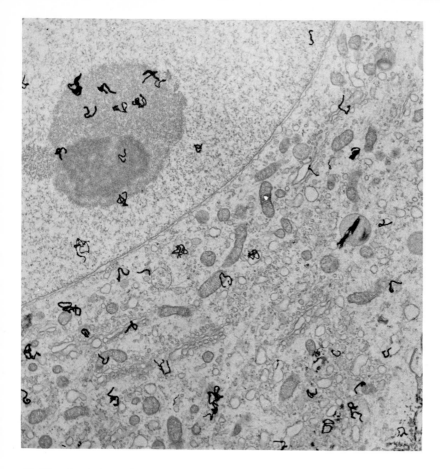

Fig.86. An electron microscope autoradiograph of a neurone from a sensory ganglion of a newt, after incorporation of tritiated histidine. The autoradiograph was prepared on a collodion-coated slide, which was coated with a monolayer of Ilford L4 emulsion by dipping. Development was in Microdol-X. The collodion membrane was stripped off the slide after development, and attached to a grid for viewing. (× 10 800) (Material prepared by Dr. M.M. Salpeter)

after about 12 weeks. Fig. 87 illustrates the sort of picture that can be obtained with NTE emulsion.

Certainly, anyone starting on electron microscope autoradiography for the first time would be well advised to use Ilford L4 emulsion. It is probably a good Idea to make this the standard technique applied first to each experimental situation. It will give most of the information that can be got from the NTE

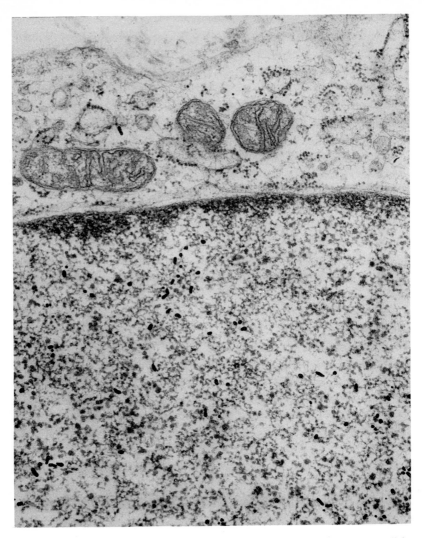

Fig.87. An electron microscope autoradiograph of part of a mesenchymatous cell from a newt, injected with [^{3}H] thymidine: it was prepared with a monolayer of NTE emulsion and developed for the highest resolution with gold latensification and Elon-ascorbic acid. (× 36 000) (From Bachmann and Salpeter, 1965)

emulsion at a much lower price in work and effort. The techniques using NTE should be reserved for those experiments in which there is a decided advantage to be gained from the increase in resolution, and in which autoradiographs with L4 have demonstrated that there is a reasonable chance of getting an adequate grain yield within the possible exposure times. Certainly if one surveys the experiments that have been published so far, the great majority use Ilford L4.

A similar survey of the method most widely used to apply the emulsion to the specimen shows that the loop method of Caro and Van Tubergen[4] has the most adherents. Most of the methods proposed in the literature are capable of giving reasonable results. The main variables are the method of preparing an emulsion monolayer, and whether or not exposure takes place with the section already mounted on a grid. These variables are linked to some extent, and it is difficult to produce predictably even monolayers on a membrane-covered grid[16] : clumping of crystals may occur along the grid bars. The alternative is to mount the sections on a flat substrate, such as a microscope slide, which has been covered with a layer of collodion, and to form the emulsion layer on this surface. After exposure and processing, the membrane, with section and emulsion attached, can be stripped off the slide on to the surface of water, and picked up on a grid for viewing in the electron microscope. This method, advocated by Salpeter and Bachmann[9], simplifies the problem of getting a uniform emulsion layer, but it has not proved very popular since a number of laboratories have had difficulty in stripping the final preparation off the slide. It is very frustrating to lose the material at this late stage, after exposures that may have lasted many months.

In the descriptions of technique that follow, the loop method and the flat substrate method will both be given for Ilford L4 emulsion: for the highest possible resolution with Eastman Kodak NTE emulsion, only the flat substrate method will be included, as it is very difficult to form a film of NTE on a loop.

PREPARING A SUITABLE SPECIMEN FOR AUTORADIOGRAPHY

Reference has been made already (p.331) to the relatively low grain densities that are usually produced by exposures that last several months. Injections of radioactive material into animals that will supply tissues for autoradiography by these techniques will often be massive. Tritium will be the isotope of choice in most cases: in making calculations of feasibility and dose, one will presumably be guided by results of scintillation counting and light microscope autoradiography. As a rough guide, one requires a minimum of 1.3 disintegrations per cubic micron of section per 10 days of exposure to get any sensible results with sections 1000 Å thick and a monolayer of Ilford L4. For sections of 500 Å and NTE emulsion, the limits of usefulness are given by 6–7 disintegrations per cubic micron per 10 days.

The extraction of labelled material from the tissue by fixation and embedding was discussed at length in Chapter 7. As a first approximation, fixation with glutaraldehyde and post-fixation with osmium tetroxide will preserve proteins and nucleic acids reasonably well, while most of the smaller molecules will be lost from the specimen. The preservation of fats is more difficult: this field has been recently reviewed by Williams[17] . Fixation in osmium tetroxide gives the best results, with retention of nearly all the phospholipids, and variable amounts of other lipids.

The embedded block is sectioned in the usual way. The thickness and reproducibility of the sections is of considerable importance if any sensible analysis of the grain distributions is needed. It is usual to assess the thickness by observing the interference colour of the section as it floats on the water surface behind the knife edge[18, 19] . Williams and Meek[20] have drawn attention to the variations in section thickness that can be obtained by this method which obviously relies on the subjective judgement of the observer. If the conditions of observation and illumination vary, the same observer may award a section a different colour. Some error can also occur as the section is transferred to and flattened on the grid or microscope slide, particularly if chloroform vapour is used to spread the section, with sections of identical initial thickness ending up covering rather different areas. For really accurate work, the section thickness should be measured by interference microscopy when it is on its support. The simplest way of doing this is by incident light: the upper surface of the section reflects sufficient light for the difference in path length between this surface and the support to be accurately measured. Interference measurements by transmitted light are also possible. An experiment by electron microscope autoradiography represents a sizeable commitment in terms of time and money, and it is very little extra effort to cut a large number of sections and reject those which do not fall into a narrow range of thickness when measured interferometrically.

Williams[17] has drawn attention to variations in thickness within individual sections, which can be visualised by shadowing techniques. Red blood cells, bacterial cells and bundles of collagen fibres are often raised above the general section level. Not only can the section thickness vary, but also its density, particularly after fixation in osmium and staining with heavy metals. The effects of these systematic variations in thickness and density through a specimen on the efficiency of the autoradiograph have not yet been calculated.

The choice of section thickness will vary from experiment to experiment, and will largely be dictated by the radioactivity of the tissue, as discussed earlier (p.335). It is clear from Fig. 22 that section thickness has a greater influence on resolution than the crystal diameter of the emulsion. Improvements in resolution should be looked for first by reducing section thickness, and only then by switching from Ilford L4 to Gevaert NUC 307 or Eastman Kodak NTE. There is absolutely no point in using the latter emulsions with sections as thick as 1000 Å.

(a) Preparing a specimen with adequate contrast

Ideally, the section should be as thin as possible, and it will be viewed together with a support film and a layer of processed emulsion. These are not the best conditions for getting a micrograph of reasonable contrast, and a number of recommendations have been made at one time or another for ensuring adequate viewing conditions. Salpeter and Bachmann[9] stain their sections in uranyl acetate followed by lead citrate before putting on the emulsion layer. As we saw in Chapter 7, prestaining carries certain risks, of removing radioactivity from the section and of introducing chemical groups which will interfere with the emulsion during exposure. Prestaining in this way must be followed by the evaporation of a thin layer (50–60 Å) of carbon over the specimen before applying the emulsion, to protect against chemography: even without prestaining, the carbon layer is a good idea, as osmium compounds in the tissue may also affect the emulsion.

Other authors prefer post-staining. Caro and Van Tubergen[4] recommend uranyl acetate after photographic processing, while several authors have suggested a combinaton of lead staining with removal of the gelatin of the emulsion – the paper of Revel and Hay[21] is an example. Post-staining carries with it the possibility of stain deposition in the gelatin, and the removal of gelatin has obvious dangers in the removal or displacement of silver grains. Cleanliness is at a premium, whether stains are applied before or after exposure, and stain precipitates in the specimen should be avoided like the plague. If, as sometimes happens, a particulate precipitate is produced, it is perhaps less frustrating before emulsion coating than at the end of months of exposure. All in all, the prestaining technique of Salpeter and Bachmann[9] seems the best (Figs. 86 and 87).

(b) Supporting the section during application of the emulsion

Caro and Van Tubergen[4] placed their sections on collodion-coated grids, with the collodion film backed by a thin layer of evaporated carbon. The grids were then attached to a microscope slide for ease of handling, using double-sided tape. This method is satisfactory if emulsion layers preformed in platinum loops are to be placed over the section, but not so good if a dipping technique is intended, as the emulsion is likely to collect round and even to some extent under the grids, and the control of emulsion thickness becomes difficult. Exposure on the grid leaves a very simple sequence of operations to prepare the autoradiograph for viewing after photographic processing.

References p. 353

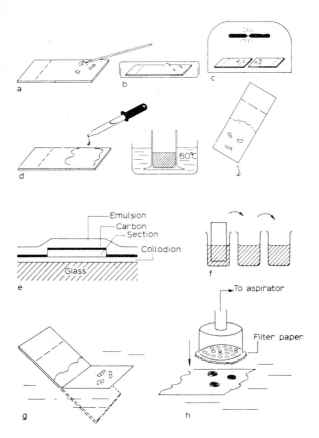

Fig.88. The sequence of procedures for preparation of electron microscope autoradio-graphs. *(a)* The ribbons of sections are mounted on a collodion-coated slide. *(b)* The slides are dried in a dust-free atmosphere. (*c*) A layer of carbon, 50–60 Å, is applied over the sections. (*d*) The diluted NTE emulsion is pipetted on to the slide, and drained off again, leaving a very thin layer over the slide. (*e*) A diagram to show the various layers on the slide during exposure. (*f*) After exposure, the emulsion is developed and fixed. (*g*) The collodion membrane, carrying sections, carbon layer, and developed emulsion, is stripped from the slide on to the surface of distilled water. (*h*) Grids are placed over the sections, and the membrane with sections and grids on it is picked up from the water surface and dried, ready for examination in the electron microscope. (From Salpeter and Bachmann, 1965)

The alternative flat substrate method[9] (Fig. 88) involves mounting the section on a slide that has been coated with collodion, and stripping collodion, section and emulsion off the slide in order to mount them on a grid after photographic processing. This is the method of choice if a dipping technique is to be used, and it seems likely that the use of a flat support simplifies the preparation of uniform emulsion layers. The difficulty with this method is stripping the sandwich off the slide after processing. Some laboratories have little trouble at this stage, others find it almost impossible. Several steps in the procedure seem to improve the chances of success.

First, the glass slide should be reasonably clean: it should be washed in detergent and rinsed thoroughly, then dipped in alcohol and dried. Soaking the slides in chromic acid may etch the surface and make stripping very difficult. Next the slide is coated by dipping it once in a 0.5% solution of collodion in amyl acetate. The thinner the final collodion layer, the better the contrast of the final preparation in the electron microscope: on the other hand, thicker layers may prove easier to strip and to handle. The section is floated out on the collodion-coated slide on a drop of distilled water, taking great care not to touch the collodion membrane while transferring the section. After removing excess water and drying the slide in a dust-free atmosphere, the section can be stained for 2–5 min in 2% aqueous uranyl acetate, followed by 8–20 min in Reynold's lead citrate[22] , if desired. Staining can be carried out with the slide lying flat in a petri dish: the solutions are pipetted on and the dish covered. After flushing the stain off with distilled water, the slides are dried in a dust-free atmosphere again, and a layer of carbon 50–60 Å thick is applied by evaporation. The carbon film must be of reasonably predictable thickness from specimen to specimen: this can usually be controlled by placing a piece of white porcelain with a drop of vacuum oil on it in the evaporator, and judging by eye when the carbon film is just thick enough to make the oil drop visible against the porcelain background.

After applying and developing the emulsion layer, the slide is soaked for 15–30 min in distilled water. Then, with a razor blade, the collodion membrane is scraped from the edges of the slide, and the slide slowly immersed at an angle of about 20° in a dish of distilled water. The membrane should float off the slide on to the water surface. If it fails to part company anywhere from the slide, the slide should be put back into distilled water for a further period, which can extend almost indefinitely until the membrane is willing to separate. Some try to cut the membrane around the sections with a scalpel: this nearly always sticks the membrane to the slide along the line of the cut, and is best avoided. If the slide is allowed to dry out between processing the emulsion and stripping off the membrane, the latter step gets much more difficult.

The flat substrate method can give difficulty, but it is in routine use in several laboratories without loss of material through failure to strip. In may be that the source of collodion is critical: it may also be much more difficult to strip a freshly-prepared membrane from a test slide than one that has been exposed for 6 months. (See also NOTES ADDED IN PROOF, p. 360.)

Other methods for supporting the section through autoradiography have been suggested. A plastic slide with a hole in it, covered by a collodion membrane, has been used[3, 23]: it is simple to manipulate, but the membrane may belly or even tear when emulsion is applied. Williams[10] mounts the sections on collodion-covered grids which are then attached to the tapering end of small corks. Emulsion layers formed on loops[4] are then placed on the grids, and the corks put into the ends of short lengths of plastic tubing for exposure.

APPLYING THE EMULSION LAYER

We have already seen that Ilford L4 will be the emulsion of choice for most experiments (p.332). Its properties allow it to be applied either by a dipping technique, very similar to the ones used at the light microscope level (Chapter 16), or as a preformed layer. In order to get reasonably good resolution, a monolayer of silver halide crystals is required, but it should be a closely packed monolayer. A layer of crystals with gaps in it reduces the efficiency without any gain in resolution, and there is evidence that the crystals in such an incomplete layer can move on immersing the layer in water[16]. A satisfactory monolayer is illustrated in Fig. 89: for L4, it should contain 45–50 crystals per square micron, for NTE about 400 per square micron. Vrensen[24] has drawn attention to the increase in efficiency obtainable with a slightly thicker emulsion layer, at little cost in terms of resolution.

Whatever method is chosen to apply the emulsion, unexposed layers should be examined in the electron microscope from each experiment, to confirm that closely packed monolayers are in fact being produced.

(a) The loop method

This was described by Caro and Van Tubergen[4]. In brief, a dilution of L4 emulsion is prepared by melting 10 g emulsion in 20 ml distilled water at 45° for 15 min in a 300-ml beaker. When the emulsion is uniformly dissolved, the beaker is cooled for 2–3 min in ice-cold water. A platinum wire loop, with 4 cm diameter, is dipped in the emulsion and slowly withdrawn: the emulsion should gel at once into a homogeneous membrane which can then be touched on the support carrying the sections. Gross swirling patterns in the emulsion will result if it is not cool enough on forming the film on the loop: if it is too cold, a layer that is far too thick can be picked up. With experience and frequent checking of unexposed layers in the electron microscope, satisfactory monolayers can be prepared in this way. Caro[25] has suggested slight modifications to the basic method to improve the uniformity of the emulsion layers. An expandable loop

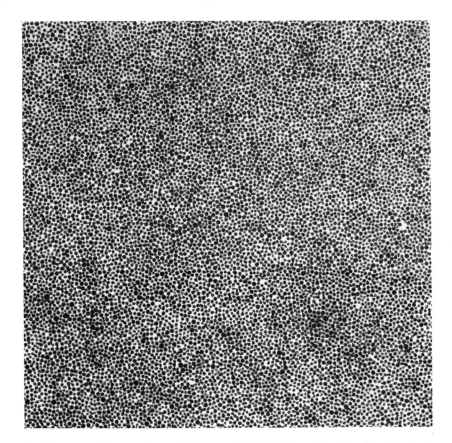

Fig.89. A packed monolayer of Eastman–Kodak NTE crystals viewed in the electron microscope. Such a layer gives a silver to pale gold interference colour on the slide, and is the ideal to aim at in high resolution studies. (✕ 15 000) (Material prepared by Dr. M.M. Salpeter)

made from a syringe has been proposed to simplify the picking up of emulsion[26] . A detailed description of the method is given on p.348.

(b) The dipping technique

This should really only be used if the section is supported on a flat surface, such as a slide. The detailed method for Ilford L4 is given on p.349. With a flat substrate such as a slide, Salpeter and Bachmann[9] have shown that the emulsion thickness can be checked by the interference colour of the dried layer: a packed monolayer of L4 gives a purple colour (Fig. 90). The final dilution of the molten emulsion can be adjusted until test slides show the correct colour in a fairly wide band across the slide. Interference bands can even be seen under safelighting with practice, though their colour may not be accurately judged without the use of test slides observed in the light. The final criterion of a suitable layer is, as always, its appearance in the electron microscope. It is possible to check the layers on experimental slides by taking them out of the darkroom after development stopbath and rinsing, but before fixation[16].

The physical characteristics of Eastman Kodak NTE make it very difficult to form satisfactory layers in loops, and this emulsion should be applied either by dipping, or by pipette. The gelatin content of this emulsion is too high to give packed monolayers of crystals, so initial removal of excess gelatin is necessary. The technique for NTE is given in full on p.351.

Other methods of applying emulsion in monolayers have been suggested including centrifugation[6, 7]. I can see no obvious advantage in this technique, though it would seem quite acceptable. Methods of preparing layers of silver bromide crystals on the surface of the specimen have been discussed briefly in Chapter 2: to date the evidence presented to show that these methods are satisfactory are not convincing, and they are best avoided.

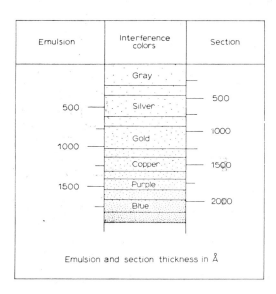

Fig.90. A table indicating the thickness in Ångstrom units that corresponds to various interference colours of section and emulsion. A monolayer of Eastman–Kodak NTE emulsion has a silver to pale gold colour: a monolayer of Ilford L4 is purple. (From Bachmann and Salpeter, 1965)

(c) Conditions of drying and exposure

As with any other emulsion, latent image fading is favoured by the presence of water and of oxidising agents. With a monolayer, every crystal is in contact with the gas in which exposure takes place. Though L4 can be exposed in dry air for up to 2 months without latent image fading[16] , longer exposures are best carried out in an inert gas such as nitrogen or argon. With Eastman Kodak NTE, drying and the exclusion of oxygen are needed to prevent fading, even with shorter exposures.

A recent paper has drawn attention to the efficiency of exposure *in vacuo* in preventing fading and chemical desensitisation[27] . It may be that this step could be profitably used in electron microscope autoradiography, where efficiency is at such a premium and it matters to accumulate every possible developed grain.

Since chemical interaction between stained section and emulsion is known to occur, and fading of latent images is favoured by a reduction in crystal diameter, it makes sense to expose control sections of non-radioactive material alongside experimental sections, in the same way as for light microscope autoradiographs. Any increase in grain density above background levels over the control section indicates positive chemography; any reduction of grain density over the section by comparison with the emulsion away from the section, in a specimen given a hefty dose of beta radiation before exposure, indicates negative chemography; any drop in overall grain density with increasing exposure time in material given beta radiation indicates generalised fading of latent images.

THE DEVELOPMENT OF ELECTRON MICROSCOPE
AUTORADIOGRAPHS

At the light microscope level, development presents few problems: almost any developer can be used, and the selection of suitable conditions is straightforward. With the electron microscope, this stage of autoradiography assumes far greater importance. A high efficiency is very desirable, with every available latent image developed. At the same time, a large developed grain is a nuisance, obscuring underlying detail and making the resolution worse.

Kopriwa[28] studied a number of developing agents with Ilford L4 and Gevaert NUC 307, and concluded that Metol—hydroquinone developers such as D-19b gave the highest efficiencies with reasonable backgrounds. Unfortunately, D-19b gives very large developed grains with L4. Microdol-X was for a long time a fairly standard developer, on the basis that it gave smaller grains (Fig. 86), but the efficiencies with it are lower than with D-19 or D-19b. Elon—ascorbic acid gives small developed grains, but results in a rather low efficiency. The physical

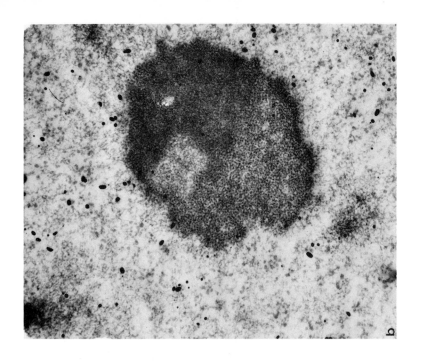

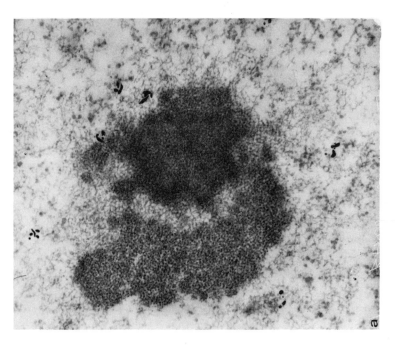

developer, *para*-phenylenediamine, was proposed by Caro and Van Tubergen[4], who showed that it could give very small developed grains that were comma-shaped, with the point of the comma indicating the site of the latent image: they claimed for it an efficiency comparable to that of Microdol-X. In other laboratories, however, results with *para*-phenylenediamine have not been very reproducible[28, 16], and it has not been widely used.

One procedure which improves the efficiencies of the developers that give small grains is the intensification of latent images by treating the emulsion with gold salts before development. This was first used in this context by Salpeter and Bachmann[9], and a recent improved method is described by Salpeter and Szabo[29]. Fig.23 presents a table of results from Dr. Salpeter's laboratory on the relative merits of different developers, and the improvement in efficiency that results from gold latensification with NTE emulsion can be readily seen: the sort of picture that results is illustrated in Fig. 87.

Developers that give very small silver deposits at the site of latent images can produce spuriously high efficiency values, since a crystal that has been hit by a β particle may contain several latent images, resulting in a cluster of 3 or 4 small grains within a small radius (Fig. 91). Such clusters should be treated as a single grain in the analysis of autoradiographs, and in calculating efficiencies[9, 29, 30].

Variations in efficiency from one laboratory to another, and even within the same laboratory, have often been surprisingly large. Vrensen[24] lists a number of literature reports which show, for instance, that a monolayer of L4 exposed to tritium and developed with Microdol-X has quoted efficiencies of 4–10%. In the same paper, he publishes data to suggest that self-absorption is likely to be a significant factor in the range of section thicknesses used at the electron microscope level. This last statement is out of line with the physical data based on the energy spectrum of tritium, and yet is derived from apparently careful work. It prompted a re-examination of efficiency measurements by Salpeter and Szabo[29], which has raised some very interesting points. First, there is no evidence for self-absorption with tritium in sections up to 1 000 Å in thickness. However, the efficiency of autoradiography was found to be related to the *density* of latent images in the emulsion layer. At low densities, the efficiency was high: as the mean distance between latent images fell at higher radiation

---

Fig.91. Autoradiographs of nucleoli from mesenchymatous cells of the newt after incorporation of [³H] thymidine. (*a*) Prepared with a monolayer of NTE emulsion developed in Dektol. (*b*) Prepared with a monolayer of L4 emulsion developed with *p*-phenylenediamine. The smaller grain size of (*b*) gives an impression of great precision: in fact the resolution of (*a*) is the better, because of the smaller crystal diameter of NTE. (× 28 000) (Photographs provided by Dr. M.M. Salpeter)

Authors	Emulsion and thickness	Developer	Efficiency (%)
Bachmann and Salpeter, 1967	L4 monolayer	Microdol X	10
	NTE monolayer	Dektol	4–5
		Gold–EA	12–13
	NTE double layer	Dektol	8–9
Kopriwa, 1967	L4 (overlapping	D 19 b	9
	(monolayer	Microdol-X	4
	NUC-307 (overlapping	D 19 b	10–11
	(monolayer	Microdol-X	0.8
	NTE (overlapping	D 19 b	3–4
	(monolayer	Microdol -X	0.2
Wisse and Tates, 1968	L4 monolayer	Microdol X	10
		Gold-EA	55
Vrensen, 1969	L4 (overlapping	D 19 b	34–38
	(monolayer	Gold-EA	29–35
	NUC-307 (overlapping	D 19 b	15–19
	(monolayer		
Salpeter and Szabo, 1972	L4 (overlapping	Microdol X	10–20
	(monolayer	D 19	20–30
		Gold-EA	22–28

Fig.92. A summary of efficiency values for tritium in electron microscope autoradiography taken from the literature. Note that conditions of exposure and development are not directly comparable, even when the same developer was used: this is particularly true of gold–EA, where the developer may be made up to different formulae. As emphasized by Salpeter and Szabo (1972) efficiency varies with the final grain density. All these values must be regarded as approximate only.

doses, so also did the efficiency. This effect was seen at densities at which the probability of double hits was demonstrably negligible, and in conditions which precluded latent image fading. It looked as if, at development, small latent images near a larger developing grain could be suppressed, in conditions which may have developed them if no other latent image were near. This effect might well explain Vrensen's results with increasing section thickness[24], where the higher grain densities predicted from the thicker sections were not realised. Microdol-X seemed to be particularly sensitive to this effect: D-19, and gold latensification followed by Elon—ascorbic acid both showed higher efficiencies than Microdol-X and less reduction in grain count at higher grain densities.

This odd effect is very puzzling. There is a great deal of evidence from light microscope autoradiography to show that grain density is directly proportional to radiation dose up to far higher levels than those at which Salpeter and Szabo were working. It is just possible that the monolayer of crystals used in the electron microscope techniques is responsible.

For the user of electron microscope autoradiography, it seems that a Metol—hydroquinone developer such as D-19, or Elon—ascorbic acid after gold latensification are the best choices.

The preparation and viewing of the processed autoradiograph

These stages raise few problems, apart from the ever-present requirement for the utmost cleanliness. A stop-oath of 1% acetic acid, or even a distilled water rinse, can be followed by fixation either in buffered 30% sodium thiosulphate (p.181) or in a commercial fixer. The beam current should be kept low during viewing: it is possible to evaporate off the silver grains if one's enthusiasm is excessive, and a torn support film due to uneven heating of the specimen assumes the dimensions of a major tragedy at the end of a process often lasting many months.

THE COLLECTION AND ANALYSIS OF DATA FROM THE AUTORADIOGRAPHS

This subject has been dealt with at length in Chapter 11, so it will not be repeated here. In most experiments with electron microscope autoradiography, it will not be possible to identify the source of radioactivity in the section just by eyeballing a few areas. The relatively low grain densities that are usually produced and the inevitable scatter of grains around the source will combine to make it essential that some statistical analysis must be carried out. The information available from other techniques will often make it easy to frame a hypothesis, while the data presented by Salpeter, Bachmann and Salpeter[31] will help in predicting the grain distributions around the structures suspected of being radioactive. If it is difficult to predict confidently that any particular structure is radioactive from outside evidence, then the "wheel of chance" method of analysis proposed by Williams[17] may have to be used. Once again, if a Williams' analysis suggests that one or more groups of structures are labelled, it may still be necessary to compare the observed grain distribution around them with those predicted from the Salpeter model system, if one is to assess their degree of radioactivity accurately.

References p. 353

Analysis is tedious, but it seems reasonable to invest this extra time in getting the utmost out of an experiment that is anyhow quite a lengthy and expensive performance.

DETAILED DESCRIPTIONS OF TECHNIQUES

Autoradiography of tritium with Ilford L4 emulsion by the two techniques described below should give a resolution with a HD value of about 1450 Å for a section 500 Å thick, or about 1650 Å for a section 1200 Å thick[31]. The efficiency should be between 20 and 30% (Figs. 23 and 92). This emulsion has a shelf-life of at least 3 months. The silver halide crystals have diameters for the most part between 1200 and 1400 Å. The appropriate safelight is Ilford 'F 904' or Wratten 'OC'.

Suggested darkroom conditions are a temperature of 18–20° and a relative humidity of 45–50%.

(a) The loop technique[4, 25]

Take a grid which has been coated with a collodion film, over which a thin layer (50–60 Å) of carbon has been evaporated. The specimen is mounted on this film, and carefully dried. The grid is then attached by a small piece of double-coated masking tape (Scotch tape No. 400) near one end of a microscope slide: up to 4 grids can be mounted on each slide.

Take a 50-ml bottle of L4 into the darkroom and stand it in a waterbath at 45° until it is molten: take it out to allow it to gel again.

When the specimens are ready for coating with emulsion, take them into the darkroom. The emulsion can be weighed out for melting and dilution, or measured out volumetrically using the procedures outlined on p.310. If the emulsion is to be weighed, take 15 g and melt and mix it with 15 ml water in a 300-ml beaker, standing in a waterbath at 43–45°. If it is to be measured volumetrically, take about 8 ml of gelled emulsion into a 25-ml measuring cylinder, and stand it in the waterbath until it melts: this will take about 10 min. Pour from this 4 ml of molten emulsion into a second measuring cylinder, and transfer this to a 300-ml beaker that holds 15 ml distilled water.

When the molten, diluted emulsion is homogeneous and smooth, transfer the beaker to an ice-bath for 1–5 min, then into a waterbath at 20°. The emulsion should have the correct consistency for use from 10–20 min later, *i.e.* it should gel immediately on being picked up in the platinum loop.

The loop, which should be of thin platinum wire, should have a diameter of about 4 cm, and must be clean. Dip it in the emulsion and withdraw it slowly, picking up a thin film of emulsion over the loop, which should gel at once, giving an emulsion film which looks uniform. Take one of the slides with grids mounted on it, and touch the end nearest the grids against the film, which should fall from the loop to cover the grids. With experience, the gelling of the emulsion film can be recognised, and the transfer of the emulsion between the two waterbaths and the icebath continued to keep it at the correct consistency.

Place the emulsion-coated slides in an open slide-box in a desiccator over dried silica gel overnight. Next day, the boxes can be closed and taped, and placed in a refrigerator at 4° to expose. If long exposures of over 3 months are anticipated, or latent image fading is a problem, the boxes should be filled with dry nitrogen, argon or carbon dioxide: in addition, a small packet of drying agent can be added before closing the box.

All processing solutions should be freshly made up and as clean as humanly possible. For a simple method of development giving large developed grains, use D-19 developer, full strength, for 2 min at 20°, in a petri dish, and place the slide in the dish, emulsion up, lying horizontal. Then transfer the slide to distilled water for 30 sec, to 1% acetic acid for 10 sec, and to fresh distilled water for 30 sec. Fix in Kodak rapid fixer or in buffered 30% sodium thiosulphate (p.181) for 3 min. Finally, wash in 3 changes of distilled water, for at least 1 min each.

To stain the preparations for viewing, prepare a 1% solution of uranyl acetate in distilled water: mix 70 ml of this solution with 30 ml absolute ethanol just before use. Immerse the slide in this solution for 10–45 min, washing the stain off afterwards with distilled water. Allow the slide to dry in a clean atmosphere.

Finally, cut the emulsion around the grids with a fine scalpel. The grids are now ready for viewing.

(b) The dipping technique[9, 11]

3 × 1 inch microscope slides should be carefully cleaned with alcohol and dried. They are then coated with a thin layer of collodion by dipping once in a 0.5% solution in amyl acetate. A ribbon of sections is floated out on the surface of a drop of water on the slide, taking care not to damage the collodion membrane in doing so. The sections should be one-third of the way from one end of the slide. The drop of water is then drained off. The section thickness can be estimated from the interference colour (Fig. 90), while the sections are still floating on water in the microtome trough.

The sections are next stained. A suggested routine is immersion for

2–5 min in 2% aqueous uranyl acetate, followed by 8–10 min in lead citrate[9]. Alternatively, 2–3 h in uranyl acetate alone may be used. Staining is performed by placing a few drops of stain over the section, and flushing it off with distilled water after the stated period. Care must be taken to prevent evaporation of the staining solution from the slide. The slide with stained sections on it is coated with 50–60 Å of carbon. It is then ready for autoradiography.

The steps in preparing the L4 emulsion for dipping should follow the sequence outlined on p.310. The initial dilution of the emulsion should be one part emulsion to 4 parts water. The diluted emulsion, in the dipping jar, should be cooled to 25° and held at that temperature.

Taking a blank slide, dip it once in the diluted emulsion, removing it slowly and evenly, and holding it vertical. Allow the slide to dry in the vertical position, and take it out of the darkroom to examine the emulsion layer. An area of the slide, approximately one-third of its length in the bottom half of the slide, should be uniform in appearance. From the interference colour of the emulsion layer, its thickness can be estimated (Fig. 90). It will probably be thicker than the 1500 Å (purple interference colour) which represents a monolayer. The emulsion should be further diluted, if this is the case, until test slides show the correct thickness of emulsion has been achieved.

When the correct dilution of emulsion is ready, dip the slides with sections on them in identical fashion, leaving them vertical to dry.

Drying and exposure conditions have been described already on p.349 Development can follow the steps outlined on the same page, using D-19 developer: alternatively, the following procedure can be used. This gold–Elon–ascorbic acid recipe will produce fairly large developed grains, without visualising individual latent images within each grain. It may give slightly more reliable efficiencies at different radiation doses to the emulsion than the development with D-19 (ref. 29).

Throughout this recipe, the distilled water should have been previously boiled and cooled, after adding a few drops of bromine.

A 2% stock solution of gold chloride ($AuCl_3 \cdot HCl \cdot 3H_2O$) is made up in the distilled water: this stock solution will keep for up to one month in a plastic bottle at 4°. Immediately before use, 1 ml of this stock solution is diluted in 100 ml boiled distilled water, and the pH is adjusted to 7.0 by adding 0.5 N NaOH dropwise. Potassium thiocyanate, 0.25 g, and potassium bromide, 0.3 g, are then added and dissolved, and the solution made up to 500 ml with distilled water. This solution should only be used between 1 and 8 h after making.

To make the developing solution, dissolve the following, in order, in 150 ml of the boiled distilled water: Elon, 0.45 g; ascorbic acid, 1.5 g; borax, 2.5 g; potassium bromide, 0.5 g; sodium sulphite, 7.5 g. Make up the final solution to 500 ml with boiled distilled water.

The developing process should be carried out with all solutions at 20°, using the following routine:

Gold thiocyanate solution	5 min
Distilled water	rinse
Elon–ascorbic acid developer	4 min
Non-hardening fixer	1 min
Distilled water, × 3	30 sec

Salpeter and Szabo[29] found a considerably lower background with this developing process than with the D-19 routine which gave a comparable efficiency.

Without allowing the slide to dry after its final rinse, place it in distilled water for 15 min. Then, with a scalpel or razor-blade, scrape the emulsion and supporting membrane from around the edges of the slide, and strip them together gently from the slide on to the surface of distilled water, emulsion side uppermost. While the membrane is floating, place grids gently on the emulsion over the ribbons of sections. Then pick up the membrane, with emulsion and grids, from the surface of the water. This can be done quite simply using a perforated filter plate attached to an aspirator (Fig. 88), with a filter paper over the perforations. The membrane can be sucked gently against the filter paper and removed from the water. The aspirator is then turned off, and the filter paper, with membrane attached, taken off the filter plate and placed on a flat surface to dry, in a position protected from dust. Finally, the membrane is cut around the grids, which are then ready for viewing.

Autoradiography with Eastman Kodak NTE emulsion

The shelf-life of this emulsion appears to be around 2–3 months. The halide crystals are 300–500 Å diameter. It is sensitive to low-energy β particles only, and, while useful for tritium and iodine-125, is unlikely to be sensitive enough for isotopes of higher energy. The appropriate safelight is Wratten 'OA'.

With the technique to be described, the predicted resolution has an HD value of 800 Å for a section 500 Å thick, and 1000 Å for a section 1200 Å thick[31]. Exposure times should not exceed 12 weeks, as background may be expected to increase noticeably from then on. Each silver grain represents approximately 10 disintegrations in the source.

Specimen preparation is the same as that outlined above for dipping in Ilford L4, except that the sections should show grey or silver interference colours (350–500 Å thick).

The gelatin content of NTE emulsion is too high to give a uniform monolayer. The first step in treating this emulsion is therefore to concentrate the silver halide crystals.

Take 1 g of NTE, add to it 10 ml of distilled water, and heat, with gentle stirring, in a waterbath at 60°. When it is completely dissolved, transfer it to 4 centrifuge tubes, warmed to around 40°. These tubes are then placed in an ordinary laboratory centrifuge the rotor of which has been warmed with a hair dryer, and centrifuged until the supernatant is quite clear.

Take each tube from the centrifuge, chill it by placing its bottom for about 20 sec in contact with melting ice, and pour off the supernatant. Melt the concentrated emulsion in the first tube by placing the tube back into the waterbath at 60°, and add to it 1 ml of distilled water. Swirl it around gently to mix it thoroughly. Then, transfer the contents to each of the other tubes in turn, melting the emulsion in each in the same way. Transfer the final dilution to a small (10-ml) graduated cylinder, and leave it standing in the waterbath at 60°. Repeat the rinsing of the tubes with a second 1 ml of water.

Take a test slide, and, with a medicine dropper, place 3 drops of the molten, diluted emulsion on it, pour them off back into the graduated cylinder immediately, and stand the slide upright to dry for a few minutes. The thickness of the emulsion layer can then be checked by taking the slide out of the darkroom and noting the interference colour in the area where sections are situated on the experimental slides. A monolayer should have a silver to pale-gold colour (Fig. 90). If the emulsion is too thick, it should be diluted empirically until the correct emulsion thickness is obtained. It is advisable to check the packing and thickness of silver halide crystals in the emulsion layer by direct observation in the electron microscope, until the procedure has become established.

When test slides appear to be satisfactory, as judged by their interference colour, cover the experimental slides in the same way, and leave them for 30 min in a vertical position to dry. Drying and exposure should follow the steps given on p.349, except that exposure with a drying agent in an inert gas is now essential.

Development should be by gold latensification, followed by a variant of the Elon–ascorbic acid developer. As with the process on p.350, all the distilled water used should first have been boiled with a few drops of bromine, and allowed to cool. The stock solution of gold chloride is made up as on p.350, and used to make a solution of gold thiocyanate in exactly the same way: the final solution is unstable, and should only be used between 1 and 8 h after preparation.

After exposure, dip the slides in distilled water, then into a 1:20 dilution of the gold thiocyanate solution for 30 sec, and rinse again in distilled water. The slides go then into developer.

The developer is made up with Elon (Metol), 45 mg, absorbic acid, 300 mg, borax, 500 mg, and potassium bromide, 100 mg, made up to 100 ml with distilled water. The developer is very unstable and its effectiveness changes very rapidly with time in the first few hours. After 5 h, it remains fairly constant up to 48 h, however.

With the developer at 24°, 8 min development should produce grains about 500 Å in diameter. The size of the developed grains can be adjusted by varying the time of development.

Following development, the slides are rinsed, fixed and washed as described on p.351. Stripping the emulsion and its support off the microscope slide in preparation for viewing follows the same procedure as for Ilford L4.

REFERENCES

1   A.G. Malmon, *J. Theoret. Biol.,* 9 (1965) 77.
2   J. Liquier-Milward, *Nature,* 177 (1956) 619.
3   S.R. Pelc, J.D. Coombes and C.C. Budd, *Exptl. Cell Res.,* 24 (1961) 192.
4   L.G. Caro and R.P. van Tubergen, *J. Cell Biol.,* 15 (1962) 173.
5   L.G. Caro, *J. Cell Biol.,* 15 (1962) 189.
6   J. Koehler, K.K. Mühlethaler and A. Frey Wyssling, *J. Cell Biol.,* 16 (1963) 73.
7   G.F. Dohlman, A.B. Maunsbach, L. Hammarstrom and L.E. Appelgren, *J. Ultrastruct. Res.,* 10 (1964) 293.
8   P. Granboulan, *J. Roy. Misroscop. Soc.,* 81 (1963) 165.
9   M.M. Salpeter and L. Bachmann, *J. Cell Biol.,* 22 (1964) 469.
10 M.A. Williams, in D.H. Kay (ed.), *Techniques for Electron Microscopy,* 3rd ed., Blackwell, Oxford, 1972.
11 M.M. Salpeter, in M.A. Hayat, (ed.), *Principles and Techniques of Electron Microscopy,* Vol. 2, Van Nostrand/Reinhold, New York, 1972.
12 T.C. Appleton, in L.J. Roth and W.E. Stumpf (eds.), *The Autoradiography of Diffusible Substances,* Academic Press, New York, 1969.
13 S. Hodson and J. Marshall, *J. Microscop.,* 91 (1970) 105.
14 A.K. Christensen, in L.J. Roth and W.E. Stumpf (eds.), *The Autoradiography of Diffusible Substances,* Academic Press, New York, 1969.
15 A.W. Rogers, *Phil. Trans. Roy. Soc. London. (B),* 261 (1971) 159.
16 L. Bachmann and M.M. Salpeter, *Lab Invest.,* 14 (1965) 1041.
17 M.A. Williams, *Advan. Opt. Elect. Microscop.,* 3 (1969) 219.
18 L.D. Peachey, *J. Biophys. Biochem. Cytol.,* 4 (1958) 233.

19 L. Bachmann and P. Sitte, *Mikroskopie*, 13 (1958) 289.
20 M.A. Williams and G.A. Meek, *J. Roy. Microscop. Soc.*, 85 (1966) 337.
21 J.P. Revel and E.D. Hay, *Exptl. Cell Res.*, 25 (1961) 474.
22 J.H. Venable and R. Coggeshall, *J. Cell Biol.*, 25 (1965) 407.
23 C.C. Budd and S.R. Pelc, *Stain Technol.*, 39 (1964) 295.
24 G.F.J.M. Vrensen, *J. Histochem. Cytochem.*, 18 (1970) 278.
25 L.G. Caro, *J. Cell Biol.*, 41 (1969) 918.
26 J.N. Telford and F. Matsumura, *Stain Technol.*, 44 (1969) 259.
27 W.C. Lewis and T.H. James, *Phot. Sci. Eng.*, 13 (1969) 54.
28 B.M. Kopriwa, *J. Histochem. Cytochem.*, 15 (1967) 501.
29 M.M. Salpeter and M. Szabo, *J. Histochem. Cytochem.*, 20 (1972) 425.
30 H. Weber, *Acta Biol. Med. Ger.*, 22 (1969) 159.
31 M.M. Salpeter, L. Bachmann and E.E. Salpeter, *J. Cell Biol.*, 41 (1969) 1.

APPENDIX

Useful data

Avogadro's number $= 6.025 \times 10^{23}$

1 curie $= 3.7 \times 10^{10}$ disintegrations per sec

$\qquad = 2.22 \times 10^{12}$ disintegrations per min

1 microcurie $= 3.2 \times 10^9$ disintegrations per day

1 day $= 8.64 \times 10^4$ sec

$\pi = 3.1416$

$\epsilon = 2.7183$

At a specific activity of 1 mC/mmole, 1 disintegration per day is given by 1.88×10^8 molecules.

At $1\mu C/g$, 1 000 μ^3 of tissue will give approximately 3.2 disintegrations per day.

The relations between the mean track length (L) in μ, the initial energy of a β particle (E) in keV, and the mean number of grains in its track in G5 emulsion (G) are given by the following equations.

$\log L = 1.59 \qquad \log E - 1.51$

$\log G = 1.19 \qquad \log E - 0.74$

$\log G = 0.747 \qquad \log L + 0.385$

THE OPTIMAL ALLOCATION OF EFFORT IN GRAIN COUNTING
BETWEEN THE LABELLED SOURCES AND BACKGROUND

To use these charts, first obtain a rough estimate of the ratio of counts over the labelled sources to be studied to counts over background: this ratio is the abscissa, p. The values of K indicate the number of similar labelled sources which will be examined: other values of K can be interpolated. The ordinates show the optimal number of grains to be counted for three stated values of the coefficient of variation (CV). Use graph (a) to determine the number of background grains to count, and graph (b) for the number of grains over the sources.

To use these charts for photometric estimations of grain density, or any other parameter of emulsion response, it is necessary first to convert the readings from arbitrary units into the corresponding number of grains. (From England and Miller, *J. Microscopy*, 92 (1970) 167).

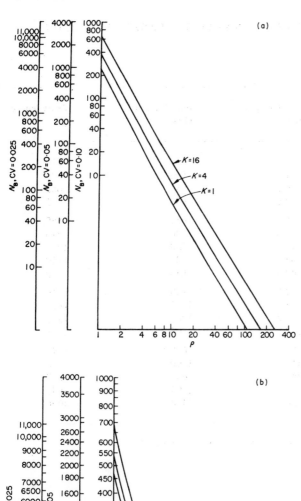

(a)

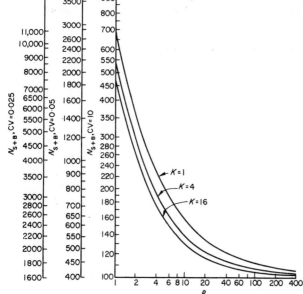

(b)

THE MEAN TRACK LENGTHS OF β PARTICLES IN ILFORD G5 EMULSION
(DENSITY 3.815)

Initial energy (keV)	Track length (μ)	Initial energy (keV)	Track length (μ)
10	1.0	450	517
20	2.9	500	600
30	6.0	550	685
40	10.0	600	775
50	14.7	650	860
60	20.2	700	940
70	26.3	750	1035
80	33.2	800	1120
90	40.5	850	1210
100	48.5	900	1310
120	65.7	1000	1490
150	96.2	1200	1840
170	117	1400	2215
200	152	1600	2590
250	215	1800	2950
300	286	2000	3300
350	362	2200	3640
400	438	2400	4000

Values taken from range-energy curves of P. Demers, *Ionographie*

PHYSICAL DATA ON ISOTOPES IN COMMON USE FOR AUTORADIOGRAPHY

Isotope	Half-life	Particle	Particle energy (keV)	γ-Rays
Calcium-45	165 d.	β	250	None
Carbon-14	5760 y.	β	155	None
Chlorine-36	3.03×10^5 y.	β	714	None
Cobalt-57	270 d.	I.C. electron	14 (83%)	Present
Iodine-125	60 d.	I.C. electron	35	X-rays present
Iodine-131	8 d.	β	250 (3%)	Present
			330 (9%)	
			610 (87%)	
			810 (1%)	
Iron-59	45 d.	β	130 (1%)	Present
			270 (46%)	
			460 (53%)	
			1 560 (0.3%)	
Phosphorus-32	14.2 d.	β	1 710	None
Sodium-22	2.6 y.	Positron	540 (89%)	Present
Strontium-90	28 y.	β	540	None
Radioactive daughter,				
Yttrium-90	64.2 h	β	2 250	None
Sulphur-35	87 d.	β	167	None
Tritium				
(Hydrogen-3)	12.3 y.	β	18.5	None

These figures are based on data published by the United Kingdom Atomic Energy Authority, *The Radiochemical Manual,* 2nd ed.

NOTES ADDED IN PROOF

Chapter 7, p. 121. first par.

A recent paper by Richter and King* has drawn attention to the main difficulty in staining autoradiographs of plastic-embedded material, which is that heat is generally needed to get stain into the section, and this may well remove the layer of processed emulsion. They have suggested hardening the emulsion layer with a 5% solution of formaldehyde after photographic processing. This certainly facilitates staining through the emulsion with a wide variety of stains, such as those suggested by Grimley, Albrecht and Michelitch**.

*C.B. Richter and C.S. King, *Stain Technol.*, 47 (1972) 268.
**P.M. Grimley, J.M. Albrecht and H.J. Michelitch, *Stain Technol* , 40 (1965) 357

Chapter 10, p. 185, last par.

A simple and inexpensive photometer for the evaluation of optical densities in X-ray film autoradiographs of macroscopic specimens has recently been produced in the Research Laboratories of Smith, Kline & French Ltd., Welwyn Garden City, England*. It enables one to evaluate relative grain densities on, for instance, whole-body autoradiographs very rapidly and with sufficient accuracy to be useful.

*S.M. Cross, personal communication.

Chapter 11, p. 216, par. 2.

An extended treatment of the analysis of autoradiographs at the electron microscope level has just been produced by Blackett and Parry*. This promises to be a most valuable extension of the original concepts of Williams [17]. In this method, prints at constant magnification are prepared of the autoradiographs, and a regular lattice of points is superimposed. These points are taken to be the sites within the specimen at which radioactive atoms have disintegrated during exposure, in a hypothetical random distribution of radioactivity throughout the specimen. A computer program is prepared from the idealised curve of Salpeter *et al.*[9] for the distribution of silver grains around a point source, from the known *HD* value of the autoradiograph, and from a set of random numbers from 1–360. This programme generates a value for the distance from each of the hypothetical point sources at which a hypothetical grain is to be expected, and a corresponding number of degrees to indicate the direction relative to a fixed reference plane in which the grain is to be found, starting from the point source. These hypothetical grains then have circles of radius *HR* placed around them, and tables of items are constructed in just the same way as that described on p. 214 by Williams[17]. A comparison of the frequencies with which items occur in *HR* circles around observed grains with those predicted from the hypothetical grains indicates at once if the observed grain distribution is random or not.

The power of this admittedly more complicated procedure is the ease with which non-random grain distributions can be compared with predicted distributions based on the hypothetical grains. If it is suggested that the observed distribution is due to all the radioactivity lying within two components only — say the rough endoplasmic reticulum and the Golgi body — then the hypothetical point sources lying over these components only are studied, and the hypothetical grains from these points used to generate a predicted distribution. It becomes relatively simple to test many different hypothetical distributions against the observed distribution, without the necessity to approximate each source to a simple geometrical shape, and without the need to make a fresh series of measurements of distance from grains to each component as its probability of being a source of radioactivity is being considered. For instance, one can very simply test the hypothesis that all components of a cell are equally labelled except one, by excluding hypothetical point sources overlying that component from the analysis. This type of hypothesis would be impossibly difficult to test by the Salpeter-type of analysis, which works so elegantly for situations in which only one component is labelled[13,14].

The work of Blackett and Parry* clearly represents a major advance in the very difficult field of analysing electron microscope autoradiographs of sources whose effects on the emulsion overlap.

*N.M. Blackett and D.M. Parry, *J. Cell Biol.*, in the press.

Chapter 18, p. 339, last par.

If it proves impossible to strip a valuable autoradiograph from its supporting slide, it may help to score around the area of slide bearing the sections, using a sharp needle, and very carefully to place a single drop of a 1 in 100 dilution of 40% hydrofluoric acid in distilled water along the score mark. Care should be taken to avoid the acid spreading on to the upper surface of the slide over the sections. After a few minutes, the acid is rinsed off in distilled water. This is usually sufficient to start the separation of membrane from glass slide*.

*D.M. Parry, personal communication.

Index*

*EM = electron microscope; ARG = autoradiograph.